Children's fiction

Flight Underground
The House in the Waves
Hostage!

Fiction

The View from Mount Dog
Gerontius
The Bell-Boy
(also published as That Time in Malomba)
Griefwork
Ghosts of Manila
The Music

Non-fiction

A Very Personal War: The Story of Cornelius Hawkridge
(also published as The Greedy War)
Mummies: Death and Life in Ancient Egypt
Playing with Water
Seven-Tenths
(also published as The Great Deep)

Poetry

Option Three
Dutch Alps

AMERICA'S BOY

AMERICA'S BOY

A Century of Colonialism

in the Philippines

James Hamilton-Paterson

A John Macrae Book

Henry Holt and Company   New York

Henry Holt and Company, LLC
Publishers since 1866
115 West 18th Street
New York, New York 10011

Henry Holt® is a registered trademark
of Henry Holt and Company, LLC

Originally published in Great Britain in 1998 by Granta Books

Library of Congress Cataloging-in-Publication Data
Hamilton-Paterson, James.
America's boy: a century of colonialism in the
Philippines / James Hamilton-Paterson.—1st American ed.
p. cm.
Includes bibliographical references and index.
ISBN 0-8050-6118-5 (hb.: alk. paper)
1. Marcos, Ferdinand E. (Ferdinand Edralin), 1917–1989.
2. Philippines—Politics and government—20th century.
3. Philippines—Foreign relations—United States.   4. United States—
Foreign relations—Philippines.   I. Title
DS686.6.M35H35   1999   99-27569
                                                                              CIP

Henry Holt books are available for special promotions and
premiums. For details contact: Director, Special Markets.

First American Edition 1999

Printed in the United States of America
All first editions are printed on acid-free paper.∞

1   3   5   7   9   10   8   6   4   2

for
Mark Cousins and Parveen Adams

Then a new era began for the Filipinos. Little by little they lost their ancient traditions, the memory of their past. They forgot their writing, their songs, their poems, their laws, in order to learn by rote alien teachings they did not understand: a morality and an aesthetics different from those the race had inherited from its climate and ways of feeling. They went into a decline, belittling themselves in their own eyes. They became ashamed of what was their own and their nation's in order to admire and praise whatever was foreign and unintelligible. Their spirit became dejected and surrendered.

José Rizal, *Filipinas dentro de cien años* (1889)

It is accepted in the Philippines that from baptism to death one needs godfathers for everything – whether to get justice, obtain a passport, or to carry on any kind of business.

José Rizal, *El Filibusterismo* (1891)

Contents

Acknowledgements

The longer one lives somewhere, the harder it is to know whom to thank for most of what one learns. Indeed, it becomes clear that unattributable knowledge is the largest and most significant part of what one knows. It is the product of wandering, of uncounted hours spent walking through untouristed zones: of long, solitary rambles in cities reading graffiti, fragments of posters and street furniture; of living in the provinces, attending to the sounds of work or picking over the jetsam on beaches. These raw tokens become memorably fleshed out by chance acquaintances, by fragments of conversation with all manner of touts, tarts, urchins, provincial governors, bus drivers and peanut vendors. By such means, over long years, a country's distinctive flavour becomes fixed in the mind. So when it comes to singling out individuals for especial thanks, it feels as though behind each cited person stood a horde of the unacknowledged: nameless, shadowy figures busy with vignettes of their existence.

Having made an effort to disentangle this book's roots from the soil that nourished it, I am happy to extend particular thanks to the following – two of whom I have never met and know only through their work: Roquito Ablan, Gene and Carmila Alcantara, Benjamin Alfante, Zeneida Amador, Benedict Anderson, Irene and Greggy Araneta, Arturo Aruiza, Fernando Balatbat, Jonathan Best, Karina Bolasco, Sheila Coronel, O. D. Corpuz, Adrian Cristobal, J. V. Cruz,

Rodolfo Cuenca, Tina Cuyugan, Randy David, Conrado de Quiros, Ricardo de Ungria, Amando Doronila, Rod Dula, Jerry Esplanada, Al J. Farretta, Alma Fernandez, Bonifacio Gillego, Jim Gomez, Louie Gonzalez, N. V. M. Gonzalez, Raffy Guerrero, Noel Historillo, Froilan Hong, Nick Joaquin, Frank and Tessie Sionil José, Lucrecia Kasilag, Fred Kluge, Clody and Julie Lauresta, Jaime Laya, Larry and Nonnie Lelang, Evelyn Lim, Teodoro Locsin Sr., Teddy Boy and Louie Locsin, Tony Lopez, Armando Malay, Dick Malay, Ricardo Manapat, Ed Maranan, Ferdinand Jr. and Lisa Marcos, Imelda Romualdez Marcos, Jose Medina, Carmen Guerrero Nakpil, Ricardo Nepomuceno, Ambeth Ocampo, Leonilo Ocampo, Satur Ocampo, Charlson Ong, Blas Ople, Oscar Orbos, Joan Orendain, Neal Oshima, Romy Parreño, Charlin Petrotta, Danton Remoto, Edmundo and Carmencita Reyes, Jolly and Julie Riofrir, Ruth Roa, Anding Roces, Ding Roces, Beth Day Romulo, Miriam Defensor Santiago, Zenaida Seva, John Silva, RayVi and Wendy Sunico, Jun Terra, Rigoberto Tiglao, Kerima Polotan Tuvera, Bernardo Villegas, Monique Villonco, Krip Yuson, Jessica Zafra, Enrique Zobel de Ayala, Jaime Zobel de Ayala.

I am deeply indebted to Bonjin Bolinao, whose astonishing net-working abilities are exceeded only by her kindness and generosity. I can only hope that neither she nor her sundry contacts will feel they have been misrepresented or short-changed by what I have written.

Neil Belton's editorial presence has been, as always, exigent and unerring as well as inspirational. And for ensuring a vital mini-mum of professional orderliness in my dishevelled and peripatetic life, my agent Andrew Hewson of John Johnson Ltd. deserves special gratitude, as he has these many years past.

Where this book is concerned, though, my biggest debt is to Maribel Ongpin and her family (which of course extends to her in-laws Bobby and Monica and their family, as well as to Deanna Ongpin-Recto). Without being fulsome there is no way of acknowledging adequately such an *embarras* of hospitality, help, patience and time. It is simpler to express my gratitude for a first-rate library as well as for a rare quality of moral sternness and intellectual rigour which time and again has stood in the way of serious misapprehension or sloppy generalization. My lasting regret is that I never met Mrs Ongpin's late husband, Jaime. Lewis Gleeck wrote that Jaime's tragic death was 'the severest judgement yet rendered on the Aquino government'. Time passes and recriminations fade. Yet even a person who never knew him can now appreciate that Jaime Ongpin was triumphantly something which (as I hope this book will indicate) it is not always a straightforward thing to be: a genuine Filipino patriot.

Obviously, nobody I have mentioned above is responsible for the views I express, some of which may indeed strike them as unwelcome if not actually wrong. The right to be pig-headed and intransigent is an author's own, and one he jealously guards.

Small portions of Chapter 2 are expanded versions of passages in my introductory essay to *The Philippines: A Journey Through The Archipelago* (Singapore, 1996).

Grateful acknowledgement is also due to the creators of the book *Si Malakas at Si Maganda*, published by Jorge Y. Ramos in 1980, and above all to its illustrator, Leonardo Cruz. The others associated with the project were Remedios F. Ramos, E. Arsenio Manuel, Florentino H. Hornedo and Norma G. Tiangco.

Chronology

1521	Magellan 'discovers' the Philippine archipelago
1565	The first Spanish settle in Manila, initiating 333 years of Spanish colonial rule
1762–4	British troops occupy Manila during Seven Years' War
1807	Basi Rebellion, Ilocos Sur
1861	Birth of José Rizal
1872	'Gomburza': the Spanish authorities execute three Filipino priests, Frs. Gomez, Burgos and Zamora for alleged complicity in the Cavite Mutiny
1882	Rizal's first trip to Europe. Enrols in Madrid University
1887	Publication of Rizal's first novel, *Noli Me Tangere*
1891	Publication of Rizal's second novel, *El Filibusterismo*
1892	Founding of the Katipunan, a radical Filipino political association
1892–6	José Rizal banished to Mindanao in internal exile
1896	Execution of José Rizal
1896–7	Philippine Revolution
1898	Gen. Emilio Aguinaldo proclaims Philippine Independence Spanish–American War Treaty of Paris: Spain formally cedes the Philippines to the US for $20m

1899–1902	First Philippine Republic under President Aguinaldo Philippine–American War, heralding 46 years of *de facto* US colonial rule
1917	Birth of Ferdinand Edralin Marcos
1929	Birth of Imelda Romualdez
1935	Manuel Quezon becomes first President of the Philippine Commonwealth (1935–44)
1941/2	Japanese invade and occupy Philippines until defeated in 1945
1942	Fall of Corregidor. Bataan Death March
1943–4	'Puppet' presidency under Japanese administration of Jose P. Laurel
1944–6	Presidency of Sergio Osmeña
1946	The Republic of the Philippines gains full independence
1946–8	Presidency of Manuel Roxas
1948–53	Presidency of Elpidio Quirino
1949	Ferdinand Marcos elected to Congress
1953–7	Presidency of Ramon Magsaysay
1954	Marriage of Ferdinand Marcos and Imelda Romualdez
1957–61	Presidency of Carlos Garcia
1961–5	Presidency of Diosdado Macapagal
1963–8	US Presidency of Lyndon Baines Johnson Major US military engagement in Vietnam
1965	Ferdinand Marcos elected President
1969	Ferdinand Marcos re-elected
1972–81	Martial law
1983	Benigno ('Ninoy') Aquino assassinated
1986	'Snap' election. Victory claimed by both President Marcos and Corazon Aquino. So-called 'EDSA Revolution'. Cory Aquino sworn in as President (1986–92). Ferdinand Marcos sworn in as President. Marcos deposed and exiled to Hawaii
1989	Death of Ferdinand Marcos in Hawaii
1992–8	Presidency of Fidel Ramos
1995	Imelda Romualdez Marcos elected to Congress as Rep. of the First District of Leyte

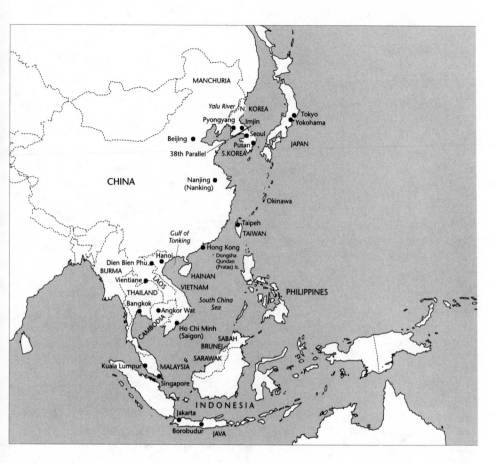

S. E. Asia

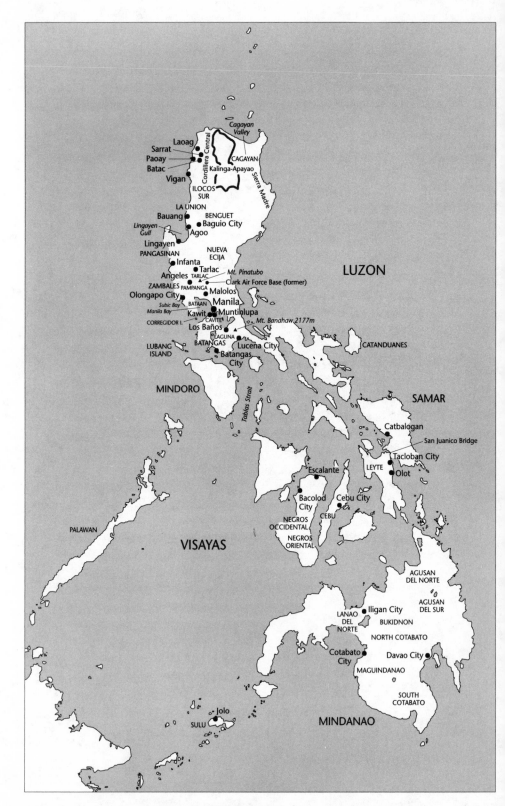

The Philippines

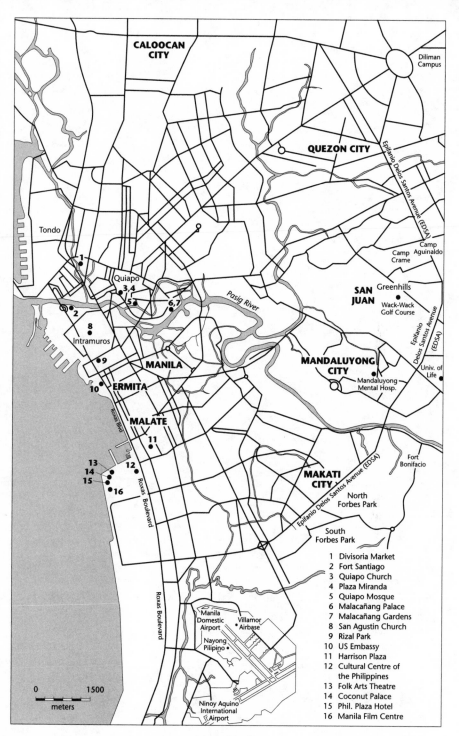

Metro Manila

1 Divisoria Market
2 Fort Santiago
3 Quiapo Church
4 Plaza Miranda
5 Quiapo Mosque
6 Malacañang Palace
7 Malacañang Gardens
8 San Agustin Church
9 Rizal Park
10 US Embassy
11 Harrison Plaza
12 Cultural Centre of
   the Philippines
13 Folk Arts Theatre
14 Coconut Palace
15 Phil. Plaza Hotel
16 Manila Film Centre

Introduction

As a nation the Philippines is not well understood in the West, suffering as it does from a confused image. This owes much to a sad and complex history which saw the archipelago fall beneath the successive dominion of Spain, the United States and Japan before belatedly achieving independence in 1946. The country that emerged was an anomaly, widely perceived politically as an American satellite while at the same time being the only formally Christian state in Asia. By appearing not to fit comfortably into the bloc of neighbouring nations that includes China, Vietnam, Thailand, Malaysia and Indonesia, it tended to slip through the highly selective grid of Western public awareness. From the mid-sixties onwards, however, this conceptual no man's land steadily acquired notoriety, if not a geography, by being the *locus* of a famously exotic ruling couple: Ferdinand and Imelda Marcos. Their story, as sporadically seized on by the international media, was played out in largely journalistic terms: unbridled corruption, wild extravagance, brutal dictatorship and a sensational, if not sticky, end.

It is just a dozen years since an apparent turning-point in post-war Philippine history. In February 1986, after the so-called 'EDSA' or 'People Power' revolution, the Marcos family was helicoptered out of Manila's Malacañang Palace and flown to exile in Hawaii. Such images as the world has today of the Philippines are mainly rooted in the events of that resounding weekend, which were widely covered by the international media. The assassination of Benigno ('Ninoy') Aquino on his homecoming in 1983 had already established the basic grammar and vocabulary for all discourse during the 'revolution': a Manichaean casting of the Marcoses as an evil needing to be purged from the country by the forces of good, as represented by Aquino's widow Cory and her Church-backed followers.

In the next few years many books were published about the Marcoses, taking their cue from this simplistic polarization. Few indeed showed much wariness of the thick religious sauce that had been poured over cold political events. The majority were journalistic works concerned with exposing the various crimes and scams of the twenty-year regime. Some of the investigation was excellent, some of it shoddy. In all, though, it could not but reinforce EDSA's Manichaean view, despite the fact that President Aquino's polity was meanwhile revealing itself as something less than an army of light. In general, the authors' methods appear to have involved dropping by Manila for a few weeks with a research assistant or two, briefed to scatter among the administrative classes, interview disgruntled grandees and listen to gossip. This made for some splendid stories, many of which wound up printed as fact without much in the way of rigorous checking.

The exiled Marcoses themselves were in no position to query or refute the allegations. Ferdinand was terminally ill; Imelda was being harried by lawyers as a prologue to her indictment and trial in New York under a RICO (Racketeer Influenced and Corrupt Organizations) statute violation. Their credibility, like that of their associates who had not turned their coats or otherwise repented, was nil. In the Philippines itself it was in everybody's interest to heap the deposed President with as many items of the nation's dirty linen as possible: this being especially true of those who had so recently worked for him. The point to be made does not so much concern the accuracy of the individual stories that further encouraged the exiled family's demonization, as something more subtle. Namely, that books written in this period tended to share a specific viewpoint, seeing everything in the slanted light of the times. And as with any oblique lighting, it inevitably left pockets of deep shadow.

*

The little Philippine village where I have been living, on and off, for the best part of twenty years could itself be said to dwell in shadow. This is partly the fault of the spotlight that is forever fixed on Manila, where most news is generated, leaving the bulk of the country in relative obscurity. But another part of the shadow comprises a good deal of what was not illuminated by all those books about the Marcos years. In my provincial oubliette I kept encountering fervent wishes for Ferdinand's return. The Marcoses, or at least their local party representatives, had to some extent penetrated village life. No matter how physically distant the President had been, some token of his personal voltage had seeped through to every last *barrio*, or village, in the country. In many regions this was probably the first time such a thing had ever happened, so remote and aloof could the capital feel from elsewhere in the archipelago. (In a forgotten interview of 1969, none other than Senator Ninoy Aquino described it thus: 'Manila is an *imperium in imperio*, a republic within a republic, and that Manila is as alien to the Philippines as Hong Kong.')[1] When Marcos went, the sense of a patron or a godfather went too. As Mrs Aquino took over, that already tenuous central government presence withdrew. Her photograph replaced those of the Marcoses in the village school and the *barangay* (village) hall, but that was all. The whole community felt as though it had moved further away from the centre of things, back to the old self-sufficient marginality of pre-Marcos days.

That many ordinary Filipinos missed the Marcoses (although few would admit it to foreigners) should come as no surprise. Rural folk everywhere are notoriously conservative and often value the old order, however little it did for them, over some brave new regime that has installed itself in the far-off capital. For over twenty years the Marcoses had run the Philippines from Malacañang Palace; they had long since come to seem like fixtures. True, rumours of corruption and chicanery had filtered through to the furthest province, but what of it? They were to be expected. There had never been a Filipino government without its whispers of mal-practice and criminality. That was politics, local or national. More to the point, ordinary people had the distinct impression that the Marcoses had at last put their country on the international map. Thanks to all that moving and shaking by wily old Ferdinand, and thanks equally to Imelda's antics and high-glamour diplomacy, the Philippines was no longer some obscure Southeast Asian nation like Laos that nobody could quite place. Nor was it merely a vast American aircraft carrier permanently at anchor off the coast of mainland Asia. Whatever his domestic faults might have been, Marcos had given the country a measure of pride and independence and a proper foreign policy of its own . . . People in the village were pretty vague about the exact details of Marcos's foreign policy, but they did retain the image of a man with his own nationalistic agenda. 'He had balls,' they said succinctly. 'He was clever. Only he had the nerve to snub the Americans – not once, either, but over and over again,' adding darkly: *That's what did for him.'* This was one of their principal theories for the President's downfall. The other was that his wife was to blame. 'He was ill, poor man, and Imelda simply took advantage of his sickness by making her own power-play.' That would be a paraphrase. The unexpurgated version over glasses of palm toddy was couched in more macho terms, the traditional male myth of the good man undone by a woman, by Woman herself – the scheming, devilish principle whose fatal allure-made-flesh drags its hapless victims towards that Venus flytrap, the *vagina dentata*. I think it was then that I first began to feel sorry for Mrs Marcos.

As the years following EDSA went by, and President Cory Aquino was succeeded by Ferdinand Marcos's own cousin, President Fidel Ramos, I began to miss an account of the Marcos era that would investigate these patches of darkness: something that would explain how an alleged monster could still command degrees of wistful or belligerent loyalty at grassroots level. Ideally, the sort of account I was hoping for would not treat recent political history solely from the usual perspective of American corridors of power. I was curious to learn what the connection was between Marcos and ordinary Filipinos – the men and women of the rural *barrios* who grew the country's rice and went to cockfights and sewed their children's dresses for Flores de Mayo parades. After all, in spite of the vast disparity in wealth, they shared a cultural heritage. Finally, in default of the text I wanted, I began to pursue my own enquiries. I soon realized that the Marcoses would only become comprehensible when put into a much longer context than was fashionable, and seen against a background of coconut palms and paddy fields as well as of executive office furniture. And in due course I found I had written a book of my own.

For the sake of convenience I have decided to use again the name 'Kansulay' which in an earlier book, *Playing with Water*, disguised the provincial village I was describing. For the purposes of this present book, 'Kansulay' is less a disguise than a fabrication based on several communities I have known in the Southern Tagalog region. The same goes for its fictitious inhabitants, none of whom represents a living person. Such a device enables sweeping generalizations to be made about 'the provinces' from beneath two cloaks of anonymity: one which conceals the village where the author still lives, and another which partially shrouds that author, who is not always the 'I' of his own discourse.

It will be noticed that, whereas the references of printed sources are given, verbal quotations are sometimes anonymous. This usually means that the people concerned only agreed to being quoted provided they were not named. Occasionally I have decided that attribution would be indiscreet or unmannerly. In all cases, though, the quotations are verbatim unless otherwise indicated in square brackets.

AMERICA'S BOY

1

Digging a well in Kansulay

They were digging a well in Kansulay up by 'Turing's patch'. This name commemorates a certain Arturo who died years ago, possibly back in the sixties or even earlier, and who by some quirk had owned a hectare or so of coconut trees in an area that otherwise formed part of a local landowner's estate. Turing's patch lies alongside the stony track leading inland away from the coast and heading for the interior's dense green hills. The track itself follows the valley of the small river that over many millennia has washed soil down from the hinterland and deposited much of it within half a mile of the sea, forming in its valley a broad 'V' of paddy fields whose emerald-green rice plants blazon its fertility. Up by Turing's patch the 'V' is still narrow and instead of irrigated fields old stands of coco-palms stretch patchily away for miles inland on steadily rising terrain.

The track here appears quilted by the morning sun filtering down through overhanging fronds and branches, the embedded stones and hollows variously highlighted and shaded in scalding blotches. The ridged, fibrous pillars of surrounding palm trunks with their staggered scars of footholds ascending to the crowns give one the impression of being more indoors than out, strolling the glades of some immense basilica. This hackneyed image is only strengthened by the beams of sunlight that slant down as from clerestory windows. Into these pale bars pass momentary insects and the smoke of cooking fires from nearby huts, drifts of motes rising lazily, winking in and out of visibility as they traverse the shafts of light. Sounds have a ringing, precise quality here. Instead of being dampened by so much woodwork they bounce about the smooth columns and are reflected back down by the vaulting palm-ribs overhead. Cocks crow; a buffalo groans down by the river; someone chops wood. There is the sudden clatter of an iron lid on a cooking pot and a harassed mother's exclamation, 'Lintik ka!' followed by a child's laughter. The clarity of the sounds is extreme, like a digital recording of a thousand years ago. These surroundings are something more than dumb foliage. This is an intelligent landscape that resonates to the intelligences that are a part of it.

The track itself can be read for its inscriptions of daily living. A dozen years ago it was little more than a footpath. Then someone had the idea of bulldozing a road to the nearest sizeable inland village, a handful of miles as the crow flies but many more as dictated by steep ravines. It was a bad idea, more a pretext for someone to get his hands on local government funds than a seriously useful project, as was borne out by the fact that even when it was still a novelty nobody used the road. It was never surfaced, the raw cuttings made by the bulldozer's shining blade were never shored up, there was no maintenance. Typhoons came and went, cuttings collapsed, bends fell into chasms so steep that earth lodged in the crowns of palm trees below while trees whose roots had been exposed toppled across the track itself. Nowadays barely two-thirds of a mile remain passable in a vehicle. The occasional jeepney or motor tricycle brings a new mother back from the hospital to her home in the outback of Kansulay, or a hired truck may fetch some felled bamboo or a load of timber. Otherwise the road has reverted to being what it always was – a trail. Even where the track remains clear at the Kansulay end, a secondary path winds its way within the road's wider margins. It is the line of least resistance beaten by bare feet and bicycles, avoiding the sharper lumps of stone.

This softer, muddier trail can be scanned for evidence of the tidal nature of Kansulay's diurnal life. Children's footprints going down to school in the morning are planted on those of adults who went in the opposite direction an hour earlier to feed their livestock in the forest. A dark brown loaf of fresh buffalo dung between two smooth indentations show where Inso has taken his beast down, harnessed to a *paragos*, the crude wooden sled with hardwood runners he uses for hauling sacks of rice or copra. He has a job this morning: a contract to haul gravel from the river bed to where they are laying the foundations for a house beside the coastal road. The hoofmarks cut across the bald tyre-tracks of Carding's absurd bicycle which is now leaning against a nearby palm. Its size is suitable for a child of ten. He rides everywhere on it, splay-kneed and with the handlebars coming somewhere between his thighs, twice a day fetching fresh *tuba*, the palm toddy that drips from the cut flower into a bamboo container. His whistling and occasional ribald remarks come from far overhead, up among the fronds he temporarily shares with golden orioles and the rest of the avian and insect life that centres mainly around the canopy of leaves. This same track provides much other evidence to beguile the amateur Holmes: fragments of *Komiks* pages, a torn school exercise; half a civil service exam script whose conical furl shows it was used to hold the boiled peanuts sold by itinerant vendors; a darkening bloodstain that was probably from one of the myriad toads and frogs that live in the paddy fields and are always being squashed in the dark, their corpses gobbled up later by foraging pigs.

Here at Turing's patch, standing on the track and facing inland, we find one flank of the valley rising steeply to our immediate left. It is a semi-jungle of coco palms, the occasional noble mango and ylang-ylang, vines and shrubs of all sorts including bananas and the ubiquitous 'Imelda'. This last is a weed whose proper name no one seems to know. It forms thick tangles as deep as a European nettle-bed and produces pale, whitish-blue flowerets of no great distinction. According to the locals it is an import – a plague weed that suddenly appeared from Africa or somewhere about twenty years ago and has been rampaging ever since, stifling native varieties of plant. 'It is called Imelda because it's absolutely useless,' a villager said. 'It has no value to man or beast that we can discover. Not even goats will eat it, *kasi mabaho*, it stinks. It has no medicinal properties. It just gets everywhere. So we called it Imelda.' An alternative version says it is called that because of some specific project of Imelda Marcos, the former First Lady: something that went wrong, like another idea of hers to introduce a foreign species of *hito* (a freshwater catfish) in the hope of developing a rural fishpan industry with something besides tilapia. The fish were big, up to two feet long, but apparently they turned out to be poisonous. They became known with grim amusement as '*hitong Imelda*'. Whatever the truth, the gently mocking name leaves behind it a faint residue of sadness whenever it is spoken, as of a good intention that went wrong.

To the right of the track is a scattered group of thatched huts for whose inhabitants this well is to be dug. Behind them lies an eighty-metre strip of palm plantation before one arrives at the river itself, beyond which the other side of the valley rises: more trees and vines, bananas and Imelda, through which chickens and pigs and children forage with shouts and loud crackling noises. This river is the focus of Kansulay's perennial water problem, for it is visibly shrinking year by year. In *Playing with Water* I described standing knee-deep in it to fill a plastic jerrican or to wash clothes at a time when buffaloes eroded deep wallows for themselves beneath its shady banks. No more. Barely a dozen years later the river no longer even fills its own broad bed but follows a shrunken, secondary course. In this it resembles the path winding its way within the greater width of the track, following the line of least resistance. It now meanders in trickles among boulders it so lately covered. Only after heavy monsoon rains are the same boulders useful as stepping stones.

The precise cause of this drying up of the village's lifeline is still not known, though sensible and plausible reasons have been advanced, all of which probably play a part. One is that the snail's pace of land reform has obliged more and more people living in the interior to become *kaingineros* or slash-and-burn subsistence farmers. Such a system yields potash-fertilized soil and good crops for a year or two, but the bare scars it leaves on steep volcanic hillsides soon erode. The pinkish laterite soil washes off in the rains, sliding downwards and often carrying with it untouched portions of forest. The denuded areas spread and even when left alone regenerate slowly where the fertile topsoil has gone. In the long run, of course, even exposed rock will turn to soil because laterite is nothing more than weathered volcanic rock; but such geological timespans are of no comfort to mere mortals. Meanwhile, the silt washed off the hills clogs the river system by filling up the watercourses, which in turn leads to the useless dissipation of tributaries in the forest where they soak away into deep-lying groundwater.

The result is that instead of being a river that runs productively and steadily throughout the year, Kansulay's source is now a creature of extremes, mostly a feeble trickle but occasionally after flash-floods a dangerous tawny spate that crashes seawards through the village with a terrifying roar, undermining coco palms and ancient stands of bamboo and depositing a fatal layer of silt over delicate offshore corals.

The rise in *kaingin* is one theory; another is that copper-mining activities in this island province's centre have altered the river system's catchment area. Since an entire mountain has already been removed by over twenty years' round-the-clock bulldozing this seems perfectly likely. And a third theory is the one heard increasingly around the world, and which panders so perfectly to that immemorial farmer's grumble that the weather isn't what it used to be: global climatic change. In Kansulay's case this seems the least probable. The monsoons still arrive, slightly variable from year to year as they always were, with or without damaging typhoons; and in the dry season the tropical sun still pours its rays with almost audible force, like a brass gong being beaten overhead. Still, whichever combination of theories one fancies, the hand of man is surely behind the undeniable fact that a coastal village is being deprived of its fresh water supply, which was the very reason for its being sited there. And the hand of man ultimately means politics. Kansulay's inhabitants are in no position to engage in wrangles at such a rarefied level, which is anyway located in distant Manila in the air-conditioned offices of powerful bureaucrats wearing filmy *barong Tagalog* shirts in front of whom no farmer could imagine himself standing, awkwardly twisting his calloused fingers in an access of embarrassed humility. (*Oho, opo,* yes sir, yes sir; and out into the bright sunlight and the traffic's roar, having achieved nothing but to get your name dangerously onto someone's yellow legal jotter? Forget it!)

So the alternative to losing the river is to dig wells. But this river turns out to be the problem yet again because almost anywhere in the valley's V-shaped debouchment has in the past been its bed. The river has wandered about, now on one side and now on the other. If one sinks a well anywhere near its present course the chances are good that at about twelve feet down one will encounter a blackish silt which gives even an abundant water supply a disagreeable smell. This is hydrogen sulphide formed in the layers of decaying vegetable matter carried down by the river hundreds – even thousands – of years ago. That is the trouble with small hand-dug wells: one can't go much below twenty feet to where the deeper seams of pure water lie. Strangely, the wells down in the village proper nearer the beach produce better water. One well dug a few years ago is within thirty metres of the high tide mark, yet the water is perfectly sweet. But this, while interesting, is of no help to the group of villagers living up at Turing's patch. It was decided to try digging their well in the valley floor right next to the track, eighty metres from the diminished river.

It so happened there was hardly anyone among the families who stood to benefit from the well who could help with its digging. Several of the men were too old; of the younger ones two had occupations in the forest that left them with little spare time and less energy; the rest were women and children. So the *barangay*'s *tanod* (an elected official who acts as a sort of village 'prefect' or general enforcer) assembled a cheerful gang of otherwise unemployed youths. Appeals to their *bayanihan* spirit, which is supposed to make everyone chip in their stint of free labour for the good of the community, had fallen on deafish ears. They consented to work only in return for *merienda*, cigarettes and beer money. Filipinos, who make much of this *bayanihan* principle, tend to over-praise themselves for it. The idea of people in a community as small and inter-related as Kansulay helping each other out with such things as house-moving and well-digging is hardly peculiar to the Philippines; yet they often speak of it rather as they do of their hospitality, as though it were a phenomenon they had pioneered and which remains practically unknown anywhere else in the world. The mistake is to treat *bayanihan* and hospitality as though they were simple virtues of national character such as can be listed in a tourist brochure, whereas in fact they represent highly complex structures of social relations. (The very word *bayanihan* has its roots in *bayan*, which can mean a town or a nation or the public or the motherland; a *bayani* can be a hero, a patriot or a voluntary labourer.) Such social virtues are never as simple as they appear when neatly codified, being heavily contaminated with secondary meanings and overtones of approbation, or indebtedness, or masculinity, or sharing, or whatever else. Strains often appear when they are invoked, as the well-diggers exemplified; though in this case one took into account the fact that a foreigner was associated with the project whose comparative wealth would quite rightly have figured in the equation of their social conscience. If it was partly his idea, why shouldn't he pay?

The diggers began and by lunchtime had made a sizeable hole. Butterflies blundered into the lattice of light-beams above the path, were momentarily trapped, fell off into shadow leaving a flash of intense colour. The earth mounding up around the mouth of the pit was studded with Hope mentholated cigarette butts ('"Hope" because you hope they won't give you cancer,' as someone inevitably remarked. It was an old joke, long since worn to the sort of pleasantry that expresses no more than a vague cultural solidarity, much as 'Good-bye' no longer means 'God be with you'.)

By evening the diggers were down to about ten feet without, however, the least trace of water. At twelve feet the following day the buckets of soil being hauled up by helpers standing around the lip contained shards of blackened pottery. Instructions were shouted down and the diggers went more carefully, finding charcoal and the handle of some sort of vessel, a thick terracotta ring incised with a pattern of half-moon gouges that might have been made with a long thumbnail. There was a good deal of excitement among the men, though they were reluctant to say out loud what was obviously running through their minds: buried treasure.

'Buried treasure' is such a constant preoccupation in the Philippines that it constitutes a distinct cultural and psychic space. There are several people in Kansulay who believe they know where treasure is buried – mainly on the beach, it seems. The problem about digging it up is that it is protected by *bantay-ginto* or 'gold guardians', terrifying spirits with long fangs who are usually the souls of those who were put to death after burying the gold so as to preserve the secret. Many people have seen these *bantay-ginto*, which can be a threat even if one is not in search of gold. The theory goes that these guardians grow weary with their long, lonely vigil by the sea and sometimes fly about at night, taking the shape of bats or small birds. Thus mobile, they are anxious to do a swap with the soul of an unwary person, especially if he or she is secretly searching for the treasure. There is an old man in a neighbouring village down the coast who they say has the soul of a *bantay-ginto* from the sixteenth century, his own having been snatched when he was fifteen and condemned to enforced guardianship of a heap of gold bars beneath the beach. This man is said to wander the strand at night, the *bantay* soul that inhabits him troubled by its human embodiment and penitential towards the human soul it usurped. He is constantly searching for the soul he lost as a boy. One imagines him walking and walking the beach, hopefully scanning the brilliant starfields overhead, expecting any of the fruit bats that flutter and dart around the coconut palms fringing the shore to be his missing self, yearning to return to its original, but now aged, body. Perhaps he wakes in the dead of night and listens to the bats quarrelling in the fronds above his house, their angry cries so high-pitched they sound, to elderly ears, more like hisses than squeaks. Does he really believe his former self is struggling to gain entry? Or is he long resigned to dying with a sixteenth-century soul?

And why sixteenth-century, particularly? Here is a clue to the whole iconography of this Filipino obsession with treasure. In 1574 a notorious Chinese corsair named Lim Ah Hong came very close to sacking Manila and driving out the Spanish colonists, who had been seriously consolidating their possession of the Philippines only since 1565. Lim was driven off but skulked in the archipelago, raiding settlements and carrying on in a generally piratical manner. Legend asserts that in the course of so doing he amassed a great treasure which, in order not to put all his golden eggs into one basket, he scattered about the islands in places known only to him. The *bantay-ginto* he put in charge of these sites were precisely calculated to be of maximum effect against Filipino counter-spells since they were Chinese. Today, one needs to win people's confidence for many years before anyone in Kansulay will talk about these savage spirits without affecting the sceptical amusement they judge appropriate for discussing the supernatural with foreigners; but once that barrier is down their descriptions are both serious and detailed. These guardians are clearly forms of dragons, with their long teeth, glaring eyes and fiery breath which can sometimes be seen as blue flames hovering around a treasure site. (I have never seen these flames; but given that in the area where Kansulay's river flows into the sea there are small lagoons of trapped and stagnant water above the high-tide level, each full of rotting vegetation, there seems no reason why methane should not form and produce will-o'-the-wisps.) Being essentially foreign devils, therefore, these dragon spirits are proof against even the most powerful local shaman, who can at best only defend him- or herself against attack but never overcome them and take the gold.

What is interesting about the whole Lim Ah Hong treasure legend is that it exactly prefigures the modern myth of Yamashita's treasure, the caches of untold wealth looted by the Japanese before and during the Second World War that Ferdinand Marcos himself so assiduously tried to track down and – many believe – found. We shall deal with this equally obsessive quest in a later chapter; for the moment it is enough to indicate that in the imagination of Kansulay's villagers the two myths are conflated into a single phenotype of buried wealth protected by terror and sheer ingenuity.

The idea of buried treasure is, of course, hardly peculiar to the Philippines, and in its commonest boy's-adventure form represents no more than the 'if only' daydreams most of us have indulged at some time. A contemporary version might involve winning the lottery, although that smacks of the inhuman randomness of a computer rather than the brilliant romance of ancient maps, scheming minds and guardian demons. Nevertheless, there is a sub-text here that is peculiarly Filipino. It arises from this nation's tortured history of having endured the domination of no fewer than three colonial powers, the chiefest of which being Spain. These islands were 'discovered' by Ferdinand Magellan in 1521, named for Philip II of Spain (who had financed the expedition) and colonized from 1565. Whatever the Catholic friars did in terms of suppressing an existing culture – and there is still much contention about this – the irreducible fact is that until quite recently the Philippines had no written history that was not compiled by foreigners with their own agenda. It therefore seems likely that Lim Ah Hong has attained his legendary status at least partly for home-grown nationalistic reasons: he was a fellow-Easterner who came close to dislodging the Westerners from their conquest. (This same spirit honours the tribal leader Lapulapu for killing Magellan in Ceba in 1521.) As a Hispanicized town, Manila was a mere nine years old in 1574, although as a Tagalog trading settlement it was centuries older. Had Lim actually succeeded in taking Manila it is likely that the whole of Filipino history would have been different, for Spanish lines of communication were hopelessly stretched and the conquerors far too thin on the ground to mount a serious military campaign. (Fourteen years later there were still only 800 Spaniards in the entire archipelago.)[1] Why might not this sense of how nearly things could have turned out differently touch a faint but deep chord of longing somewhere in the Filipino psyche? In which case Lim Ah Hong's famous treasure scattered so widely about the archipelago is not just gold but represents 'the past'. This is the unwritten Filipino past, the accumulated riches of a pre-Spanish culture since dismantled and lost but always searched for. The metaphor extends still further, in that even today powerful foreign devils have a habit of capturing the souls of Filipinos in search of their true inheritance. Western academic practice is seen by many modern Filipino scholars as having hijacked an indigenous knowledge, a home-grown account of cultural history, either subtly moulding it for its own purposes or radically misunderstanding it.

I have never quite had the courage to air this theory to a Filipino academic, mainly because it touches on the supernatural. Some scholars tend to be a little terse with Westerners expressing interest in such things, perhaps because they think they detect an element of patronage. Many educated Filipinos would be only too happy to gloss over those aspects of their own popular culture they see as holding the nation back by shackling it to an iron ball of mediaeval mystification, folk beliefs, and anything else that smacks of a pre-scientific age of stick-rubbing and forest-dwelling. One takes their point while persisting in the conviction that beliefs (like social virtues) are never simply about what they profess but always embody metaphors.

The well-diggers, meanwhile, had perceived that these blackened fragments of pottery they had unearthed were not portents of treasure and began to be genuinely interested. One of them fitted the pieces together, and although there was much missing the unmistakable outline of a familiar round-bottomed cooking pot took shape on the path beside the hole. 'It's just a *palayok*,' somebody said. It was true: one could go to town on any day and buy the identical object from the market there. An archaeological site, then, rather than treasure trove. Even here, reason still ruled. Mading said: 'They were just people like us. *Uling at palayok*, charcoal and cooking pot, ordinary people. We haven't any gold and neither did they. How does a poor farmer living in the woods get his hands on gold?'

'They didn't have Chinese ceramics, either,' agreed Pusoy, referring to the tradeware from the Asian mainland that was bartered in vast quantities before the Spanish arrived. This still turns up all over the place in archaeological sites and in the wrecked remains of Chinese junks that scuba divers are constantly finding silted into the seabed around the Philippines' coastline. Identical celadon bowls fill Manila's antique shops; the better pieces wind up in private collections and museums (from where they often mysteriously migrate to private collections). But here in Kansulay we are obviously dealing not with foreign history but with local, with the 'rude forefathers of the hamlet'. We wondered who these people might have been, and when. We also wondered whether in those days this hearth was on the river bank instead of eighty metres away. For the first time it was possible to see the villagers speculating about their own roots, regarding the sooty fragments at their feet with a novel emotion, a real curiosity about the past. Had there been a village in those days? Might it even have been called Kansulay? The evidence was buried twelve feet down, which made it feel immeasurably old. But perhaps it wasn't all that old after all, though nobody had any idea at what rate the river's silt is deposited nor whether a simple mudslide had buried a *kainginero*'s campfire earlier this century. Without carbon dating or an archaeologist we could only speculate. But there was no one present who was not struck by the cooking pot's unchanged design. The next time any of us was in the market he would view those stacks of new *palayok*, nestling in straw, quite differently.

'I think,' said Mading at last, 'it was hundreds of years ago. I bet there was always a little settlement *sa ibaba*, down there,' and he shot his lips towards the invisible coast beyond the palms and paddies. 'I think there were always people living here and *sa ilaya*,' meaning inland in the far and equally invisible hills. 'They lived on the banks of this river because in those days – remember what it was like when we were kids, even? Deep and clear enough to drink. We all got water from the river. Imagine what it must have been like hundreds of years before.'

And immediately some began building up an imaginary scene until one could practically see the outline of an idyll that might only have existed before the coming of outsiders, of the Spanish, or maybe of Adam and Eve. The others leaned on their shovels and looked stolid, too unused to this sort of speculation to know how to contribute. *In those days* – Mading warmed to his subject – *in those days* the river was deep and crystalline and full of fish, over-hung by feathery stands of bamboo which creaked gently in the breeze off the sea. In those days, of course, nobody cultivated coconut palms in vast plantations of neatly spaced trees since there was no need to be commercial. Instead, the original jungle would have crowded to the river bank and settlers would have hacked clearings for their *bahay kubo*, their bamboo-and-thatch huts on stilts. These homes would have been identical to the present-day versions right here at Turing's patch except for being lashed together with *batbat*, strips of vine bark, instead of nylon fishing line. Mading's vision was idyllic because naive. It fantasized a rural past of plenty – with abundant fish in river and sea, with fruit and game in the forest – in place of poverty and hardship; in short, before one only master grasp'd the whole domain, in Tom Paine's phrase.

This impromptu fantasy beside the track was geographically structured by the twin co-ordinates of *sa tabing dagat*, or along the seashore, and *sa ilaya*, along the riverbank. Since one visualizes rivers as flowing into the sea more or less at right angles a shape emerged in the air which framed this discourse, like a 'T' lying flat. The village would be at the junction of river and coast. Its social and trading connections lay up and down the coast and along the river into the interior where there were other villages on its banks. Nothing was said about crossing the sea or, indeed, about crossing the province. There were but two axes to existence: *tabing dagat* and *ilaya*, along and up, and both lay beside water. This topo-graphical detail is highly particular to the culture. Mading's sylvan idyll, on the other hand, was internationally recognizable. In European literary terms, for instance, it was that of the Greek and Roman authors who had extolled unspoilt rural (as opposed to urban) living because of its genuineness. Artless shepherd boys and hard-working country folk lived in unthinking harmony with nature. Two thousand years later English literature in particular rediscovered these bucolics with an eagerness that grew as the Industrial Revolution's dark satanic mills made the contrast with rural peace and harmony all too obvious. By the late eighteenth century the British *bahay kubo*, or thatched cottage, was well established and sentimentalized as the *locus gratiae*. Indeed, the worse rural poverty became, the more the Victorians sugared the scene until iconic pictures of rose-girt cottages with cosy thatch and diamond-paned windows were as ubiquitous as today's parallel daubs in Manila's tourist shops. These modern canvases are typically of idealized evening scenes: a farmer ploughing a paddy with a water buffalo while in the background his humble home (but in its way a palace!) is outlined against a lurid sunset sky. In both the English and the Filipino version the political and cultural message is the same, equally potent, equally falsifying. Via an implied sermon on the virtues of simple living the viewer is invited to suspend disbelief, in the first case, in such things as the Enclosure Acts and starvation rural wages, and in the second, absentee landlords and starvation rural wages. Today, of course, most of Britain's thatched-and-trellised cottages are in the hands of the nostalgic middle class and go for stupendous sums of money, whereas many millions of rural Filipinos still live in thatch-and-bamboo huts, most of them longing for a cement-block structure with a sheet iron roof the better to resist typhoons.

At this point *merienda* arrived and the Edenic vision of pre-Conquest living went all to pieces like the unearthed cooking pot. Work on the well duly resumed, but at eighteen feet – more or less the safety limit for unshored holes in this soil – there was only the blackish ooze of former river bed. It meant two days' exertion had been all for nothing. Yet finding the pot had after all been something. It had made several young villagers momentarily thoughtful, even moved by the idea of being part of a long continuity in that place. It is hard for Europeans accustomed to brick and stone to imagine how different the sense of a landscape must be where the vernacular architecture is so temporary. Wooden structures in the tropics are prey to termites and typhoons. Only houses built around four thick hardwood legs have much chance of surviving beyond ten or twenty years, and most ordinary *bahay kubo* do well to reach six or eight years without radical repairs. It is therefore quite unusual for an adult rural Filipino to be able to walk past a house and say 'That's where I was born.' This must induce a different interior landscape to that of a European who can point to entire towns of sixteenth-century buildings, written records going back a thousand years and more, artefacts from twice that, the past clearly visible – even intrusive – at every turn of the way.

Yet many Filipinos, like the people of Kansulay, still actively live their own past without knowing it. They do so by being caught up in a way of life dictated by climate and landscape that has probably changed comparatively little since pre-Spanish times. Their mental geography is still remarkably structured by the idea of riparian living, whether by a river or the sea. This is, after all, what one would expect of a sea-going people of largely Malay stock who first arrived in these islands in 18-metre longboats called *balangays*, an entire village to a boat captained by its headman. Having discovered a propitious spot on a coast or up a river mouth, they landed and re-founded their village (still known today as a *barangay*, the old name having been resurrected by President Marcos to describe the basic administrative unit and to replace the Spanish *barrio* or *sitio*). As the historian O. D. Corpuz points out, water pervades the names of places and peoples all over this archipelago:

> Our forefathers located their settlements along river, lakeshore and seacoast. Even in the hinterland the settlements tended to parallel mountain streams; the houses were strung out like a ribbon along a body of water. This explains the prominence of water-related terms in Filipino place names. *Pampang* means river bank, and from this is derived the name of Pampanga Province. Cebu owes its name to *sugbu*, which also means river bank. *Agusan* means 'where the water flows'; it is the name of Agusan Province. Catanduanes province is named after the river Catandungan. Iligan City in northern Mindanao owes its name to *iligan* or *ilidan*, which means coast. *Danao* means lake or flooded area; it is the origin of Lanao, Maranao, Mindanao, Maguindanao. The Tagalogs are people from the river, after *ilog*. *Sug* or ocean current is the origin of Sulu; thus the Taosugs, the incomparable sea warriors who fought the Spaniards for three hundred years, are 'people of the sea'. *Baybay* means shore or beach; it was the name of several coastal villages in various islands; it was also one of the old names of Leyte Province.[2]

Exactly how different the physical Kansulay village was at the end of the Marcos era in early 1986 when compared to its pre-Conquest state (if, indeed, it did exist then) is hard to judge; yet it is not impossible to make some intuitive guesses. One of these would be based on the state of its communications with the rest of the province. The progress of the province's roads reveals that only very recently has anything approaching modern mobility become a matter of any importance. When the author first came here in 1981 the 'national road' around the island's perimeter started bravely from the little capital town as a ribbon of concrete that faltered just beyond the outskirts. Apart from some local patches of tarmac and paving around the coastal towns, this main road was unmade. In the rainy season whole sections of it degenerated into huge pot-holes full of mud, while fords were often impassable. In those days one could still take a *calesa* from the capital's marketplace to Kansulay, some eight kilometres away. These were Spanish-style horse-drawn vehicles with two tall wheels which generally bore their passengers high and dry over the worst bits, no matter that the horse ended up wearing mud gaiters up to its hocks. In the dry season the dust was uniformly invidious, regardless of how one travelled. Over the years, with painful slowness, the road's macadam surface crept outwards from the capital until it reached this *barangay* in the mid-eighties, at about the time a deeply ill President Marcos lost office so spectacularly.

The road's fitful progress could be seen as a barometer of several things, among them foreign aid, government funding, pork-barrel handouts and corruption. Government funds are few and far between and tend to run out well before a project is finished. So a proudly announced section of highway can peter out just short of a crucial watersplash which for decades has demanded a proper bridge. Pork-barrel funds are similarly unreliable and highly seasonal, tending to be spent on flashy public works to pay off old political debts or when there are local or Congressional elections in the offing. And as for corruption – well, the province's perimeter road mirrors it faithfully if one can discover the huge sums that have been earmarked for its construction over the years. Nobody – least of all a minister or an official in the Department of Public Works and Highways – would ever expect anything more than a low percentage of any funding actually to be translated into surfaced roadway. (The same principle holds good for all other government departments.) Funds have to pass through many hands, to which agreed percentages stick. Four hundred and fifty bags of cement may be despatched (out of the 1,000 ordered), of which 300 might reach the site. Once repairs to the foreman's lavatory have been considered, as well as the patio for his wife's coffee mornings, and a contribution made to the local *barangay* captain's cement stockpile for building the basketball court which will gain him a second term of office, there may be 150 bags left for the road. It has always been thus. It was so well before the Marcoses came, it was so while they were in office, and it is still so today.

Whatever else the progress of the province's perimeter road suggests, it has clearly not been a matter of vital priority. This in turn hints that the local economy did not depend crucially on the export of fresh produce to Manila. Perfectly true. The province's only real industry was copper mining and the foreign company concerned built its own local road and communications network. Otherwise, the only products of marketable surplus were, and still are, fish and copra. Practically all the industrial fishery in the province's waters is that of powerful consortiums based in Manila, Batangas and Lucena City – in other words, outsiders. And as for copra, since it is virtually non-perishable it finds its way from the forest at its own pace to the warehouses of small-time buyers who dry it further and store it until the market price makes it worth parting with to dealers from outside the province. In brief, what all this shows is that the local economy is still mainly a matter of self-sufficiency. The province consumes pretty much all it produces, and always has. Individual *barangays* like Kansulay are but small reflections of the same principle.

In fact, self-sufficiency has always characterized life in these parts, which probably explains why one can still hear older people lamenting the passing of the Marcoses and their twenty years in power. This is not because they had ever made any of the locals wealthy, but because when they were in Malacañang Palace the poor were able to obtain certain basic medicines free under Mrs Marcos's 'Botika sa Barrio' scheme. Cynics can argue (and have) that this was simply part of the Marcoses' game plan for currying favour with the grassroots electorate. But the people of Kansulay were less interested in motives than they were in antibiotics for their children and themselves. When Corazon Aquino took over as President it was not only her instinct to scrap anything her predecessors had done, but the World Bank and the IMF insisted she suspend costly social schemes – at least until the economy had been rescued. Again, the rural poor were incurious about the rationale. All they saw was a sudden lack of free basic healthcare.

So we can stand on the track by Turing's patch, beside the redundant hole the men are filling in again, and be moderately sure that the cardinal points of this way of life changed little until the mid-1980s since there was no reason for them to have done so. We know from fading carbon copies of local historians' typescripts that the first public 'passenger truck' was introduced as far back as 1918 for short runs around the capital town, and that the first cinema opened there the following year. It seems that a second cinema, the Liwayway ('daybreak') Theatre, opened in 1924, but few people appreciated films in those days and the early silent movies were not profitable (though the Liwayway Theatre was not itself demolished until 1958). Nowadays there is only the Chinese-owned Lucky 7 in town, supplying an ever-popular diet of martial arts and torrid romance. Yet little of this would have touched Kansulay, separated as it was from town by several miles on horseback or on foot, as well as by a largely cashless economy. The first television came to the village in about 1985, but it was run off a cumbersome series of jeep batteries with a converter. In any case it was used less as a television than for showing video movies with a 'Betamax' (the superseded format still gives its trade name to videos to this day) which had been brought back from Saudi Arabia by Kansulay's first overseas contract worker. This man had returned, practically black with the sun, bearing with him marvels of technology that occasioned the sort of intense curiosity Sir Walter Raleigh's potatoes and tobacco must have aroused at the Court of Elizabeth I. Mains electricity was scanty in Kansulay before 1990 and until recently was mostly confined to houses along the coast road. The first private telephone arrived eighteen months ago. There is not a dishwasher or washing machine in the village. The plates, like the laundry and the children, are washed under the nearest pump. Such signs of twentieth-century modernity as exist in Kansulay are still to some extent novelties, and the twentieth century itself will have long passed before everyone in the village has access to the basic amenities. Such as, no doubt, a decent water supply.

That is the physical Kansulay. But there is good evidence the social Kansulay may also have been asleep in itself for centuries before Marcos came to power in late 1965. One suggestive indication of how static it still is as a society is that it is nearly impossible to do anything to it without causing it upset, even if the action has been officially requested. Put in a well, and somebody's nose is out of joint because it's not on *his* land. Help a child with its school fees, and expect to receive letters telling you that 'you ought to know' how the child's parents, though smilingly benign when you are in residence, become ogres of vanity and snobbery once you have left, supercilious to former friends they feel they now outrank. The smallest and most natural favour, as from a friend to a friend, somehow tips a hair-sensitive balance and sends jealous gossips from door to door. Were rural communities always like this, everywhere around the world, since before recorded history? Probably so; which is no doubt why it is a perennial relief for the young especially to escape to the unjudgemental anonymity of the big bad city. Even drugs and thugs are preferable to Eden's virtuous malice. Kansulay's fierce ripples of parochial passion, masked as ever by the friendliest, most open gazes, wash to and fro as across some rock pool, distorting the face of anyone bent over it who imagines he can play the part of benign observer, occasionally helping toppled creatures back to their holes with a cautious fingertip. Either he must submerge himself in the pool or stay far away; there is no middle course of drifting in and out, humbly playing God. By the very delicacy of this pool, by its sequestered extremism, one knows it to be pristine. Gratifying as this idea is, the actuality proves deadly to any lingering idealism about human nature. From this fact alone it becomes clear why Filipinos' own descriptions of their *bayanihan* system will never do. Nothing in a village ever could be that simple, so naively without motives and consequences. There is no such thing as pure altruism in a small community.

Kansulay's landscape, and that of its hinterland, still pervades the *barangay* and its thinking to an extent almost unknown now in the 'developed' world. The people's skills are rural. Children learn young how to care for livestock, to find wild honey, to look for and dig up *burot* (a kind of sweet tuber surrounded by thorns). Some even know how to make fire. Everyone, male and female, can use a *bolo*, the ubiquitous machete-like knife, often with great skill. It is astonishing to watch a man square off the end of a post or a tree trunk using nothing but a *bolo* and leave a face so smooth and crisp you would swear it had been sawn. Some years ago there was a BBC radio programme which concerned an archaeological dig in Britain at a Bronze Age site in the East Anglian fenlands (probably that at Flag Fen near Peterborough).[3] The diggers had unearthed baulks of timber thousands of years old and well preserved by the bog they were in. The archaeologists were excited by what the different varieties of wood told them about Britain's ancient landscape, but even more so by the skill of the ancient artisans. They agreed that history would have to be rewritten because it was perfectly clear to them that the lengths of wood had been sawn rather than chopped, and it was previously thought that saws were unknown to these people. Here were these trunks, cut smoothly and at perfect right angles. Anyone with even a rudimentary experience of carpentry knew such a thing was impossible using a chopping motion, especially with a bronze axe. One visualized these experts with their anoraks, clip-boards and measuring tapes and longed to tell them to forget academia for a week, to buy an air ticket and find their way to the rural Philippines where on any day they could see real live human beings doing with a simple knife what those early Britons had also known how to do.

Clearly, the villagers of Kansulay are not separate from their landscape and the sundry skills it has imposed on them for generations. Since most of the Philippines is still more like Kansulay than it is like Manila or Cebu City, even an account of recent political history would make little sense if it overlooked landscape as irrelevant. It would be like discussing Berber or Inuit politics without referring to desert or Arctic. Standing as we presently are among the dapples on the track up at Turing's patch, listening to the sounds of foraging animals and sniffing the breeze from the forest laden with heavy rot and hidden blossom, it is easy to see how this landscape can inhabit a people historically and psychically so that even after a generation of living away from it in a slum in the nation's capital, traces of rural attitudes and behaviours can still be found which, like the breeze from the forest, persistently scent their lives.

2

A history told by foreigners

Until recently, the Philippines' history was that of its colonizers, written by foreigners in a foreign tongue. There is plenty of archaeological evidence to show that the archipelago has been inhabited for the last 30,000 years at least, but the first written references to it are in Chinese state documents that refer sketchily to trading relations (all those porcelains!) between the tenth and fifteenth centuries. Here the significant thing is that the Chinese traders found themselves dealing not with a country that would later become known as 'the Philippines' but with various ports-of-call scattered throughout a group of islands. It is clear that there never was a proto-Philippines in the sense of a political entity with some sort of centralized administration – no Angkor Wat, no Borobudur. At the most there were fiefdoms with local chiefs. There are a few other vague references from the time of Marco Polo onwards (his uncle Maffeo headed a Venetian trade mission to China in 1260–9); but as a moment's reflection will show, it was hard for returned travellers in those days to explain precisely where they had been. Crude magnetic compasses existed, but much of the globe was still blank to European sea-going explorers who in any case had no way of fixing their longitude accurately until the eighteenth century. Travellers tended to plot their journeys by references to the various courts they visited, and these are often hard to identify at 700 years' distance.

Where the Philippines is concerned there are virtually no proper accounts of its indigenous peoples before late sixteenth-century Spanish friars began keeping records of their communities and writing reports for their superiors in Manila and Spain. It is exactly this dearth of documentation that led to forgeries in the nineteenth century. The late William Henry Scott stated the matter with characteristic baldness: 'No Philippine historian has yet published a prehispanic document of uncontested authenticity . . .'[1]

From the first, the Spaniards' colonization of this archipelago was quite different from their conquest of Latin America. The sheer sailing distance of Manila from Madrid meant a journey via Mexico, with an arduous overland trek intervening between risky crossings of both the Atlantic and the Pacific. For the next two centuries and a half the galleon supply route sailed unreliably between Acapulco and the Philippines. In a sense Philip II's new acquisition became the colony of a colony because throughout those 250 years the Philippines was actually governed from Mexico. It tends to be overlooked how many different foodstuffs and words which today's Filipinos think of as either indigenous (maize, pepper, papaya, tobacco) or Spanish (*tocayo, sombrero, palenque*) are actually Mexican in origin. Even less is it remembered that two of the commonest and most intimate Filipino words (*nanay* for 'mummy' and *tatay* for 'daddy') were imported from the Mexican Indian language Nahuatl.[2] Genes also made the Pacific crossing abundantly in both directions.

These dangerously stretched lines of communication between metropolitan Spain and its latest colony severely restricted the numbers of travellers, so there was never a mass migration of adventurers, bureaucrats and military to the Philippines as there was to South America. This in turn meant that the archipelago was never really conquered in its entirety. None but the most zealous missionary could penetrate to the mountain tribes living in remote isolation in, for example, the middle of Mindoro or the high Cordillera, while the thinly spread military were obliged to give up their attempts to subdue the 'Moors' in the Moslem south, in Jolo and Sulu and parts of Mindanao. There, the local *datus* (princelings) and petty sultanates were far too well entrenched, trading from easily defended fiefdoms up sheltered estuaries amid thick jungle. And there they still were, not much changed, when Joseph Conrad described them in his novels at the turn of the twentieth century. Even today, people in certain parts of the country still refer to the *habagat* – the southwest monsoon – as the 'pirate wind', commemorating an ancient fear of the seasonal gales that brought crews of marauding Moors up from their southern strongholds, attacking the galleon trade and carrying off slaves even from the northernmost parts of Luzon. Many of the defensive watchtowers the locals built can still be seen.

Those southerners owed their Islamic influences to Arab traders from the Indian Ocean, while Indians themselves had some slight cultural sway elsewhere in the Philippines. This was at least partly religious, and had percolated overland across Asia to Indochina before making the leap across the South China Sea. It survives discreetly, mainly in vocabulary. Among the Sanskrit loan words whose arrival in the Philippines must greatly have pre-dated that of the Spaniards were two for deity or royalty: *bhattara* and *devata*. By the time the Spanish missionaries arrived these words had taken their present-day forms of *bathala* and *diwata* and were applied to a wide selection of idols and spirits. Optimistically, the earliest priests assumed they described the local equivalent of their own Judaeo-Christian god (they were all too wrong), so that today the Tagalog word for God is Bathala. However, in this as in so much else the Filipinos' true spiritual pluralism showed triumphantly through, since the word can equally mean a false god or an adored woman, just as *diwata* means a lovely maiden or a fairy. A more obviously Hindu influence can be discerned in the name of the capital town of Pangasinan Province: Lingayen. This derives from the *lingam*, the phallic symbol of Siva, and the Spanish priests were obliged to make the pragmatic gesture (which all the great monotheistic religions have had to make in a variety of ways) of assimilating the fertility dances associated with the *lingam* into Christian ritual. Today's dancing devotees have simply redirected their songs from a giant phallus to the co-founder of the Poor Clares, St Clare herself.

A second factor lay behind the peculiar way in which the country came under Spanish rule. Unlike in South America there were no myths of El Dorado, no great mines of silver and precious stones. The result was that there were no brutal and greedy conquistadores looting the country from end to end. Instead – and uniquely – the Philippines was largely subdued and administered by *los frailes*: friars of various Catholic orders whose official task was that of conversion. The Spanish Crown's grandly ambitious aim was nothing less than the spiritual conquest of Japan and China, and only incidentally that of the Philippines, which was viewed more as a stepping-stone. Describing himself as 'an instrument of Divine Providence', Philip II regarded it as a matter of moral scruple that this 'barbaric archipelago' should be won for Christ by the Bible rather than by the sword. A measure of the mission's success is that the Philippines became, and remains, Southeast Asia's only predominantly Christian country. This alone would ensure it a later history different from that of other colonized countries in the region.

Spanish colonial policy towards the Philippines in the sixteenth century is often made to seem like a private whim of Philip II, albeit backed by a religious motive. That is to overlook the intellectual, spiritual and political ferment in Europe at the time colonization was taking place. The conversion of the Far East to Christianity had full papal backing, not merely that of the Spanish Court. Many of the friars who went to the Philippines had probably studied with men and women we now know as saints. In Spain, the late Renaissance was in full flower. Both Teresa of Avila and John of the Cross were very much alive, though not yet canonized. (It is interesting that the notional Filipino 'common man' is named after John, this mystical theologian and virtual founder of the Discalced Carmelites. Britain's John Smith (or John Bull) and America's John Doe are in the Philippines Juan de la Cruz.) Ignatius of Loyola, the founder of the Jesuits, had himself died only in 1556. His Society of Jesus was an essential intellectual prop of the early counter-Reformation, the movement hastily set up by Roman Catholicism to combat Martin Luther and the Protestant Reformation. The Vatican's new policies were set out in the three sessions of the Council of Trent (1545–63), several of them concerning the need to spread the Catholic version of the gospel overseas. Ignatius's Jesuits were prominent in foreign missions; his friend and fellow Basque Francis (later St Francis) Xavier was nominated papal nuncio for the East and in the last ten years of his life went to Goa, Ceylon, Malacca, the Moluccas, the Malay peninsula and Japan, finally dying in China in 1552.

All this is a reminder that the Spanish friars whose job it was to mould the Philippines into a spiritual and political entity must have been an odd mixture. Some would have been highly sophisticated intellectuals seeing their task as part of a broad strategy by the Church militant to reach as much of the globe as possible before the Protestant heresy did. The majority, though, were no doubt like majorities everywhere and were profoundly unexceptional men. They were the Church's foot-soldiers, separated from their own peasant backgrounds by a few years' seminary living and probably less than brim-full with proselytizing zeal. In fact, many of them might have resembled the nineteenth-century ne'er-do-well sons of middle-class British families who were saved from disgrace at home by being packed off to the colonies to try their hand at sheep farming in Australia. By what right does one assume this? Simply by the historical fact that the Philippine revolutionary movements that finally gathered to a head at the end of that same nineteenth century were initially a reaction to over 300 years of friar abuses, often so brutal and so gross one can only conclude that at least some of the men concerned must have been shipped from Spain and Mexico as a convenient way of dumping the Church's embarrassing, semi-criminal element in a Far Eastern oubliette. A less damning way to look at it might be to say that since communications with Europe were so intermittent (an exchange of letters might easily take two, even three years) and the priests in the Philippines so scattered and isolated, many of them could – and did – maintain an almost Kurtz-like existence in the communities they ruled like petty kingdoms, unchallenged and largely unsupervised for years at a stretch.

From the late sixteenth to the late nineteenth centuries, therefore, the Philippines was effectively run by a foreign church. The task these Spanish friars had set themselves was prodigious: nothing less than the 'cultural cleansing' of an entire population. Their view was that the natives' primordial and benighted ways must swiftly be replaced by the Christian, humanistic ideals of Renaissance Europe. The early priests discovered that a written syllabary showing Indic influence already existed, belying their instinctive charges of barbarism, but they marginalized this writing system as inadequate and replaced it with the Castilian alphabet. Nationalists used to claim, and some still maintain, that the friars systematically eradicated a glorious and widespread Filipino system of writing. This is demonstrably untrue, since a version of it survives to this day among the Mangyans of central Mindoro. That aside, the evidence for general literacy rests on precisely two Spanish documents (those of the Jesuit Pedro Chirino in 1600, and of an administrator, Antonio de Morga, in 1609), the second of which clearly relies on the first. Chirino's assertion goes, in part:

> So given are all these island people to writing and reading, that there is scarcely a man, and much less a woman, who does not read and write in the characters used in Manila.[3]

A modern historian such as Corpuz discounts the whole idea. Firstly, he finds it absurd that a phenomenon like universal literacy should have gone unremarked in the preceding seventy-nine years, and secondly he asks how that literacy could have arisen in the first place. This commonsensical argument is indeed persuasive. People living in small, self-contained communities like Kansulay would simply have had no need to write. Unlike in China there was no centralized state needing a bureaucracy; and in place of anything remotely resembling an organized church were local shamans whose rites needed no writing. All this apart, the Church was not stupid. Its administrative task in a country of over 7,000 islands was daunting enough without destroying an established system of communication that might have made things easier. It never, for example, suppressed the local languages in order to make everyone learn Spanish. Quite the reverse; it obliged its friars to learn the dialects and strenuously prevented the *indios* from learning Castilian. No; the reason why the syllabary was ignored was that it was too vague for record-keeping. Certain sounds could be transliterated in various ways; and while this might have been all right for story-telling, where the context would have made the correct reading obvious, it was less reliable when it came to people's names. Names were, above all, needed for administration: names on documents, names on contracts, names on parish rolls.

This reveals the strange dilemma in which the Spanish colonizers found themselves. Until they arrived there was no such thing as a national identity in these islands. There were just groups of people living in *barangays* by the sea, by the river, or *sa ilaya* in a tribal patchwork. The foreigners could not recognize or administer people whose tribal and family identities existed indelibly in the mind but not on a page. The *indios* were in no doubt about who they were; each could position him- or herself in an immensely complex web of genealogies (unlike the European social system, Filipino familial descent is equally matrilineal and patrilineal). But those who knew each other perfectly well as 'Father of So-and-So' or 'Daughter of Thingummy' presented an impenetrable, fluid face to their colonizers, who had to assign them 'proper' names in order to administer them. Whether consciously or not the Filipinos resorted to parody. Some took typical Spanish names, often that of the priest himself. Some wittily appropriated the names of immensely famous and aristocratic Castilian families. Others adopted names of individual saints or of all-purpose Christian import such as 'De los Santos'. This was a splendid ploy. The friars could scarcely object; but for the secular administrators who laboured in their wake, faced with umpteen Johns of the Cross, it must have been a nightmare. In matters of justice, finance and public order it led to chaos; in things like marriage it could imply an outrage to morality since under the cover of twenty-eight people in one village all named Mendoza it was impossible for a priest to be certain about degrees of consanguinity. The thought that he might shortly be marrying a girl to her own uncle in conformity with some cheerful pagan practice was not reassuring.

Being effectively nameless by all being called the same was a brilliant expedient on the part of the oppressed. By as late as 1849 the Spanish authorities were reduced to ordering names to be formally assigned to all those without one. The local *alcaldes* (mayors) usually made things easier for themselves by designating a letter of the alphabet to each pueblo and requiring everyone to adopt a name beginning with that letter. Even today there are small towns where most of the family names start with the same letter; a tribute to tenacity of place as well as to an ancient and ingenious civil disobedience. It should be added that the Spanish were not above playing games of their own, occasionally assigning Filipinos 'joke' surnames such as 'Bizcocho' (biscuit) and 'Cagas' ([he] shits).

The Church's missionary task, meanwhile, proceeded apace. The old tribal pantheons of gods and the deep-rooted animistic beliefs had somehow to be eliminated, whether by decrees and beatings, or – as in the case of the *lingam* – by assimilation. Filipinos must initially have been deeply bemused by the language question. It was not strange that their conquerors should speak their own language among themselves, but that their unfamiliar religious rituals should be conducted in yet another new tongue – Latin – must have struck them as odd indeed. What kind of gods were these that had to be addressed in a separate language? Especially when the priest told you that the three gods were really one, whom you should consider as your Father. Nobody had ever heard of talking to their own fathers in a separate dialect reserved especially for talking-to-fathers. The whole thing was baffling. And since it was baffling, the process of Christian conversion took the friars a long, long time. As is now apparent, it was never wholly achieved; the native culture was too ancient and went too deep. A Filipino priest who used to celebrate Mass in Kansulay until a few years ago remained a firm believer in *nuno* (tree- and water-spirits) as well as in *duwende*, the goblins who live in ant-hills in the woods. One might say that the Holy Trinity and the *genii loci* had achieved a sort of Mexican stand-off, the degree of compromise being nicely illustrated by the fact that the goblins have a Spanish name.

There is no doubt that in the first enthusiastic decades of their presence the friars' achievements were considerable, and they did promote some of the ideals of European humanism as well as literacy. But the years passed and the initial impetus flagged. There must have been several reasons for this, including the archipelago's extreme remoteness from Europe and the likelihood that many of the friars were themselves lacklustre, if not actually barbarous. And not only the friars became lax. The Spanish military cannot have been quite on top of things, either, for during the Seven Years' War the British occupied Manila from 1762 to 1764, only returning it (along with Havana) in exchange for Spanish Florida. During these two years many of the Sepoys the East India Company had brought with their military deserted, and even today there are said to be people in the nearby towns of Cainta and Taytay whose faces supposedly exhibit Indian features.

To return to the friars: well before the turn of the nineteenth century the friarocracy had fallen very far from its founders' ideals. The various orders owned huge tracts of land and wielded absolute power over the *indios* as well as over the Spanish military and civil governors. The Church bled the already impoverished peasants still further with tithes and taxes and indulgences. Many of the friars kept mistresses and had illegitimate children. Indeed, a large proportion of the mestizo blood in modern Filipinos' veins (including, one should note, those of Imelda Marcos herself) comes from those avowedly celibate men of God. No matter that there had always been among the priests men of great saintliness, humanity and courage. Long before the nineteenth century's revolutionary end there were popular revolts and uprisings against the brutality and hypocrisy of individual friars and their local regimes.

By then, though, other things were beginning to change. In the face of increasing economic pressures the Spanish authorities found themselves obliged to open the country to international trade. Even so, social practices and civil rights remained far behind the times. The first Filipino *ilustrados*, the educated middle-class boys who began trickling to Europe in the latter half of the nineteenth century, soon noticed two things that sharpened their nationalism. The first was the developmental gulf between the mother country and her Far Eastern colony that showed only too clearly what a backwater Spain had allowed the Philippines to become. And secondly, those who went on to France and Germany and Britain couldn't help noticing how far Spain herself lagged behind northern Europe. They returned to Manila both thoughtful and angry. Nor was it only Filipinos who noticed the backwardness of their own country. Visiting entrepreneurs and travellers were equally astonished, half enchanted and half repelled. As late as the mid-1890s, an American visitor to Manila was amazed to be able to witness a public garrotting: a festive occasion well attended by an eager crowd that included dainty young mestiza ladies giggling in their Sunday best.[4]

Today's visitor to the Philippines will find, in practically every town of the archipelago, a statue of the national hero, José Rizal. Viewed historically, Rizal was one of the great Asian nationalists of the same generation – he, Gandhi, Tagore and Sun Yat Sen were all born in the 1860s. Yet Rizal was unique, and would have been so in any country at any time. His middle-class provincial boyhood nurtured a great poetic sensibility, while his intellectual achievement when still a teenager turned out to be crucial to his country's subsequent history. For it is a strange fact that despite his fellow *ilustrados'* observations in Spain and elsewhere of the Philippines' backwardness, and despite the growing discontent of Juan de la Cruz, the Filipino 'common man', it seems that no one before Rizal had made the perceptual leap of blaming the friarocracy itself for this state of affairs. It is hard to believe, yet it is a measure of the absolute power the Catholic Church and the Spanish Crown wielded over the minds of their Filipino flock. To query the actions of a friar was to question the Church itself; to question the Church was to doubt the legitimacy of the Spanish Crown. Thus any complaint against a wayward priest led logically to charges of sedition being brought against the plaintiff. Yet it was not the barbarities inflicted on those accused of treason that prevented thought, so much as the idea of rebelling against the mother country. This constituted an effective mental block to all except the adolescent Rizal, whose insight was that the abuses of individual friars were less important than that his country was ruled by foreigners. This notion was so radical and so taboo he initially dared not speak of it to his own conventionally minded parents for fear of offending them, though he did find a sympathetic ear and – later – a brave and loyal supporter in his elder brother Paciano.

Rizal was himself partly scared as well as excited by his own revolutionary conclusion, and there is reason to think that even when he died he was still torn between reformism and outright rebellion. Restlessly, and convinced his life would be short, he resolved to learn as much as he could about his country and its distant 'motherland'. While qualifying as a doctor he twice went to Europe, a typical *ilustrado* who soon became a most untypical polymath, befriending scholars all over the continent and becoming fluent in several languages. At the same time he was writing and talking, above all to other Filipino exiles in Madrid, whose efforts at consciousness-raising constituted the propaganda wing of a proto-revolutionary movement. 'One man opposing a society / If properly misunderstood becomes a myth' wrote Wallace Stevens acutely,[5] and the misunderstanding and myth-making about Rizal started in this European period of the 1880s, not least in his close friendship with the young scholar Ferdinand Blumentritt in Germany, a sojourn that many years later was to give rise to the bizarre rumour that Adolf Hitler was Rizal's illegitimate son.

By then, living on hardly any money, half-starved and half-frozen by European winters, Rizal had begun the novel that made him famous. More immediately, *Noli Me Tangere* was to make him infamous, with its pungent satire on the Church in the Philippines and its shocking details of friar abuses. He departed Europe leaving all who met him deeply impressed and moved by his brilliance and determination. He returned home more than ever certain that his country would never develop until it was free of Spain and the friars. He wanted nothing less than independence, a conviction that had been reinforced by having seen so much of Europe for himself. He was appalled at how far Manila lagged behind Madrid in terms of intellectual freedom. As he had his old scholar, Tasio, explain in *Noli*: 'We in the Philippines are at least three centuries behind the chariot of Progress; we are scarcely emerging from the Middle Ages. That is why the Jesuits, who in Europe are reactionaries, look like progressives to us . . .'[6] Even so, it needs to be pointed out that 'benighted' Spain's colony was the only one in Asia to have had a university in the nineteenth century, whereas the supposedly 'enlightened, advanced imperial powers provided in the same Southeast Asian region [. . .] no real universities in French Indochina, the Dutch East Indies, or British Malaya and Singapore until after World War Two.'[7]

Rizal's second novel, *El Filibusterismo* (1891), contained a more nakedly revolutionary message which not only assured its young author notoriety among his own *ilustrado* class but made his writings central to the growing working-class revolutionary movement. Yet Rizal himself always drew back from calling publicly for revolution, and still more from advocating premature armed struggle. There are still Filipinos who consider he betrayed the revolution he had done so much to set in motion; but theirs is perhaps an ideological zeal too easily felt by non-participants from the safety of a century later. Not only that, it ignores the complexity of Rizal's youthful sensibility. He was above all an intellectual, a poet and radical thinker. The scion of a comfortable *burgis* upbringing, he came to acknowledge himself as ill-adapted to the practicalities of overthrowing a state, even had he wanted to, and it is doubtful whether he ever managed to achieve a private reconciliation between what his intelligence told him was necessary to free the Philippines and an instinctive shying-away from the implied matricide of committing himself to the overthrow of *Inang España*, Mother Spain. Even after he had been banished by the Spanish authorities into internal exile in a remote part of Mindanao (1892–6), it seems likely he went on believing in an essential Spanish benevolence and good sense that could still make possible the Philippines' gradual transition from colony to independent state without bloody confrontation.

Yet in the end there was no benevolence and even less good sense. Rizal's writings had freed too many others to think the unthinkable. The 'Propaganda Movement' that men like Marcelo del Pilar, Lopez Jaena and Rizal himself had organized in the 1880s had politicized thousands of Filipinos, by no means all of them of the *ilustrado* class. Some of these became dissatisfied with what they saw as little more than a reformism that merely allied itself with Spanish liberals in Europe, even though in a famous essay of 1890 (*Filipinas dentro de cien años*) Rizal foresaw that 'one fateful and inevitable day' the Philippines would have to declare independence and become a republic. By mid-1892 the Katipunan revolutionary movement was holding secret meetings under its leader, Andres Bonifacio – later to be known as the 'Great Plebeian'. (*Katipunan* means 'association' in Tagalog. The society's full name meant 'The Most Exalted and Most Honourable Association of the Sons of the Country'.) Bonifacio and his followers were irrevocably sworn to the armed overthrow of Spanish rule. In the critical years of Rizal's banishment to Mindanao, and in the absence of his restraining intellectual presence in Manila, the Katipunan movement became rapidly more powerful and its influence more extensive. It grew especially in the provinces to the north of Manila, the great agricultural heartland of vast haciendas and friar lands that was already a focus for peasant rebellion and which would remain so for the next century.

Eventually, with revolution in the air, the Spanish – by now panicky and frustrated – laid vengeful hands on the person they ultimately blamed for all this. Rizal was arraigned for treason and condemned to death. The medical man of letters who had never so much as lifted a sword in anger (though he was an accomplished fencer) spent his last night in the condemned cell writing his most famous poem, 'Ultimo Adiós'. Early next morning on 30 December 1896, José Rizal was led out to Manila's killing-ground of

Bagumbayan, in the Luneta Park. There, wearing an incongruous bowler hat and facing Manila Bay with his arms tied at the elbow behind him, he was shot in the back by a firing squad, a traitor's death. He was thirty-five. His last words, clearly audible to bystanders, were 'Consummatum est', Christ's own last words, a phrase that many have since taken as proof that Rizal had not repudiated the Mother Church, whatever he felt about Spain. Observers did notice that after the fusillade the squad of Filipino soldiers did not instantly raise the customary cheer of 'Viva España!'. Instead, a strange and awkward silence fell – of shame or else in recognition of a deed that had irrevocably set something in motion whose outcome would dwarf all those present. Only then did the obligatory cheers ring out. It is anybody's guess as to whether any of the firing squad knew that they had just helped bring to an end nearly four centuries of Spanish empire in the Philippines. From the Spanish point of view it turned out to be the worst thing they could have done; from Rizal's it was his crowning achievement. In that instant he became a martyr, his suffering and sacrifice popularly likened to that of Christ. His words and ideas flew like wildfire. Local uprisings turned into mass revolt. In 1898 the brilliant Katipunan general, Emilio Aguinaldo, proclaimed independence from the balcony of his house in Kawit, Cavite (which is still standing), and by the year's end the First Philippine Republic's constitution had been adopted by the Revolutionary Congress in Malolos, Bulacan. Early the following year General Aguinaldo was sworn in as President of the First Philippine Republic.

If there really were such a thing as poetic justice, the poet Rizal's story would have ended with the overthrow of the colonial administration and the creation of an independent Philippines. But fairytale endings are everywhere in short supply. This one was stillborn for a variety of reasons, the overwhelming one being that it had the fatal misfortune of coinciding with the Spanish–American War, which in turn proved to be the genesis of America's overseas empire (her land empire having been secured by wresting it from its native peoples). Even without this unforeseen event that was destined to have such a profound effect on the Philippines, it is not clear that the First Philippine Republic would have lasted. The fact was that the Katipunan's revolutionary forces were a loose amalgam that from a distance – or from a Spanish perspective – might have looked like a consolidated movement, but actually was riven with fractures. These fissures included many of the classic ones of revolutionary movements: leaders who were ambitious for personal power (Andres Bonifacio, 'the Father of the Revolution' was executed for 'treason' by General Aguinaldo's revolutionary government); difficult lines of communication that resulted in a geographical patchiness where organized cadres were concerned; vast disparities in education and understanding of the ideology at stake; similar disparities in military skills and provisioning; the presence of charismatic local religious leaders whose devout peasant followers often expected divine battalions to drop from the sky to their aid; and deep divergences along class lines between what the small but powerful middle class wanted from Spain's departure and what the peasant masses were expecting of the revolution.

In any case, the First Philippine Republic collapsed as the Americans took a hand in the making of the country's history. In the United States the westward push of settlers had reached the shores of the Pacific by the 1850s. There was only one way to go, but that would require a powerful – even global – maritime presence such as Britain had established to maintain her own empire. By the mid-1890s, following the depression of 1893, American domestic disquiet suggested a decisive foreign adventure would be a useful way of easing the pressure. To President McKinley his country's manifest destiny was clear: it lay in an overseas empire. The only problem was finding someone to fight. It sounds cynical to say that America in the 1890s needed a war, but it did. 'Fortunately,' as Gore Vidal remarks, 'Cuba wanted to be free of Spain; and so the United States, a Goliath posing as David, struck down Spain, a David hardly able to pose at all, and thus Cuba was freed to become a client state, the Philippines conquered and occupied, and westward the course of empire flowed.'[8] At the time, Senator Albert J. Beveridge usefully cleared up a few points for any ideologically challenged American democrats:

God has been preparing the English-speaking and Teutonic peoples for a thousand years [to be] master organizers of the world. He has made us adepts in government that we may administer government among savages and senile peoples.[9]

Even so, the idea of a country founded on principles of freedom and democracy deliberately picking a fight with another country just to acquire an empire did not sit easily with the American people. Indeed, until four months before the Spanish–American War, President McKinley himself was assuring Congress that the United States would never annex Cuba since 'it would go against the American code of morality and it would be an act of criminal aggression'. To help reverse this sort of attitude a press campaign began, with Joseph Pulitzer's *World* and William Randolph Hearst's *Journal* printing articles about the economic benefits for everyone, conquerors and conquered alike, should America ever find itself reluctantly obliged to gain an empire. It was an early instance of a supposedly free press being used by the government to sway mass opinion in favour of an adventurist policy that went violently against both the letter and the spirit of the Constitution. (More than sixty years later the same device would be used, for a while successfully, to ensure public backing for the undeclared war in Vietnam.)

The ensuing Spanish–American War was to last a scant eight months, and in its victory and timeliness was viewed by US Secretary of State John Hay as a 'Splendid little war'. It was just cruel luck that in 1898 the Philippines' struggle for independence should have coincided with this righteous imperialism. The Americans spotted their advantage at once. The Spanish were far from home, their ships were old, their credibility was lost among their former Filipino subjects, their forces were occupied with a growing popular insurrection. The Americans contacted the Filipino nationalist forces and offered them a deal. In exchange for their help in routing the Spanish from the archipelago, they said, the United States would ensure the Philippines' independence. There was much debate among the *Katipuñeros*, who by that time had effectively bottled up the Spanish High Command in Intramuros, the walled citadel in Manila. Many of them considered they could manage quite well without American help, having come so far on their own, and were loath to enter into pacts with any more foreigners over the future of their country. But they were overruled and the deal was done. Barely two years after Rizal's execution, Commodore Dewey sank the decrepit Spanish fleet in Manila Bay over breakfast. Eugene Fitch Ware, the sometime lawyer and poet (or maybe sometime poet and lawyer) struck the right note of chirpy triumphalism in his 'Manila':

> *Oh, dewy was the morning, upon the first of May,*
> *And Dewey was the admiral, down in Manila Bay;*
> *And dewy were the Regent's eyes, them royal orbs of blue,*
> *And do we feel discouraged? We do not think we do!*

Meanwhile, an extraordinary deal was done between the Americans and the Spanish. In order that the latter should not have to resist a full US–Filipino assault on their remaining forces, they sued for peace but in a manner that had to do with face-saving on both sides. The Spanish insisted they should be financially compensated for gracefully yielding up their territory to *force majeure*, while the Americans, who had clearly always intended to hang onto the Philippines regardless of any deal they had done with Bonifacio's forces, salved their conscience by turning themselves into simple purchasers, and paid. In this fashion the Philippine Islands and their entire freight of souls changed hands like any piece of real estate for $20 million, made over at the Treaty of Paris in December 1898.

Spain's three-and-a-half centuries' hegemony was finished at last; yet the Filipinos who had fought so decisively to help the Americans rid them of their mutual enemy were astonished to discover that their new allies had no intention of leaving after all. Washington's imperial expansionists were viewing the Philippines as an essential stepping-stone (how history repeats itself!) for American exporters with an eye on the 'Great China Market' (then as now!). This was, of course, the same motive that had led the British to acquire their foothold in Hong Kong back in 1842. However, so bald an act over half a century later merited an official explanation. No sooner was the annexation of the Philippines a *fait accompli* than Washington's rewriting of motives and events began until a disinterested observer might have been excused for thinking that the entire Filipino people had, as one, fallen to its knees to beg for American rule. Certainly the very first clause of the Jones Bill (enacted in 1916), drafted to clarify US intentions *vis-à-vis* questions of Philippine independence, was to read:

Whereas it was never the intention of the people of the United States in the incipiency of the War with Spain to make it a war of conquest or for territorial aggrandizement; . . .

Unfortunately for Washington it seemed a great many Filipinos had indeed misunderstood its lofty motivation. Once the deed was done and the Spanish had left, the Americans had to turn their attention to defeating their former comrades-in-arms whom they now labelled 'insurgents'. As soon as these political realities were made plain, the incredulous President of the First Philippine Republic and his newly appointed government found themselves having to repel the interlopers they had recently welcomed as allies. Their military opposition, though inventive and often heroic, was – like the Republic itself – doomed from the moment when President (still General) Aguinaldo was captured in 1901. At this point the class divisions in Filipino society took on a real importance. A mestizo middle class had been slowly building itself for years, founded on Filipinos with a better-than-average education who had patiently learned how to make themselves indispensable to the overstretched Spanish administration. The canniest ones had wangled themselves clerical jobs in the offices governing friar lands, those vast haciendas and tracts of prime agricultural land that the Church had annexed over the centuries. Gradually, the odd hectare became 'lost' in redrawing a map, a clause was 'overlooked' in copying a land title, and the foundations of a new landed élite were stealthily fashioned. Towards the end of the Spanish period there were mestizo hacienda owners whose children were the *ilustrados* who went abroad to complete their education. After 1898, in the power vacuum that formed in the wake of the defeated Spanish, a proportion of these middle-class Filipinos made it clear they would vastly prefer representatives of an 'advanced' society like America to fill it rather than what they saw as illiterate, rag-tag revolutionaries, no matter how patriotic their rhetoric. The new gentry had no desire to live in a country governed by people like their own estate workers. One of the more perceptive American administrators of the day spotted the outer fringes of a quicksand of social dynamics:

Neither Congress nor the [Philippine] Commission reckoned with the ignorance of the common people nor with the opposition to the acquisition of land by poor Filipinos . . . on the part of their richer and more intelligent fellow-countrymen . . . The cacique does not wish his labourers to acquire land in their own right, for he well knows that if they did so they would become self-supporting, and it would cease to be possible for him to hold them as peons, as is commonly done at present . . .[10]

(*Plus ça change*. The dawdling process of land reform, still very far from complete a hundred years later, testifies to the accuracy of this observation.)

The war that ensued between the new American colonials and their cacique supporters on the one hand, and the Filipino guerrillas and freedom fighters on the other was protracted and bitter. Although the dates of this Philippine–American War are usually given as 1899–1902, it actually lasted until at least 1906 and guerrilla encounters went on throughout the first decade of the twentieth century. By the end, over 4,000 American and 16,000 Filipino troops had lost their lives, but the overwhelming casualties were civilian. Modern scholars estimate that almost a million non-combatant children, women and men died, mainly of disease and starvation.[11] It arguably remains the United States' least-known war. In certain respects it was to be refought more than sixty years later in Vietnam, where not only strategies such as 'hamleting' had been pioneered in the Philippine–American War, but even vocabulary ('gook').

If this was a time of anguish and betrayal for many Filipinos, it was the beginning of a badly muddled period for the United States as a champion of democracy. Plenty of thinking Americans had the gravest misgivings about their already vast country's adventuring in quest of a new imperium. It seemed after all that Uncle Sam was behaving no better than George III had. Mark Twain, for one, was deeply ashamed and outspoken, saying after Dewey's walkover victory in Manila Bay that the stars and stripes of the American flag ought to be replaced with a skull and crossbones. 'We cannot maintain an empire in the Orient and maintain a republic in America,' he said simply. Theodore Roosevelt, who became President in 1901 after McKinley's assassination, was equally though differently unequivocal from the depths of the war with the Filipino 'insurgents':

Every argument that can be made for the Filipinos could be made for the Apaches. And every word that can be said for [President] Aguinaldo could be said for Sitting Bull. As peace, order and prosperity followed our expansion over the land of the Indians, so they will follow us in the Philippines.[12]

But it was not only Americans themselves who were divided over this business of a democratic republic suddenly finding itself becoming imperial. The very ideology of their Constitution was put under extraordinary pressure. One mark of this was official uncertainty about which governmental department in Washington ought to administer the Philippines, since no one could bring himself to come right out and copy Britain's example by setting up a full-blown Colonial Office. The name alone was far too indiscreet. A Filipino historian put this dilemma well as he described the Americans tacitly approving the new imperialism while refusing to face its implications:

Proof of this reluctance, of course, abounded. For one thing the imperialists had to sugar-coat the economic basis of imperialism with such idealistic phrases as 'mission', altruism, destiny . . . Americans could not bring themselves to admit the reality of their empire or to refuse outright the erection of an imperial structure commensurate with their new role. [. . .] The political leadership failed to recognize the need for an additional agency to promote efficiency and centralization. This administrative blindness was most disconcerting to the imperialists; hence they satisfied themselves by establishing an inconspicuous bureau [the Bureau of Insular Affairs] buried among the divisions and offices of the War Department.[13]

Thus it was that the US administered the Philippines through the Bureau of Insular Affairs for thirty-six years, doing its utmost to ensure that the dread words 'colony' and 'colonial' were never used. As for the sugar-coating Cruz refers to, some prime examples were produced by Lt-Col. Clarence R. Edwards, the BIA's head in the early days (his parents were friends of President McKinley's), who was positively lyrical when in full flight. To him, the Philippine venture was 'the grandest altruistic work ever attempted by man. . . . Call it destiny, if you will, say that it was Providence, if you prefer, but a humanly unpreventable tide swept the Philippines into the protection of the United States.'[14]

Like the Spanish before them, the Americans found they had inherited a daunting territory. Troops and administrators alike found themselves balked by densely jungled mountains slashed by deep ravines, as well as by thousands of scattered islands where communication was dependent on boats, which in turn were subject to availability and weather. Even today it is easy to imagine the problems they faced. The jungles may have receded but the mountains and ravines, the sea and the weather remain unchanged. And if today the capital still feels remote to most people living in the provinces, Manila at the turn of the century actually and unironically *was* an *imperium in imperio*, a sort of lightning conductor through which awesome American power fizzed and crackled while the bemused *provincianos* looked on from a distance as at a storm on a far horizon that was destined, sooner or later, to break over every last head in the country. Yet even as the Americans' 'pacification' of the *indios* went on, so did the arguments back in Washington. The Democratic Party's platform was for the Philippines' immediate independence. Thoughtful and articulate people said bluntly that it was ludicrous hypocrisy to preach 'little brown brother's' freedom even as he was being rounded up and his village burned, just as it was to talk about his 'prosperity' while American entrepreneurs were being doled out thousands of hectares of valuable friar lands.

The Republican Roosevelt resisted such arguments with fresh rhetoric; but the fact that issues of principle were being debated which went to the heart of the United States' Constitution was symptomatic of deep American ambivalence over the whole venture, which by now included other ex-Spanish possessions such as Cuba. The American conscience having thus been pricked, it resulted in an irony that connoisseurs of history's cynicism will savour. One of the ways in which Washington contrived to present itself as a liberator was by making sure that the perfidy of the Spanish friars in the Philippines was well known. The reaction to nightmare stories of mediaeval repression and abuses was, predictably, a wave of Protestant sympathy that culminated in a missionary and educational movement to put Filipino souls back on course after centuries of perversion. Having been mis-missionized the first time, they now needed corrective re-missionizing. One result, apart from a good few Protestant zealots descending on the archipelago, was more than a thousand idealistic young Americans who responded to a Presidential appeal for volunteers to help set up a free public educational system in the Philippines. These became known in the islands as 'Thomasites' after the USS *Thomas*, the converted cattle boat that brought the first 600 to Manila in 1901. Hartzell Spence, in his 1964 Marcos hagiography, summarized their pedagogical achievements with his usual felicitous partiality:

> The Thomasites gave the Filipinos in one generation the highest percentage of literacy in Asia. They taught in English from American texts which emphasized political freedom and democratic institutions. Students learned by rote the Gettysburg Address and Washington's farewell to the troops along with sections of *Hiawatha*. . . . The acceptance of democracy, the respect for learning and for educators characteristic of Filipinos today, was a labor of love which the Thomasites bequeathed to the Philippine peoples.[15]

A Filipino writer, Florentino Dauz, viewed the Thomasites' as well as the American missionaries' reading lists rather differently. Taking Malcolm X's distinction between the 'field Negro' and the 'house Negro' he wrote:

> Your missionaries, their teachings enforced by physical violence against school children, forced us to read the life of Booker T. Washington, a house Negro . . .* God Bless America. The Gettysburg Address. Patrick Henry. Jefferson. The Grand Central. J. P. Morgan. Jay Gould. John D. Rockefeller. This catechism was meant precisely to condition the tympanic membrane to hear the same things, and dull the senses in preparation for the ultimate teachings which were yet to come.[16]

* Booker T. Washington (1856–1915) was a Black American teacher and reformer whose civil rights campaigning earned official approval since he advocated industrial education rather than political agitation.

The inclusion of Longfellow in the Thomasites' curriculum showed real wit. Hiawatha had become pretty much the best-known figure in American frontier literature since Natty Bumppo and Uncas had done their stuff in *The Last of the Mohicans*. This sentimentalized portrait of a Native American evidently struck the Thomasites as the perfect model for inducing the right attitude in a fresh supply of *indio* tribespeople. The literary preferences of these early teachers lives on in a way that would have given them great satisfaction. One day in the middle-eighties I wandered into Kansulay's little school when classes were out and found the 'Thought for Today' written up neatly on the blackboard in pink chalk. Normally this would have been a pithily edifying phrase such as 'A cat may look at a king.' Today it was a slab of dear old Longfellow on the gender question:

> As unto the bow the cord is,
> So unto the man is woman,
> Though she bends him, she obeys him,
> Though she draws him, yet she follows,
> Useless each without the other!

This had been popular with Malacañang Palace's image-makers a few years previously when someone, probably leafing idly through a book of quotations for fresh inspiration on how to counteract widespread rumours of Marcos marital shenanigans, had hit on this as a perfect expression of the First Dyad's relationship: Ferdinand and Imelda going inseparably together like, well, a horse and carriage. In any case it was pretty innocuous since Kansulay's ten year olds understood practically no English.

Back in 1901 the average Filipino must have been deeply baffled. What had started out as a long-overdue campaign to oust the Spanish friars had led, via José Rizal's martyrdom in the name of his country, to a second occupation by aliens and a bloody war. But were the Americans liberators or the new enslavers? Were the Filipinos themselves going to turn out to be beneficiaries or losers? It is perfectly true that many Filipinos, then as now, were not nationalists at all, and yearned only for the day when the United States would confer statehood on their archipelago, absorbing it once and for all. (If Hawaii, they were to argue later, why not the

Philippines?) Others, the principled as well as the disaffected, brooded uneasily on McKinley's notion of 'benevolent assimilation' as well as on the implications of 'manifest destiny'.* American uneasiness alone would be enough to guarantee the Philippines' remaining forever outside the Union. No amount of triumphalism could ever blot out Mark Twain's feelings of shame. In one way or another this ambivalence has dogged both countries ever since. A historian's conclusion makes a sad postscript to a venture that has so deeply affected two nations: 'Before long everyone, even Theodore Roosevelt (who had been influential in bringing about their annexation), agreed that the Philippines were an expensive nuisance and their conquest had been a mistake.'[17]

Once the natives had been pacified, the new colonizers made considerable investments in the country's infrastructure and institutions, some of which survive to this day. The Philippine National Bank, for instance, was created in 1916 in the days of Governor-General F. B. Harrison (whose own name lives on in a Manila shopping centre, Harrison Plaza). The fledgling PNB seemed from the start to set an unfortunate precedent. After several untrained Americans had been the Bank's presidents, including a Mr Samuel Ferguson whose 'ignorance of banking was inclusive', circumstances 'came to mean that an organization containing not a single trained banker, not one single man familiar with bank detail, was handling and investing $150,000,000 of values. And, there being no bank examiners, no one was keeping check.'

> They [the Filipino politicos] were like a child with a new toy. They laughed and cried over it, hugged it and kissed it, fondled it, rocked it to sleep and then woke it up and jumped on it, banged it with a club, ripped it open and pulled the stuffing out.[18]

* A phrase popularized by the Democrat journalist John L. O'Sullivan. In 1845 he wrote that it was America's 'manifest destiny to overspread the continent allotted by Providence for the free development of our yearly multiplying millions'. At the time, 'manifest destiny' was seen as justifying the possession of Texas (1845), California (1850), Oregon (1859) and Canada (postponed *sine die*). As time went by, the phrase's implications, like US ambitions, were expanded to cover the acquisition of an overseas empire at the century's end.

The New York accountants Haskins and Sells were employed by the Wood-Forbes fact-finding Commission in 1921 to audit what was by then a banking disaster. 'The investment made by the Philippine Government in the capital stock of the Philippine National Bank has been completely lost . . . [and] . . . the bank has operated . . . in violation of every principle which prudence, intelligence or even honesty could dictate.' This report of 19 May 1921 set the PNB's main losses at $37,544,500, a prodigious sum for it to have mislaid in fewer than five years. Haskins and Sells' report went on: 'The foreign department [of the PNB] operated under the supervision of the Vice-President (M. S. Concepcion, son of the Bank's president) [and] was found to be conducted very inefficiently and dishonestly, necessitating criminal action against the heads of the department . . . The accounting of the bank generally has been extremely bad. Even where proper records had been devised they were generally carelessly and inaccurately kept. There was no record to show the total liability of any customer . . .'[19]

This sort of thing would never for a moment have been tolerated in the United States. Why, then, was it allowed to go on under an American administration abroad, if not because there was at the heart of the whole American enterprise in the Philippines a deep ambivalence, a repressed uneasiness with its own motives that cashed out as an unwillingness to make a real effort? It was as though by not calling the Philippines a colony the United States could avoid a thoroughgoing colonial responsibility for what went on there, and could even reassure its critics that it was, as much as possible, allowing Filipinos to run things in their own fashion.

However, there is no question that the Philippines – an 'expensive nuisance' and a colony by any other name – did profit greatly from American tutelage. The sundry American administrators, bureaucrats, advisers, business people, teachers, doctors and missionaries in the Philippines included the usual proportion of people of goodwill and good faith, often immensely idealistic and eager to counteract any lingering suggestion that their presence was unwelcome by demonstrating the advantages of American liberal democracy. From 1910 or so (by which time military 'pacification' had long been achieved) until the outbreak of the Second World War, Washington spent enormous sums of money on infrastructural projects. Schools, hospitals, roads, bridges, airstrips and ports

all came into being; but just as important as the buildings themselves were the ideas they embodied of a *public* right. Schools
especially, once they no longer functioned as an arm of the Catholic
Church, began slowly spreading a novel degree of literacy as well
as new liberal ideas among the younger population. It was a
system that disseminated its own propaganda too, of course, in
the shape of allegiance to a new mother country and a new flag; but
it did so by means of a cheerful dynamism that was much more to
Filipino taste than had been the dour beatings and pronounce-
ments of the friar schools.

In these same two decades many businesses were set up by
American entrepreneurs, eager to take advantage of the almost free
hand on offer. Great empires came into being in such sectors as
mining (gold in Benguet, for instance) and agriculture (copra,
tobacco and – most notably – Del Monte's pineapple estates). Many
Americans became very rich; but so did many Filipinos, especially
those of the cacique class who had got off to a head start in terms of
accommodations with the new order. In a sense, installing US-style
business practice was the easy part. Somewhat harder to implement was Washington's plan to set up a US-style governmental
system so that as much administration and responsibility as possible might devolve on Filipinos themselves. Behind the ringing
phrases about democracy was the usual dream of every colonial
power: of a peaceful, industrious satellite nation ruled by locals
who knew where their best interests lay, beavering away beneath
the indulgent eye of a Governor-General while the colony's wealth
flowed in a steady stream back to the mother country. To this end,
the Americans began nurturing certain home-grown politicians
who had emerged at the top of the heap from the turmoil of the
failed revolution: men like Manuel Quezon and Sergio Osmeña.

The case of Manuel Quezon nicely illustrates the extraordinary
ambiguity of relationship between a native politician and an occupying power, not least in Quezon's friendship with the MacArthur
family that was destined to have such weighty historical consequences. Quezon was nothing if not a committed Philippine
patriot. He had fought with General (and President) Aguinaldo to
resist the American invaders. Having been appointed in early 1900,
General Arthur MacArthur was the Philippines' military governor
at the time of Aguinaldo's capture. Six years later Manuel Quezon

and Sergio Osmeña were both members of the Immediate Independence Party, whose name proclaimed its patriotic aim even as its tolerated existence testified to a democratic rather than a revolutionary agenda. Quezon, already distinguished by his political dexterity as well as by intelligence and cacique breeding, was exactly the sort of local boy the Americans were eager to groom for government. In 1909 he was appointed Philippine Resident Commissioner in Washington, returning to Manila in 1916 to take up the Senate presidency.

Meanwhile, General Arthur MacArthur's son Douglas had served for a while in the Philippines as a young officer, in 1905 accompanying his father as his aide to Tokyo. Thereafter he enjoyed a distinguished military career, being much decorated in France in the First World War. In 1930 Douglas MacArthur was appointed US Army Chief of Staff. He was in many ways a strange, even romantic figure for a chief military bureaucrat in a gritty and competitive capital like Washington. He yearned for the relaxed days of his youth in the Philippines on the yonder side of the horrors of trench warfare in France. He must have looked back to a nearly Edenic time in a tropical paradise where the part of his life that had not been spent winning the country for America was very gracious and easy-going indeed, full of mansions and servants. As a patrician Republican Douglas MacArthur felt himself completely out of step with the 'New Deal' Democrat Roosevelt, who won the US Presidency in 1932 – an incompatibility that was mutual.

In Manila, despite years of assimilation and Americanization, the old Rizalian ideal of a fully independent Philippine republic had never completely faded, neither at grassroots level nor in the hearts of men like Manuel Quezon. By 1934 modern Filipino history had reached a crucial point when, following intensive nationalist lobbying in Washington, the Tydings-McDuffie Act was passed which provided for the creation of a Philippine Commonwealth for a ten-year transitional period, after which complete independence would be automatic. In 1935 the Commonwealth duly came into being with the election of an all-Filipino administration that in terms of domestic affairs was largely autonomous. The US Governor-General in Manila at the time, Frank Murphy, might have represented the real power behind the throne, but it was a power exercised for the most part in a discreetly 'hands off' manner.

Thus it was that Manuel Quezon was elected President, his Vice-President being Sergio Osmeña. Together they presided over a US-style Congress of two Houses. In 1934, on learning that over in the United States Arthur MacArthur's boy Douglas was coming up for retirement as Army Chief of Staff, and anxious about the military threat he believed Japan was beginning to pose to the Philippines, Quezon had gone to Washington to ask for MacArthur's services as a strategist. Washington was happy to oblige. For his own part, MacArthur was only too pleased to escape Washington and the prospects of imminent retirement to take up a glamorous posting in Manila as his old friend President Quezon's proconsul. Once there, he soon persuaded Quezon to create a new title for him (since Roosevelt had refused to do any better than 'Military Adviser to the Commonwealth'): Field Marshal of the Philippines. He even designed his own uniform: 'black trousers, white tunic, and a braided cap, the whole costume spangled with medals, stars and gold cord like a matador's suit-of-lights'.[20] His own patrician background made close friendship with the old colonial oligarchy far more congenial to him than Washington's political minefields had ever been, and he and Quezon became very close. He much admired the intelligence with which the new President steered a course between the dictates of his fervent Filipino nationalism and those of the pragmatic cohabitation with Washington necessary for these last ten years of US tutelage. Quezon was also an excellent organizer and commander, and it was maybe this that gave his new Field Marshal the mistaken impression that his own job was something of a sinecure. At all events MacArthur clearly spent more time on social rounds in his Ruritanian finery than he did on efficiently organizing the defence of the Philippines.

Historians have blamed General Douglas MacArthur for not taking full advantage, in late 1941, of the ten hours' warning he was given after the Japanese attacked Pearl Harbor. Certainly the Japanese caught his small air force unprepared and on the ground. They landed along the western coasts of Zambales and Pangasinan (in the Gulf of Lingayen, the place of the *lingam*) and the Bataan peninsula soon fell. The surviving American troops, most of whom were Filipino conscripts, were walked in the notorious 237-kilometre

Death March to concentration camps in Tarlac province. Thousands died in terrible circumstances in the first months of the war. General MacArthur fled his stronghold on Corregidor Island in Manila Bay, vowing famously to return. By early 1942 the Philippines once again found itself subject to a new foreign government, yet another colonial power.

The fact that Filipinos were now caught up in the Second World War merely gave a painful urgency to old and unresolved issues. Now whose side were they on? American promises for the Philippines' full independence, the transition period for which had begun in 1935, were now on indefinite hold. So would the Filipino best serve his country's interests by collaborating with these new Japanese masters, or by resisting them? Was the patriotic Filipino a quasi-American or – at some deeper level – a patriot of a nation that so far existed only in dreams? It was a profound moral dilemma. By this time the country's Americanization was quite marked, not only by the way in which the English language had supplanted Spanish but because so many young Filipinos had spent years in the United States at university or military colleges like West Point. Everything in the previous forty-four years, including *The Song of Hiawatha*, had confirmed their belief in the supremacy of American power, both economic and military. Yet in the space of a few weeks, beginning with Pearl Harbor, Americans had been routed from their possessions all over the Far East and Pacific and seemed to be in full retreat. Filipinos had noted the equal routing of the British from their strongholds like Singapore and Burma and wondered whether this might in fact be the end of Western imperialism in the East. With the easy Japanese defeat of MacArthur and his abandonment of the Philippines to its fate, some element akin to awe in the attitude of Filipinos towards the Americans died, never to be resuscitated. The Japanese expertly played on these suspicions that the Statue of Liberty actually had feet of clay. Cannily – as they integrated the Philippines into the rapidly expanding Japanese empire, the so-called 'Great East Asia Co-Prosperity Sphere' – they claimed that their troops had finally freed the Philippines from the colonial domination of Westerners. Filipinos were true Easterners, like the Japanese. It was a deep alliance of the blood that no amount of indoctrination by foreigners could efface. And once again, many Filipinos were responsive to this fresh rhetoric of liberation.

Besides, there were pressing matters of everyday pragmatism, of *pakikisama* – that highly valued Filipino virtue of being able to get along with people in a smooth and unruffled manner. The thing about the Americans was that they were no longer here, whereas the Japanese most certainly were. Therefore one had to get along with them as painlessly as possible. This was less collaboration than common sense.

It would be naive to think today, nearly sixty years later, that these issues are long dead and academic. (One need only look at France and Switzerland, where the question of who collaborated with the Nazis is still very much alive.) National traumas have a habit of living on, even when there are few left alive with any direct memory of them. It is hard to understand the precise mechanism by which this happens. In some mysterious way a people's hurt evokes a defensive strategy, which in turn becomes a national attitude and ends by being an aspect of the culture. In present-day Filipino public life it is possible to read, in the right historical light, a long succession of injuries and their scar tissue. It is like a palimpsest, a document many times erased and written over, the traces of whose earlier versions may still be glimpsed by those so inclined. The less patient will simply reach for the nearest moral judgement.

In the Second World War, the division of Filipinos into at least two minds was reflected by the widespread resistance to the Japanese occupation. Many took to the hills and joined up with fighting units, as the young Ferdinand Marcos did in Northern Luzon. Some of their older compatriots already had guerrilla experience. In the thirties, peasant protest at worsening relations between landowners and their tenants, as well as over increasing hardship, had led to the formation of labourers' organizations and to occasional violent acts such as crop-burning. These unions, intimately connected as they were with the local terrain, were nodes of invaluable experience around which a more general struggle could be organized. A guerrilla organization was formed known as the *Hukbalahap*, a composite name which translated as the People's Anti-Japanese Army. The ensuing warfare threw up the usual extreme cruelties and exposed all the predictable heroisms and villainies of family loyalties, private fidelities, concealed class warfare, old scores, betrayals, turncoatism and collaboration.

It is safe to say that, of all the traumas Filipinos had collectively undergone since the moment Magellan landed, the Second World War was by far the worst. In 1945 General MacArthur did return, landing in Leyte to fight his way back across the archipelago – some scholars now say quite unnecessarily given the inevitability by then of Japanese defeat. Yet the Japanese put up an extraordinary resistance, none more so than those units in Manila. There are those who take this as simply a measure of their extreme loyalty to the Emperor, citing diehards like Lt. Onoda Hiroo, the last known 'straggler' who went on obeying his orders in the jungles of Lubang Island scarcely fifty miles from Manila until 1971 (he was finally induced to surrender by the Japanese Ambassador hovering above him in a helicopter, assuring him over a loud-hailer that the war was over and he had the Emperor's assurance that it was OK to stand down. A similar diehard, Shoichi Yokoi, was to surrender the following year in the jungles of Guam, having made his clothes out of tree bark for twenty-seven years. He returned to Japan saying 'Shamefully I have come back home alive' and died in 1997). Other historians claim there was a darker reason for the Japanese stand in Manila, which was that by concentrating the Americans' efforts it bought time for special units to hide the last of Yamashita's treasure elsewhere in the islands.

One might as well deal with this business of the Yamashita treasure here and now and get it out of the way. There are as many versions of it as there are interested parties, but as far as one can gather the theory goes roughly as follows: Japan invaded Manchuria in 1931, using as a pretext the so-called Mukden Incident – an explosion on the Japanese-controlled South Manchurian Railway. Thereafter, its military conquest of East Asia continued with the gradual occupation of strategic areas of China. The pace of conquest accelerated with the taking of Laos in 1941, Japanese forces then moving swiftly to occupy as much territory as they could including, of course, Hong Kong, Singapore, the Philippines and all Indonesia. On the way they raided the national banks and treasuries, stealing any private wealth they could find and creaming off the profits of the different black market gangs and triads they encountered. By the time the Philippines had fallen in 1942 they had allegedly amassed a vast 'snowball' of gold bullion, coins, pearls, diamonds and all manner of wealth. One would have thought that, until the Americans had recovered from Pearl Harbor enough for their warships to begin making the oceans unsafe for Japanese shipping, much of this wealth could easily have been sent back to Japan in instalments, making an accrued treasure unnecessary; but this is too cheerless a prospect for treasure freaks. In one way or another, therefore, this giant snowball of loot was apparently trundled into the Philippines, where the Japanese considerably added to it by ransacking gold mines such as those at Benguet as well as whatever Douglas MacArthur and President Quezon had left in the Central Bank.

When in due course it became clear that the Japanese were losing the war they apparently took the decision that, whereas they could be induced to relinquish all their other conquests, they were determined at all costs to hang onto the Philippines. General Yamashita was then posted to Manila to supervise the archipelago's defence. This soldier had had an odd war, having made a brilliant start by becoming known as the 'Tiger of Malaya' for leading his 30,000 men down Malaya, across the Strait of Johore and on to Singapore, where he faced down Lt.-Gen. A. E. Percival with his 80,000 men. In a dazzling piece of psychological warfare, Yamashita had sat down with Percival and, with a mixture of bullying and complete bluff, induced Percival with his vastly superior forces to surrender. The fall of Singapore made Yamashita a great popular hero in Japan, although he was never allowed a triumphant return to Tokyo. Years before, he had fallen out with the Prime Minister, General Tojo, and now found himself transferred thousands of miles north to Manchuria and relegated to an obscure outpost there until 1944. By then Tojo and his Cabinet had resigned, and with the war going badly for Japan the Tiger of Malaya was recalled and posted to Manila, where he took control of the Fourteenth Army. It was therefore while he was in command of the Japanese forces in the Philippines during the closing months of the war that a decision was taken to divide up the supposedly incalculable quantities of Asian treasure and hide it in secret caches spread throughout the archipelago. (This, of course, is an obvious congruence with that sixteenth-century pirate, Lim Ah Hong.) General Yamashita was not personally involved in this: the 'Yamashita treasure' only bears his name because it was hidden largely during the months of his command.

Whether the Japanese fought the Battle of Manila partly as a delaying tactic is still not clear; but according to one theory it did buy enough time (while concentrating the Americans' efforts on the city) for dedicated bands of Japanese officers to be able to supervise the hurried digging of pits and tunnels elsewhere in Luzon in which gold bars and barrels of jewels could be stashed. The various hiding places were apparently constructed with great craftiness, protected by every sort of trickery: false maps, blind tunnels, a few gold bars left as decoys, shafts that flooded when a baulk of timber was removed, and poison gas or explosives to be triggered by an unwary searcher. There is an account of such things, plus a description of a treasure-hunt in the late 1980s on Corregidor Island and in Fort Santiago, in Charles C. McDougald's book *Asian Loot* (San Francisco, 1993) which one can wholeheartedly recommend to treasure enthusiasts. It is set firmly in that charmed world of old maps and characters of such transparent shadiness their word can only be accorded absolute trust. Another author, Dick Russell, wrote in *The Man Who Knew Too Much*: 'As late as 1986, a team of high-ranking US military personnel was reportedly in the Philippines in search of the buried bullion. One of these was General John Singlaub, the CIA's deputy chief in South Korea during the Korean War and later tied into the Iran–Contra scandal . . .' Obviously, there must be something in it.

At the end of the war, all this would have been neither here nor there to the wretched Manileños trapped in the city. Admiral Sanji Iwabuchi's Manila Naval Defence Force received and wholeheartedly implemented the following orders for the period 23 December 1944 – 14 February 1945:

When Filipinos are to be killed they must be assembled in one place and disposed of, with the proviso that ammunition and manpower must not be wasted. Because the disposal of dead bodies is a troublesome task, they should be collected together in houses scheduled for burning or demolition. They should also be thrown into the river.[21]

In early 1945 the Japanese marines, faced with defeat, 'went on an orgy, raping, shooting, bayonetting, beheading and burning alive tens of thousands of unarmed Filipino citizens'.[22] It is from this period that stories abound of babies being thrown into the air and impaled on bayonets as a game played by Japanese soldiers. Meanwhile, those Manileños who escaped the attentions of the Japanese were being bombed and strafed from the air by the Americans. The battle left the city of Manila virtually destroyed, while the last of the Japanese high command surrendered up north in Baguio. If the Americans saw themselves as saviours, then it was perhaps in the same sense that a US Army major in 1968, speaking of the smoking ruins of Ben Tre, a town in South Vietnam he was fighting to defend, famously said to a reporter: 'It became necessary to destroy the town to save it.'[23]

With salvation like this, who needs perdition? – a question that must have been asked by Filipino survivors not just of the Battle of Manila but of the entire war. By the end, it is probable there remained not a single family anywhere in the country that had not known loss, while thousands of families had vanished entirely. And once again, history was about to repeat itself. The post-war world was shaking down into new power blocs. The Americans and the rest of the Allies found themselves squaring off to the Soviet Union, until lately their comrade-in-arms against the Axis powers. In the Philippines the Huk guerrillas, who throughout the occupation had fought heroically from the inside after the Americans had fled, now found themselves labelled by the returning Americans as 'Communist insurgents'. Even as full independence was finally granted in 1946 an American-backed Philippine military campaign began, aimed at mopping up the guerrillas in the hills who had outlived their usefulness and had suddenly turned from being gallant allies into the enemies of freedom and democracy. It is not clear if most Filipinos, including the first President of the (independent) Republic of the Philippines, Manuel Roxas, fully comprehended the extent to which they were hostages to a power-play that was truly global, just as they had been in 1898. After China went Communist in 1949 the Philippines was for the moment less valuable to the Americans as a stepping-stone to the vast potential market of the mainland than as a strategic base for US forces, a vital link in a chain of such bases designed to run entirely around the Communist world like a cordon sanitaire that would contain it as well as guaranteeing no part of that world was in theory unreachable by the bombers of

Strategic Air Command. Probably few Filipinos perceived the political realities as clearly as did the ex-Huks now being chivvied through the hills. Exhausted and decimated as they were by years of jungle-living and skirmishing with the Japanese, there can have been few of them with the energy to espouse Communist ideology with a view to continuing the struggle for a fresh objective. On the other hand, most of them must have been properly sceptical about what Philippine independence (officially declared in 1946) could possibly mean in circumstances that made it clear the Americans still called the shots from the huge bases they retained in Olongapo, Subic Bay and Angeles, Pampanga. They certainly appeared to regard President Roxas as no more than a puppet.

A resistance to the new status quo lingered on throughout the fifties in the form of guerrilla activity which brought whole towns temporarily under Huk control, moving closer and closer to Manila. This had the effect of frightening people off the land and into the capital. It also brought direct CIA intervention which became a major factor during Magsaysay's presidency. This sort of destabilizing skirmishing continued into the sixties when a worsening domestic economy in the hands of the new Filipino oligarchy coincided with Mao's Great Proletarian Cultural Revolution (1966–8). By now the Huks as such were no more, given that their very name was no longer applicable; but their Communist successors, as the New People's Army, were very much in existence up in the hills or in the rustling canefields of the vast sugar estates of Negros. They, at least, recognized that the United States had lost interest in Filipino democracy – had, in fact, lost interest in the Philippines except as an essential military foothold off Southeast Asia and as a lucrative arena for American business (Del Monte's vast pineapple estates, for instance, had been acquired even before the turn of the century when, following an opportunistic enquiry, the American Governor-General in Manila elected to ignore the statute limiting landholding to 1,024 hectares and made over a large area of Philippine public land to the US Navy, then ordered the Navy to sublet 20,000 hectares to Del Monte. This was not dissimilar to Dole Pineapple's helping to end the monarchy in Hawaii, declaring a republic, and then insisting that the United States annex the islands – which it did in 1898. Men like Sanford Dole were the true kings of the banana republics of the future).

In fact the NPA guerrillas commanded a good deal of sympathy if not actual assistance from many educated Filipinos, including the more radical clergy, whose moral support ran from expressions of nationalist sentiment to revolutionary zealotry. This was the time of Marcos's first term as President (1965–9), when quite a few well-brought-up middle-class students abandoned their degree courses and went off to join the NPAs. A good proportion of them were not Communist at all but merely youthful idealists who identified with Juan de la Cruz in his sufferings at the hands of a still feudally minded élite. They, too, were under no illusions about the Americans having ceded their power to an independent Philippine government. Indeed, to the present day it is still commonly understood that no Philippine administration or chief executive has ever taken office without Washington's approval and active connivance.

Certainly it is open to anyone to query matters of emphasis in so brief a résumé of Philippine history. What cannot be disputed, however, is the relevance of this anguished past to every aspect of today's country. Whether or not the threat of Maoist Communism was ever as real as Washington and Manila claimed, when Ferdinand Marcos declared martial law in 1972 he did so with Washington's express approval. This was in order to give himself the extraordinary powers he said he needed to put an end to Communist-led subversion. It can scarcely have been irrelevant to his decision that it empowered him to remain in office indefinitely. Once again Filipino guerrillas and Filipino armed forces skirmished bloodily in the hills, and once again historic questions were raised. The country that had been known as 'the showcase of democracy' lived for over eight years under American-backed martial law, with its suppression of habeas corpus and human rights, its electoral fraud, constitutional tinkering, censorship, jailings and torturings. These years between 1972 and 1981 left a deep mark on an already scarred national psyche, a wound which the 'EDSA Revolution' of 1986 did nothing to heal. Twelve years later, many Filipinos argue that the revolt which sent the Marcoses into exile had a parallel with the 1896 Katipunan Revolution in that both were essentially led by the *ilustrado* class, and both leaderships soon sold out their own radical element in order to maintain the status quo. To such critics, the 'People Power' that heroically stopped Marcos's tanks was more of a middle-class revolt led by liberals and bankers fed up with the mortally ill Marcos's mis-management of the economy and the consequent devaluation of their assets.

The old questions remained. What *was* democracy really about? Come to that, what was a Filipino? Who owned the nation's flag to which one's children daily pledged their loyalty at school? Did the chain of command end at the President's desk in Malacañang Palace, or did the buck not stop until it had reached the President's desk in the Oval Office of the White House? How could the urgent importance to the United States of its military bases in the Philippines be ignored, both in the Vietnam War and in the larger context of containing Communism? In which case, what did Philippine independence mean? And aside from that, was the country really being run in order to make it a better place for Juan de la Cruz and his wife to bring up their children in peace and a smattering of prosperity?

Even if Juan de la Cruz did not actually voice such questions each day they formed, and still form, a vital part of his awareness. They arise directly from a grievous past, much of which is too recent to be ignored, too painful to be forgotten. If this chapter has sounded a polemical note, dwelling on the more glaring abuses of Spanish, American and Japanese imperialism alike, it is for the sole purpose of trying to represent something which few historians seem prepared to talk about: the sheer confusion that successive generations of Filipinos have felt when confronting the latest invaders with their fresh protestations of altruism that scarcely concealed naked self-interest. One does not for a moment discount the advances and benefits these invaders brought, any more than one wishes to deny that great numbers of individual foreigners have been utterly genuine in their love of the Philippines and the Filipino people and have wished them nothing but well. For every awful tale there are abundant stories of deep friendships and sac-rifice on both sides, of inter-marriage and all sorts of alliances and relationships, often forged in the teeth of doctrinaire opposition or outright danger. Even obscure Kansulay has its mixed memories. There was wartime horror when three men from a town a few miles down the coast were rounded up by the Japanese for allegedly having given succour to Huk guerrillas. On Christmas Day 1942 they were paraded around the little grid of streets wearing 'confessional' placards around their necks, made to dig their own graves and executed. It shocked the province and has not been forgotten to this day. Yet neither has the friendly and religious Captain Takimori, the Japanese provincial commander who, for too short an incumbency in the capital town, took an interest in local customs and beliefs and made his officers return all the religious statues and little treasures they had looted from churches and houses.

The point is that it is precisely this bewildering conflict of emotions that has left its indelible mark on an entire population. Had Filipino history been one long catalogue of monstrous and unrelieved tyranny it might arguably have been less muddling and complex in its psychic legacy. As it is, though, a largely non-literate people with an array of animist and other beliefs was suddenly subjected to waves of foreigners preaching a God of Love even as they whipped and garrotted, announcing democracy and liberty even as they reneged on a pact and declared war, and claiming Asian blood-brotherhood even as they turned the country into a prison camp. Nevertheless, this tends not to be spoken about as constituting a national *problem*, even though, if this were the case-history of an individual, a reasonable modern person would think it unlikely that any child could have undergone such a background of betrayal and rejection and still have grown up at ease with itself and its position in the world.

3

Ferdinand Marcos makes
a good start

After such a necessarily crude overview of Philippine history, it might be useful at this point to have an even balder biographical outline of the man who became President in 1965 – Ferdinand Edralin Marcos.

Born 1917, law graduate with top Bar honours 1940, briefly interned by the Japanese 1942, subsequently getting by until 1945. Congressman 1949, Senator 1959, President of the Philippines 1965–86. His first term of office was marked by a 'technocratic' style of government that concentrated on building roads, schools, hospitals and other neglected areas of the infrastructure. Re-elected 1969. In 1972, in response to leftist dissent much influenced by Mao's Cultural Revolution (1966–8) as well as to more general lawlessness, he declared martial law with the full support of Washington. At first this probably had the support of a majority of Filipinos as well. The law and order situation improved dramatically for a while even though Marcos's martial law regime, despite its brutalities, was a good deal more liberal than other Asian equivalents. This period also saw the launch of his new political party, the KBL, which embodied his ideological vision of a New Society. But as martial law wore on for almost nine years, becoming increasingly unpopular, the New Society seemed to most people more and more to resemble the old. Marcos's Constitutional Convention, which effectively rewrote the Constitution to give Marcos virtually unlimited power and tenure, aroused deep hostility and scepticism. By 1980 he had been secretly diagnosed as fatally ill. From now on, albeit with remissions, his health would steadily decline and with it his grip on events which he had once controlled with consummate ease. In 1983 the Philippines was in grave economic crisis, the same year that saw the assassination of his only credible political opponent, Benigno Aquino, on his return from exile in the United States. This event, provoking widespread condemnation both at home and abroad, can be seen as having sealed Marcos's political fate. In 1985 he called for a snap election to justify his claims of legitimacy for continuing as President. The prospect of yet another Marcos term of office precipitated the 1986 *coup d'état* by Juan Ponce Enrile and Fidel Ramos (respectively his personal lawyer and cousin) popularly known as the 'EDSA Revolution'. The Marcos family were banished to Hawaii by President Ronald Reagan, whose support had continued until Ferdinand's last day in office. He died in exile, 1989.

The future President Marcos was born in 1917 in Sarrat, Ilocos Norte. Seventy-nine years later I was given a guided tour of the area by an old friend who is himself an Ilocano, although one staunchly opposed to Marcos from at least his declaration of martial law in 1972 until the end of his presidency. He is endlessly cynical about the dead President. He is also endlessly proud of being Ilocano, a cultural solidarity which now and then spills over unintentionally to include the man whose embalmed body we are about to visit in Batac, a town only about ten miles from Sarrat. On the long drive up from Manila this friend was a fund of scandalous stories and observations, but the real enthusiastic flow began only once we had crossed the Agno River in the north of Tarlac province. Before that we passed the Aquino family's Hacienda Luisita which Cory, when she succeeded Marcos as President, had in a fit of absent-mindedness committed herself to including in the nation's pressing land reform scheme. This was a lapse she later and firmly corrected by retaining every last square metre of the enormous estate. 'Trouble here recently,' my friend observed gleefully. 'It was in the papers, did you see? Some of her wretched tenants were complaining they were kept so poor they'd been forced into prostitution.' His scepticism about Marcos extends firmly to Ferdinand's successor.

An hour or so later we crossed the Agno. My friend expanded visibly. 'Ah,' he said with a sigh of satisfaction. 'We are now in the Ilocos. I smell my home.'

'I thought this was still Tarlac?'

'Oh, forget lines on the map. The point is, these people round here –' he waved a hand at the window towards the knots of labourers in the fields – 'they're Ilocanos. You look, in a few miles you'll soon see the difference . . . Now, *there* – you see those houses? They're just *nipa* huts, aren't they? Regular *bahay kubo*. But see how neat they are? Everything tidy, the yard swept, the fences mended. You'll never see that down in Manila or in your province. The Tagalogs are basically sluts and slovens. Go on, admit it; you've never seen Tagalogs live like this, have you? Oh, the *odd* one maybe, the one-in-a-million. But never a whole village. Look at this . . . And look at the fields, too. Everything neat, the crops well-tended, every last square metre in use, everyone busy. No fields lying fallow because nobody can be bothered to plough them. Nobody goofing off in the shade like the Tagalogs . . . We're a different race up here. That's the whole point about Marcos. You must get that straight. He was an Ilocano to the bone. That's why he appointed all those Ilocanos to the armed forces. Of course. He knew he could trust them. You know what they used to say in those days when a military man was passed over for promotion? "He comes from the wrong side of the Agno."'

He breaks off to observe of the bus we are stuck behind, 'You see that name? That fleet's owned by a provincial governor. He's a famous drug addict and a sex pervert. He beats and tortures his women. He is a sadist. It's all in the newspapers . . .'

After a while we reach Pangasinan province where my friend was born and he explains how his family had been part of the late-nineteenth century migratory wave of Ilocanos who had flooded southwards. Land had always been a problem for Ilocanos; the twin provinces of Ilocos Norte and Ilocos Sur are crowded between the sea and the mountains of the Cordillera Central. Many of those migrating south were actually headed east to the green and under-populated Cagayan Valley but had to go the long way around because the intervening mountains were impassable to their waggons. 'My God, they were poor in those days. Buffalo carts with wood wheels. Barefoot . . .' At this point my friend confesses to having a mild shoe fetish because he himself had been sent barefoot to school (in the early thirties when a pair of child's shoes cost ₱1.50) where he was once humiliated by having to receive a prize, clumping up to the stage in wooden clogs amid titters. Here he admits himself sympathetic to Imelda Marcos's own obsession with shoes, which has similar origins. The world mocks without knowing the injury of a childhood shame. (In nearly every culture, it seems, shoes become a rather obvious symbol of economic status, and one frequently notices Filipinos looking at feet almost before they look at faces. They can spot real leather at a glance. Evidence of class stigma lingers on in different vocabularies. Not for nothing did the French version of such wooden clogs or *sabots* give the word 'sabotage'. Today the word for clogs, *bakya*, has become a downcast, unrevolutionary adjective meaning 'low-rent', 'tacky', 'poor' or 'old-fashioned'.)

My friend had indeed been *bakya*, but as an intellectual and a socialist he is now proud of it. As an Ilocano he evidently feels the solidarity for his people's history of one who has for years been living exiled from Arcadia down in that Tagalog stronghold, Manila. We stop at Agoo, just over the La Union border, where he eats hugely of some blackish food he says was a favourite of Ferdinand's. When we are under way again I have to admit that the atmosphere up here is different. It is not like the Philippines I am familiar with. The roads are good (thanks, of course, to Marcos), the fields are indeed well worked and neat. Motor scooters abound, a rare enough sight back in Manila for their presence up here to be noteworthy. My friend explains that they're smuggled. The capital of Ilocos Norte, Laoag, is only about as far from Taiwan as we have just driven from Manila. 'Chinese genes,' he says. 'Lots of them here, we're so close. Smuggling, ancient trade links, ties of blood and character. That's the secret. Ilocanos are like the Scots, frugal, hard-working, hard-headed . . .'

The heat beats inward through the window glass onto my right cheek. It is that dozy, early-afternoon moment for siestas and an absence of strenuous reflection. My friend goes on drowsily singing the praises of all things Ilocano, plainly happy to be home, as proud of this landscape as he is sad that his cradle tongue, Ilokano, has become rusty. 'You look at the houses of the poor down south,' he keeps saying. 'I've never been to that village of yours – what is it,

Kansulay? – but I'll bet it's slovenly. Southern Tagalog, right? Bound to be filthy and demoralized. Look at these houses. Up here it's not demoralizing to be poor, you see. There were never any big haciendas like in Pangasinan and Tarlac. People could own their little plot of land and work it for themselves. You look when we get to Laoag. On the covered market they put up a notice, I expect it's still there. "*Bawal sa Tamad sa Laoag*": "Laziness Forbidden in Laoag". Imagine, in the Philippines! You can see we Ilocanos are a race apart.' I am too sleepy to protest that this civic gesture – a Tagalog phrase, at that – can be seen nowadays all over the Philippines. It doesn't seem to matter; I have got the underlying Ilocano message loud and clear. *We are different.*

We stop in a succession of towns along the coast to look at old Spanish churches. Some have had the original stucco stripped off their exteriors to expose thin bricks laid horizontally as well as patches of rubble and bodge, which is why they were rendered in the first place. This rare sight of bricks in a largely brickless country reminds me of Italian churches that have lost their stone facings and show how their original builders had been equally rough and ready. I wonder aloud whether there is stonework missing which someone has incorporated into his own home, like a house in Cairo in which I once stayed whose foundations were largely built of facing slabs from the Great Pyramid. My friend sets me straight. At least, I presume him to be correct when he says:

'It wasn't stone, it was plaster. It was Imelda Marcos who had it done. It was an idea from her later phase, in the early eighties. She'd abandoned her Filipino nationalist period and had caught a sort of Euro-Renaissance snobbery from her arty American friends like Van Cliburn and the Italian-born Cristina Ford. She started collecting lots of paintings – not wisely and not well, unfortunately; she was badly advised. She also began changing views and buildings that didn't match her fantasies. She set-dressed quite a lot of the Ilocos, you'll see. She just got this urge to antiquify, never mind how inauthentic the results. You wait till we get to Vigan – she whitewashed the entire town. I'm not kidding. I guess she thought it looked more Spanish that way. A Hollywood version of the Mediterranean, you know? So with this church she took off the plaster and exposed the brickwork. Did you know she also decided that all Manila should be re-roofed in tile? Imagine – there's scarcely been a single tiled roof in Manila since the Second World War, when every last one was smashed. When she was Governor of Metro Manila she passed a law instituting compulsory tiling. Nothing came of it, of course. She'd overlooked the total lack of tile factories.'

We soon come on Vigan which, the hand of Imelda Marcos notwithstanding, cannot fail to give a European a small *frisson* of homesickness in this land of cement block construction mostly dating from the last fifty years. It is a largely intact Spanish town, prettified here and there and inevitably with the faint whiff of the museum about it. However, there is at least one genuine museum that really does evoke the Spanish period since it has not yet fallen into the hands of the heritage industry. This is the birthplace of Father Burgos, who, in the company of two other priests, was executed in 1872 by the Spanish at the urging of the friars as the alleged instigators of the Cavite Uprising. The three priests – Gomez, Burgos and Zamora – are known collectively as Gomburza. A typically Filipino contraction, this, 'Gomburza' became the secret password of Bonifacio's Katipunan, for the priests' martyrdom was a harbinger of the 1896 Revolution. They were radical only to the extent that they were urging the Filipinizing of the Church, and were thus initiators of the Philippines' first proper reform movement. Fr. Gomez was seventy-three; Fr. Burgos was thirty-five; Fr. Zamora was thirty-seven. José Rizal's elder brother, Paciano, had studied with Fr. Burgos at Manila's Dominican college, San Joseé, and became his favourite pupil. When Burgos and his two companions were led out to the garrotte at Bagumbayan, the selfsame place where José Rizal was to be shot twenty-four years later, it represented a turning-point in the lives of youths like Paciano, as it did in Philippine history. It was an extraordinary thing that the Holy Church could publicly strangle three of its own ordained priests, one of them a venerable old man, by means of an iron collar and screw. A black cloth was thrown over their heads and, beneath it, their necks were broken one by one. A dark and violent thing, Spanish catholicism. As Rizal himself once remarked sardonically of Spain: 'The land of Goya.'

We wander through Fr. Burgos's birthplace past a series of horrid but fascinating oil paintings of the Basi Rebellion of 1807, an Ilocano uprising provoked by the Spanish government's prohibiting the locals from brewing their own traditional drink, *basi*, and obliging them instead to buy it from government stores. The crude paintings were done by an amateur some twenty years later, but his detailing of what had happened to the revolt's ringleaders suggests he may have been an eyewitness. The heads of the executed men are depicted being sawn off and put in iron parrot cages for, presumably, exhibition. The parrot cages remind me of the cloth thrown over Burgos's head in Bagumbayan in 1872. By a mental leap no doubt suggested by all this mediaevalism I suddenly recall the case of the Catholic priest mentioned by the anthropologist Michael Taussig. This man, in the early part of the *twentieth* century, burnt a woman alive in northern Peru because she was accused of being a witch.[1]

The house in which the future martyr was born is charming, random, rambling, airy and genuinely old, full of beguiling odds and ends in no particular order. Downstairs there is a gallery of famous sons and daughters of Ilocos, including Ferdinand Marcos. His portrait is that jaunty photograph taken of him looking very young, wearing a Second World War glengarry and beaming cockily. Beneath this is printed the whole official martial-law-era biography, including the story of his being the most decorated Filipino of the war. This is Marcos in the old, unreconstructed version. It has escaped the Cory-era revisionist's blue pencil that stripped him of his medals and reduced him to the barest historical necessity of having been 'the country's Sixth President (1965–86)'. The censorship practices of free societies are always more interesting than those of totalitarian regimes. So far as the Burgos Museum is concerned the last fifteen years might never have happened. I like its dusty unwillingness to bring itself up to date. But then, up here in Ilocos political correctness has local implications of its own where a famous Ilocano is concerned.

Eventually we reach the town of Batac, an orderly-looking place. This is the heartland of Marcos country. The name Marcos is not especially obtrusive but, like the elephants somebody was once absolutely forbidden to think about, lurks constantly just beneath the mind's horizon. Outside the town hall is a vast banner that reads 'Home of Great Leaders'. My friend dusts off his Ilokano to good effect and we are directed to a couple of colonial-looking brick houses with *capiz* shell windows on the river bank. Either they have been beautifully restored or else – as my friend suggests – entirely invented by Imelda, as were dozens of 'ancestral homes' during the Marcos incumbency. It was a rich period for the instant dynasty. Again, there are no notices other than a small sign saying only 'No Cameras and Hard Objects inside the Mausoleum'. This discreetness is in conformity with the widow's wishes that her husband's body should not become a tourist attraction. For twenty pesos' *merienda* money we find someone to fetch the key. Quite suddenly my friend refuses to come in and goes back to sit in the car. Too many painful memories too difficult to explain.

When the door to the mausoleum is unlocked I am met by a gust of Mozart's *Requiem*, specifically the 'Rex tremendae majestatis'. Inside it is gloomy and chill, an igloo made of tufa blocks, domed and with a polished marble floor like black ice. This circular chamber might be far underground, a lost cavern like that of King Arthur or the Seven Sleepers. It is the temporary resting-place, or unresting-place, of Marcos. He is lying in state in a glass case lit by subdued spots. An inscription at his feet reads only 'Ferdinand Edralin Marcos – Filipino', this time not for reasons of censorship but because it is the correct modest mode for a national hero. Above his head hangs a large embroidered presidential seal. Batac's once and future king is wearing a white *barong*, black trousers and shiny black pumps, and lying on a thin white-sheeted pallet and pillow as though on a hospital trolley. Across his chest is a red sash with a large star, as well as a lot of medals (which no doubt stubbornly include all the ones he was accused of having awarded himself. This is a highly contentious corpse). His face is very pink, with the texture of a Barbie doll's, the outcome of the embalmer's art. The Marcos family is said to have engaged the same Russian experts who are responsible for maintaining Lenin's incorruptible state. There is something touching about how small he is. It is in the Grim Reaper's normal repertoire of tricks to leave the lifeless notably shrunken, but Ferdinand was a small man to begin with and one is reminded of Renato Constantino's acute, if merciless, remark: 'Imelda's statuesque figure is responsible for the President's elevator shoes and pompadour hair-do.'[2]

The Mozart goes on and on; we are looped into eternity, temporarily. The restraint of the place is impressive. A member of the

Marcos family was later to tell me that when Ferdinand's body was finally allowed back from Hawaii in September 1993 Imelda was 'too strapped for cash' to build something to rival St Peter's Basilica in Rome and was obliged to settle for this modest simplicity. As a matter of fact it works well, being both dignified and touching, even as it begs the question of why this dead man can't be buried but must go on lying here in the cold and the dark (no *lux perpetua* in here: the dim lighting goes off when the door is closed, like that of a fridge, along with Mozart. The refrigerator stays on. Currently there are problems about unpaid electricity bills). The answer, as to everything in this country, is politics. The Marcos family quite reasonably wants him buried in Manila alongside other Philippine presidents. Cory Aquino, herself widowed by the dead man's regime if not by Ferdinand himself, was vindictively adamant that not even his dead body should be allowed back into the country. Even her successor Fidel Ramos, who is Ferdinand's own cousin, fellow Ilocano and ex-head of his Philippine Constabulary in the martial law years, relented only after his friend's body had already been lying in its Hawaiian refrigerator for four years, and then merely to the extent of allowing it no nearer Manila than Batac. The theory was that the sort of funeral his widow would give him could pose a threat to national security. It probably would have done, too, since after a few years of Cory Aquino many Filipinos had begun to look back with unexpected nostalgia. In any case, here the corpse goes on lying, not like Edward I's wife Eleanor of Castile who lay for a night at Charing Cross as the last stage of her funeral cortège before being buried in Westminster Abbey, but in a kind of necropolitical limbo. Whatever else, it shows this small neat man to be definitely one of the undead.

Outside it seems excessively hot and bright. There is a woman with a careworn, peasant's face standing there, demure in a white dress. She asks me if I have come to see *Apo*, the Chief. I say I have. 'We often speak with him. He is in heaven. *Si Kristo po at siya ay isa* [Christ and he are one].' I later discover this calm lady is a member of the Alpha Omega sect to whom Ferdinand appears, sometimes during trances and sometimes in dreams, to tell them to love one another and wait for his return. She produces a small coloured picture of Marcos-as-Christ, his hands – complete with the stigmata – pointing to the Bleeding Heart radiating beams of light from the middle of his breast. In a spiritually eclectic culture it is nearly impossible to be blasphemous. Behind me the thick wooden door of the tomb gives off nothing but silence as it awaits either Mary Magdalene or the electricity company's bailiffs.

Da Apo, then, was born just up the road in 1917, and was destined to be contentious even in so involuntary an act. His father, Mariano Marcos, was taught as a child by the Thomasites in the first classes they held in Ilocos Norte and grew up trilingual in Ilokano, Spanish and English, which might seem the perfect metaphor for a Filipino's divided loyalties. He became a teacher before graduating in law and was then elected Congressman for the Second District of Ilocos Norte. Ferdinand's mother, Josefa Edralin, came of an *ilustrado*, landowning family and had likewise been a Thomasite pupil in the same little primary school as Mariano. In due time she graduated from the University of the Philippines. Thus there was nothing really of rags-to-riches about young Ferdinand. Both his parents were of reasonable status socially, and by prevailing provincial standards well-to-do.

It is not easy now to sort out the historical from the hagiographical where the Marcos family is concerned. A background that in anybody else would have been deemed fairly unremarkable for a bright, ambitious boy from the provinces was glossed and reworked, even from before his 1965 election victory, by commissioned writers, ex-boyhood companions, college friends and fellow Ilocanos with an eye to immortality, not to say a job in Malacañang Palace. As his Presidency wore on and he awarded himself the extraordinary powers of martial law these accounts began to take on the retrospective trappings of destiny, such that the infant Ferdinand was born immediately after a thunderstorm, that wise old women predicted greatness from the shape of his skull, that the boy soon began demonstrating superhuman intellectual precociousness as well as feats of endurance and marksmanship, while exhibiting from the first a moral character that would have shamed Baden-Powell.

All this may safely be ignored, except for the marksmanship. Of far more consequence are the simple facts of where and when he was born. It was only nineteen years after the uncompleted

Revolution, when the Spanish had finally gone and the Americans had taken their place. Every adult in Sarrat and Batac whom young Ferdinand knew when growing up would have had vivid memories of Rizal's execution in 1896 and the momentous events that followed. Most of the men would have been combatants – if not in the Revolution itself then in the Philippine–American war that followed. Batac had at least two illustrious sons: General Artemio Ricarte, an important figure in the Katipunan revolutionary movement, and Gregorio Aglipay, a revolutionary priest. Aglipay was an interesting man whose childhood, like that of José Rizal, had been indelibly marked by the executions of Fathers Gomez, Burgos and Zamora back in 1872. His conscience had turned him into something of a guerrilla, fighting first against the Spanish and then the Americans. In a sense his spiritual nationalism was the logical outcome of 'Gomburza's' campaign for a Filipinized clergy, for in 1902 he went on to found the Philippine Independent Church, more generally known as the Aglipayan Church. This organization, which still exists today all over the Philippines but especially in Ilocos Norte, aimed for a home-grown Filipino – as opposed to Roman – catholicism. The infant Ferdinand was baptized by Bishop Aglipay himself, which made him an Aglipayan almost from birth (he was only baptized a Roman Catholic when three years old). In small towns like Sarrat and Batac everyone knew everybody else: Aglipay was a friend of Ferdinand's father Mariano, and took a particular interest in the boy. Moreover, the maternal grandfather, Fructuoso Edralin, was a cousin of another distinguished warrior, Antonio Luna, Commander-in-Chief of the Army at the time of his death in 1899. Both men fiercely resisted the American invasion. Consequently, little Ferdinand must have grown up in a pungent emotional climate. For one thing the rugged landscape abounded with tales of heroism and resistance, of the Ilocano's independent fighting spirit. A scant eighteen years before he was born most of Sarrat's able-bodied menfolk had marched off to attack the American forces who had taken the local capital, Laoag. Armed only with *bolos* and sharpened bamboo staves they succeeded in breaking through a palisade before being largely wiped out by gunfire. Their leader was Jose Ver, almost certainly a relative of the man Ferdinand would one day appoint his security chief and head of the armed forces. In 1936 a large monument to the heroes of Sarrat would be built in front of the town hall, but in Ferdinand's childhood Bishop Aglipay's imposing church in Batac exemplified this same nationalistic tradition in spiritual guise.

That was one half of the picture. The other was that by the 1920s a certain pragmatism had long since supervened at a civic level. The Americans were clearly there to stay for the foreseeable future. The best had to be made of a bad job, which to many Ilocanos came to seem less bad than they had at first thought. In the early part of the century Ferdinand's grandfather, Fabian Marcos, was appointed Mayor of Batac. He had been giving Spanish lessons to the American occupation forces, and once in power used his influence to negotiate a deal with them for that first batch of Thomasites who taught his son Mariano and his future daughter-in-law Josefa. Thus the boy would have grown up in an atmosphere whose degree of overt tension is now hard to assess, but which contained two apparently conflicting strands which must have found an echo in his character: as it were, the heroes of Sarrat and *Hiawatha*. It is quite possible there never was a seamless synthesis between the two, only a sort of emulsion whose constituents would separate out from time to time throughout his life and political career. Of course this kind of dichotomy was not peculiar to Marcos but can be seen everywhere in Filipino culture, which generally makes far less strenuous attempts than Western culture does to resolve such intellectual conflict. Most Filipinos can hold conflicting views without evident discomfort, switching from one to the other as the need arises (nowhere more obviously than in religious matters). If it is a behaviour learned from a bitter history then it has served Filipinos well; but it is equally an Eastern way of dealing with the world. The Mayor of Batac did a deal with the Americans. He would have been a lousy mayor if he hadn't, given the circumstances; and if it led to a future of Hiawatha and Green Cards it was still a lot better than anything the Spanish friars had provided in 300 years.

To say that Marcos as President never forgot his roots would be merely to understate the obvious, even though the hypothetical direct question 'Do you consider yourself an Ilocano first or a Filipino?' would have elicited from him a diplomatic response that depended on the circumstances, on the questioner and the expected reply. In a sense he answered it in his actions – at least, at a domestic level. He not only built in his home province the best roads in the country, he stocked the armed forces of the Philippines with Ilocanos. Many of the people closest to him throughout his administration were relatives and family friends: sons and daughters of the Ilocos. At this point it is essential to note some peculiarities of the Filipino social system. To base one's patronage and appointments on familial relationship has obvious advantages in terms of trust, loyalty and predictability. One has an expectation that people from one's own extended family will think and behave in a certain way, unlike those from outside the clan who may well have hidden agendas (such as advancing their own families). Besides, the concept of nepotism loses much of its force if applied to a kinship system that is cognatic, or bilateral, and recognizes relationships far more distant than the grandson implied by the word's origin.

> The family has long been at the centre of Filipino society. As in most parts of Southeast Asia kinship is essentially bilateral; that is, ancestry is traced through both the mother's and the father's line. Effective kinship ties are maintained with relatives of both parents. A bilateral system gives a potentially huge number of living kin, especially as five to ten children are not uncommon even today in each nuclear family of each generation. The only effective limitation on recognized kin is the number of relatives with whom an individual can sustain close interpersonal relations; 'kin' is a network of dyadic ties.[3]

It might be added that kin can be still further expanded to include the 'fictive kin' who are acquired through the *compadre* system of sponsors at weddings and baptisms. Through one's *kumpare* and *kumare* one gains access to, and a relationship with, still other extended family networks. A mere *barangay* captain might easily have thirty 'godchildren'; a professional politician might acquire hundreds, to all of whose families he has a duty, just as they would have the reciprocal duty of voting for him. This is above all a social system that depends on the notion of the *padrino*, the *apo*, the godfather; the boss to whom people are bonded by blood ties and debts of obligation. O. D. Corpuz put the matter succinctly, if regretfully, when he observed 'it may be said that in every Filipino president beats the heart of a tribal chief.'[4]

Such, then, are the alliances that can undercut broader ideological and political affiliations in the Philippines, and Ferdinand would have grown up assimilating them with Doña Josefa's milk. In addition he would have learned another important social concept, the so-called *utang na loob*. The phrase translates literally as 'inner debt', and it indeed contains something of the English-language concept of 'indebtedness', with the intensifier that a person's *loob* is more than just 'inner' and can take on the attributes of both heart and soul. This implied distinction between the 'inner' and the 'outer' person is extremely important to Filipinos who, unlike most Anglo-Saxons, seem to feel under no pressure to reconcile differences between their 'inner' selves (which may not be compromised) and their public selves. Once again, the notion of synthesis is alien. This may be the reason for one of the more impressive of Filipino attributes, which is the ability to sell oneself without any sense of personal loss. The *loob* remains unsullied.

The way in which *utang na loob* goes beyond an English sense of mere indebtedness is in its implication that the debt can never be fully discharged. Most debts are not crudely financial, of course, and their very unquantifiability makes them all the more unrepayable. Thus a cycle of mutual indebtedness builds up throughout the vast family network, not onerous, precisely, but unignorable. The only way out would be to renege, refuse, walk away. That leads to the gravest charge one Filipino can level at another, that of being *walang hiya* or without shame. To lack that sense of shame, which must stem from having a properly functioning *loob* or inner self, is to become an outcast so far as that network of relationships is concerned. Here we are emphatically not being sidetracked by anthropological niceties into some academic backwater. This intricate social system has large-scale political consequences that can lead to complete misunderstanding when the Western press comes charging out of its corner, swinging. A Filipino acquaintance puts it well:

> Filipino politicians utilize political patronage in exchange for votes at election time, thus introducing the Filipino *utang na loob*

element into a Western political system put into operation in the Philippines by the Americans. The political system, from *barrio* level to the national machinery, functions blissfully, largely on *utang na loob*, despite impinging contradictions from theoretical principles and tenets of the Western political model . . . This model expects the political system to be determined by 'issues', but *utang na loob* has a stronger pull. [The] ambivalence between . . . *utang na loob* and the tenets of democratic elections marks the volatile and footloose Philippine political system.[5]

It has even been suggested that the strange relationship which successive post-war Filipino governments have had with Washington owes much to a national, collective sense of *utang na loob* towards the United States for having brought the Japanese occupation to an end. The idea of Uncle Sam as *padrino* might also explain the anger Filipinos have frequently felt when the US has appeared to renege on obligations of its own towards a country with which it has so many blood ties. The great *padrino*, going his own sweet international way, has appeared to his little brown brothers as *walang hiya*.

Ferdinand Marcos, then, was destined to be contentious even at birth. This is because of an old rumour taken up by the American author Sterling Seagrave in his 1988 book, *The Marcos Dynasty*. Fans of Mr Seagrave no doubt recognized that research for his earlier book, *The Soong Dynasty*, overlapped that for the later. The central hypothesis of both books is of an immense Chinese conspiracy whose tentacles almost outreach even the author's imagination. This is not precisely the 'yellow peril', that conspiracy-by-copulation or Malthusian nightmare in which the West of the 1890s had foreseen itself swamped by Eastern hordes; nor yet is it the conspiracy of Fu Manchu, the wily and inscrutable Oriental created by the British novelist Sax Rohmer in 1913 as a sort of Mandarin Moriarty. Rather, Seagrave's is a theory that has tight, family-based triads and secret societies of pronounced right-wing leanings amassing vast fortunes, largely through crime syndicates, while using their power to infiltrate the criminal and governmental circles of an expanding empire of Southeast-Asian countries – including, of course, the Philippines. On second thoughts we may be dealing with Fu Manchu in his final, 1959, version. In *Emperor Fu Manchu* (1959) Rohmer, who by then had decamped to the United States, turned his hero-villain into a villain-hero and, in deference to the prevailing post-McCarthy ethos, made him a dedicated anti-Communist.

At all events, in order to make Ferdinand Marcos an important part of this web and, by so doing, explain his entire career as having been in the service of Chinese masters, Seagrave says categorically that Mariano Marcos was not his father. The real father, we are told, was a young Chinese law student at the University of the Philippines (UP) named Ferdinand Chua who impregnated Josefa Edralin. On discovering this, Chua's family sent him packing to Fukien to look for a proper Chinese wife, while Josefa's family hurriedly arranged a marriage to her classmate Mariano Marcos. Chua duly returned from Amoy with a Fukienese wife, graduated from UP and rose to become a municipal judge in Laoag. Seagrave notes that the Chuas were the wealthiest Chinese family in Ilocos Norte, 'part of the great Chua clan, the sixth richest and most powerful clan in the Philippines, numbering among its members many millionaires and several billionaires'. After the Second World War this clan became a prominent supporter of Chiang Kai-shek in his losing struggle with Mao Zedong and, joining similar KMT loyalists in Manila, the Chuas helped form a new Federation of Chinese Chambers of Commerce, thereby concentrating the business and trading links of the most influential Filipino Chinese under one umbrella organization. Of Ferdinand Marcos's putative Chinese father, Seagrave has this to say:

> If this version is accurate, and the essential details have been confirmed repeatedly by various independent sources, it would help to explain many peculiarities and inconsistencies in the official Marcos story. Such as the fact that Josefa was seven years older than Mariano, the fact that he spent little time with her and the children over the years, that he mistreated and abused Ferdinand as a boy, but was affectionate toward her second son Pacifico, and that Mariano's career advanced in ways that can only be explained by the intervention of a powerful but invisible patron. This would also explain why Ferdinand Marcos seriously considered himself to be a direct descendant of the Chinese pirate

Li Ma-hong. There was no Chinese blood in Mariano's family, and only a little in Josefa's.[6]

The point one would make is not that this is stupid, because it isn't, but that ten years later it still remains unconfirmed. Either it is correct or it is not. One can detect no radical shift in thinking among Filipino politicians and intellectuals brought about by Mr Seagrave's theory, as might have been expected had it broken over their heads with the force of revelation. In the aftermath of the 'EDSA Revolution' no holds were barred when it came to denigrating the Marcoses. It is likely that a good many Filipinos would willingly have embraced the idea that Ferdinand maybe hadn't been so completely one of them after all but a Chinese – if not full-blooded then blood-indebted. (There is, of course, a good deal of latent anti-Chinese feeling on the part of Malay Filipinos, 'the Jews of Asia' being one of those recurrent whispered phrases.) Furthermore, those who knew the family well assert that his brother Pacifico and his sister Elizabeth both looked exactly like him, which is unlikely had they not shared the same father. If one declines to spend much time in trying to refute Mr Seagrave's hypothesis it is simply because it is not the interesting part about either Ferdinand Marcos or the Philippines.

Instead, we can move on to 1935 when Ferdinand was eighteen. He had just finished his first semester at UP when he found himself under suspicion of murder. This is where the question of his marksmanship comes in. The background to these melodramatic circumstances was that his father – or maybe stepfather – Mariano had been defeated in 1931 when he ran for a third term in Congress. Worse, he had even lost in his home town Batac to a young upstart named Julio Nalundasan. Suddenly Mariano was out of a job. He was so depressed he was not even able to manage the family law firm but instead took a job down south in Davao, Mindanao, which is about as far from Ilocos Norte as it is possible to get in the Philippines. But in 1935 he returned home to run for Congress once more. In the interim there had been some interesting changes at national political level. His old nemesis Julio Nalundasan was now running on Manuel Quezon's Nacionalista ticket. Quezon, after almost twenty years as Senate President, was about to become the first President of the newly created

Commonwealth of the Philippines. In terms of political power in the two pre-war decades, Quezon was second only to the American Governor-General. Clearly, Mariano's prospects of success against a candidate backed by Quezon were slender, and were made slenderer still since he was running for the Republican Party, headed by none other than Bishop Aglipay. By now Aglipay was an old man, and had lost much of his appeal. In the event Nalundasan won handsomely. Provincial politics being what they are, his supporters were not content with victory but decided to rub Mariano's nose in it. In the back of a car they rigged up a coffin in which sat two effigies labelled 'Marcos' and 'Aglipay'. The car then roared triumphantly around the little streets of Batac tooting its horn to the applause of the crowds. It made a special discourtesy call outside the shuttered Marcos house where the mockery reached a new pitch. Inside the house a bleak decision may or may not have been taken.

Three nights later, while cleaning his teeth on the verandah of his house, Julio Nalundasan was shot in the back with a .22 bullet. He died within minutes. Two days after that Ferdinand returned to his studies in Manila. He was already known as one of the best pistol shots in the university, and since the defeated Mariano had been in Laoag at the time of the murder suspicion naturally fell on his son. Yet mysteriously he was not arrested for another three years, just five months before he was due to graduate from law school. By then, like several of his classmates, he had enrolled in the reserves of the Philippine Constabulary and was a third lieutenant. He was jailed, then bailed, finally tried and found guilty 'beyond any reasonable doubt', and given a minimum sentence of ten years. Then, within a few days of beginning his sentence, he was informed that President Quezon was willing to offer him a pardon – a decision that to this day has not been explained except by Sterling Seagrave, who hazards that 'Quezon had long since been advised of the special relationship that existed between Ferdinand [Marcos] and Judge Chua, and that a deal had been cut.'[7] Seagrave's theory is that Quezon's presidential term would be ending in less than two years and, if he decided to run again, the Chua clan's support could be critical.

In any case Ferdinand now did something quite extraordinary. He turned down the presidential pardon and voluntarily returned to Laoag jail where he spent six months playing table tennis in between writing his own appeal brief, a mammoth document over 800 pages long. In the months following its submission he took his Bar finals, also from jail. He not only passed these but came top, with the highest score on record. Perhaps inevitably he was accused of cheating, whereupon he insisted on a viva voce re-examination to clear his name, which only confirmed the original result. Not long afterwards Associate Justice Jose P. Laurel (who oddly enough had also been convicted of murder at the age of eighteen and acquitted on grounds of self-defence) handed down a verdict of acquittal on the brilliant young graduate. The next day a triumphant Ferdinand Marcos returned to the Supreme Court to take his oath as a fully fledged lawyer.

So – did he or didn't he kill Nalundasan? Was the young Ferdinand a murderer or not? The case has never been satisfactorily resolved. By the time he was the President in Malacañang Palace the official line was that since he had been acquitted, he was clearly innocent. But no great effort was ever made to quash the rumours, no doubt because he realized that in a nation which sets great store by a macho image the lingering suspicion would do him more good than harm at the polls. Beyond question he had made an auspicious start to his career. The affair had earned him much publicity, as had President Quezon's own interest in the case. The rejected pardon, the top scholar who wrote his own successful appeal from jail, his sensational acquittal – all these had gained Ferdinand national recognition. The dark rumours that refused to go away only added spice.

It certainly seems like astonishing good fortune that an ex-Congressman's son from the sticks should have acquired the support of the President himself. In lieu of a better explanation, Sterling Seagrave's theory that this is explained by Ferdinand's true paternity undeniably has a certain plausibility, though it does leave one pertinent question unanswered. If Mariano was not Ferdinand's real father, why would the boy have committed murder to avenge his honour? Macho codes demand that a man settle his own scores rather than let a teenaged stepson (whom he allegedly never much liked) do the dirty work. It should be added that my Ilocano friend who drove me up to Batac had been at college with Nalundasan's son José, who used to say that never for one moment did he doubt that Marcos was his father's killer. On the other hand, there is a picture extant showing a smiling José being warmly folded in a Marcos embrace somewhere in Malacañang Palace.[8] Both men look relaxed and happy and Ferdinand, in particular, is beaming expansively in a way he seldom did in public. And there we shall let the matter rest.

Retrospectively, it can now be seen how these pre-war dramas presaged much that was to come, both in substance and in tone. So often there would be an equivocal event from whose murk Ferdinand would emerge not merely victorious but having substantially advanced his interests. And nearly always his success can be traced to an adroit use of the law. In this he was certainly not unusual, although better at it than most. In a country that has always had an extraordinary preponderance of lawyers among its ruling élite the law is constantly invoked to muddy and obfuscate. Thanks no doubt to Mariano Marcos's own legal practice, his son learned young that both law and religion provide suitable forests for the Filipino where he may skulk and slither and shine in constant fluidity. Even more satisfactorily, these were forests planted by foreigners, by Westerners who had brought with them Latin, the peculiar dialect reserved for God and the law. This was a gift to Filipinos, who were already masters of camouflage and evasion. Now, whenever danger threatened, they could take cover in thickets of Latin, buying time, misleading, joking, mocking, turning things to their advantage; rewriting events until they took place in some never-never land, a jurisprudential Oz. Just as uncomprehended phrases of the Latin Mass were garbled by peasants into spells, love potions, curses and mystical flummery, so even today the solemn remnants of Roman law still serve to bewilder or strike fear. Threatened officials bluster about 'certiorari writs'. A police chief does not sack a useless subordinate, he files a petition for mandamus against him to make him do his duty – in other words an enforcement by law to compel law enforcement. It is brilliantly Filipino. And of course practically no one of any social or political clout ever comes close to going to jail. Even the most appalling crimes arousing public outcry disappear into that enchanted land where judgements and appeals are bounced back and forth between one court and another like a tennis ball in a stupefying rally, until the defendant dies of natural causes or runs out of money, and the public's outrage has long been superseded by fresher protest at grosser crimes.

With the suppleness that characterizes Filipinos taking up residence in strange terrain Ferdinand Marcos grew up to be a consummate woodsman in this foreign forest. His 800-page appeal brief was one demonstration of his mastery at an early age. Another was the way in which so many of his actions now seem to us cloaked in indeterminacy. About him there was always, finally, something that was not quite clear. One now suspects that this may also have been his own experience of himself.

4

The Second World War

The Second World War came to the Philippines, as it did to Hawaii, Hong Kong and Malaya, on 7 December 1941. Ten hours after they had attacked Pearl Harbor in Hawaii the Japanese bombed Clark Field, the US Army Air Force base in Pampanga, fifty-odd miles north of Manila. Despite the warning the Americans were caught napping. Of their entire air force in the Far Eastern theatre, over half the bombers and one-third of the fighters were destroyed on the ground at Clark in a matter of minutes.

And yet three years before, none other than the Communist Party of the Philippines had issued a manifesto warning the country that a Japanese invasion was imminent. At a more general level the likelihood of war had been openly gossiped about since 1940. Officially, however, the attitude on the Allies' part seems to have been one of sublime complacency. As one Manila resident, Marcial Lichauco, put it at the time: 'The people residing in the Philippines – Americans, British, Dutch, Swiss, Spaniards, Chinese and the Filipinos themselves – [were] not ready for this war. They simply could not conceive that Japan would dare face the combined forces of America and Great Britain.'[1] Eighteen days later the Japanese flag was flying over the US High Commissioner's Manila mansion and martial law had been declared.

The fall of Manila in so short a time, preceded as it has been by Hongkong, is a terrible blow to the white man's prestige in Asia and the Far East. There can be no excuses. Troops, planes, tanks, guns and supplies began pouring into Manila many months before war began. That Japan could occupy Luzon is not exactly a surprise – the island is not a fortress like England is today; but that the Sons of Nippon should have accomplished this feat in twenty-five days while, at the same time, they are engaged in an all-out offensive against British Malaya and China seems un-believable. It is but another instance of over-confidence and unpreparedness on the part of the democracies.[2]

The diarist was all the more shocked for knowing the United States well. In 1923 he had been the first-ever Filipino to graduate from Harvard. He and his American-born wife were to survive the war in Manila, and he lived to be the Philippine Ambassador to the United Kingdom at the time when Marcos first became President in the mid-1960s. In those early days of 1942, and from the depths of gloom and bitter surprise at the straits in which it seemed 'the white man's' arrogance had landed them, ordinary Manileños like Lichauco could only observe the visible evidence of military unpreparedness on the Americans' part. They were not to know that US secret service agencies such as the Counter Intelligence Corps were much better prepared and had already installed 'sleeper' agents against just such a Japanese invasion. Prominent among these were two 'Nisei', American citizens from Japanese families, Richard Sakakida and Arthur Komori. Sakakida was destined to have a charmed life, managing after months of the most brutal interrogation to convince the Japanese that he was one of them and had no connection whatsoever with the US mili-tary. Thereafter he spent the remainder of the war smuggling out crucial information from the heart of the Japanese High Command in Manila.[3] The particular significance of Sakakida and others like him to this present account of Marcos's war will become apparent in due course.

Even before they reached Manila the Japanese had bombarded towns and cities throughout Luzon with tons of leaflets that read: 'In order to advance their imperialistic cause, America seized your country forty years ago and, since then, you have been abused, exploited, neglected and, what is worse, have been treated as an inferior race.' It was the start of an attempt to win Filipinos' hearts and minds as fellow brown-skinned Asians, an attempt that did have a limited degree of success in certain quarters. Those who seemed most susceptible were petty officials and local politicians as well as members of the rural élite, particularly owners of great agricultural estates and haciendas such as those in Central Luzon. Obviously, these were precisely the kinds of people whose co-operation the Japanese were going to need to run their regime at local level. It would probably not be unduly cynical to attribute a degree of pragmatism and self-interest to the motives of many such converts to the New Asianism, and when after the war the time of reckoning arrived for those seen as having been 'collaborators' there was no lack of accusers. Yet for true Filipino nationalists who were only waiting with impatience for the United States to grant full independence, the issue must have presented them with a dif-ficult dilemma in those early days of the war. When the Japanese Propaganda Office in Manila trumpeted the fall of Singapore it must have seemed to many that independence would either have to be postponed indefinitely or else accepted from non-American hands:

'You, Filipinos, Burmese, Indians, Indonesians and Malayans,' reads the proclamation, 'must stand up and face without fear the sacred duty of grasping without hesitation this God-given opportunity which may never come again. Stand up and co-operate in the creation of a new Asia for the Asiatics.'[4]

But it was not long before the true nature of the Japanese attitude towards their fellow Asiatics became painfully apparent, what with the public slappings, beatings and kickings, and the circulated dia-grams on the correct way to bow to a Japanese officer. When the Japanese political police, the Kempei Tai, began their atrocious interrogations in the old Spanish dungeons of Fort Santiago, most intelligent Filipinos can have been left with few illusions. Any lin-gering notions of racial solidarity had also gone by the board on the Filipino side, and the physical peculiarities of the invaders were soon noted and parodied. For the duration of the war one of the slang names for a Japanese soldier was *komang*, which has no

English equivalent but by analogy would mean 'bow-armed'. Outside Manila, especially in the fields and villages of Central Luzon, resistance was already beginning:

Independence for the sake of independence [. . .] was not the key issue for most people in [the] resistance. They wanted the Japanese out because of what the new regime had done to their lives – the fear, death, destruction and repression were worse than anything people had known before. The Japanese and Filipino authorities were their own worst enemy, for they did little to win popular support but did much to turn people against them.[5]

While all this was taking shape in the first few weeks of the occupation, things on the military front were going from bad to desperate from the Fil-American point of view. The Japanese landings had bottled up the entire Philippine Army in the Bataan peninsula on the far side of Manila Bay, with the American and Filipino top brass in still further retreat off the peninsula's tip on the fortress-island of Corregidor. It was clear from the start that the 95,000 Filipino and American USAFFE (United States Armed Forces in the Far East) troops would wait in vain for the relief they expected daily. The formerly invincible Allies were being routed all over Southeast Asia and were in no position to send help to anyone. General Douglas MacArthur had been obliged by the Japanese destruction of his air and naval forces to fall back on War Plan Orange-3, which originally dated from 1904, the time of the Russo–Japanese War. WPO-3 had envisaged American forces defending only Luzon, as a last resort retiring to Bataan for a protracted defence of Manila Bay and allowing the US fleet in Hawaii a generous six months to come to their rescue.[6] In that sense one could say things were now going according to plan; but the General's extraordinary failure to ensure the strategy was properly provisioned in advance had led to an almost complete lack of supplies and equipment. By early April USAFFE men were down to an average daily ration of 800 calories if they were lucky. Ninety percent of the Philippine Army was without boots. Three months of bitter and unrelenting combat had left the survivors exhausted and ill. On 9 April Bataan fell in what was then the single greatest military defeat in American history, and some 76,000 Filipino and American survivors were force-marched north and east to intern- ment camps in the Death March that killed roughly half their number. Somewhere among these rag-tag columns of defeated men was the future President of the Philippines, Ferdinand Marcos. They left behind them the beleaguered island of Corregidor from which the current President, MacArthur's friend Manuel Quezon, had been smuggled away to exile in the United States even as the General and his staff were evacuated to Australia. The fort was clearly doomed, and MacArthur had left his deputy, General Jonathan Wainwright, to shift for himself as best he could while uttering his immortal farewell, 'I shall return.' One of those cap- tured when Corregidor fell was the CIC agent, Richard Sakakida, who had been acting as MacArthur's personal interpreter and translator, although of course the General had no idea of his true identity.

How MacArthur had explained to his friend the President the ease with which Japan invaded his country is anybody's guess. They had spent some weeks together in close proximity, hunkered down in the command post buried deep in the tunnels of Corregidor Island as worsening news from the Bataan peninsula across the strait came in a steady stream. MacArthur could later claim with some justification that in hanging on for those desperate four months his 'battling bastards of Bataan' had fought a more heroic defence and inflicted more damage on the Japanese invaders than had any comparable Allied army in the Pacific region at the time. That was true; but it rather overlooks the strategic disaster that had put them in such a hopeless position in the first place. For this MacArthur must take the blame, as he also must for issuing a proclamation that help was on the way when it wasn't, thereby falsely raising the men's hopes and causing a slump in morale later on.[7] In fact it was not merely Roosevelt who had doubts about MacArthur's character as a man. It turns out that his generalship and military competence were being privately doubted even as the Japanese were landing in the Philippines. In the cause of Allied solidarity, fellow officers like Dwight D. Eisenhower tended to con- fine their criticisms to their diaries, which in Eisenhower's case were only published in 1981. In January 1942 Eisenhower, who was about to take command of US troops in Europe on his way to becoming Supreme Commander of Allied Forces and eventually President of the United States, wrote in his diary that MacArthur was 'as big a baby as ever. But we've got to keep him fighting.'[8] Eisenhower was himself a good enough soldier to know that the men's assessments of their officers seldom erred. MacArthur was known to his men as 'Dugout Doug' (during the entire battle for Bataan he visited the front only once[9]) and a widely circulated couplet went into a little more detail:

> Dugout Doug's not timid, he's just cautious, not afraid;
> He's protecting carefully the stars that Franklin made.[10]

Even as the under-supplied USAFFE forces in Bataan were falling to the combined onslaughts of the Japanese, malaria, dysentery and malnutrition, MacArthur had talked President Quezon into reappointing him Field Marshal of the Philippines, with full perks and back pay, once the war was over.[11] Even more extraordinarily, Quezon presented him with a cash honorarium of half a million dollars.[12] Not long afterwards a US submarine was summoned to Corregidor, loaded with twenty tons of gold and despatched to Australia. It seems never to have been established whose gold this was. It presumably belonged to the Philippine Treasury, the remaining contents of which was sunk in Manila Bay to prevent the Japanese from getting their hands on it. On the other hand the gold might have been more in the nature of a private nest-egg sent ahead of MacArthur, who sailed from Corregidor on 11 March for a Del Monte plantation in Mindanao and thence flew to Australia. With him were President Quezon and Vice-President Osmeña, whose joint duty in exile was to represent the Philippines' legitimate government, a stipulation of Roosevelt's. Left on Corregidor with the luckless General Wainwright and the others was Manuel Roxas, the man both MacArthur and Quezon fancied as Quezon's presidential successor. Roxas, though now wearing a brigadier-general's uniform, had been appointed Quezon's Secretary of Finance back in 1938. A lawyer by profession, he was always torn between the twin careers of politics and the law. In the latter capacity he was in practice as the partner of Marcial Lichauco, whose journal entries open this chapter. Before the war ended Quezon died of TB in his American exile and Roxas did indeed succeed him in 1946 as the first President of the fully independent Republic.

A month after MacArthur's departure Eisenhower made a diary entry on 10 April: 'Corregidor surrendered last night. Poor Wainwright! He did the fighting in the Philippine Islands, another got such glory as the public could find in the operations.'[13] Douglas MacArthur's most remarkable achievement was to turn this whole unpropitious series of events into a mammoth public relations triumph such that he ended the war a national hero, receiving the Congressional Medal of Honour for his defence of Bataan and Corregidor. Part of this was down to some resonant communiqués he had issued on the outbreak of the Pacific War, and part to the often fanciful but always carefully crafted broadcasts from Bataan and Corregidor by his faithful propagandist, Carlos P. Romulo. (Romulo was arguably the Philippines' leading journalist at the war's outbreak, when his friend MacArthur commissioned him a major and later an aide-de-camp. On Corregidor he was a broadcaster with the USAFFE radio station until he left for Australia with his mentor. Later still, he was to become the Philippines' Ambassador to the UN, President of the University of the Philippines, and finally Ferdinand Marcos's Secretary of Foreign Affairs.) Most of all, though, MacArthur's triumphant reputation – which became increasingly rickety from his death in 1964 until the publication in 1981 of Carol Petillo's devastating biography – was due to an overwhelming desire on the part of the American and British publics for a hero at a critical time of defeat. MacArthur played the part to perfection, rounding it off in 1944 with bullish photo-op pictures of himself wading ashore à la John Wayne from a landing craft on Leyte, complete with the well-rehearsed and wholly predictable quotation, 'I have returned!' (As Margot Asquith remarked in not wholly dissimilar circumstances, 'If Kitchener was not a great man, he was, at least, a great poster.') In addition to being given the Medal of Honour and referred to as the 'Lion of Luzon', he was named 'Number One Father of 1942' – a title curiously reminiscent of similar accolades which the Soviet Union and, later, Communist China liked to bestow on their own favoured citizens.

MacArthur's history cited here offers an uncanny parallel with Ferdinand Marcos, not least for the motif of surreptitious gold.

Marcos wound up at the end of the Death March a PoW in Camp O'Donnell, Tarlac, as ill and exhausted as anybody else. Somehow in the next three years he, too, managed to become a hero of almost MacArthurian proportions with a heroism that, like the number of his medals, went on increasing long after the war had ended. This was likewise due to a skilful sculpting of facts, the tossing of a judicious smoke grenade here and there, and outright lies. At an ordinary human level this is not hard to understand. When a fledgling politician is crafting his public image in a nation about to receive its full independence, it is even less surprising.

Sunday, June 28, 1942:
Out of approximately 40,000 Filipino prisoners in camp O'Donnell, 18,000 have already died and many are so weak that they cannot be moved. The Japanese Military Authorities have, therefore, announced that, to show their friendship to the Filipino people, they will release the sick prisoners who are strong enough to walk. The names of about 3,000 men have been published in the newspapers and they will be allowed to leave a few hundred at a time. One relative or friend of each prisoner will be permitted to go to the camp for that purpose.[14]

The significance of this announcement was that it enabled Marcos to get out of the PoW camp in which he was languishing. As the sick prisoners were released their names were listed throughout that summer in the *Manila Tribune*. The name of Ferdinand E. Marcos appeared nowhere, however. Maybe he was not sick but fell instead into a second category of prisoners the Japanese were releasing but which Lichauco does not mention: those whose families had co-operated with the Japanese military authorities. Ferdinand's mother, Josefa, collected him from Tarlac on 4 August and took him at once by train to Manila. On the way, she is supposed to have told him that his father Mariano was under house arrest back home in Batac 'for refusal to join the Japanese civilian government in Ilocos Norte'.[15] However, according to a US Army intelligence report in the files of MacArthur's command, Mariano Marcos, far from rebuffing the Japanese, had actually taken part in a ceremony welcoming them to the provincial capital, Laoag, early that year. Then on 17 July, barely a fortnight before Ferdinand's release, Mariano had spoken eloquently at a pro-Japanese rally in Batac. This being so, the conclusion seems unavoidable that the Japanese released the son from the PoW camp because the father was co-operating. From that moment, the story of Ferdinand's war ceases to be a single intelligible, sequential account. Instead, it splits into two versions so different they often barely even touch: that of the myth-makers and that of the debunkers.

Chief among the myth-makers was Ferdinand himself, who, when planning to run for President in 1965, commissioned an American writer named Hartzell Spence to write the sort of biography likely to appeal to the Philippine electorate. Painstakingly briefed and endowed with a vivid if predictable imagination, Ferdinand's post-war Boswell sketched a widescreen canvas of practically non-stop derring-do. This takes place in an anecdotal terrain somewhere between the windy plains of Troy and the Hollywood lots of MGM. We are in the 'with one bound he was free' school of adventure, in which our hero single-handedly wipes out nests of Japanese machine-gunners, carries out daring rescue missions though mortally wounded, organizes a resistance of plucky guerrillas in the hills into an élite fighting force he names *Ang Maharlika* ('The Aristocrats'), who . . . But you get the picture. Not a cliché of the genre is overlooked. There is even the obligatory sweetheart (a Filipino-American female guerrilla named Evelyn who saves Ferdinand's life by stopping a Japanese bullet meant for him) and the obligatory torture scene. The whole thing is more like a 'B' movie script than a serious account of one man's odyssey through three years of brutal and divisive history that brought his country to ruin; and in 1969 he did indeed have it turned into the jungle epic *Maharlika*, timed to coincide with his bid for re-election that year. The torture scene, in Hartzell Spence's expert hands, is worth quoting. It follows directly on from Ferdinand's and Josefa's arrival by train in Manila after his release, where he was re-arrested by the Kempei Tai and taken to Fort Santiago for interrogation – ostensibly about what he might know of the plans some classmates of his had hatched to form a guerrilla band and escape to join MacArthur in Australia.

His interrogator, who was revealed as a secret-police colonel, lost his affability finally. The three soldiers who attended him, at a signal, threw Ferdinand to the pallet that was raised off the floor, and jammed a rubber tube into his mouth. Water was pumped slowly into his body until he thought he must surely burst. Now the colonel jumped on him with both knees. Water, bile, blood, excreta from stomach, kidneys and bowels spurted from every orifice of his body. He knew that he was about to die. Who could survive such torture? Stubbornly he decided to go bravely. He refused to speak.

This exasperated the Kempei Tai colonel, who gave him another round of the water cure. Then another. During the pumping, Ferdinand's bulging eyes saw the electric light bulb over his head grow larger and hotter, and seemingly come closer until it was in his face. Then the colonel would jump on his stomach, and the light would recede. The pain of the water pressure was too fierce to be borne. After a while Marcos became numb to it, and no longer felt the variations of its intensity. Covered by the filth from his body and the emissions of the torture, he lay in a pool of vileness. He had no idea how many times the ordeal was repeated – over and over, until he lost consciousness at last.[16]

It is hard to guess how much of this was supplied by Ferdinand himself and how much came from Spence embellishing what he was told. What is noticeable in the above account is a complete absence of private detail, some oddity that might have burned itself into the victim's memory. Instead, for all the blood, sweat and excrement it reads like hearsay. There is nothing here we have not read before somewhere, and which we do not expect. Possibly this was merely a failure of Spence's inflammatory style. Spence was not just any old hired hack, however. He was originally a United Press man who during the war founded and edited *Yank*, the US Army weekly. He then went on to edit the US Armed Forces' journal *Stars and Stripes*. His credibility in the Pentagon was very high, so his version of Marcos's war gave a semi-official imprimatur to the story and the book itself was freely distributed to US embassies and government agencies worldwide, as well as to the American press. Spence's summing-up of Ferdinand's war was unequivocal:

Before he was twenty-five he had won more medals for bravery than anyone else in Philippine history, had suffered the heroic

Battle of Bataan and its aftermath, the infamous Death March, and the mediaeval tortures of the Japanese secret police.[17]

This was the official version, which from the time of Marcos's first presidency (it was published in 1964) had the status of gospel both in the Philippines and the United States. A 1966 cover story in *Time* magazine took its cue from Spence:

> [Marcos's] idea of intelligence duty was to prowl behind the Japanese lines, often in his personal Oldsmobile sedan, probing for weak spots. He found one on Bataan's Mount Natib, a Japanese military battery that was lobbing 70mm shells into US General Jonathan Wainwright's beleaguered defenders. Marcos and three privates scouted the battery, trailing two near-dead Japanese artillerymen to it, then cut loose. They killed more than 50 Japanese, spiked the guns and escaped with only one casualty. Marcos won the first of a brace of Silver Stars for the operation, and a few weeks later was recommended for the US Medal of Honour for his part in the Defence of the Salian River. But the recommendation was never filed with Washington, and Marcos failed in becoming the only Filipino to win America's highest military award.[18]

The debunkers' version of Ferdinand's war started precisely because this barrage of myth-making left a good few Filipinos quite unconvinced, even outraged. Among these was an association of those who had survived Fort Santiago and the Japanese interrogations. They hotly disputed his claim that he was ever tortured there and refused to accept him as a member of their group. After he had become President of the Philippines in 1965 such voices became judiciously muted in public, at least, if not at reunion dinners. It was only after martial law had become oppressive enough in the late seventies to have driven his opponents exiled in the US into organizing the Movement for a Free Philippines that Marcos's incredible war record began to be subjected to serious scrutiny. The original work was done by Bonifacio Gillego, who wrote an article about his 'fake medals' in the Filipino newspaper *We Forum* in 1982. Boni Gillego is today a Congressman on the verge of retirement, an ex-soldier of the old and most honourable school. His asset was that as a retired military man (with, it must be said, good friends in the CIA) he was in touch with all sorts of men of the same generation who had served in the war. Some came to his attention when they wrote to check a story while busy on their own memoirs of famous engagements such as Mt. Natib, the Salian River and Bessang Pass. Others simply met at reunions and swapped stories. Boni Gillego was the first to examine systematically and critically the anomalies in each one of Marcos's supposed exploits and awards, although much of the credit that was his due went, predictably, to the foreign journalists who developed it.

His *We Forum* article (which earned the news-sheet closure) was widely disseminated in the US by the Movement for a Free Philippines and the information taken up by American investigative journalists such as John Sharkey of the *Washington Post*, whose access to US military archives was perhaps better and more practised than Boni Gillego's. By now it was 1983, and in the wake of Ninoy Aquino's assassination that August a kind of open season had been declared on Marcos by the American press. The *Washington Post*'s 'Outlook' section led with Sharkey's demolition of Ferdinand's claims to war honours:

> When Philippine President Ferdinand E. Marcos visited Washington in September 1982, Defence Secretary Caspar W. Weinberger* presented him with a case displaying US medals supposedly awarded him in World War II, and President Reagan complimented him at a special ceremony for fighting 'valiantly' on the US side against Japan.
>
> A Philippine government publicity brochure describes Marcos as 'his country's most decorated soldier,' with more awards (32) than the 27 credited to American World War II hero Audie Murphy. Allegedly included in these decorations are two US Silver Stars and a Distinguished Service Cross.
>
> However, an 18-month effort to verify Marcos's claims to high American decorations raises serious doubts about whether he actually was awarded them . . . Nor could any independent,

* Weinberger had himself served on General Douglas MacArthur's Intelligence staff during the Second World War.

outside corroboration be found to buttress a claim made in Philippine government brochures that he was recommended for the US Medal of Honour because of his bravery on Bataan, as a document in his US military file suggests.[19]

The open season on Marcos continued. The darling of *Time* magazine, vintage 1966, had quite suddenly become an ogre, being compared with the late President Somoza of Nicaragua. This media campaign was to intensify up to, and even beyond, the moment Ferdinand left office in 1986. Early that year, a bare fortnight before the snap election on 7 February, the *Washington Post* and the *New York Times* both ran front-page stories saying US Army investigations had concluded that Marcos's 'Maharlika' guerrilla unit was a fiction and that 'no such unit ever existed as a guerrilla organization during the war'.[20] Worse was to come. It was alleged that not only had he never been tortured by the Japanese, but he had, like his father, sided with them.

What was interesting about these revelations (apart from the way they conveniently overlooked that the sole printed source for the tales of Ferdinand's heroism had been Hartzell Spence's *Time*-endorsed version on which the 'Philippine government brochures' had drawn) was their timing. Still more interesting was what that implied about the preceding twenty years' silence on both sides of the Pacific, when Marcos's US Army files were 'mislaid'. Sterling Seagrave (whose chapter on Ferdinand's war provides a good general, if one-sided, overview of the whole dismal episode) noted that 'subsequent congressional investigation determined that the Pentagon, after mischievously burying the records for decades in a Midwestern vault, had just as mischievously slipped them back into the archives where they belonged, to await McCoy's serendipitous discovery'.[21] (The reference is to the investigative scholar Alfred McCoy, whose research formed the basis of the new revelations about Marcos having collaborated with the Japanese.)

An uneasiness still lingers around most public discourse about the Second World War in the Philippines, and has its origins in an issue of far more general weight than that of one man and his medals – that of *collaboration*. This collaboration is, of course, primarily that of certain Filipinos with the Japanese. But in Ferdinand's case it is not just that, although as we shall shortly see it gave him the political base on which he constructed his future career. It is also the connivance of the United States with his myth-making, the endorsement of a story that the US Army had known to be untrue as early as 1948 after he had twice applied to have his 'Maharlika' unit officially recognized and his claims had been rejected as 'distorted, exaggerated, fraudulent, contradictory and absurd'.[22]

This is where the CIC agent mentioned earlier, Richard Sakakida, comes in, together with many others like him. When a war ends in almost unlimited bloodshed, chaos and destruction, as the Second World War did in the Philippines, it is perhaps easy to imagine that nothing remains of what has gone before: no coherent memories, no evidence, nothing but a clean sheet and a fresh start. Certain characters can, as it were, stagger from the smoking ruins believing themselves free to invent a new past, thinking that amid the general anarchy and turmoil their recent activities will have gone unnoticed and therefore unjudged. But of course a great many people did survive, including Richard Sakakida himself, with their memories not only intact but vivid. Once having managed to convince his Japanese captors that he was loyal to Japan, Sakakida had lived for three years on the constant edge of discovery. His very life depended on having an intimate knowledge of the anti-Japanese resistance in general and guerrilla activity in particular. He was, after all, scanning the Japanese Army's own top secret files on an almost daily basis. It is therefore beyond believing that he would never have encountered the name of Ferdinand Marcos or that of the 'Maharlika' unit had even a tenth of their stirring exploits been genuine. But this is a consistent theme: Marcos's name goes practically unmentioned in all contemporary accounts. The man who claimed that General MacArthur had personally told him after the war that but for him Bataan would have fallen three months earlier does not appear even in the General's own reminiscences. In 1986 the former USAFFE Army captain who had directed a guerrilla unit in Pangasinan province, Ray C. Hunt, was tracked down and asked his opinion. It turned out that he did remember Marcos since he had once arrested him on suspicion of collaboration with the Japanese and for engaging in buy-and-sell activities. For this, Marcos had actually faced a death sentence for the second time in his life, and on this occasion was saved only by the personal intervention of

Manuel Roxas, another future Philippine President. As to Ferdinand having led his own band of guerrillas, Ray Hunt said: 'Marcos was never the leader of a large guerrilla organization, no way. Nothing like that could have happened without my knowledge . . . This is not true, no. Holy cow! All of this is a complete fabrication. It's a cock-and-bull story.'[23]

It is a very strange thing that successive administrations of the world's most powerful nation should have accepted and publicly praised one man's self-assessment, and with little more authority than that individual's own assurances. The reason can be summed up in one word: Vietnam. Since this word explains so much of the twenty years' relationship between Washington and Marcos it is perhaps not very surprising; yet the sheer effrontery of the cynicism still has the power to shock. Even the radical Filipino historian (and sometime Benedictine monk) Ambeth Ocampo admitted to being astonished when he recently unearthed some further evidence:

> While browsing through declassified US State Department documents I read many confidential telegrams exchanged between the US Embassy in Manila and Washington. In one telegram concerning pointers for the [forthcoming] Marcos state visit [to Washington] in September 1966, Marcos was described as: 'A genuine war hero, a very attractive personality and a great public speaker. We have in this visit a large amount of capital, centring around the image he can project about Vietnam and, as President Johnson has said, about the vitality of the new Asia.'
>
> What I did not realize before was that the US ambassador insisted on the awarding of two medals to Marcos. In a confidential telegram dated September 6, 1966, he said that Marcos: '[H]ad never received the Distinguished Service Cross. Accordingly, I suggest Washington may wish consider giving decoration to Marcos during visit, perhaps in White House ceremony. Gesture would be much appreciated here and would help point up for American public fact of Marcos' wartime heroism under US flag. [. . .] Allied to foregoing, I would hope when Marcos introduced to Congress for joint session speech that mention will be made of his distinguished war record with US forces and decorations awarded him.'

When the State Department brought the matter up with the Defence Department it was discovered that there was no record of Marcos being awarded any medals. The alarm bells should have been ringing, but the US needed Philippine support for the Vietnam War and kept silent. On September 8, 1966 a confidential telegram sent to the US ambassador in Manila said: 'We have determined that Army ready and willing go ahead with presentation Distinguished Service Cross and Silver medals on basis that Marcos' US Army records do not, repeat, not show he ever received them . . .'

Washington knew Marcos was sporting medals he had not officially received but they played along. [. . .] Eventually, Marcos himself was asked about the medals because a *Time* correspondent said he admitted not having them: '. . . Marcos told me that Zich of *Time* magazine had been mistaken and that he, Marcos, had received both the Distinguished Service Cross and the Silver Star. There is, therefore, no reason for any presentation in Washington.'

From the documents cited above and many others, the Marcos war records could have been shot down as early as September 1966, but it took 20 years to expose the fraud . . .[24]

In actual fact it took nearer forty years, since the deception could have been exposed back in 1948 had the military authorities not had their hands full of vastly more important matters. Some time later, of course, the relevant file 'disappeared' at a whim of the Pentagon's. In the exchange of telegrams quoted above, therefore, one suspects there may be confusion about the ambiguity of the word 'received'. The 8 September message from Washington to their ambassador in Manila could – and probably should – be read as having meant that according to Army records Marcos had never been physically *presented* with the DSC, not that he had never been awarded it. Still, since we now know from his Army file that the status of the citation itself was dubious, to say the least, there must have been some fudging going on in Washington. Maybe his file had already been 'mislaid'. The clear overall impression remains of an official determination to play up the Marcos war record for all it was worth, since 'We have in this visit a large amount of capital, centring around the image he can project about Vietnam . . .' This simply confirms what has long been apparent: that Ferdinand Marcos no less than the Filipino people was little more than a hostage to yet another piece of American overseas adventuring. It remains for us to determine how much freedom he actually had.

All this takes us prematurely into the future, far ahead of the years 1942–5 when the issue of collaboration often boiled down to a question of day-to-day survival. Not surprisingly, the Philippine population ran the gamut between the Huk guerrillas' outright opposition to the Japanese and active support for their presence. In between were a hundred agonizing shades of *pakikisama* (that Filipino virtue which sets a high premium on smooth social relations regardless of circumstances), of grudging cohabitation, of resignation, of dumb resistance and surreptitious civil disobedience. Edging towards the 'active support' end of the scale were those who decided to profit from the Japanese and their war needs. At the extreme of active support, of course, were those Filipino politicians who headed the so-called puppet government while President Quezon and Vice-President Osmeña in the United States represented the legitimate Philippine Government in exile. The Japanese, having abolished all existing political parties, had instituted a single party known as the Kalibapi (*Kapisanan sa Paglilingkod sa Bagong Pilipinas* – the Association for Service to the New Philippines). In October 1943 the Japanese granted the Philippines its independence and in grand open-air ceremonies the Second Philippine Republic was inaugurated with Jose P. Laurel as President. (This was the same Justice Laurel who, a few years earlier, had acquitted Marcos of the Nalundasan murder.) Also prominent in the new administration were Jorge Vargas, lately President Quezon's executive secretary, and Benigno Aquino. The Aquino family, in particular, appeared to represent an extreme case of fractured loyalties. As head of this wealthy cacique clan, Benigno's father, General Servillano Aquino, had been a celebrated patriot who in 1899 had opposed the American occupation by choosing 'to continue the strife by individual action'.[25] Forty-four years later his son Benigno took a different view of a foreign occupation. (And *his* son, Benigno Jr. or 'Ninoy', was of course destined to die on the tarmac of Manila International Airport in 1983 in opposition to the current political status quo.)

After liberation in 1945 no opprobrium was too great to heap on the heads of 'active collaborators' and 'puppets' like Laurel, Aquino and Vargas, whom the Japanese had flown out to Japan to escape capture by MacArthur's forces. But at the time, thoughtful and informed Filipinos like Marcial Lichauco saw their behaviour – and especially Laurel's – in a much more complex and sympathetic light. As every page of his diary shows, Lichauco was no friend of the Japanese occupying forces. But he had been close friends for years with men like Laurel (another lawyer) and Roxas (his own legal partner) and saw them as people of considerable integrity whose conscience and patriotism obliged them to be pragmatic. Laurel had just survived serious wounding in an assassination attempt while playing golf a few months earlier, an attempt that ironically did much to convince the Japanese of his pro-Japanese bona fides, when in September 1943 Lichauco wrote in occupied Manila:

To his most intimate friends Laurel has explained his attitude. He has no doubt in his mind that the United Allies will win the war but he fears it may take between five to ten years before Japan can be brought to her knees. Meantime, the problem facing the Filipino people is that of survival and he therefore considers it his duty to do what he can to appease the Japanese militarists and help alleviate the sufferings of the Filipinos and the further privations which, no doubt, are in store for them in the future. In the second place, Laurel believes that no matter how thoroughly beaten Japan may be at the end of this war, the Japanese nation can never be obliterated and, sooner or later, the Japanese people will rise again and become a power in this corner of the world. Consequently, he does not think it advisable for the Filipino people to permanently incur the hatred of the one hundred million Japanese who are such close neighbours of ours. He realizes that in accepting the Presidency of the puppet Republic, some of his countrymen will get the impression that he is collaborating with the enemy, but Laurel is willing to run that risk because he is convinced that someone must head the government which the Japanese are determined to set up here. One thing he is determined to accomplish, and that is to prevent the Japanese from conscripting Filipino soldiers to fight against the Americans.

'I prefer to be shot,' he said, 'rather than agree to such a proposal and I believe I can stall the Japanese long enough to save
our young men from fighting their friends.'[26]

To us at the century's end Laurel's attitude might appear emi-
nently reasonable and, in the circumstances, morally courageous.
He also seems to have been commendably far-sighted in what he
has to say about Japan's certain defeat and equally inevitable resur-
gence in East Asia. Understandably, the Americans were obliged to
take a rather different view. Little more than a week after Laurel's
inauguration as unwilling President, Roosevelt replied to his
request that the United States recognize the Philippines' independence with a resounding 'No'; on which Lichauco, beleaguered in
Manila, comments tartly:

> It is all very well for President Roosevelt to discredit the Filipinos
> heading the puppet government that has been set up here. It is
> easy to be brave when the enemy is 10,000 miles away. It is easy
> to say that the only true officials of the Filipino Government are
> temporarily in Washington. But how can 18,000,000 Filipino
> people live in these Islands without some form of government?
> *Someone* must head the government here unless, of course, it is to
> be substituted by an organization run entirely by Japanese offi-
> cials and such irresponsible and discredited Filipinos of the past
> who would be only too glad to jump at the opportunity to
> assume positions of power.[27]

It is scarcely possible to exaggerate the moral discomfort of the
position in which the majority of Filipinos now found themselves,
with old questions of national identity and allegiance again predominant. Once the war was over, of course, and Japan defeated, it
was as though nobody had ever really doubted the outcome or
where their loyalties had always lain. But at the time things were a
good deal more equivocal, not least because of the constant fear of
informers, spies, torture and reprisals.

Up in the hills and on the plains of central Luzon, the Huk resistance guerrillas had fought an unrelenting war which would have
been quite impossible without massive local support. As it was,
they became well enough organized to constitute an independent

regional government of sorts with its own elected officials, legal system, communications network and even newspaper.[28] Their engagements with the Japanese tended to be well planned and efficient, employing disciplined strategy rather than the hit-and-run 'freebooting' tactics favoured by other irregular units (such as Marcos's putative 'Maharlika' group). Indeed, the Huks tended rather to look down on other guerrillas, especially those in the so-called 'USAFFE squadrons'. These were composed chiefly of USAFFE men who had either avoided being captured in Bataan or had subsequently escaped from a PoW camp. Some squadrons were commanded by Americans – a handful of the several thousand stray American and other Western stragglers hiding in the hills all over the archipelago. The Huks were often scornful of these units, which they accused of self-interest and shirking. They said the USAFFE men were mainly interested in avoiding contact with the Japanese, being content to skulk and sit out the war in order to receive their back-pay and pensions once it was over, meanwhile subsisting on common thievery from local peasants. They referred to them dismissively (with typical linguistic felicity) as 'tulisaffe', a punning combination of USAFFE and tulisan, the historically loaded word for a common bandit. It should be noted in passing that the Huk guerrillas were confined to central Luzon (Bulacan, Nueva Ecija, Pampanga, Tarlac and Laguna provinces, to be precise). Outside that area, both northward in the Ilocos and southward through the bulk of the archipelago, there was an array of groups largely operating on a local basis. These ranged from scattered fighting outfits to 'lost commands' of misfits, the disaffected, and the frankly criminal more interested in turning the presence of the Japanese to their private advantage by enriching themselves and settling old scores.

The Huks' main hatred, like that of most resistance groups, was directed less at the Japanese than at those Filipinos they saw as collaborating. These included local politicians and petty officials as well as members of pro-Japanese associations such as the Kalibapi, which gave the Japanese political support, and the Makapili, whose network of informers helped the military. Above all, though, the Huks loathed the newly reconstituted Philippine Constabulary, whom they viewed as nothing more than the puppets' mercenaries. Such people, when they fell into guerrilla hands, seldom made quick or easy deaths. The claim that Ferdinand Marcos – and there-fore Spence – had made about his father Mariano gallantly resisting the Japanese in Ilocos Norte was embellished with an account of Mariano's death as a guerrilla late in the war. 'Failing to break him, the Japanese bayoneted him and suspended his body from a tree. Two days later, Ferdinand visited the scene, but his father's remains were gone. They were never found.' Reality, however, was rather different, as Sterling Seagrave later established by talking to an eye-witness. Mariano, who had publicly sung the Japanese forces' praises in Batac, had actually fallen into the hands of a guer-rilla unit commanded by an American, Major George Barnett. Even more unfortunately for him, Barnett's unit included several friends and relatives of the late Julio Nalundasan, the man who had beaten Mariano in the 1935 election and whom Ferdinand was convicted of having shot. Under interrogation, Mariano confessed that it was Ferdinand who had put his name forward to the Kempei Tai, the secret police. (This probably explains how Ferdinand had obtained his release from Camp O'Donnell.) After a month or two as the unwilling guest of Major Barnett, Mariano was tried for war crimes and sentenced to death for having worked for the Japanese from start to finish (it was now early 1945). The wretched Mariano might well have wished for a simple bayoneting. The man whose custom it had been in his middle twenties 'at six each evening to put on a tan military uniform with a Sam Browne belt, holstered sidearm, riding breeches and boots, and strut around [Sarrat] village square cracking a riding crop on his thigh'[29] made a very unmilitary death, though a traditional one. He was hitched to four water buffaloes and torn apart, his shredded limbs and torso then being hung, dripping, on a tree. A similar fate would probably have awaited his son had not Roxas intervened in the nick of time.

What did Ferdinand Marcos *really* do in the war, then? Briefly, once he was out of Camp O'Donnell he took his chances, like many another young Filipino. Much of his autobiographical war record might be fiction but there is little doubt he did move about, his life inevitably structured by the events going on around him to the extent that he was occasionally caught up in guerrilla activity. His character was opportunistic rather than passive. He would never have elected to stay at home either in Ilocos Norte or in Manila, docilely building a legal practice on the foundations of his Bar examination triumph, unless there had been nothing better in the offing.

But there was something better, in a sense. There was the radical disruption offered by the war and the Japanese occupation, and social disruption makes for social mobility. His Ilocano blood and his family's political background equally led him to where profit might be made and power found. As regards the first tendency, his overriding need as a rolling stone would have been survival, a way of getting by. Ray Hunt's accusation that Ferdinand had been condemned to death for his involvement in buy-and-sell rackets not only makes sense in the circumstances, it is borne out by other documentary references. By 'buy and sell' Hunt did not mean ordinary wheeler-dealing. After all, anyone in wartime might be reduced to the survival tactic of dabbling in the black market. The accusation specifically meant dealing directly with the Japanese, selling them things which, as the war dragged on, were strategically vital and in increasingly short supply. (One such thing was iron, and towards the war's end iron bars were treated more like gold. It seems that the need for iron often justified demolishing perfectly good buildings simply to steal the reinforcing rods buried in the walls and ceilings.)

Many Filipinos bitterly resented their fellow countrymen's buy-and-sell activities with the Japanese, and those involved were prime candidates for charges of collaboration once the war was over. Marcial Lichauco himself refers with scorn to those who dealt with the Japanese; but for oratorical thunder one has to turn to another lawyer, Francisco A. Delgado, who followed up the cessation of hostilities in 1945 with a blistering memorandum to Tomas Confesor, the new Secretary of the Interior, on how the briefly reinstated Commonwealth government ought to deal with those who had collaborated with the Japanese. For him, these 'buy and sell tycoons' merited a special category of their own:

> During the three years of Japanese occupation, a number of our countrymen, and many resident aliens, tempted by the ease with which they could sell practically anything to the Japanese Army and dazzled by the numerical enormity of the sums which they amassed, plunged headlong into the ugly racket commonly known as buying and selling. The goods bought by the Japanese

were of course those which they could use in the pursuit of their military campaign. Hundreds became millionaires overnight. Many, on the other hand, were forced into this business because that was the only way whereby they could save their families from starvation . . .

While a number of Filipinos engaged in this racket, most of the 'big shots' were the alien residents in the Philippines. While the Filipino 'buy and sell' addicts scampered pell mell for pickings, the foreigners conducted their manoeuvres in a more organized, systematic and astute manner. The East Indians, who, before the war, 'salaamed' to Britain and the United States, discovered the 'Open Sesame' to fabulous riches. They raised the banner of the 'Assad Hind'; hailed Subhas Chandra Bose as their leader and protector; and shouted 'On to Delhi!' from their princely carriages and their stores overflowing with goods. The Chinese saw their chance, and so they waved the banner Wang Ching Wei* as the Japanese waved back with newly printed military notes. The Jews, who took refuge in this country because they were ostracized and driven out of Germany, suddenly reassumed their German nationality and stuck 'Swastika' banners on their cars while they stuck fat bundles of money into their pockets . . .[30]

From the general tone it can readily be appreciated that Ferdinand would have known his activities could prove fatal if he were ever caught – which, as we have seen, he was. The near-miraculous intervention to save his life by Manuel Roxas who, as soon as the war was over in 1945, became the last President of the Commonwealth and then the first of the Republic, brings us to the second of Ferdinand's natural inclinations: that of gravitating towards political power. Here again his Ilocano inheritance sheds some light. Mention has already been made in the previous chapter of that celebrated son of Batac, the revolutionary General Artemio Ricarte, the stories of whose exploits against the Americans Ferdinand would have heard at Josefa's knee. In 1901 the defeated

---

* This refers to the KMT (nationalist Chinese) figure whose Japanese-sponsored government ruled in Nanjing from 1940–5.

Ricarte had categorically refused to take the oath of allegiance to the United States, so the Americans banished him to Guam and later to Hong Kong. However, he chose finally to live in Yokohama, only returning to the Philippines during the Japanese occupation. Once there, he became a co-founder in 1944 of the Makapili, whose informers guerrilla groups like the Huks held in special contempt.

It is not obvious why this aspect of Ferdinand's background is not accorded greater weight by historians. He had grown up in a province a long way from Manila, in an atmosphere whose attitude towards the still-recent American occupation was ambiguous, to say the least. Ricarte was only the most locally celebrated example of many Ilocanos whose inability to square their patriotism with swearing allegiance to the United States had driven them into outright exile, into smouldering acquiescence, or into closer alliances with the Chinese and the Japanese – who in any case had always had strong connections with these northern provinces. As a Filipino, Ferdinand would instinctively put family, friends and region before his country, which is what any civilized person does ('If I had to choose between betraying my country and betraying my friend, I hope I should have the guts to betray my country,' as E. M. Forster rather too piously said). When Ferdinand's war record came to be critically investigated in the 1980s, though, the task fell largely to Americans, most of whom had conceivably never read E. M. Forster. More to the point, they not only had been on the winning side in the war against the Japanese but, like the British, had the extraordinary good fortune never to have suffered the agonizing moral test of having their own country brutally occupied by the armed forces of a foreign power. The lenses through which they scrutinized this terrible and confusing period of Filipino history, therefore, had an inbuilt polarization. In this clear but slanted light it appeared to them that the majority of Filipinos had felt a deep loyalty to the Americans and had variously fought for, or longed for, their return. Those who hadn't were traitors: puppets and collaborators who cynically chose to side with the enemy for personal gain.

Yet although this was presented as a truism, it was not entirely true. The majority of Filipinos undoubtedly did support the Americans, but not necessarily from any deep sense of loyalty. They wanted the Americans back in order to drive the Japanese out. After all, life for most Filipinos before 1941 had not been especially rosy. (What Kansulay's old people remember – without much emotion – is great hardship, agricultural wages held at bare subsistence level, unremitting labour and virtually no medical facilities. To that extent their lives had changed hardly at all since the time of the Spanish.) Seen in this context, the American regime had not been popular so much as the known devil that is broadly tolerated, much as the British in India were, an assessment that was not invalidated by thousands of personal friendships between individuals on both sides. As the war went on, though, and Japanese rule became more oppressive, the Americans' lengthening absence undoubtedly made Filipinos' hearts grow fonder. There was no question but that the Americans had been in all respects more agreeable than the Japanese; but as Quezon had famously said, 'Better a government run like hell by Filipinos than one run like heaven by Americans.' In addition to which, the image of the United States had taken a severe beating even before the Fall of Bataan. It was not just that the Americans had been militarily defeated; they also seemed thereafter to have abandoned the Philippines to its fate a little too easily. One day, when President Quezon was impotently holed up on Corregidor, he turned bitterly to Charles Willoughby, one of MacArthur's aides, and exclaimed: 'America writhes in anguish at the fate of a distant cousin, Europe, while a daughter, the Philippines, is being raped in the back room!' This was certainly what he himself felt, but whether he spoke for the entire nation is less sure. A year later, though, Marcial Lichauco recorded a brilliant assessment by a Japanese officer of how things stood – brilliant because it showed an unusual understanding of the Filipino gift for dissembling. The occasion was a parade in Manila on the first anniversary of the Fall of Bataan:

> Among those in the grandstand was a fairly well-known [Filipino puppet-] government underling who had helped organize the show. In his eagerness to court the friendship and favour of the Japanese official who sat beside him he turned to the latter and said: 'I think there is little doubt now that the great majority of our people are pro-Japanese. I should say that ninety percent of them at least understand Japan's true objectives in fighting for the unification of Greater East Asia.'

But the officer turned to him rather deprecatingly and replied:

'You are mistaken, – I am afraid that forty-five percent of the population continues to be pro-American, five percent are pro-Japanese, while the remaining fifty percent are comedians.'[31]

By the mid-eighties, with American journalists taking their cue from the State Department and fitting Marcos for a black hat even as President Reagan was stubbornly insisting on his white one, such niceties of history went by the board. By then they all knew what to think about the Pacific War and alleged wartime collaborators like Marcos. The effect of their sweeping, though unconscious, judgemental attitude was to assess Ferdinand's war as an open and shut case of the most simplistic kind of self-interest, seen against an implied background of heroism and sacrifice on the part of his compatriots. The reality, as we can imagine, had been a good deal less clear-cut and infinitely more painful.

If, as seems likely, Ferdinand did recommend his father to the Japanese as being favourable to their cause, how might we assess his motives? If Mariano had already made his welcoming speech in Batac, surely recommending him would have been superfluous? On the other hand, if Mariano had already made his new allegiance clear, his son was presumably wise to take advantage of a *fait accompli* and thereby get himself out of the PoW camp. This was surely where the politics came in. He was, after all, well connected thanks to the Nalundasan case and his Bar exam triumph. Barely two years earlier President Quezon himself had offered him a pardon in his murder conviction. Now, of course, Quezon was in exile in America. But there was still the judge who had pleaded so eloquently and successfully to the Supreme Court to uphold his appeal, Jose Laurel, his *semblable* if not his *frère*, who had also been acquitted of murder when he was eighteen.

Laurel was himself an interesting and complex man, as Lichauco's assessment indicated. Like Ricarte, he was a convinced nationalist who had always been fundamentally opposed to the American presence in the Philippines. (It should be remembered that theirs was not some local piece of hard-headed intransigence: in most of colonized Asia at the time – in India, Burma, Malaya, Indonesia, China and Indochina – there were strong anti-imperialist movements, all of which would achieve their goal of independence in the next few decades.) For a Filipino to have been anti-American until 1942 (and even after) was by no means as *outré* as American authors saw it in the 1980s. Well before the outbreak of war Laurel, who in 1938 was awarded an honorary doctorate of Jurisprudence by Tokyo Imperial University, had been legal consultant to several Japanese industrial companies with large investments in the Philippines. It is known that Ferdinand was hospitalized in Manila in June 1943 with what his brother Pacifico, a doctor, diagnosed as a gastric ulcer and fever; it is also known that his hospitalization coincided with that of Laurel following the assassination attempt on Wack-Wack golf course. It is too much to suppose that the two recuperating men did not spend time together. Each had something the other wanted. As far as Ferdinand was concerned Laurel – who was about to become puppet President – necessarily had usefully close links with the Kempei Tai as well as friendships with high-ranking Japanese that pre-dated the war. And from Laurel's point of view, Marcos had by then all sorts of contacts with guerrilla groups from Ilocos to Leyte that could provide information about the purely criminal outfits the Japanese (and therefore Laurel himself) had an interest in breaking up. Ferdinand was, additionally, deep in Laurel's debt for his pre-war acquittal. It was an *utang na loob* he could not have ignored without dishonour.

When, after the end of the war, Laurel and the others were brought back from their refuge in Tokyo and tried as collaborators, Laurel was acquitted under President Roxas's Proclamation no. 51, which granted a blanket amnesty to most of those accused of collaboration. Many Filipinos have since expressed satirical views about what they saw as a lot of collaborators being exonerated by another collaborator. Ferdinand Marcos, whose reputation as a war hero was by then under intensive construction, was doing his utmost to avoid being publicly lumped in with those who needed amnesty. Yet his wartime dealings with both Laurel and Roxas (who until he pleaded the heart condition that was to kill him a few years later had been the preferred choice of the Japanese as puppet president) must have enmeshed him in a complex web. They had all of them squeaked through into this strange climate of exoneration, if not of forgiveness. In the new moral and political status quo it was in their interest to connive at the sanitizing of each other's past. That Ferdinand's powerful wartime friend Roxas was back in political business with a clean slate and running a new Republic undoubtedly gave him a good base from which to operate, for he was already thinking ahead.

In that sense Ferdinand's war was something of a personal triumph even without all the comic-strip heroics he was to add as a top-dressing. In the next four years until he was first elected to Congress there must have been some awkward moments when he was unsure whether the persona he had invented for himself would be exploded. But as time went by and his ties with the men the Americans had anointed as the new regime grew closer, he must have felt himself increasingly safe. What effect his war had had on him at a psychological level is another matter. One would have thought he was surely left with at least two sources of profound guilt, the first of which being a bogus war record. This secret, which of course both he and the Americans shared, would acquire the status of mutual blackmail when he came to be President, a complicity he and Washington could each hold over the other's head. What might have started out as nothing but youthful braggadocio – a little embellishment here, some dramatic details there – slipped out of control and gradually hardened into a fiction that, by the time he was briefing Hartzell Spence for the definitive version, was brazenly bolstered by alleged quotations from MacArthur himself (recently, and safely, dead in 1964). Since their history's sundry betrayals and lies have rendered most Filipinos sublime cynics, all politics in the Philippines are pure *palabas*, sheer spectacle, into which Ferdinand's fanciful skill with the greasepaint fitted without difficulty as an adroit and original gambit. The people who felt most deeply about the issue were the authentic scarified survivors of Fort Santiago's underground torture chamber, as also the genuine battle heroes. They never forgave him. (What was more, such people never had been deceived. Frank Sionil José, the renowned writer and proprietor of Manila's La Solidaridad bookshop – which throughout the Marcos martial law era was a refuge for dissenting intellectuals – offered the following vignette: 'One of Marcos's closest old friends was Commodore Nuval. Each year, at the time of Ferdinand's birthday, Nuval would come to the bookshop to choose three books as gifts for him. One year it happened to coincide with a ceremony commemorating the Battle of Bessang Pass, in which Ferdinand the "war hero" had claimed he was very much to the fore. Nuval was in my shop and we were gossiping about this and he laughed and said: "Ferdy was never at Bessang Pass." This would have been in 1966 or 1967. It was made doubly absurd because that same September a girl came to the shop, the daughter of Major Conrado B. Rigor, who was the true hero of Bessang Pass, as every Ilocano knew. She was in tears because of the way Marcos had usurped her father's heroism.')

The other source of guilt Ferdinand may have had difficulty dealing with was his father's death. Had Mariano, that perennially unsuccessful man, brought about his own downfall? Or had his son directly contributed to it by recommending him to the Japanese as a man they could deal with? Either way, Mariano had died for having dealings with the Japanese, while the equally guilty Ferdinand had not. The mere fact of his death, and in so spectacularly unpleasant a manner, might surely have been reason enough for Ferdinand to insist with increasing vehemence on a far more palatable version of events. His father had been a hero; he himself had been a hero. Who was counting? (And by then, who dared count?)

And what, finally, of that other hero, the mighty champion of the free world, General Douglas MacArthur? There was an extraordinary outcome of his return to the Philippines, one that Roosevelt could never have imagined when he had thankfully sent him off to be Quezon's military adviser in 1935. It depended on the United States, in 1945, being almost entirely preoccupied with Europe in the wake of the Nazi defeat and in the quick resettling of the Western world into fresh alliances. To put it bluntly: Japan had been nuked into submission and the Eastern Pacific would have to take care of itself for a while. The carving up of Europe into Eastern and Western blocs, with ex-allies swiftly turning into Communist enemies, more or less monopolized American attention. Almost by default, therefore, MacArthur was given a free hand to arrange his former fiefdom according to his taste. His personal support was crucial to getting his old friend Roxas approved by Washington and elected. So also was his capricious withholding of US aid for the reconstruction of the Philippines until after the election, thereby making the aid virtually contingent on Roxas becoming President. Thereafter, the $2 billion in aid was fought over by various groups of vultures who had good links with the new ruling élite of

MacArthur and Roxas. Only very little of this fabulous sum (at mid-1940s value, too) actually went into rebuilding the Philippines' shattered infrastructure and economy. To illustrate just how bad things were, it is perhaps better to rely on an American author for a final description, beginning with what happened to the $2 billion:

Instead of revitalizing the economy, much of it ($150 million by one estimate) went to rehabilitate a few privileged American-owned businesses and import–export companies. Six million dollars went to rehabilitate the fabulously rich Benguet gold mines, in which MacArthur held stock. Beer baron Andres Soriano, MacArthur's wartime aide-de-camp, was a Spanish citizen, but quickly took Philippine citizenship as the war approached. Then, one day after Pearl Harbor, MacArthur made him a colonel in the US Army and arranged to get him instant American citizenship. In 1946, when Soriano's San Miguel brewery urgently needed bottle caps, MacArthur had the War Department fly 20 tons of caps across the Pacific. So things were.

Everybody was on the make. Millions of dollars' worth of consumer goods flowed into Manila just for the maintenance of the US Army. One quarter of these goods ended up on the black market. GIs working with civilians sidetracked trucks, powdered milk, pistols, stockings, typewriters, and cigarettes. Two months after Yamashita's surrender, over $1 million in US Government-owned goods were seized when police broke up a Manila ring. After that it became serious.

'It may well be,' journalist Robert Shaplen observed, 'that in no other city in the world was there as much graft and conniving after the war.' The Surplus Property Commission, intended to dispose of excess US military property, became the preserve of Roxas backers. Washington industrial lobbyists contrived to make it illegal to bring surplus war goods home. Thousands of jeeps, tanks, planes and munitions went on the market in every former combat zone. President Roxas offered Washington 1 peso for 90,000 tons of surplus ammunition stored on Luzon. The State Department fumed, but turned the munitions over. Tons of US Army scrap metal in the Philippines were sold to an American concern through various fronts for a mere $335,000. The deal was arranged by MacArthur's associate, former High Commissioner Paul McNutt, whom Filipinos called the 'Hoosier Hitler'.

While politicians and businessmen grew wealthy, Manila's balance of payments deficit with the United States jumped to over $1 billion. 'The future of the islands is not bright,' commented an American magazine. 'The United States is responsible for the situation and should do what it can to rectify it.'[32]

Today, many Filipinos date the tacit acceptance of theft and corruption at government level from this period, as well as the final demoralization of a people who had suffered so much. From then on, they claim, no public figure was likely to be taken seriously or believed, no official expected to be trustworthy, no politics to be viewed as anything more than the spectacle of a corrupt élite playing musical chairs among itself. It may indeed suit diehard nationalists to view the corruption surrounding the Americans' administering of post-war aid as the root of much subsequent social and political evil in the Philippines, but the truth is less conveniently simplistic.

The fact is that Filipinos themselves needed no lessons from Americans on political intrigue and corruption. In the old days the Spanish had made frequent references to Filipinos' blithe ruthlessness when given petty ascendancy over their fellow countrymen, and visiting Americans from the turn of the century onwards had recorded their own amazement at the unashamed corruption and brutality often displayed by local functionaries. It could be argued that these were simply the disdainful observations of foreign colonials with a vested interest in portraying benighted brown people incapable of governing themselves, but the weight of evidence is against such a view. Certainly a writer like Katherine Mayo was acting more as a sceptical journalist than as an American apologist when she visited the Philippines in the early twenties. Her resultant book, *The Isles of Fear – The Truth about the Philippines* (1925), frequently shows her sympathies to have lain with the wretched *indios* as they laboured not so much beneath the American yoke as beneath that of their own kind: local headmen, small landowners, politicians and bigwigs. If at the end of the Second World War the battered Philippine people were often more sceptical than optimistic about their newly independent country's political future, it was surely because they recognized that an all-Filipino political process was unlikely to be other than corrupt. They would have realized that the opportunities the recent war had offered for unscrupulous self-advantage on the part of so many people with political ambitions could only have made the outlook gloomy. In the event, their cynicism was amply justified.

It may well be that this immediate post-war period did in some way further polarize the electorate into those who ran for office and those who grew the rice (to caricature it somewhat). It was the moment when, in recognition of the way in which the war had weighed equally heavily on all levels of Filipino society, something like a true democratic spirit might have taken shape. But as will be seen in Chapter 7, such attempts as Juan de la Cruz made to vote his own representatives into government (in this case Democratic Alliance candidates in Central Luzon in 1946) were thwarted and crushed with the utmost crudeness. It is hardly surprising that ordinary folk, finding themselves rebuffed by their own newly independent nation's polity, were driven back into taking shelter behind the peasant defences that had always proved so powerful a refuge in the past: all manner of superstitious beliefs and charismatic religious practices, which here and there became allied to grassroots revolutionary movements. It was a liminal world the fledgling politician Ferdinand Marcos would reveal that he understood perfectly.

5

The haunting of Kansulay

For all its sudden plunging down to where clear streams run through green tunnels and daylight leaks between overhead leaves like a precious distillate, the general trend of the path has been upward for two hours. My guides have kept up a swift pace while my eyes see little but their bare heels printing themselves over and over. I tag along as best I can. People accustomed to going barefoot have differently shaped feet, broader, the toes used individually for gripping. My own toes might as well be welded together in a flap designed only for propelling me forward. My guides are hardly old, but already their feet are an illustration of the local, semi-jocular dialect expression for 'barefoot': *nakaluya*. *Luya* is ginger, and the reference is to the foot resembling a root of ginger with its splayed, bulbous rhizomes flecked with dried mud. Despite the slime of the trail, though, their feet remain stubbornly clean, as though they were both strolling a basketball court. My own rubber sandals are clotted with mud.

After two hours we emerge on an upland slope where the coco-palms have thinned and the red volcanic soil supports guava bushes as well as the *kugon* grass used for thatch. At our feet the forest-tops shimmer in the afternoon sun, the lively shine of leaves falling and rising in a series of valleys towards the range that hides Kansulay and the blue South China Sea. Those are the same valleys through which I have come, slipping and floundering in forest deeps cut off from the sun.

'*Mahiwagang lugal,*' someone observes. An enchanted place.

It is a strange sensation when a patch of terrain asserts itself. This is not like one of those landscapes gazed across whose lyrical moment is inseparable from the onlooker's mind. The ordinary slope is unexceptional in its view, yet it gives off a disquieting air suggestive of sentience, as though it always had something to be busy with whether anyone was watching or not. Perhaps after all this is nothing but self-suggestion; I have already heard it described as a special place. Yet I also have a rueful history of failing to sense what everyone else seems to feel on cue.

Up here on this tropic slope, however, there is no need for such misgivings. The very air insists on recognition. The long tresses of *kugon* on a neighbouring hillside part to let stray quick breezes run up through them, as though at stalk level hidden creatures were silently racing. On our hill the air is peculiarly still. My guides watch the grasses without speaking. Eventually I ask them if it is true that *tintang luya*, the black ginger allegedly grown by shamans for their rites, comes from this area. The question goes unanswered. 'I've never seen black ginger, have you?' one asks with an equivocal smile before leading off around the shoulder to where, behind a clump of *madrekakaw* trees, the cave opening lies. It is a mouth at a slant, slightly taller than me and narrow, admitting just enough light to show a silt floor angled downwards. This is soft and takes our footprints clearly. Some burnt stubs of coconut-frond torches lie about, together with scattered and scorched stones from a cooking fire.

The cave has a reputation. The Japanese did not land on this island until July 1942, which gave the locals six months to consider who might take to the hills and who might stay put and sweat out the impending occupation. Even so small a province has its comparatively inaccessible places, and before the year was out resistance fighters were using this cave as one of their bases. The three local men already mentioned as having been paraded around town before being executed on Christmas Day 1942 were suspected of belonging to one of these guerrilla units. The odd fact is that, try as they might, the Japanese never did find this particular cave. Others they found, but not this one. That and the cave's proximity to a larger one used for secret underground rites in Holy Week is a reason for its peculiar fame. For it is said that our cave has the power to hide its own mouth. In this way it is possible for someone

it wishes to exclude to look behind the *madrekakaw* trees and see
nothing. This ability of the opening to seal or conceal itself at will is
one curiosity; another is the assertion that people who visit it in the
right spirit may come and go without leaving footprints on its silty
floor. I have heard it said that the guerrillas who used it during the
war carried *anting-anting*s or charms that allowed them to live here
without tell-tale evidence. I have met an old warrior who claims his
unit used it until late 1944. He describes the site with perfect accuracy, but says the cave they lived in is not the one I am now visiting
because whenever he and his comrades entered it in the old days
they would find themselves in a place they couldn't recognize.

I have already discussed this with my guides, who assure me
that this is the only opening. Is it perhaps connected to the bigger
cavern they use during Holy Week? They couldn't say. Even the
youth who has been on one of those week-long subterranean fasts
and has spoken with Jesus Christ and the queen-enchantress Maria
Malindig is not sure. Suppose we make palm-frond torches and
follow it down as we had planned? Neither reluctant nor enthusiastic, one goes off to look for fallen fronds and soon we are filing
down into this crack in the earth, trailing smoke and sparks. There
are numerous greasy boulders to scramble over and the downward
passage continues for what might be a hundred metres. Disturbed
bats whirr about our heads and there is an ammoniac smell of
guano. We come upon some rusted metal that might have been
anything. Ammunition canisters? Mess tins? I am still thinking in
terms of a war more than half a century ago. The mud floor is free
of all marks other than those of bat droppings and the tracks we
ourselves are leaving. Presumably rainwater must regularly flow in
to leave a perpetual *tabula rasa*. The torch gives out and the second
is lit from its last flickers. We must go back.

'What happens if you go on?'

'Nobody knows. Maybe nobody has ever been. Or somebody
knows and does it all the time.'

'All the caves in this province are connected,' says my other
guide. I have known him since he was a child but down here he
sounds like a stranger.

'Even the one under Malindig?' I ask, referring to an immense
cave rumoured to be beneath the mountain at the other end of the
island, a good twenty miles away.

'Especially that one.'

'And is that where Maria Malindig lives?'

'Maybe sometimes.'

The old ex-guerrilla had said he and his comrades had once had 'an action' with a party of Japanese soldiers and had taken some casualties. Eight of them had managed to get away and return to this cave half-dead with hunger and fatigue. No sooner had they entered the cave, though, than they were greeted by a beautiful woman who invited them to rest. Once they were seated the woman began laying before them great plates of food and pitchers of fresh water. The men ate and drank until they were full, then fell asleep. When they awoke the cave was dark and bare, but they were still sated and remained neither hungry nor thirsty for the next three days. The old man said this had never been explained. He said no more, except to retail one last fragment of his half-forgotten war. The Philippine Republic which the Japanese had declared in October 1943 under Laurel's puppet administration had had a single political party, the Kalibapi (the Association for Service to the New Philippines). He said this cave had been the headquarters of the Kali*da*pi, the *da* standing for *Dating*, which would render as The Association in Service of the *Former* Philippines. He would not explain further, only smile. Consequently I cannot get the weight of this at all. Was it just a light pun, or a token of something deeper and more mystical, perhaps associated with this cleft leading towards the province's heart? A yearning for a distant past before all foreign invaders came?

After I had returned from our jaunt to the cave (where we had definitely left footprints, suggesting we had visited it in the wrong spirit), the expedition simply joined an already long list of inconclusive experiences that Kansulay had afforded me over the years. Sometimes I wearied of my dumb-brick rationalist role, of so faithfully playing the part of the only guy in town who knew there was a perfectly good explanation for odd happenings which people were half proud to see baffled me. I found their proprietorial attitude provoking, as though they had carefully arranged the life of the village (*hocus-pocus! abracadabra!*) as a grand illusion, a conjuring trick, just to watch the foreigner's jaw drop. (And if so, what an adroit reversal it was of the usual picture of the bumpkin-from-the-sticks taken to a great city and overwhelmed by the marvels of technology!) There had been the occasion of the meeting one night in somebody's hut when Ka Rody, a local shaman, had spoken from a trance in three distinct voices, one of them a child's and another a woman's, purporting to be those of the legendary royal figures associated with this province's mythology. Chicanery, of course, I told myself as I stood obdurately in one corner, silently playing my James Randi role as ghostbuster-general. But that was before the twelve lit candles clumped closely together in a circle on the table began to go out, one by one, with metronomic regularity until the last three went out simultaneously. No strings, no concealed blowing, no flickering of neighbouring candles only two inches away; not even any last wisp of smoke from the wick. Worse, the candles had been my own contribution. When I asked if I should bring anything somebody had suggested candles. I had bought them myself in the market that morning: ordinary slender, yellow candles tied in a bunch by their wicks. Well, there was bound to be an explanation, just as there would be for the din of a large party which had once woken me and my companion in the middle of the night. We had lain and listened to the clatter of plates, the familiar drunken singing, the bursts of laughter, and I wondered sleepily whose birthday it was before realizing what something more alert in me had long since noticed: that the sounds were coming from uphill, behind my hut, where there was nothing but a steep slope buried beneath thick tangles of Imelda-weed and dense forest growth. ('Don't be scared,' my companion had said in the darkness. 'It's only *mumu*. They like to play tricks sometimes.') These were, I later learned, forest *mumu* as distinct from the sea *mumu* that sometimes frighten Kansulay's fishermen at night with the sound of a baby crying nearby as they sit far out on the still sea beneath the stars.

But it was wearisome all the same, being reduced to saying over and over again that there was bound to be an explanation, deciding that such a thing would not have happened had I only just arrived. It is interesting how easily one takes on the intellectual colouring of one's surroundings. The city's gross rationalism becomes oddly flimsy after months of living in the woods and being with people whose lives are bounded by perceptions different enough to give off this unsettling air of inconclusiveness. Usually their intelligence seems utterly modern as they deal cunningly with boat engines and ailing television sets. Then suddenly, almost in mid-sentence, it is as though they were still inhabiting a lost century with an entirely different set of skills and knowledge. Yet each intelligence lives at ease with the other. We expect too much of rationalism, just as others expect too much of the mysterious. In any event, one is tired of trying to provide over-neat syntheses. A culture's secret peculiarity lies in its discontinuities, and these are all too easily smothered by whatever sweetish or sourish sauce an outsider pours over to make them homogenous and palatable.

What is disquieting about Kansulay is, I sometimes think, what is disquieting about Filipinos in general, including their polity. It is a certain liminality – a living on a boundary, now flirting with one side and now the other while yet managing to maintain a peculiar stasis. I have no idea if this elusive balance leads anywhere, nor even if that matters. It awakes a private image in me, half dream and half memory. It is like catching sight of someone in the depths of a forest, a brown face barred and dappled by sunlight falling through fronds, standing very still and watchfully. It is someone I feel I recognize, and I take a step forward in greeting. Yet in that instant's change of perspective there is also a change of light, revealing with a shock that no one is there after all, that what I had taken for a person is only part of a tree trunk. Has he melted silently away, or was he never there? Ruefully I retire. Only years later am I able to perceive that it wasn't a tree trunk, either, but the house of a spirit. A training in Western journalism does not qualify us for such perceptions, and certainly not on a national scale.

This brilliant elusiveness, the watchfulness of the figure in the wood and the tree spirits – these are not just a mystical glaze applied to the matt lives of Kansulay's people by an outsider hoping to compensate for his own lack of a soul. They are part of the daily fabric of life, audible, observable, tangible. In *Playing with Water* I mentioned overhearing the village men making ritual requests (*'Tabi nuno!'*) to spirits to move aside as they crossed a stream or chopped a tree. This still goes on, as does the wearing of *anting-anting*. Many babies have odd little cloth-wrapped pellets on a string around their necks. Boys and young men, especially, carry amulets to ward off danger. These may be pinchbeck medallions showing a variety of mystical symbols derived from an eclectic range of Christian, pagan and Masonic images (the eye-in-a-pyramid that bizarrely appears on the back of the US $1 banknote is popular). Some amulets contain spells written on scraps of paper and then encased in gum. Amid such variety a small cross or crucifix is simply one more talisman. Young men sometimes wear a .223-calibre M-16 bullet around their necks in accordance with macho fashion. The local market sells a neat combination of the secular and the religious that consists of a stylized brass bullet with a cross-piece of metal inserted near the top, at once crucifix and projectile. These are much fancied by adolescent boys, no doubt because the bullet also has a groove scored around it near the tip to make its phallic connotations still more evident.

Marcos's fanciful war record had been made more credible by a story that became known all over the country, which told that Bishop Aglipay himself had once inserted a talisman in the form of a splinter of wood into Ferdinand's back. This, it was claimed, had not only enabled the Lion of Ilocos to survive his war exploits but had also brought him the necessary health, wealth and fortune to become President even as it warded off potential enemies. Yet again, it is impossible to say where the truth of this tale lies. The insertion of such a talisman is not itself implausible, especially in the provinces, but neither is it incompatible with a completely cynical use of the supernatural to enhance the general Marcos myth. Ferdinand was himself quite superstitious, especially about dates and numbers, and became a knowledgeable and adept numerologist.

In Kansulay, spells and charms have a perennial fascination. It is not always easy for an outsider to judge their status because most people will deny knowing any or believing in such things. Nevertheless, there they are. They exist as a clandestine scripture, written in the shaky capitals of marginal literacy on the silver-backed liners of cigarette packets or else in little home-made breviaries cut down from school exercise books with pink-and-blue lined pages. They are often completely opaque. At the end of Chapter 3, commenting on the unintended aspects of the gift of Latin to the Filipino mind, I remarked on the garbling of the Latin Mass as central to such spells. So it is; but it is something more than just misheard and misunderstood phrases from a pre-Vatican II (i.e. pre-1960s) ecclesiastical world that for Filipinos stretched back to the sixteenth century. It is bound up with all sorts of *sub rosa* political statements.

Here, we are back with issues that José Rizal satirically targeted in his first novel, *Noli Me Tangere* (whose title is of course itself a quotation from the Vulgate of Christ's words). Its chapter 32 entitled 'The Sermon' is almost entirely about language and comprehension, while at the same time being a devastating description of a late nineteenth-century church service clearly drawn from the life. He writes in Spanish, the language of the Franciscan, Padre Damaso, who is giving the sermon; but Rizal's advantage is that he also speaks excellent Tagalog, which is more than his character does, so he can assess the sermon's impact on the *indios* in the congregation. Father Damaso delivers the first part of his sermon in Spanish and the second part in his eccentric Tagalog, 'for', says Rizal in a mischievous reference to the Apostles, 'as the Bible says: *Loquebantur omnes linguas*, "they spoke every language."' Damaso begins with a Latin text which he quotes accurately from the Vulgate Bible he is using, and off he starts in Spanish. But it is not long before he shows that his own grasp of Latin is weak when he tries to drop in the Ciceronian tag that to err is human (*errare humanum est*) but garbles it to '*errarle es hominum*' in a failed learned gesture. It may be that no one other than Rizal notices, however, least of all the Tagalog-speaking peasantry over whom the Franciscan's rhetorical tirade of Spanish is now pouring:

'So listen, all of you, with your hearts' and souls' ears, so that instead of the Lord's words falling on stony ground to be gobbled up by the birds of hell you may yourselves thrive and sprout like holy seed in the field of our venerable and blessed father, St Francis! You, you great sinners, you prisoners of those Moorish pirates of the spirit who lie in wait on the ocean of life eternal in their mighty vessels of the world and the flesh: yes, you who are weighed down by the chains of lust and sensuality, oarsmen in hellish Satan's galleys! Look over there with all due conscience at the one man who can rescue souls from the Devil's captivity: our brave Gideon, our valiant David, Christianity's triumphant Roland and heavenly *guardia civíl*, braver than all policemen put together, present or future –' (here the *guardia* Lieutenant frowned) '– yes, Lieutenant, *even* braver and stronger! A man who, unarmed but for a wooden cross, dauntlessly overcomes the eternal Bandit of Darkness and all Lucifer's gang and who would have wiped them out for good had such evil spirits not been immortal! This wonder of Divine Creation, this impossible marvel, is our Blessed St James of Alcalá himself who – to resort for a moment to a metaphor since, as somebody once said, such figures are helpful for understanding the incomprehensible – despite being a great saint was finally just a common soldier, a mess steward in our invincible army which the Blessed St Francis commands from Heaven and in whose ranks I have, by God's Grace, the honour to serve as a corporal or sergeant.'[1]

Unfortunately, the *indios* in his congregation have caught nothing of this foreign oratory except scattered phrases such as '*guardia civíl*', '*tulisan*' (bandit), 'St Francis' and 'St James'. However, they had all noticed the police Lieutenant scowling and assumed from Father Damaso's gestures at that point that the priest was scolding him for not going after the local bandits. They could well imagine that between them the two saints he mentioned could easily deal with the matter since apparently there was a picture in the Franciscans' convent in Manila showing St Francis repelling the pirate Lim Ah-Hong's attempted Chinese invasion during the early years of the Spaniards' rule, using only the girdle of his habit. Rizal remarks that '[a] good few of the faithful cheered up and gave thanks to God for this help, never doubting that after he had dealt with the bandits St Francis would also do away with the *guardia civíl* . . .'

The whole episode is an acute observation of how people will try to make sense of a foreign language by catching at a few words and then constructing a meaning that reflects their own preoccupations. The wish that St Francis himself might disband the *guardia civíl*, that hated and brutal instrument of the friars' rule, is especially tragi-comic. Rizal's contemporaries would also have spotted the mention of bandits as significant, for the growing problem of *tulisanes* was a widespread indication that the Spanish authorities were losing their grip on civil unrest. Also escaping the modern reader, probably, is the significance of the rhetoric about 'the Moors', the Moslems in the southern Philippines. Since the Spanish had notably failed to subdue them either militarily or spiritually,

priests seldom lost an opportunity to present them as natural enemies of Christ and habitually conflated all Islam with the pirates
who periodically came sailing up from Mindanao, terrorizing the
sea-lanes and coastal communities. (Centuries of such Church
propaganda have left their disastrous mark on the politics of today.)
It seems to me not impossible that Rizal included this as a subtle
way of suggesting that doctrinally, at least, the friars were stuck
immovably in the Middle Ages, still fighting the Crusades.

That, at any rate, is the Spanish part of the sermon. Eventually
Father Damaso changes gear and switches to Tagalog. Or rather, to
his own version of Tagalog, which his thick Spanish accent mangles
beyond recognition. Rizal notes that whereas the priest had carefully written down the Spanish portion, 'Father Damaso ad-libbed
[in Tagalog] not because he knew the language any better but
because, judging rural Filipinos to be ignorant of the art of rhetoric,
he was not afraid of making a fool of himself in front of them. . . .
He began with *Maná capatir con cristiano* [for *Mga kapatid kong
Kristiyano* or 'My brothers in Christ'], followed by an avalanche of
untranslatable phrases. He spoke about the soul, about hell, about
mahal na santo pintacasi [our dear Patron Saint], about *indio* sinners
and virtuous Franciscan priests. "Golly!" exclaimed one of the two
irreverent listeners from Manila in an aside to his companion, "I'm
off. This is all Greek to me."'

To drive the point home, Rizal has already had Father Damaso's
peroration take him to the subject of St James of Alcalá's miraculous acquisition of a foreign language. 'Before he died he spoke in
Latin without knowing the language! Marvel, you sinners!, you
who study Latin but who can't speak it and despite whippings
will die without speaking it! To speak Latin is a gift of God, which
is why the Church speaks Latin. I myself speak Latin! . . .' Father
Damaso's own Latin, as we have seen, is not beyond criticism; but
to err is, after all, only human.

This chapter of Rizal's certainly shows the value of literature in
shedding light on the otherwise dry and misleading historian's
assertion that the Spanish friars gave Filipinos their religious instruction in the local dialect. The legacy of utter mystification is here
before me as I write: a collection of various spells and charms from
Kansulay from which a handful may be quoted. Some are intended
to be said ritualistically (repeating them a prescribed number of

times, usually three or seven, and at certain hours); others are to be declaimed when needed. Still others, like the following cure for stomach-ache, need to be physically applied:

MUOG MUTOG
MADUROG
EGUZOM
Ho. Ho. Ho.

This is written on thin paper – cigarette paper would do – but in pencil, not ink or ballpoint. The paper is then pressed lightly on the stomach. *Muog* and *Mutog* are Tagalog words meaning, respectively, a 'lair'/'bastion' and 'to crush'. I am told *Madurog* means swollen, but it is possibly a Visayan rather than a Tagalog word. 'Crush the swelling in the lair' conveys a message of sorts, albeit not a very soothing one. 'Eguzom' is an obvious corruption of the Latin *Ego sum*, which most probably originates in one of those Biblical utterances by Jehovah, as when he tells Moses '*Ego Sum Qui Sum*' – I Am That I Am.[2] The Santa Claus effect at the end is puzzling but possibly signifies either a mis-copying of 'Xto' (for 'Christo') or, more likely, a stylized instruction that one should cross oneself three times. If so, it might even be a misreading of the Tagalog *Ito*, meaning 'this' or – in this case – 'thus'.

A 'Prayer to ward off someone's evil intentions' goes:

MITIM GLADIUMIN
BAGINAM MIHI PATER
NON VIVAT ELIUM HOMPAC
ROMDUM

The first three words are clearly Christ's command to Peter on his arrest in the Garden: '*Mitte gladium tuum in vaginam*' ('Sheathe your sword'). The 'b' for 'v' is typically Filipino, since 'v' does not exist in Philippine languages. Of the rest, *Mihi Pater* ('to me, Father') and *Non Vivat* ('let him/her/it not live') make no contextual sense, and of the rest I would suggest only that *Hompac* is probably a corruption of the words of the Creed, '*[et] homo factus [est]*', the 'p' for 'f' likewise being a Filipino characteristic.

There is a spell nearly three times as long as this which is designed to calm a fierce dog, although in the circumstances of being attacked by the brute it is hard to see how one might have the time or presence of mind to say it all aloud. And finally we can quote a useful spell for making someone fall in love with you:

SATOR ARIPO TINIT OPERA BOTOS
MOM MIAM TULGUM DOMINUM ABALATUM
PESTIGOS MUTUM SAKOMIA, ENO ERA CULU
[name of person] HUCCIUM PRIAM MOLON
PUSSIHIS NIMENITRI TARUM ADITA
CHRISTUM, SUSI NOBIRAC SEPETAME ME
GALELEO EGOSUM

Of this, only the first and last lines seem capable of much elucidation, though having Galileo (of all people) usurp Jehovah's words is a remarkable piece of lese-majesty. The first line does have a certain mysterious force, however. It is a slightly corrupted version of a famous palindrome of obscure mystical significance that can be found inscribed in mediaeval churches all over Europe. It should read *Sator Arepo Tenet Opera Rotas*, which literally means something like 'The sower Arepo keeps the wheels in motion'. It is normally written as a magic square:

S A T O R
A R E P O
T E N E T
O P E R A
R O T A S

In this way it can be read from back to front, top to bottom, bottom upwards, in columns or sequentially. It will be seen that the word TENET forms a cross in the centre. In addition, the words conceal the anagram of 'Pater Noster'. (I discovered they can equally be made to form the malediction '*Te perterreat Satanas!*' or, 'May Satan terrify you'. Anyone can play these games.) It is easy to imagine a priest beguiling the members of his *indio* flock with this curious and ingenious little charm which was sometimes associated with the Jesuits although it pre-dates their founding. (In passing, I should mention here that one Tagalog word for magic or sleight of hand is *salamangka*, in honour of the Jesuits' home town. English preserves something of the same sense in the word 'Jesuitical', referring to casuistry. Charles III, aware of anti-clerical strains in Spanish society, expelled the Jesuits from Spain and its colonies in 1767, a decree which filtered through to Manila the following year. Two days later the Jesuits in the Philippines were given their marching orders and their property was confiscated. A Kansulay friend of mine, talking about the origins of the province's cathedral, mentioned a legend that its site had once been famous for the *suwita* who lived there. When I asked what *suwita* were, he said 'Parang duwende 'yon', meaning they were like goblins. Since the cathedral dates from the eighteenth century it seems to me quite likely that these cunning imps were actually thinly-disguised *Hesuitas*. There is also a Tagalog word, *suwitik*, meaning sly, cunning or tricky. I have no doubt about its derivation, though the renowned Filipino lexicographer, Vito C. Santos, thinks it is Chinese in origin.)

Spells like these can easily be dismissed as parody prayers, the cod Latinisms being what Chinese whispers did to the Mass in the days before it was said in the vernacular. At that level they can be seen as touching efforts by the powerless to ape their masters' superior magic, the essence of all magic being nothing more than incomprehension. Thus they are quite literally hocus-pocus, which is itself a phrase once used by European conjurors at the climax of their act to signify the presence of magic. The parallel is still closer when it is discovered that 'hocus-pocus' is almost certainly a parody of *Hoc est Corpus* ('This is [my] Body'), Christ's own words of consecration at the Last Supper and the climax of the Mass when – if one believed in Transubstantiation – the moment of maximum magic occurred and the wafer was literally changed into flesh.

Are these spells, then, nothing more than an ignorant imitation of priest-speak? Partly, maybe. But other factors are involved that make it less easy to patronize and dismiss these small incantations as just the superstitious gibberish of barely literate peasants. For one thing they are documents of social history. Since Mass has not been said in Latin for a generation, the majority of Filipinos will no longer associate that language with priest-speak. If it was moribund before, it is now a dead language as far as they are concerned and it is hard to see how it would any longer suggest power. Secondly, at the time the spells evolved they were parody prayers and therefore must have contained an element of mockery, given that we know priests were not held in universal admiration and respect. Maybe we should allow there was no conscious satirical intent behind the formula 'Galileo Egosum', that it was only a chance coupling of two plausible-sounding phrases. Maybe we should also discount deliberate playfulness in a nonsense word like 'MIX-IVIC' which occurs in another spell and which one strongly suspects derives from nothing more arcane than an attempt to pronounce Roman numerals. But what we are left with is constantly-repeated evidence of *lack*. At some point the Church's official formulas were not enough; they didn't work, or they didn't address the problems that really interested people, such as toothache and rabid dogs and love. To that extent, therefore, the spells usurped a piece of social (or even spiritual) territory which the Church might have believed was within its own power but which was not, and to that same extent they were being subversive. When they are said with the correct fervour and in the correct form, with the right number of repetitions, crossings, and sips of water, something of the formal Church is left in tatters, just as Rizal's parody of a priest unintentionally parodying his own doctrinal language also leaves behind an unexpressed hollowness, as of power being dismantled.

Kansulay's liminality fascinates because it allows people to be simultaneously satirical and devout, sceptical and fervent – to us, an astonishing intellectual feat. It also fascinates because it extends through so many registers besides the medical and the spiritual. Life in the village is a daily refutation of the Western concept of 'alternative', with its suggestion of either/or expressed in such phrases as 'alternative medicine' or 'alternative religion'. Kansulay's version would be closer to 'parallel medicine' or 'parallel religion', a distinctly Filipino solution to the problem posed by otherwise having to make a false choice. The people of Kansulay were being post-modernist centuries before the West invented the concept. There is even a certain liminality about their approach to mechanics, amounting to an amazing ingenuity for keeping an engine running that appears to have little to do with mechanical theory. Indeed, it is an attitude that simultaneously accepts and rejects a technology that was once alien but which has long since become naturalized. It admits the nuts and bolts, as it were, while discarding the maintenance manual. What looks to an outsider like the compulsive sabotaging of hi-tech Western objects and their subsequent 'Filipinization' is a powerful way of putting him in his place. It is powerful not just because it politely but firmly declines certain prerequisites normally considered mandatory for the successful functioning of an engine, but because it seems to operate against what the outsider perceives as the user's best interests. Surely it is in the villager's interest that his pump should work, his jeep run, his radio make sounds? Yet it is not uncommon to see brand-new vehicles with loose wiring already exposed beneath the dash or looped like fresh intestines around a motorbike's handlebars, as if the truck- or tricycle-driver found it impossible to operate his vehicle without first demythologizing it with familiar 'lash-up' emergency arrangements, even though these are mechanically unnecessary. This is, in effect, the engine-as-body, mechanics as psychic surgery. Distressingly, it nearly always works. In Kansulay's world the often-repeated phrase 'lack of maintenance' is less an explanation than a spell. It sometimes seems that the Filipino tendency – in sharp contrast to how anthropologists and other Western academics explain ritual and all other forms of social behaviour – is towards *dis*order; yet life in Kansulay often shows that this is its own form of order, poised on a mysterious boundary.

One last illustration of this will bring us back to where we started, to the caves which are themselves on an edge between two worlds. It concerns an incident that took place nearly twenty years ago and coincided with my first arrival in the village. In those days I understood even less of what was going on than I pretend I do now, and since I did not yet know any of the people involved I remembered only the bare outline of a story that had gripped the village for days. Two little girls had gone to the forest to look for fruit and had disappeared. The whole village turned out to look for them but they had vanished. A day later they were spotted miles down the coast, wandering along the road away from the village. They were brought back and all was well. That much I remembered.

Recently I heard this story again, retold by a villager I had not seen for the last fifteen years. This was Dorcas (whose beautiful, old-fashioned name had so struck me at the time), a friend's daughter who had decamped to Manila when she was eighteen, married a much older Australian and gone off to live in Melbourne. Over the years she had raised a family there, returning only rarely to visit her parents in Kansulay, none of these trips coinciding with one of mine until last Christmas, when we both met again. On the face of it Dorcas had changed radically (although remarkably little physically) in that she was now no longer a Filipina girl but an Australian woman fluent in English and fully qualified in some kind of paramedical skill by which she earned her living. The contrast in outlook between her and her brothers and sisters who had remained in Kansulay was marked indeed, though I was to discover that it did not go very deep except in matters of material expectations and a Rizalian sense of outrage at the backwardness of her own native village.

Over the Christmas period she recounted two stories, the one about the missing children and another from her own adolescence. In order to retell the incident of the girls she brought their mother to my hut – a lady I knew only by sight and whom I had never until then associated with the story. Together, in a mixture of English and Tagalog, they gave the following account:

The two sisters, then aged seven and ten, had gone to the beach to bathe, and afterwards had walked up to the woods to look for guavas. It was later reconstructed (from accounts by villagers who glimpsed them but had thought nothing of it) that they had come back down again carrying the guavas bunched up in the fronts of their T-shirts. It appeared they had forgotten where they lived and who they were. They set off southwards along the coast, not on the road itself but slightly inland, 'sa tabing niyugan', along the edge of the coconut plantations. While the rest of Kansulay turned out to search for them the two children meanwhile walked and walked, passing two towns, on through the night. This was obviously a later reconstruction; and yet when the girls' mother went with the *barangay* captain to the police station in the first of the two towns to give their description, somehow it must already have been assumed that this was a case of *possession* and not kidnapping or worse. Obviously, this was a quite different conclusion from the one most contemporary Western societies would have reached; but it should be remembered that those sorts of crime are virtually unknown in Kansulay and children roam about with the sort of freedom I can remember from my own childhood, coming home in time for supper after dropping in haphazardly at friends' houses in between forays and adventures.

Since the two girls were possessed, it was further assumed that the children would be heading south since they were obviously being ensorcelled towards a particular cave – the same Malindig Cave described earlier in this chapter as lying beneath a mountain twenty miles away. In any case the local police also assumed the children would be headed there. This 'possession' theory must somehow have been decided on quite early, else why would the captain and the girls' mother have gone to the police down the coast instead of in the other direction to the much bigger police station in the provincial capital? Come to that, why mightn't the children have been heading inland to one of the little towns where they had some aunts and uncles? Or anywhere else? It all had an over-determined air, but one had to accept the mother's account since the girls – today of course adults, one 'a tomboy' – are themselves amnesiac about where they went although they do remember the incident. Yet if they had been seen heading back from the guava bushes, why did so many people turn out to search the woods? These are imponderables.

During the night – or else the following day – the two little girls met 'a very beautiful white lady' beside the road who offered them drinks. Then at 4 p.m. next afternoon a Kansulay couple with their own jeepney were on the outskirts of a coastal town a good fifteen miles to the south and spotted the girls, saying 'Those are Até Susing's kids!' They stopped and took them on board, but not until the driver's wife had made the children throw away the guavas they were still carrying. She noticed that one of the guavas was red. (Here the mother interjected that this was highly significant and proof of the possession theory.) The driver's wife then (but how? where?) burnt all the children's clothes and dressed them in something else (where did she get two girls' outfits from?) before she and her husband drove them back to Kansulay, returning them to their home at about 5 p.m. Both girls were now able to recognize their family and their house, but as dusk fell the elder began 'changing'. Instead of being completely exhausted by her twenty-four-hour hike like her little sister and falling asleep on the spot, she became very *'malakas at matapang'* (strong and fierce), *'parang galit na siya'* (as though she were angry). She reportedly threw her father out of the window as he was closing the shutters.

They took her to consult one of the village shamans but his powers could not handle this degree of possession so they took her to another, more powerful. He needed two weeks to cure her, burning herbs and incense whose smoke she had to inhale. The parents also got the parish priest to bless their house. Before the girl was finally cured they noticed the cross she wore around her neck became very hot.

That was the story, and in a version I later confirmed by talking to the former *barangay* captain who had been involved. The interesting thing was that, though over-determined and full of the sort of details one reads in the lurid Tagalog *komiks* on sale in bus stations everywhere, it was not a self-contained family story but involved a whole village looking for lost children. Thus it intersected with 'normality' to the extent that everyone seemed agreed that the girls did indeed disappear for twenty-four hours, the parents were distraught, the police were notified, the elder girl especially seemed 'changed' by the incident until she was 'cured'. In any case an explanatory narrative would presumably have to hinge not on two ensorcelled individuals but on a bewitched community.

When Até Susing excused herself and left after giving her account, Dorcas 'confessed' or volunteered something about herself dating from when she was thirteen that really did change her life and even today still has the power to frighten her. She had never told Barry (her husband) since she knew he would dismiss it as hysterical rubbish. This account dates from before I first met her, in other words from the mid-seventies. One interesting thing was that she recounted most of the first half in Tagalog, but when the scene shifted to Australia she switched to English.

In those days her parents' landlords owned a little beach resort near Kansulay where Dorcas worked for a while as a maid to earn extra for her schooling. On one occasion some visitors from Manila were supposed to be arriving very early, so she and another maid waited from 4 a.m. in order to be able to give them early coffee and breakfast when they came.

The two girls were sitting on chairs in front of the house, whose porch light was on and quite bright, directly in front of a big old *balete* tree only about three metres away. Suddenly Dorcas became aware of the sound of a strong wind. 'I'm not sure if I was dreaming or hallucinating or what, but I saw in that tree a horrible ugly face, laughing in a menacing, sneering way. It looked like a devil with slash eyebrows – you know, slanting straight back – and short goat's horns and cat's eyes. Just the face. No body. It wasn't at all dark in front of the house because the patio light was on. I saw it quite clearly and I was petrified. I tried to turn to my friend beside me to call for help but this strong wind kept pushing against my cheek so I had to face the front. This wind sometimes changed direction, going up and down, and it made my eyelids go up and down too. I was aware that a black dress was walking around me as I was sitting there. I couldn't see a face, just this black dress. My eyes were held downwards. I guess this lasted an hour. My friend didn't notice a thing, not the wind or the devil or anything. Nothing. The guests finally turned up at around 5.30 a.m. but by then it was over.'

This episode with the wind was the beginning of a kind of haunting for poor Dorcas, one which manifested itself whenever she tried to sleep. The wind had a characteristic, terrifying sound (she later likened it to that buffeting, blustering noise made when a car window is opened half an inch at speed). Thereafter she heard this sound every night 'for thirty minutes' when trying to get to sleep. It must have been traumatic for any adolescent needing her sleep, and her insomnia became worse the more she dreaded the night-time. Her mother and father advised her to sleep during the day instead, but even when she did she still heard the wind. 'I guess I wasn't asleep because I could hear my mother sweeping under the house with the broom.' When in this state she would 'see' one of two visions, depending on which cheek she lay on. Lying on her left side she would see 'a ritual'. 'It was like the basement of a house that I could see very clearly but it was somewhere I had never been. There was a table in the middle of the room with a lady lying on it who had already been killed.' There was also a candle on the table. This was surrounded by a lot of people and there was 'this strange, heavy voice like hearing a sermon. Then I'd turn over on my right side and see a different thing. I'd see a huge white cat with long fangs that could say words although I can't remember anything it said.'

Her parents took Dorcas to the cathedral in town where a priest made her drink holy water and gave her a palm frond cross he had blessed. He also instructed her parents to make her wear dark-blue clothes at night as well as a rosary, and hold a little prayer-book on her chest when she lay down to sleep. Like everyone else in Kansulay she and her family slept higgledy-piggledy together on a fairly cramped bamboo floor, so she was not short of close company and support. Even so, 'I could still hear the wind. It was a sign of whoever was trying to possess my body. I could see myself lying there. I was just above my body, looking down. I could see the crucifix I was wearing. It was standing up on end, and so was the prayer-book. But I was protected so I wasn't harmed. I could sleep.' Here Dorcas switched to English.

'In 1986 when I had my second child (I was twenty-three) I had terrific post-partum blues when I got very weak. The problem was I couldn't sleep. I kept thinking I could hear the wind again. It was still there. My husband tried to get me to pray with him but my mouth locked shut and I would force the Bible away when he brought it near me. He became very scared one night because my voice kept changing. Sometimes I sounded like an old man, sometimes like an old woman or a child. He was scared enough to call up his brother. I can remember saying words, but whoever was saying them was not me. *Not me.* So my husband and his brother took me to the hospital that night and they gave me I think it was Valium or stronger but still I couldn't sleep. I was desperate and so sad because I wanted to hold my new baby and just sleep. I was praying for help. I thought "If this goes on I will surely die." While I was praying for sleep and help I saw two persons, two figures descending in bright white clothes. They looked alike. They both laid their folded hands on top of my head. They said "Tonight you will sleep" and poked me on the forehead with one finger, quite hard, so I fell back at once into sleep.

'Oh, I was so happy when I woke next day. I was so full of energy! Ever since that night I got better. Now each night I pray to these two persons who were so loving, just to thank them. In my opinion they were the Father and the Son. They saved me and I'm so *thankful*, so grateful. I'm not afraid of death now. I know that whenever I really need them they will be there . . . We have so much to be thankful for.'

Despite her Australianization and professional medical job, Dorcas remains psychically a true daughter of Kansulay in that she does not for a moment doubt that she was bewitched as an adolescent, had been in extreme danger of being possessed as Até Susing's little girls temporarily were, and was saved by a divine intervention that continues to protect her to this day. Certainly in the context of her story, here in the woods behind Kansulay, the knowing Western interpretations seem oddly insufficient or else like an alternative – rather than definitive – reading of her account. The thirteen-year-old whose body is 'changing' (Dorcas's own word, showing she was aware of its significance), fearing/desiring the predatory male (the devil in the *balete* – and not forgetting that *balete* trees are particularly associated with spirits) and prey to hysterical symptoms (winds and visions) couched in clearly traceable animist/Catholic imagery . . . There is no real problem with such a reading except that it denies, as always, that the experience might be more than a single patient's private symptoms. Yet no adults in her story showed bafflement at any point. The wide local acknowledgement of such stories shows they represent a common experience. Her own parents never doubted it, just as they never doubted that a priest would be more effective than a doctor. Most of Dorcas's imagery would have come from stories she had heard, comics she had read or radio serials she had listened to. Her left-sided (truly sinister) vision of a sort of Black Mass in a basement (she could never have seen a house with a basement in those days – they simply do not exist in this province) would surely have come straight out of comics whose imagery, like the features of its protagonists, is mostly 'Westernized' to accord with popular movies. Black Masses in basements always were a staple of the genre, just as they still are in those Italian *fumetti* involving *la* Cimeteria, *la* Sukia and all the rest of the pornographic girls who obligingly sell themselves to the devil in issue after issue.

Yet the source of the imagery is the least problematic aspect of Dorcas's account. Since there is no scientific way of determining whether her faith has been responsible for holding the devil at bay, we may as well take her word for it. After all, why did she recover after that single night's crisis? Are we to suppose that her single dose of whatever it was, Valium or Largactil, was more effective than she thought? But even so, there is no logical way of maintaining that controlling symptoms with Largactil is any less 'mystified' than controlling 'possession' with holy water, since nobody understands precisely what an anti-psychotic drug does, nor how it relates to voices heard and visions seen. All one can say is that both *bendita* and chlorpromazine are often effective within their respective cultural milieux.

Far more interesting is the way my friend's accounts were structured, especially that of the two children's temporary disappearance. There was a quality in it I already recognized from a thousand daily incidents and conversations: that odd disjointedness as of a narrative having been begun from somewhere other than its beginning, thereby throwing out of kilter my own culturally shaped expectations of cause and effect, of events followed by consequences. Stories are differently told here. *Because* the girls were possessed they had been able to walk so far without food and drink, had been able to pass several villages and two towns without anyone asking who they were or where they were going, had kept on through the night without either light or companion, as well as most of the following day. *Because* they were possessed the jeep driver's wife already knew to burn all their clothes and throw away their uneaten guavas before returning them to Kansulay.

That this mode of thinking is not exclusive to a distant province is shown by the frequent accounts of supernatural events in the popular press (ghosts, dwarves, vampires, mermaids, snake-twins), occurrences which sometimes have enough consequence as stories to be taken up by the more serious newspapers. Many of the eye-witness accounts have this same quality of reversed narration, of a taking for granted a general understanding not merely of peculiar events but of a world which runs differently from that elsewhere and follows different expository rules. It would be silly to think that the technocrats of Malacañang Palace during the Marcos days – or, for that matter, the executives of today's Makati Stock Exchange – also inhabit this liminal world. But on the other hand it is equally foolish to maintain that it might not inhabit *them* to the degree that it is in the cultural air they breathe. After all, the Marcoses themselves played host in the Palace to a succession of people claiming curious powers, among them the so-called Bionic Boy who – according to his own description – was for a while virtually adopted as a member of the Marcos family. We shall come to him in due course, as also to Johnny Midnite, whose mysterious 'toning' powers kept the people, the Palace, the clergy and the military all glued to their radios in the depths of martial law. About this liminality, which pervades the Filipino character, one can say it resembles the famous entity in quantum electrodynamics that only becomes either a particle or a wave when it is observed or measured. Until that instant it is neither one thing nor the other but exists in a state of sublime ambivalence or equivocation.

This conducting of a quite passionate but withdrawn village life by means of an endless series of tales – parables, even, from the fringes of an unseen world – is the quality I most miss when absent from Kansulay. One searches in vain amid the bleak rationalism of Western discourse for traces of its anarchic merriment and wonder. Away from the world's Kansulays the implacable arrow of cause and effect flies on and on from left to right, through all argument, conscious of nothing besides its own undeviating flight. When one encounters a social narrative constructed without reference to this arrow it may induce exasperation, but it can also break one into an altogether different apprehension. It is, in its way, a kind of poetry. Kansulay, with its gossips, liars, mystics, storytellers and shamans, is a village of poets whose community is its own act of creativity.

At this distance one can feel an occasional pang of pity for Fr. Damaso and all those generations of friars. Writing in 1749, a Fr. Pedro Murillo Velarde betrayed the frustrations of his doctrinal dealings with his flock. He realized that their eagerness for confession, for example, must be evidence of something other than a deep conviction of sinfulness, that he was entangled in a quite alien way of structuring thought (for all that it was also a brilliant defence, this unEuropean equivocation). Part of this, no doubt, was down to a simple lack of comprehension, even though we might guess that the Jesuit Velarde's grasp of the local dialect was better than the fictional Damaso's. But the wretched man clearly suspected there was something else going on, something he instinctively knew he would never be able to deal with:

> Only a person who has done it can describe the effort it costs to confess them [the *indios*]. Even when one has a general grasp of the sin, to try to get a specific account of the circumstances is to enter a labyrinth without a map. For they do not understand our orderly mode of speech, so when questioned they will answer 'yes' or 'no' at random, without properly understanding what is being asked, so they will produce twenty contradictions in the space of a minute.[3]

Wandering the woods on a favourite walk to a famously haunted mango tree on the river bank, I find myself speculating from time to time about the possible political consequences of all this. The more one lives in a village like Kansulay, the more one wonders how differently predicated a nation's politics might actually be from that of the fictitious 'international community'. One hears Western press reports of how this or that developing country's progress is being 'hampered' by tribalism or feudalism or some such, even as its Harvard-, Oxford- or Sorbonne-educated delegates hobnob in the UN, make advances to Washington or greet IMF heavyweights. But what is it these dignitaries truly represent? What is their relation to Até Susing, who washes her family's clothes daily in the series of sluggish puddles that was once Kansulay's river? As she squats with her threadbare skirts tucked up and chats to colleagues in the middle of a drifting raft of suds, what is Susing's connection with her neatly suited representative in the distant capital or overseas? Does her lowly presence have a faint echo in the man of state, living on as a sort of cultural DNA in his bloodstream, a bond of common ancestry, a secret affinity, a way of viewing things?

In a sense, how could it not? It must surely be a mistake to examine a developing country's political leaders while ignoring the village woman in their blood. It was characteristic of Marcos that he understood his electorate's Até Susings because he had grown up among them, despite the later image-making that invented a more prosperous background for him and built him an ancestral home. It certainly led to Manila's social élite making snobbish remarks about his provincialism when he first took office as President. I suspect it was this that the villagers glimpsed just often enough to respond to his wily appeals for their votes.

One morning shortly after my conversation with Dorcas I mention the cave that is supposed to lie beneath Mt. Malindig to my godson. He is now nearly thirty, but when he was a teenager he and I had once climbed the mountain without, as I recall, hearing anything about a cave. '*Sabi*,' he says non-committally. *They say.* 'They say the cave exists but that it is only a part.' A part of what? Of the underground truth, apparently, which is that the whole interior of this island province is hollow. Somewhere beneath us there is also a fabulous treasure: a *gintong baka*. A gold cow, no less. My godson tells me that the activities of the copper-mining company that has dominated this province's economy for the last quarter century have gradually eaten away two of the cow's legs. In early 1996 thousands of tons of slurry from the mine's tailings pit poured out through an illegally constructed tunnel and smothered the province's main river system, killing it stone dead. The ecological damage caused a state of emergency to be declared and led to the shutdown of the company's operations. 'People say it was punishment for having hacked off the *baka*'s legs,' my godson says. '*Sabi*.' Maybe it was also just deserts for disturbing the province's subterranean aquifer system which might or might not be the reason for Kansulay's river drying up. Since this same company was for years secretly owned by Marcos himself via a series of holding companies, one suspects the golden cow is actually The Golden Calf.

I ask him if the 'beautiful white lady' whom Até Susing's daughters had seen was the same person as the alluring woman in the cave who had given miraculous food and drink to the anti-Japanese guerrillas during the war. 'I expect so,' he said. 'Maria Malindig is everywhere. She is the spirit of this province. *Sabi*.' I am touched to see he is still wearing the little gold cross I gave him for a birthday years ago.

6

Imelda Romualdez, too, makes a good start

If Ferdinand Marcos came to power in 1965 as a partly invented person (and he once said he believed Spence's *For Every Tear a Victory* had been crucial to his winning that first election), his wife was almost as much a public creation in that she, too, was to have her biography face-lifted until it was worthy of her. About Ferdinand himself there is always something that remains uncertain, hidden, enigmatic. There is a tradition in the Philippines of *de mortuis nil nisi bonum*, at least in public, and maybe his current reputation also benefits slightly from this. It is bad luck as well as bad taste to attack the dead, who cannot defend themselves. But his widow, being very much alive, is not yet accorded the advantages of such reticence and *delicadeza*. There is surely no other living soul who has held such power, who hobnobbed with and charmed so many world leaders, who was once fawned upon by five American presidents as well as by journalists and gossip-columnists far and wide, and whose image is now so widely mocked and mud-spattered.

The reasons for this are many and not always simple. Among them, undoubtedly, is that Imelda Marcos was all too perfectly herself, too brimful of the entire range of Filipino faults and Filipino virtues; so that the nation, at last feeling free to view her through the Western press's eyes, turned on her latterly with 'the rage of Caliban seeing his own face in a glass', in Oscar Wilde's phrase. For it is undeniable that a good deal of the behaviour that has earned her the virtuous ridicule of Filipinos themselves is quite normal by local standards. The extravagance, the queenly capriciousness, the empty-headed partying with showbiz 'personalities' and the jetting around on international brand-name shopping sprees of the most vulgar kind – all of these are exemplified (or aspired to) daily by Manila's *arriviste* socialites. The difference is that Mrs Marcos had, and has, real substance beneath the glitz. She has never been as empty-headed as she sometimes seemed, and still less was she empty-hearted. Glaring faults, certainly; but glaring virtues, too, among which a perverse simplicity. It is impossible to meet her *à deux* without carrying away an impression of naive sincerity. This is all the stranger since she is a consummate politician and has appropriate (and well-attested) gifts, such as never forgetting names and faces, which nobodies like myself are apt to find flattering. But as the years go by one is less easily flattered as well as better at spotting such tricks of the trade. In Mrs Marcos's case, though, I do not believe they are false. She actually does like people and finds them interesting; it is touching that she so patently believes what she says, especially when not a little of it is distinctly dotty. Certainly, the one thing I had never expected was to find myself touched. She is a very complex lady indeed.

In Kansulay, any anti-Imelda feeling tended to follow a conventional sexist line, viewing her as the quintessential scheming woman who, for her own purposes, had wormed her way into a good man's heart and taken advantage of his illness. Dr Alma Fernandez of the University of the Philippines told me she had been in New York in 1990 at the time of Mrs Marcos's acquittal on all RICO (Racketeer Influenced and Corrupt Organizations) charges that had been brought against her. There and then Dr Fernandez had written an article for the Filipino newspaper *Malaya* that was something of a feminist reading of Imelda's career, her arraignment and general fall from grace. She said it had proved quite easy to do since Mrs Marcos was such a classic victim of a male-dominated society. I took her to refer to life in the upper echelons of global politics rather than in the Philippines, where *machismo* is over-valued but powerful women are a recognized type, until I reminded myself of Imelda Marcos's awful childhood as well as the ruthless way in which she was wooed, won and subsequently moulded by her much older husband.

Imelda Remedios Visitacion Romualdez was born in Manila in 1929.* Her father, Vicente Orestes, was a lawyer who worked in the family law firm (Romualdez, Romualdez y Romualdez) with his two older and far more successful brothers. By most accounts he was an easy-going man, somewhat artistic (he played the piano and sang), who favoured a quiet life. Unfortunately his first wife, Juanita Acereda – like himself, descended from a Spanish priest – died leaving him with five children to bring up. He married again, this time to a girl he selected from a convent, Remedios Trinidad. At this point all hopes of a quiet life ceased because his children much resented their new stepmother, whom they considered not only an intruder but déclassée since she was brown-skinned. Imelda was Vicente Orestes' first child by Remedios Trinidad, and four more were to follow. Long before then, open family warfare had broken out between the two sets of children to the extent that Remedios Trinidad moved out of her husband's big house and went with her children to live in the garage, sharing it with her husband's hire-purchased car, an Essex Super 6. At night the children slept on boards propped up on milk crates while their mother bedded down on a table. The last of Vicente Orestes' children, Conchita, was conceived in this garage. Half a century later Imelda's own niece, Beatriz Romualdez Francia, was to describe the position thus:

> The vacillating and enigmatic Vicente Orestes commuted between the big house with his first set of children, and the garage with his second wife and their children together. He would drop by at the garage before going to work, and then at night before retiring . . .
>
> [Remedios] sent her daughter Imelda to the big house early each morning to get their daily allowance – a modest sum. In this way Imelda began at an early age to learn the rules of a painful

---

* For the detailed outline of Mrs Marcos's biography in this chapter I am deeply indebted to three main sources: authors Kerima Polotan Tuvera, Carmen Navarro Pedrosa and Beatriz Romualdez Francia.

game and negotiate between two worlds. She learned to mediate between a father who identified himself with the Spanish and Caucasian class – who had enjoyed such privileges only a few decades before and still continued to do so under the American colonial government – and a mother who was classified with the subjugated, indigenous Filipinos.[1]

It is perhaps worth noting that this old stone house of Vicente Orestes' was on General Solano Street, practically on the Pasig River and only yards from Malacañang Palace where Imelda was to get all sorts of sweet revenge only a couple of decades later. This was one ancestral home she did not restore. On the contrary, she bought it together with the two adjacent lots, bulldozed the entire site, and turned it into a garden. All mention of a childhood spent partly in a garage as the outcast of her step-family was excised from the record until 1970, when the journalist Carmen Navarro Pedrosa dug up the unwelcome facts and published them in her remarkably brave book, *The Untold Story of Imelda Marcos*.

Since it is the lot of thousands of ordinary Filipinos to be conceived, born and to live their lives in garages and shanties, the conventionally heartless might say it was excellent training for a future First Lady, a salutary taste of how the other half lives. That, of course, is precisely how a child cannot see her own life, especially when she is not yet ten years old. This experience, and the even worse poverty that awaited her and her siblings in Leyte, must have set up within little Imelda the sorts of splits and fissures anyone might inherit from childhood stress, but which only extreme power and wealth can later magnify into the behavioural chasms that throw up on either side the monster and the angel.

In 1937 Remedios gave birth to Conchita, her sixth and last child. Feeling the onset of labour the ex-convent girl stoically took herself off in a taxi without a word to her husband in the big house and checked into the free (i.e. paupers') ward of the Philippine General Hospital. Three days later she tottered back into the garage on General Solano carrying her new baby. Her husband took it as a deliberate slight that she had vanished without telling him, and even more so that she had gone to a paupers' ward. (Beatriz Romualdez Francia says that, forty years later, Imelda Marcos took steps to cover up the fact that her youngest sister had been born in a free ward by having a Dr Reginaldo Villanueva at the General Hospital prepare 'an affidavit stating that Conchita Romualdez was born in the pay ward. Villanueva was told to cooperate and toe the line with the veiled threat that his children abroad would be safer if he acceded to [this] request.'[2] (To set against this, however, is the fact that the rebuilding of the hospital, which arguably still offers Manila's best medical services for those Filipinos too poor to pay, was one of Imelda's major projects when she eventually came to power.) Four months after Conchita's birth, Remedios died of double pneumonia and the eight-year-old Imelda watched her mother laid to rest in La Loma cemetery. From descriptions by Mrs Francia and others, the shadowy Remedios reminds me of almost anyone from Kansulay, which makes me warm to her memory. The melancholy, the stubbornness, the almost romantically proud acceptance of a garage floor instead of a marriage bed: all these are recognizably indigenous traits far distant from those of an ideal mate for the aloofly Hispanic Vicente Orestes.

By September of that year, 1938, this dreamiest of the three Romualdez brothers decided to quit Manila, where financial success had constantly eluded him. The big house on General Solano, which was anyway mortgaged, was sold. The Essex Super 6, no longer functioning and also overdue in its instalment payments, was towed out of the garage and back to the dealers. The selling up of his Manila assets barely paid his debts. His plan was to retreat to the province of Leyte where his Spanish grandfather had been a priest, where the Romualdez dynasty had effectively been founded in 1873 and where his illustrious and scholarly brother Norberto was an Assemblyman. There he intended to retire from the law and administer the estates of his more prosperous Romualdez relatives, meanwhile living off whatever income could be derived from their coconut plantations. The truth was, he had little interest in money. The double widower wanted to get well away from the city in which he had conspicuously failed to prosper and sit beside the blue, blue sea of a distant province, dipping into books and humming tunes to himself. Sixty years on this seems entirely sympathetic, although with a large family to keep it might be considered irresponsible by bourgeois standards. It certainly had undreamed-of consequences.

The move sealed the fate of his branch of the family and cast them forever as poor relations to the rich Romualdezes of Manila. This change in family status would be critical to Imelda's development and would set her ambitions even more firmly.[3]

In the ten years that followed, which of course included three of Japanese occupation, Vicente Orestes and his family moved about Leyte's little capital town of Tacloban, finally coming to rest in a Quonset hut on Calle Real. Such was Imelda's home in her formative early teens. Her father largely read the war away. When General MacArthur finally returned, landing in Leyte, Vicente Orestes took Imelda up to the local US Army camp to beg surplus materials in order to spruce up their hut. They also begged for food. They were not alone, of course. Their living conditions and diet were no doubt much like that of Tacloban's other citizens. Even before the war it had never been a place of full bellies and flush toilets. In later years Imelda quite often spoke of the hunger and poverty of those days, although she only ever did so to other family members.

> She described how her mouth would water whenever she saw neighbours who had margarine with their bread for breakfast. In her home breakfast was limited to a native roll and black coffee. The roll would not wait for late wakers, either. Food was strictly rationed, and any child who wanted more was reprimanded with 'only those who work get fed'. She remembers that her father used to save his coins in a bamboo pole so he could afford a leg of ham when Christmas came. 'If we had a slice of ham, then it was a feast.'[4]

The 'bamboo pole' might have been a door jamb, still occasionally used even today in Kansulay as the family's piggy-bank, while the yearning for margarine was to manifest itself years later in a slightly different guise. This I learned about from a friend who acted as a NAMFREL (National Movement for Free Elections) observer during the snap election in 1986. She told me that after the Marcoses had fled Malacañang Palace she had gone poking about the many outhouses and storerooms in the Palace grounds and had come upon a modest, nondescript little house tucked away among the trees. Once inside, she had found it impossible to explore further because it turned out that every room and even the hallway was stacked ceiling-high with cartons of Heinz sandwich spread in catering-sized jars. Only then did she recall having heard that Imelda had once confessed to a craving for sandwich spread because in her childhood it had seemed the very epitome of luxury and elegance and had practically symbolized the unobtainable. In its pathos there is a certain 'Rosebud' quality about this forgotten house of sandwich spread that is somehow lacking in other extravagances and oddities which had come to light and were then attracting greater attention in the newly vacated Palace, such as the gallon bottles of Dior and Guerlain scent and the bulletproof bras.

By the time General MacArthur's troops waded ashore in Leyte Imelda was sixteen and already acknowledged as the prettiest girl in Tacloban. She was much in demand for adding glamour to civic functions and she often went, heavily chaperoned, to sing for the GIs at the camp. She had a good voice and her confidence – so different from the usual *probinsiyana* bashfulness – showed the pleasure she took in an audience. One day by special request she found herself singing to a huge assembly of troops that included MacArthur himself as well as Irving Berlin, who was on tour with the USO (United Service Organizations). She was asked to sing Berlin's own song, 'God Bless America', and obliged, but on her own initiative changed the wording to 'God Bless the Philippines'. She reported the composer as being 'aghast at my impertinence' until she explained that the Philippines and America were really one world. According to her, Berlin promptly wrote another song which Imelda equally promptly sang: 'Heaven watch the Philippines/Keep her safe from harm . . . Friendly with America/Let her always be . . .'[5] Anyone might feel free to wonder a little at the self-possession and temerity of a sixteen-year-old Filipina correcting a famous American composer's song for him, as at her suspiciously well-developed nationalism at the very moment of the US landings. Possibly the account itself underwent, like Berlin's original song, some judicious minor adjustment.

Certainly the handwritten fragments of Imeldiana that survive from this period show no trace of such feisty individualism. On the contrary, they are touching in their ordinary schoolgirlishness. One is a list of the sort of biographical details teenagers think define them. She gives her nickname as 'Meldy', her motto as 'To try is to succeed!', her ambition as 'any desk work or to be a – – – – Ehem!' (for which four-spaced blank Carmen Pedrosa proposes the word 'wife'). Otherwise we learn that Meldy's hobbies were 'singing, reading, going to movies, letter writing', that her favourite subject was 'lovemaking, ha!', that her favourite dish was 'fried chicken and ice cream', that her favourite actress was Ingrid Bergman and her favourite expressions 'Nuts!' and 'Hubba! Hubba!' ('Hubba-hubba' was a classic piece of Second World War US military slang, defined as 'an exclamation of delight, relish, etc, esp. at the sight of a woman', which no doubt commended it to young Meldy who, in common with everyone else, liked to be appreciated.) Perhaps more revealing was an entry in a schoolmate's autograph book which reads: 'Dearest Polly, Keep that smile on your lips, But always put that [sic] tears in your heart. Love; Meldy.' This is accompanied by a competent little sketch of a girl with a weeping heart. It would be silly to read too much into conventional things of this sort, but the idea of hiding one's grief and presenting a smiling face to the world is indeed very Filipino (as is her English), and the Mrs Marcos of later years showed she had fully mastered this trick of Asian stoicism, which does not preclude shedding tears for effect.

Well before she became a local beauty queen ('The Rose of Tacloban') Imelda was attracting suitors, and like many a pretty girl before or after might well have settled for a prosperous husband and lived out the rest of her life in the province where her family name had distinction. But two things combined to take her back to Manila. One was the unwanted attention of a particularly insistent admirer and the other her genuine musical talent. Two Romualdez cousins in Manila, struck equally by her looks and her ability, offered to arrange singing lessons and a helping hand in the big city. In 1952, at the age of twenty-three, she left for Manila with her cousin Daniel as escort. It was a moment perfectly designed for the 'little-could-they-have-guessed' school of biography.

Thus did Imelda leave Tacloban, the small town that made her queen, that helped her bury the memory that she was Remedios's deprived child. It was time to go. Leyte had nothing more to offer Imelda. Little did Danieling realize that the trembling country cousin he accompanied on the fateful journey to Manila, with five pesos in her purse and a dirty *tampipi* (a poor native suitcase), carrying only a few skirts and blouses, held the formula for one of the most remarkable success stories in Philippine political history.[6]

In order to avoid a misleading impression (of country hick and earnest mentor) we need to recall that Daniel Romualdez was by then Congressman for Tacloban, that his trembling cousin was a famously beautiful woman of considerable interior poise, and that they did not take a steerage passage on an inter-island ferry but flew on Philippine Airlines' afternoon flight to Manila.

Once there, Imelda roomed in her Congressman cousin's house and soon became familiar with the daily ebb and flow of political grandees as well as with the general tenor of life in power-broking circles. She herself was treated more indulgently than inclusively by her cousins, who found her a job in a music store on Escolta, the old Spanish main street of downtown Manila that nowadays forms part of Chinatown. In this shop she sang to buyers of sheet music or else demonstrated pianos by playing them to prospective customers. (Forty-five years later I asked the redoubtable Lucrecia 'King' Kasilag, herself a noted composer and doyenne of the Cultural Centre's musical activities, about Mrs Marcos's actual musical ability. Was she, I wondered, what one would call a good pianist? Mrs Kasilag, a staunch Imeldista, frowned at a filing cabinet. 'Not necessarily,' she said at length.)

Imelda served in the music shop until Vicente Orestes unexpectedly turned up one day. He wanted to see how his daughter was getting along in the big bad city and found her singing to some customers. Outraged, he accused Danieling of 'selling' Imelda and insisted she be moved to a job commensurate with the dignity of a decent girl. One was promptly found her as a clerk in the Intelligence Division of the Central Bank, an institution where any decent girl might pick up a trick or two. It did, however, fulfil the teenage Meldy's ambition of 'any desk work'. After work each day she took singing lessons at the Philippine Women's University Conservatory of Music. Then, after an editor of the *Manila Chronicle* had spotted her by chance on the street, she appeared on the cover

of *This Week* (the 15 February 1953 Valentine issue) as 'the lass from
Leyte – Imelda Romualdez'. It was essentially from that moment
that Imelda became a public figure, a role she has since filled for
almost half a century. Deciding to run as Miss Manila in a beauty
contest that was itself a preliminary stage in the quest for a new
Miss Philippines, she found her own family implacably opposed
to sponsoring her. Beauty contests were vulgar affairs and
Romualdezes did not demean themselves with such things.

So Imelda obtained the backing of the president of the Philippine
Women's University, Mrs Benitez, as well as of Mrs Kasilag, the
head of the university's Department of Music. Against all predictions the title of Miss Manila went to a Norma Jimenez. Imelda
was disbelieving, then angry. Where anyone else might have
accepted fate and consoled herself with the thought that, well, it
was only a beauty contest, she went directly to the Mayor of
Manila, Arsenio Lacson, and charged that the contest had been
fixed. She must have been a formidable presence: tall, beautiful,
furious and judiciously tearful. Two days after the original press
release of Miss Jimenez's victory the following announcement went
into all Manila's major newspapers:

> Mayor Lacson yesterday disowned the choice of the International
> Fair Board and named Imelda Romualdez of Philippine
> Women's University as Manila's official candidate for Miss
> Philippines.
>
> In a letter to the director of the International Fair, Lacson
> charged violation of certain rules of the International Fair contest
> that as Mayor of Manila he would nominate the only candidate
> of the City of Manila for the beauty contest.
>
> The beauty contest committee named by Mayor Lacson
> adjudged Miss Romualdez winner of the Miss Manila title with
> 655 points. Norma Jimenez and Amparo Manuel tied for second
> place with 453 points each . . .[7]

This was a splendidly Filipino piece of in-fighting in a culture
where everything is negotiable, even retrospectively, and competi-
tion winners – like examination or election results – can be almost
indefinitely reconsidered in the light of 'delayed information' in the
form of writs, threats or plain family connections. As it turned out,

Imelda was not on her way to becoming Miss Philippines, for Mayor Lacson's overruling was itself promptly overruled. The International Fair sponsoring the contest decided that the Mayor of Manila was not eligible to choose the candidate for Manila, and reinstated Norma Jimenez. By then it no longer mattered to Imelda. What counted was what she had learned about her own will. 'To try is to succeed', indeed. For students of her later history, some significant names had entered her life as a consequence of this episode: Mrs Kasilag, Mrs Benitez and Mayor Lacson. And the girl who went on to win the 1953 title of Miss Philippines was Cristina Galang who, as Cristina Caedo, eventually became one of Imelda Marcos's famous band of private aides – somewhere between gofers and groupies – known collectively as the 'Blue Ladies'.

After this came a brief affair with an eligible young man, Ariston 'Titong' Nakpil, who was cultured (a Harvard-trained architect) and of excellent family. He had one drawback, however, in that he was already married. This marriage was in the process of being annulled (which it eventually was) but the situation produced delay and uncertainty as well as the furious opposition of Imelda's father. It cannot have been an easy time for her. Mixing with Ariston's family, who incidentally took to her and showed her great kindness, made her aware of how much of a provincial she was among Manila's élite. Her accent gave her away, while her social manners – natural and spontaneous though they were – lacked the requisite polish. She was now twenty-four, by provincial standards old enough to be aware of a clock ticking somewhere in the background, certainly old enough to marry anyone she chose, regardless of what her father thought. On the evening of 6 April 1954 she went to Congress with the wife of her distinguished cousin Danieling, who was then acting Speaker of the House. When she arrived, a Congressman named Ferdinand E. Marcos was sounding off about something on the floor of the house, but politics of that sort bored Imelda and she and her friend went off to the cafeteria to wait for the session to end. When it did, Marcos himself came into the cafeteria, took one look at her and demanded an introduction.

There followed a famous eleven-day courtship that was to become a significant ingredient in the Marcos dyad's mythology since it not only exemplified that old heart-warmer, love at first sight, but more importantly, fate. According to this, Ferdinand and Imelda were made for each other but they had anyway been destined to meet because fate itself had plans for them as well as for the Philippines, and the two strands, the private and the national, were indissolubly intertwined. (As President, Ferdinand was to 'write' the first four volumes of a projected multi-volume complete history of the Philippines called *Tadhana*, or 'Destiny', which was actually ghosted by a committee of scholars, mostly from the University of the Philippines. Apart from an inevitable unevenness in style, the series starts not badly; but it is hard to see how, had they reached the twentieth century, a certain slant in events could have been avoided. Presidents do not commission histories of their nation by accident. As we shall see, Imelda also commissioned a book, *Si Malakas at Si Maganda*, which makes explicit the predestined nature of her and her husband's relationship, as also that of the First Couple as Mother and Father to their country. But this is to leap ahead.)

We left Ferdinand Marcos in the late 1940s having had a good war. In 1949 he was elected Congressman for Ilocos Norte in his father Mariano's old district, running on a platform that included a promise to obtain benefits from the US government for all Filipino veterans of the recent war. By 1954 he was a millionaire, commuting between Congress and his leafy suburban home in San Juan in a shiny white convertible. During his first term as a Congressman the Senate President was Jose Avelino, who had himself made half a million dollars during his own first congressional term. A casual remark of Avelino's became the most famous thing he ever said. Referring to his fellow politicians, he exclaimed: 'We are not angels! What are we in power for? When Jesus Christ died on the cross he made the distinction between a good crook and the bad crooks. We can prepare to be good crooks.'

By the time Ferdinand met Imelda, then, he was an excellent crook in Avelino's sense, and conceivably in other senses as well. Like any Filipino politician he was making money by using his influence, by being a fixer, by 'facilitating' import licences and so forth, and by involvement in sundry business ventures that included tobacco-growing and cigarette-importing. In this area he had dealings with a carpetbagger named Harry Stonehill, a GI who had stayed on after the war's end and taken advantage of the carve-up of Washington's generous $2 billion in aid. Stonehill, a gifted entrepreneur, unwisely kept a 'blue book' listing people he had dealt with. Inevitably it was found and in 1962 he was to be deported from the Philippines to the sound of trumpets on the orders of President Macapagal. Among other things the blue book revealed was that Macapagal had used Stonehill's funds for his presidential campaign. Another name that cropped up in it was that of Ferdinand Marcos.[8] Apart from Ferdinand's expected activities as a wheeler-dealer in Congress there was another possible source of his sudden private wealth. It has long been assumed that he and some comrades from his alleged wartime guerrilla band, 'Maharlika', had used their links with the Japanese to find at least part of the fortune the occupiers had buried as the 'Yamashita treasure'. This is what Mrs Marcos said to me on the subject in 1997:

My husband's war comrades sold the remains of the Yamashita treasure while he was briefly in the US. [Ferdinand had gone to Washington in May 1947 as a member of a team sent by the Philippine Veterans Commission to negotiate the payment of $160 million in benefits and back pay.] He didn't get rich on that, but it introduced him to precious metals trading. By 1949 he already had 4,000 tons of gold.[9]

Four thousand tons? That is what she said, making me feel an unworldly naïf who still thinks gold is reckoned in troy ounces. Be that as it may, the Yamashita treasure has certainly been taken very seriously for the last half-century. Its relevance to Marcos-watchers is that many Filipinos, including people who worked with Ferdinand, are convinced that he found some – but probably not all – of the loot. (It is the remainder that continues to lure ex-Green Berets like Charles McDougald, ex-CIA men like Singlaub and sundry Filipino dreamers.) It is widely believed that in the last weeks of the war Ferdinand became privy to information about the hiding-places of several caches of treasure, dug them up, and once the war was over, sold them. To have become 'privy' to this sort of knowledge might seem to suggest excellent connections with the Japanese, or else an extraordinary amount of dumb luck. In any case, this allegedly formed the basis of his prodigious wealth, which was thus acquired before he went into politics. Once he was President, the theory proceeds, he used his Ilocano-dominated military to track down other caches of treasure and added those to his private hoard. And it was for this reason, it is said, that he commissioned a gold refinery in Manila: ostensibly so that the Philippines could at last refine its own gold from mines such as Benguet, but in reality so that bars of Japanese and other gold could be re-smelted into untraceable bullion before being spirited away to Swiss banks.

The counter-theory runs that this whole Yamashita treasure story is pure hokum, but has been most carefully played up by the Marcoses as a way of explaining Ferdinand's private wealth, which in fact came from far more disreputable dealings, cheatings and carpetbaggings in the aftermath of war. That is why (they say) Imelda Marcos so cheerfully bandies these huge tonnages of gold about in conversations on the subject of her husband's wealth: it is all a smokescreen. That is why (according to them) Imelda Marcos keeps harping on the notion that her husband's astuteness as one of the world's biggest private dealers in precious metals *supported* rather than undermined the Philippine economy. 'Tarquin Olivier, the son of Laurence Olivier, set up the Thomas de la Rue refinery here in Manila to refine gold . . . It was Ferdinand's private money that went to the Government and its projects . . . The PGH [Philippine General Hospital] and the LRT [Light Rail Transit] were both built without a single cent of Government funds,' she says.[10]

The observation of a Filipino with a lifelong connection with the gold industry may be appended as a final comment:

In the 1960s and until 1974 the Philippines was the free world's second largest producer of gold after South Africa – superior even to the US and Canada. It was a major product, with six or seven gold mines. The Johnson Matthey (de la Rue) refinery was set up in 1975 and enabled the Philippines to do its own refining to world standards. By law the gold had to be sold to the Central Bank. Theoretically, between about 1977 and 1982 Marcos was in a position to 'buy' all the gold mined and refined in the Philippines at a discount. Practically, he could steal the lot.

That Ferdinand Marcos was already astoundingly wealthy by 1954 can hardly be left out of the equation when it comes to considering the 'whirlwind romance' that ensued from his chance meeting with Imelda Romualdez in the House cafeteria. Decorum is usually preserved by presenting him as making all the running: the ambitious young Congressman swept off his feet by the *ingénue* ex-beauty queen. Certainly his eleven-day wooing of her now seems less of a courtship (which implies a degree of old-fashioned etiquette) than an amorous bulldozing. On the day of their first meeting Imelda was still thinking of herself as the all-but-fiancée of Ariston Nakpil. In less than a fortnight she found herself married to a rich, handsome and youngish Congressman. She agreed to join Ferdinand and a reporter friend of his, Jose Guevara, on a five-hour car trip to the northern mountain resort of Baguio. They left Manila on Ash Wednesday and on Good Friday Imelda signed the marriage certificate. I do not know whether Ferdinand had told her that as a matter of fact he was already engaged and had been living with his fiancée, Carmen Ortega, for some years in his large villa in San Juan, Manila, and had four children by her. Presumably he must have, for that engagement had been publicly announced not long before, and the same villa to which he was bringing Imelda as his new bride would surely have shown traces of its former occupant and her children, now hastily re-accommodated elsewhere. In any case Imelda apparently returned from Baguio flashing a ring set with eleven diamonds, one for each day of their courtship. (In terms of pure practicality it would surely have been hard to have had an expensive ring made to order within hours over the Easter holiday in a provincial town. Had he planned the whole thing in advance and driven up with the ring already made in his pocket, the number of diamonds privately significant to him for numerological reasons? There is something missing from this myth, just as there is from the story I was told by a fellow Ilocano of Marcos's, the Congressman Roquito Ablan. He said Ferdinand's father, Mariano, told him before the war that he had named all his children sequentially after a sentence in a school history text: 'Ferdinand Magellan was sent on the orders of Queen Elizabeth across the Pacific to seek fortune': thus, in order, Ferdinand and his siblings Elizabeth, Pacifico and Fortuna. Unless Mariano was gifted with uncanny prescience – and his failure to avoid a revolting death suggests he was not – it is improbable that he can have known in advance the genders of his yet-unborn children. But myths have their own narrative conventions.)

How is Imelda's sudden capture to be interpreted? That a provincial innocent was swept along by the glitter and determination of a rich public figure twelve years her senior and simply overwhelmed? But that hardly squares with the girl who had the nerve to go alone to the Mayor of Manila and talk him into overturning the result of a beauty contest. Clearly, a determined character was not restricted to Ferdinand. One might guess that the ticking of Imelda's inner clock had been getting louder and the Nakpil affair seemed set to drag on indefinitely. Here, by contrast, was this rich and ambitious man whom people were already tipping as a future presidential candidate, with a famous Bar reputation and an increasingly famous war record. It must have seemed like an opportunity for putting memories of garage floors, earth closets and singing to GIs behind her for good, as well as a way of showing that her father's run of bad luck was not irreversibly the lot of that particular branch of the otherwise distinguished Romualdez family.

And as for Ferdinand, what did he have to gain by marriage at this point? He was already well known as a philanderer, which had never yet done any harm to a male politician's career in the Philippines. His recent engagement to Carmen Ortega presumably meant that at the age of thirty-seven he, too, had begun to feel the clock was ticking for him. And maybe he was plain bored with his common-law family, wanted a break and chose a beauty queen. Other men have done the same. Or there again, maybe it really was a matter of true love on both sides. We shall probably never know. In any case, the church wedding that followed their hasty civil union was lavish indeed and was treated by the newspapers as a glamorous social event of public note. Some of the more overwrought copy was similar to that produced at the time of Prince Charles and Lady Diana's wedding in 1981, at least in terms of the 'fairytale' imagery. Imelda and Ferdinand made, after all, an exceptionally glittering and handsome couple.

The ensuing eleven years, during which the Marcoses lived in the well-appointed villa in San Juan, saw the birth of two daughters and a son. They also marked Imelda's transformation from a housewife into a politician's wife, a rite of passage that cost her dear. This painful moulding process was surely an instance of what would prompt Dr Alma Fernandez to a 'feminist' reading of Imelda's life in 1990, at a time when most of the Western world's press had declared open season on Marcos's widow.

When she first moved into the house in San Juan her new husband would not allow her to change anything, so presumably she found herself living with furniture and decor chosen by her husband's live-in fiancée. Most days she would travel down to Divisoria market in downtown Manila (near what was then the city's main railway terminus, Tutuban station) where she did the catering. She also bought material for her own dresses in Divisoria, suddenly finding herself having to live a remarkably social life. She was asked to model clothes for charity shows and was constantly invited to be a sponsor at weddings, baptisms and confirmations. She had the support of her own clan in that her favourite younger brother Benjamin ('Kokoy') came to live with them and was eventually followed to Manila by her other siblings. (At this time Kokoy's girlfriend was Ninoy Aquino's sister, Maur. Young Benigno Aquino Jr. had recently made a name for himself as an intrepid reporter in the Korean War, and this early link between the Romualdez and Aquino clans may, in the light of Ninoy's assassination twenty-eight years later, have represented the high spot in their relations.) Then in 1955 Vicente Orestes, now aged seventy and gaunt with lung cancer, died in Manila. At her father's death Imelda might have felt partially vindicated, for he had at least lived to see his branch of the family back on the road to social rehabilitation, thanks to his daughter's brilliant marriage. She herself was pregnant at the time. One of her nephews, watching her during the funeral, reported that she was so upset when her father's coffin was lowered into the grave she lost her footing and fell into the hole on top of it.

Perhaps the most difficult thing for Imelda to cope with was living a life in which she was expected simultaneously to be a housewife, a young mother concerned with running a family home, and a hostess to the constant stream of people who tramped through it at all hours of day and night, needing to be fed. These were her husband's political allies: agents, ward leaders and supporters, many of them uncouth by her standards and some of them frankly goons. She found herself

> . . . repelled by his kind of life, a life in which absolute strangers descended on her house and left it messed up, torn up, rent apart . . . They walked right into her bedroom, and political schedules began to be sheer physical torture. Crowning fiesta queens, she waited on one stage after another, in heat or in cold, in wind or in rain, from dusk to the small hours, until she was ready to drop. The crowds that surged through her house made all peace impossible, and one had to have a smile and a coin for every outstretched hand. The horror is epitomized in the story that, one day, handing a coin to a woman with a babe in arms, she had lifted the swaddling cloth and seen that the baby was dead.[11]

This new life also required an abrupt shift in her attitude to money. The Rose of Tacloban, who until recently had had to scrimp on meals in order to be able to afford a new pair of shoes to wear in her office at the Central Bank, later told Mrs Francia's Auntie Loring that as a young bride

> she was taken aback when one evening a stranger deposited a dirty sack in the middle of her living room. She quickly told the servant to take the sack to the kitchen, but before the fellow could carry out her order, Ferdinand smilingly instructed him to take it instead to the master bedroom. Pulling his wife aside, Ferdinand informed her that the sack contained money; he also made it clear to her that this would not be the last of its kind.
> On seeing the puzzlement and scepticism on Auntie Loring's face, Imelda went over to lift the cover from her bed. There lay a dirty-looking sack under it. She pulled it out and showed Auntie Loring how it was stuffed with money.[12]

(By 1960, the year after Ferdinand's election to the Senate, Imelda had already become accustomed to such things, even complacent, confessing to Auntie Loring: 'Money doesn't mean much to me any more . . . Our money comes in sacks. I'm tired of counting money.'[13])

Once again, to keep this culturally in proportion, it has to be remembered that Philippine politics was, and at election time still is, conducted in cash; and the nearer to the grass roots, the truer this becomes. Campaigns in particular call for prodigious quantities of ready cash, mainly in low-denomination notes. (This was why, when in 1986 the Marcoses were forced to flee the country, so many million Philippine pesos were found in their luggage by US officials who flew them out. The discovery readily lent itself to yet more stories about their having cleaned out the nation's coffers before going into exile, when in fact the money comprised KBL [the Marcos political party] cash left over from the recent snap election campaign that Ferdinand was taking home to Ilocos Norte – which he had been told was his destination. By the time the Marcoses were informed they were actually going to Hawaii, it was too late. Had they known this in advance, it seems inconceivable they would have bothered to take masses of Philippine peso banknotes to the United States, where the exchange rate at the time of the crisis – assuming they could even have found someone willing to change it – was absurdly unfavourable.)

Imelda's intense dislike of so many aspects of her new circumstances can scarcely have been made more bearable by her husband's determination to turn her into an urban sophisticate. This involved not only his giving her improving books to read with the significant passages marked in pencil on which he later quizzed her, but extended to an obsession with her tendency to over-eat. (A remark was later attributed to him to the effect that he hadn't married Cinderella to see her turn into the pumpkin.) His own interest in gastronomy was virtually nil, and such pleasure as he did take in the table extended little further than plain Ilocano vegetable dishes like *pinakbet*. His young wife, though, had many years of penury to make up for, together with all sorts of unassuaged cravings. Imelda had always known that, given the chance, she was going to be a champagne-and-*foie-gras* sort of girl; and this apparently led to a period when on Ferdinand's instruction a pair of scales was placed on the table by her at mealtimes and her allowance of food weighed out.

At the same time she began to realize that she was increasingly the butt of snobbish remarks and jokes on the part of Manila's social élite. 'Old' society, in particular, made satirical remarks about her habit of handing out identical little bottles of Jean Patou's 'Joy' to Congressmen's wives. She must also have known there were plenty of disparaging rumours circulating about her husband, too; but maybe she assumed that, as a man and as someone older, richer and more powerful than she was, his position made him feel invulnerable enough to ignore them. She herself was cut to the quick. She had, after all, lately been part of high society in Tacloban and here she was being made to feel like a parvenu straight off the ferry.

She began having severe migraine headaches for the first time in her life, alternating with bouts of lassitude and comfort-eating when Ferdinand was safely out of the house. She would lock the bedroom door and spend the day in bed, listening to soap operas on the radio and gorging on sweets. The double vision which her headaches produced began to acquire a metaphorical force – 'brought up to value honour, order, sobriety, manners and niceties, she could not abide the tumult and the disorder, the house that was not a home but a public arena . . .'14

The crisis came towards the end of the decade with a full-blown nervous breakdown. One night Imelda lay as though dead, 'cold, pale, motionless and hardly breathing'. Alarmed, Ferdinand took her to New York for three months where she saw a psychiatrist in the Presbyterian Hospital who diagnosed manic depression and told her that only she could get herself out of the state she was in. The cure, he said, lay in her changing her attitude: not merely to accept her new life but to embrace it completely, to revel in it, even if that entailed renouncing all sorts of preferences of her own. It seems that Ferdinand did offer to give up politics if she really wanted him to, but by then the doctor's course of auto-suggestion (a sort of Couéism which in those days pretty much represented psychiatry's sole armoury against mental illness of the non-chronic kind) seemed to be having an effect. To what must have been her husband's profound relief she told him he mustn't dream of doing such a thing. It was up to her to change, not him.

In a way this breakdown was Imelda's revelation on the road to Damascus in that thereafter everything changed, although it is less certain in Imelda's case whether the experience resulted in a more saintly person. It undoubtedly helped her come to terms with matters of money. Mrs Francia's mother recounted how, as godmother to the Marcoses' first child, Imee, she had often visited the house in

San Juan in those days, for she took seriously her role as the child's spiritual guardian in a milieu that struck her as perilously worldly. On one occasion Imelda took her up to her bedroom and laid out all her jewellery for her inspection, saying, 'You see, Amy, whenever I'm depressed I spread my jewels out on my bed; it cheers me up quickly.' This was the person who within the next twenty-five years would amass what was estimated to be the world's most valuable private collection of jewellery. On another day, rightly sensing that Mrs Francia's mother was wondering about the source of all this extraordinary wealth, Imelda said in a sudden hot burst of self-justification, 'You've been secure all your life. You don't know what it's like to be insecure. You don't know what it feels like to have toothache and not to be able to afford going to a dentist.'[15]

Mrs Francia published her book in 1988; Kerima Polotan wrote hers in 1969, only a decade after Imelda had cured herself of her breakdown and when the Marcoses were riding high, just completing Ferdinand's first presidential term of office. In those days the question of their wealth was not yet an issue biographers dared address (although it was much discussed by Manila's chattering classes). Thus Kerima Polotan could see the First Lady (as Imelda liked to be called) in a less complicated – or contaminated – light, more as the good wife who had overcome personal difficulties the better to be a model consort:

> Having accepted the terms of her kind of life, she never again flinched or took a step backward. Explaining it afterwards, she attempted a metaphor: '[I] was like a butterfly breaking out of its cocoon.' The headaches stopped for ever, the vague pains disappeared, and the double vision fused to become a single, concentrated look on the possible heights her husband's career might take.[16]

If this sounds too glibly like a woman deciding to sacrifice herself for her man and finding the process liberating, we should remember not only when Mrs Polotan Tuvera wrote her book but the period she is describing. By the time Cory Aquino had succeeded the Marcoses and Mrs Francia's book was published, people had long been saying that Kerima Polotan's had been propaganda, mere hagiography and whitewash; that after all both she and her husband Johnny Tuvera had served Marcos – albeit most honourably – for years. But once again, this was to let vindictiveness get the better of a sense of history. The modern women's movement did not emerge in the United States until the 1960s; Manila in the 1950s was completely devoid of any such popular liberationist notions, just as it was devoid of reliable psychiatrists. (Here one must make an exception for certain of the essays by one of the very best post-war writers, Ariston Nakpil's relative by marriage, Carmen Guerrero Nakpil. For their day, these were astoundingly advanced. Collected in one volume, *Woman Enough* (1963), they made a considerable impact; the essay on divorce, in particular, dated from the late forties and was in its way far more radical than much of the polemic the Women's Liberation Movement was producing in the US long after *Woman Enough* was published. Eugene Burdick, co-author of *The Ugly American*, paid Mrs Nakpil the ultimate compliment by lifting her entire essay 'The Filipino Woman', title and all, for a chapter in his book on Asia. He wisely died before he could be sued.) Such rare writing aside, the dominant ethos in Manila, so far as young middle-class mothers were concerned, was of stifling Spanish Catholic proprieties weirdly allied to the sort of American aspirations exemplified in Lucille Ball sitcoms: a world of feisty but ultimately submissive housewives with narrow waists and frilled aprons who coveted 'miracle' kitchens and were wonderful mothers to lovably freckled, tow-haired kids whose archetype was Jay North as Dennis the Menace. Mrs Polotan, these days a widow in her seventies, was of Imelda's own generation or even slightly older. The description she gave of Imelda's change of heart following her agonizing breakdown whitewashed nothing; it was simply of its time. (Hers remains the best-written of all the Imelda books.)

Later writers such as Mrs Francia developed their own theories as to what had 'really caused' Imelda's breakdown, the principal one being that she had been deeply disturbed 'by the discovery that the position, and at least part of the wealth, of the man she had married had been ill-gotten'.[17] In other words, she had been morally outraged and disillusioned as much as she was repelled by the lifestyle of the upwardly mobile politician she happened to have married. It is hard to know what to think about this so many years after the event, but it is a plausible enough theory. Certainly the scene in the Marcos household, with its constant crowds and cook-outs and uncouth strangers wandering about with sacks of money (that is, when they were not cutting the upholstery of her new sofa by sitting down while wearing their *bolos*) must have contrasted strangely with the decorous scene in her eminent cousin's house where she had until recently been living. Speaker of the House *pro tempore*, Danieling, was a practising politician of a very different and patrician kind.

I should like to propose a slightly different hypothesis, which is that part at least of Imelda Marcos's upset was caused by the paradoxical discovery that her new position did not vindicate Imelda Romualdez to quite the extent she had supposed. Her husband's ambitiousness, his manifest engagement in all sorts of ancillary business activities, some of which were clearly dubious, marked him out in Manila as a type. For all his wealth and growing power, he was revealed as indelibly provincial, the exemplar of rough-and-ready Ilocano politics of the variety she must have heard a lifetime of Romualdezes openly disdaining. Her own uncle Norberto, Vicente Orestes' brother, was not only a politician himself but a scholar who had been a delegate at the 1935 Constitutional Convention and who wound up as a Supreme Court justice. When he died in 1941 President Quezon called him 'truly a great man' while a Spanish language newspaper said, 'A saint has died: a just man and a perfect gentleman.' Her family, in short, were part of the old élite. It must suddenly have seemed to Imelda that the new life she had contracted with a man who was not by their definition a perfect gentleman was doomed to exclude her for ever from that particular kind of mannerly distinction. She may even have wondered whether before he died her father had guessed as much. Her 'step up', far from restoring her branch of the family to public esteem, looked like guaranteeing its enduring status as faintly pariah.

If this is correct, her recovery was absolutely characteristic and iron-willed, though arguably only the most important in a long line of decisions (both before and after she married) that exemplified a determined, 'go-for-broke' spirit. If the snobs didn't like it, they could lump it. And if they thought her husband shady then she could think of a way of rubbing their noses in it . . . For it does not quite do to place too much emphasis on a novelistic 'before and after' Imelda, of innocence suddenly corrupted. Common sense, as well as a sense of place and history, makes it obvious that she cannot have been wholly innocent even in her Rose of Tacloban days, if by 'innocent' one means ignorant of the ways of the world. She must shrewdly have observed first-hand all there was to know about accommodation, even corruption. Apart from her own family's dominant position in Leyte's politics (and provincial politics were seldom conducted even with Manila's pretence of decorousness, tending towards dirty tricks, pay-offs, and not infrequently murder), she had watched her father and the rest of Tacloban's inhabitants adjust to living under the Japanese occupation. She would have known the scams by which certain Leyteños had profited from the Japanese, just as she would people who profited by the presence of the GIs she later sang to. No doubt a few nice girls from Tacloban's convent schools had opted for dollars and romance over penurious virtue. The stakes had always been clear. Apart from which there was an old tradition that stemmed as much from Asia as from Spain, that one could lose one's heart in romance provided one did not lose one's head. A good marriage need not necessarily imply a grand passion. I do not believe a girl of Imelda's intelligence and beadiness was innocent of such knowledge; any Kansulay teenager today knows as much. Yet that does not mean that acting on it might not cause all kinds of stress. Any optimistic youngster might experience sadness on perceiving the essential starkness of the deal.

> Susie Abadilla, who accompanied Imelda at her PWU [Philippine Women's University] voice lessons, asked her, right after her marriage to Marcos, if she had loved this man deeply enough to marry him after a brisk 11-day courtship. She merely shrugged her shoulders enigmatically and said, 'Well . . .'[18]

By the time I met Mrs Marcos, of course, her story of a great romance had become immovably fossilized. Everything, from the beribboned bronze bust of her late husband in the apartment to her affectionate and even reverential references to him, made it clear that the status of their mutual love was non-negotiable. Not only was it a historical given, so was the yin–yang (Imelda's own phrase) nature of their political functioning together: 'It was like a sex act all the time, a love act. He thought of it, I implemented it.'[19]

7

Communists, nationalists
and America's Boy

The first requirement for a career in politics in the Philippines is money, and as we have seen Ferdinand had evidently taken care to lay the foundations of his future presidency sometime during the Second World War. The second requirement is contacts; and perhaps the most important of the contacts Ferdinand made soon after the war, that with the CIA, is the subject of this chapter. The implication of long-term planning on his part was often singled out in the negative biographies of the late 1980s as proof that there had always been something scheming about the man. He had been 'plotting' to become President right after the war, from before the war, from student days at UP, from boyhood up . . . Care was taken in describing the Marcos career retrospectively so that the terms used did not infringe those much-prized, Horatio Alger qualities like ambition or determination. Instead, Ferdinand was described as having been 'single-minded' (always a suspicious thing to be, with its overtones of narrow fanaticism); he was 'wily' rather than clever; he had not *as*pired to become President but *con*spired. Nor had he ever planned anything; he had always plotted.

The truth was more unexceptional. There is nothing unusual about a bright and ambitious university graduate boasting to his close friends that one day he will be President, although when a former fellow student and comrade like Leonilo Ocampo recalls this today it sounds uncannily like prophecy. Furthermore, when a

Filipino with a Law degree was ambitious in those days it virtually presupposed a career in politics. A country about to become independent offered a young man excellent opportunities for preferment as well as the prospect of having a hand in the making of a new society (and how ironic that sounds after Marcos's New Society!). What is more, anyone entering politics anywhere harbours a wistful dream of getting to the top, of becoming President or Prime Minister, even if their realistic selves know better. Given the political system of his day, then, there was nothing about Ferdinand's rise to power that was particularly extraordinary. He played the same system as did everyone else; he simply did it better than most, perhaps more ruthlessly, making some astute connections and having a lot of luck on the way. Still, thanks to his strange war and what he must have known about the skeletons in the cupboards of most of the members of the post-war Philippine government, he had an ace up his sleeve that many of his potential rivals did not have: the United States.

In 1950 a fortyish politician named Ramon Magsaysay, who had only been appointed as President Quirino's Defence Secretary a mere two months earlier, oversaw a superbly planned operation of military intelligence that resulted in the arrest of the Communist Party of the Philippines' entire Manila-based politburo. Newly elected to Congress, Ferdinand watched shrewdly. When in due course Magsaysay succeeded Quirino as President and managed to be popular simultaneously with the Filipino grass roots as 'a country boy' and with Washington as 'America's boy', Marcos must have become doubly attentive. He knew that the CIA's Edward Lansdale ('the Walt Disney of covert action', in Sterling Seagrave's felicitous phrase) had been responsible for Magsaysay's appointment as Defence Minister. Thereafter, Ferdinand could see ever more clearly the American hands pulling on the strings of Filipino politics. He realized that, independent nation or no and free electoral system regardless, the Philippines would never in the foreseeable future have a President who did not first have Washington's approval and backing. From an ambitious politician's point of view it became a matter of discovering how to play both the nationalist card and the anti-Communist card. Ferdinand Marcos thought he knew how he could become America's boy.

*

We need to backtrack slightly in order to acquire a perspective on the significance of Communism to America. The United States had emerged from the Second World War as the most industrially powerful nation on earth. From a European viewpoint America had hardly won the war by herself, having joined the fray rather late, but she had been on the side that could not possibly have won without her. It is true she had taken her time to recognize the global pretensions of the Nazi threat in Europe, and had very nearly been too late to save beleaguered Britain. But once Pearl Harbor had been attacked and Japan had made alliance with Germany, America's involvement became inevitable and – given Hitler's foolishness in invading Russia – the long-term outcome was not much in doubt. Wars are often portrayed as struggles between God and the infidel, or good and evil, or right versus might, but seldom so plausibly as in the case of the Second World War. Insofar as the notion of 'evil' had much meaning left in it, Nazism as revealed by the death camps seemed to redefine it. Consequently the Allies, unlike most victors of major wars, had a good claim to have won the moral high ground as well. This claim had been severely – many still think irreparably – damaged by America's dropping not one but two nuclear bombs on Japan in quick succession. It was pragmatic; the war was ended; the world promptly split into new power blocs separated by an 'Iron Curtain', as Churchill described it.

The Allies' notion of having had right on their side in the struggle against the Axis powers now carried over to their Cold War stance against the USSR and her satellites. (When forty years later President Ronald Reagan referred to the 'Evil Empire' he really meant it.) The Cold War, as a strategic stand-off based on the doctrine of MAD (mutually assured destruction) was undeniably dangerous and nervy. As a European whose lifetime has encompassed the whole of the Cold War my private, largely adolescent, memory is of a military affair conducted for 'our' side by NATO, interspersed with famous incidents (the downing of Gary Powers' U-2 spy plane, the Cuba missile crisis) and stories of espionage and competitive weaponry.

What I do not recall, because nothing like it occurred in Europe, was anti-Communist hysteria, which seemed to be peculiar to the United States. Stalin had long since stopped being 'Uncle Joe' of the war years and had been revealed as a genuine totalitarian monster, both brutal and sinister. The English writer George Orwell had satirized Communism generally in his 1945 novel *Animal Farm*, but by 1949 events in Soviet Russia had prompted him to the far more chilling predictions of *Nineteen Eighty-Four*. This later book embodied many of the phobias current throughout the Western bloc at that time, most particularly of police state suppression of democratic freedom so vividly exemplified in the real world by Stalin's gulags and the rigid controls that beset every aspect of public and even private life in the USSR. (Faced with 'crimes of opinion', not only did ordinary Russians need to censor their own speech, but even faces in the same official photograph might change from one day to the next.) If at public level in Western Europe such absurdities led to uneasy mockery, in NATO's corridors a much grimmer attitude prevailed that sometimes came close to reflecting the paranoia of Stalin's own state security apparatus. By the time Russia, and then China, exploded their own nuclear devices, there was unquestionably a genuine degree of psychosis on both sides in the Cold War. In the United States, anti-Communist sentiment toppled over into an outright witch-hunt. This had loud echoes in the Philippines as well as profound long-term political consequences.

The high summer of this hunt is usually seen as falling in 1953–4 with the hearings chaired by Joseph McCarthy. The Republican senator from Wisconsin claimed to have lists of the names of State Department officials and even high-ranking US Army officers who 'in reality' were Communist infiltrators. After a lengthy and notorious series of televised hearings the charges remained unproven and McCarthy's career collapsed with a Senate censure. The effect of this débâcle was not to discredit anti-Communism so much as the Republican Party, since it had appeared too loud and unserious in the face of what was seen as a desperate menace. It is not easy today to think oneself back to the attitude of, for example, the founders of the MPA (Motion Picture Alliance for the Preservation of American Ideals) in 1944 when they were opposing 'not only Communism, but the New Deal, labour unions, and civil rights organizations at a time when others connected with those causes were pulling together for the war effort, postponing their differences for the duration'.[1] The actor John Wayne, who eventually became the MPA's president, looked back in an interview to those days as having been a time when 'Roosevelt was giving the world Communism'.[2] (This was the same FDR whose heroic determination to come to Britain's aid had finally prevailed over a widespread opinion that events in Europe were none of America's business.) A future US President, the film actor Ronald Reagan, also played a considerable role in that period of Hollywood 'purges' and gave information regularly enough to the FBI to merit an informer's code number: T-10.

Between 1946 and 1948 such attitudes were central to HUAC (House Un-American Activities Committee), which was Republican-led at a time when that party controlled the House of Representatives. The controversial lawyer Roy Cohn, who was described (after his death from AIDS) as 'a native fascist, Joe McCarthy's brains [and] the legal executioner of Ethel and Julius Rosenberg' recalled the period vividly, since it was the making of his subsequent career.

> HUAC was rampaging against everything American as apple pie, particularly the movie industry. Ten screenwriters, called The Hollywood Ten, had been cited for contempt and accused of fostering Russian propaganda in movies during the forties. President Truman denounced this stuff as a 'witch-hunt' and when HUAC (led by Richard Nixon) went after Alger Hiss, Truman called it a 'red herring'.[3]

The point Cohn was making was that, contrary to the assertions of liberal historians, the Democrat Truman was just as rabidly anti-Communist as the Republicans of HUAC. In 1947 that President had written an executive order which instituted the first loyalty-security programme in US history, thereby allowing the FBI to probe the background and 'Americanism' of every government employee. The ability to see 'Reds under the bed' easily transcended party boundaries.

The Korean War between 1950 and 1953 was crucial to the hardening of the United States' anti-Communist stance, not least because the outcome was so indecisive and seemed to Washington to reek of unfinished business. (The war ended with matters standing largely as they had in 1948, with Korea still divided into two – the Communist North and the democratic South – on either side of the 38th Parallel. The conflict was decisive only for the five million or so who died.) Although sixteen member nations of the recently formed United Nations sent troops, it was clear from the first that this was principally an American show, sanctified by the UN and militarily supported chiefly by the British. In the Philippines, President Quirino committed himself to sending an expeditionary force, the 10th Battalion Combat Team. The young Ninoy Aquino, still only a boy of seventeen, was sent to cover the war for the *Manila Times*. He began like all boys by seeing the war as an adventure, but within months believed himself to have aged ten years.

The premise for the UN's intervention was when in June 1950, 'in much the same way that, during the American Civil War, the Yankees of the North had crossed the Mason–Dixon Line to impose their kind of government on the Confederacy of the South and thus enforce the unity of the nation, the North Koreans crossed the 38th Parallel into South Korea and advanced as far south as Pusan.'[4] The UN troops were under the supreme command of none other than the ex-Field Marshal of the Philippines, General Douglas MacArthur, at the incredible age of seventy. At first the war went the UN's way and by late October 1950 the Americans' Eighth Army and X Corps had passed the North Korean capital, Pyongyang, and were pushing towards the Yalu River which formed the border with China. Soon they had bottled up the remains of the North Korean Army on the river's southern bank. It all seemed over bar the shouting. MacArthur triumphantly predicted the Eighth Army would be home in time for Christmas, and the edge went off the US troops. This was just what Lin Piao had been waiting for, hidden in the mountains on the far side of the Yalu. Lin was the commander of China's First Red Army Corps, the man who only the year before had been a decisive strategist in the defeat of the Guomindang's Nationalist forces. China was about to take a hand in events.

The reverse, when it came, was as terrible a defeat for MacArthur as the Fall of Bataan had been. The Chinese forces fell on the Eighth Army and X Corps and drove them back down the length of North Korea with disastrous casualties. An article in *Time* magazine described the rout in hysterical terms:

The United States and its Allies stood on the abyss of disaster. The Chinese Communists, pouring across the Manchurian border in vast formations, had smashed the UN army. Caught in the desperate retreat were 140,000 American troops, the flower of the US army – about the whole effective army the US had . . . It was defeat – the worst defeat the United States had ever suffered. If this defeat were allowed to stand, it could mean the loss of Asia to Communism.[5]

MacArthur blustered and branded the Chinese intervention as 'criminal', but T. R. Fehrenbach wrote later that it had been at least as legitimate as the American intervention had been in the first place. 'Just as the United States had not been able to stand idly by in June when a friendly dependency was overwhelmed, in October the men in Peiping [Beijing] and the Kremlin felt they could not permit the forcible separation of North Korea from their own sphere.'[6] MacArthur hinted clearly at the possibility of nuclear retaliation, while back home hawks such as Rep. L. Mendel Rivers of Charleston, S. Carolina, called publicly for atomic weapons to be used against North Korea. Then on 1 December President Truman, who five years earlier had authorized the dropping of the nuclear bombs on Hiroshima and Nagasaki, himself announced 'we will if necessary use the atom bomb'. Horrified, the British Prime Minister, Clement Attlee, flew the Atlantic to talk him out of so disastrous a move. 'For the first time the UN cloak that the United States Government had so expeditiously woven for its action in Korea became not a support but a hindrance. . . . After 1 December 1950, the allies who had tripped unquestioningly into Korea would never again allow the United States an unlimited credit card, moral or otherwise.'[7]

Thus faced with the threat of his own allies' defection, Truman backed down. He vented his feelings by turning on MacArthur and stripping him of all his commands. A new allied offensive began again in January, once more crossing the 38th Parallel. But it had not advanced over halfway to Pyongyang when the Chinese countered with their spring offensive and overran the UN lines at Imjin. The Philippine battalion was in the thick of this fresh fighting, having been sent to help the hard-pressed British at 'Gloster Hill', which was held at the cost of severe casualties. Ninoy Aquino, now eighteen and a veteran war correspondent, reported brilliantly from this engagement. Not long afterwards he left Korea when the war ground to a halt and turned from military stalemate to negotiations which dragged on until 1953. He was greeted as a hero back in Manila for his fearless coverage of the war, and in particular for his reports on the Philippine battalion. To help him recover, the *Manila Times* rewarded him with a roving commission which he used on an extensive grand tour of Southeast Asia.

Not surprisingly, Aquino left Korea convinced of China's military might and tactical skill, which had come as a complete surprise to everybody, not least to General MacArthur. Consequently he started his journey in 1952 with his ears still ringing with dire American forebodings à la *Time* magazine about the domino theory which foresaw Communism, unchecked, toppling state after state in Asia. Indeed, when visiting Vietnam, one of his early stops, he portentously noted 'should this state fall into the hands of the Communists the Free World might as well write off Southeast Asia as LOST'. By the end of his tour, though, he had substantially changed his mind:

[H]e had found out that Communism was not uniformly a bogey to Asians, quite a number of whom equated it with liberation; and that the region in general was cool to the idea of an Asian pact against the Communists. What he had discovered was an Asia that feared not the Reds but the West, an Asia that wanted no involvement in the East–West cold war nor in the crusades of the 'Free World', and that therefore abhorred the proposed Pacific Pact as one more ploy to align it with the Americans in their battles against a rival power.

Said a wiser Ninoy at the end of his travels:

'To the Asian, the Western argument that "if Communism wins, Asians stand to lose their civil liberties" is meaningless. To the Asian now jailed by the French in the numerous prisons of Vietnam for being "too nationalistic", civil liberties have no meaning. To the Asian jailed on St John's Island in Singapore for possessing intelligence and nationalistic spirit above the average, civil liberties are likewise meaningless. The Filipino is aware of, and has enjoyed, America's benevolence; but to the rest of Asia the American looks like the Frenchman, the Britisher and the Dutchman. To Asians, these people are the symbols of oppression. And many Asians would prefer Communism to Western oppression.'[8]

The West – particularly the United States – made a crucial error by allowing the 'domino theory' of Communism to obscure the nationalist realities being played out in the ex-colonies of Southeast Asia. The British spent heavily in terms of lives, money and political repercussions in order to suppress the Communist uprising in Malaya. Then in 1954 General Giap famously defeated the French army at Dien Bien Phu. Arguably the twentieth century's greatest military tactician, Vo Nguyen Giap was later to mastermind the American defeat in Vietnam together with Ho Chi Minh. The strange thing is that from 1945 onwards the Office of Strategic Services' files clearly revealed as much as anyone needed to know about these two men: how for thirty-four years Ho Chi Minh 'had wandered the world as an exile seeking support for the independence of a country known centuries earlier as Vietnam'.[9] The head of the US State Department's Division of South-East Asian Affairs between 1945–7, Abbot Low Moffat, had been in Hanoi and knew Ho Chi Minh. He later testified to the Senate Committee on Foreign Relations, 'I have never met an American, be he military, OSS, diplomat or journalist, who had ever met Ho Chi Minh and who did not reach the same belief: that Ho Chi Minh was *first and foremost* a Vietnamese nationalist . . .'[10] Giap was of the same mould. At the age of fourteen he had joined an anti-colonial party, was jailed by the French at eighteen, went underground at twenty-four after organizing student strikes, and at thirty-one was already a widower because his young wife had died in a French jail while serving a life sentence for 'conspiracy'. None of this had much to do with the head, and everything to do with the heart. It was not Karl Marx whom the French, and later the Americans, were up against in Indochina but sheer grief and rage and an ancient patriotism. Even a twenty-year-old Filipino journalist could see as much in 1952. It was an extraordinary mistake for the West to have made, and doubly unforgivable in that they already had in their files all the evidence they needed to correct it. But that is how hysteria is.

It is difficult to overestimate the importance of this period for the ensuing decades of Philippine politics and the extent to which those politics were crucially influenced by the American fear of Communism in Southeast Asia. In the first place the Philippines dutifully – if not slavishly – cloned HUAC and came up with CAFA (Committee on Anti-Filipino Activities) which bizarrely began its own Red-baiting and witch-hunting activities just at the moment when HUAC itself was discredited in the US, its chairman, Martin Dies, jailed for fraud, and Senator McCarthy had been hounded back into the decent obscurity of Wisconsin.

Secondly, the Vietnam War, which effectively began fewer than ten years after the Korean War ended, seems in many respects like a re-run of Korea but on a far larger and more tragic scale. This time the Philippines was involved to an extent well beyond merely supplying the 'Philcag' non-combatant unit which Marcos sent in response to President Johnson's urging. Vietnam, in fact, had a profound effect on domestic Philippine politics and on Marcos's career, but in ways which only became fully apparent afterwards.

And thirdly, it is important to realize that the old colonial-era idea of Asia for the Asians – that of Rizal, Gandhi and Sun Yat Sen – was very far from dead, and there were plenty of Filipinos like Ninoy Aquino who found inspiration in it. 'To the Asian,' he wrote, 'democracy and oppression are synonymous. Democracy in Asia is almost on the 13th step of the gallows.' The irony was that in the next thirty years he was to become Marcos's only plausible political rival, to be labelled as a Communist, to be jailed under martial law and finally topple down those thirteen steps onto the tarmac at Manila International Airport with a bullet in his brain, the victim of Marcos-era democracy.

What, then, was the nature of the Communist threat in the Philippines before 1950? The answer, with nearly half a century's hindsight, is 'negligible', if by Communism is meant classical Marxist–Leninism dedicated to the overthrow of the state and capable of mustering enough popular backing to succeed. The CPP (Communist Party of the Philippines) was founded in 1930, and from then until the sixties drew the vast majority of its support from landless tenant farmers, chiefly those of Central Luzon. These were exactly the same people who formed the bulk of the Hukbalahap guerrilla resistance to the Japanese in 1942–5, and were very far from being atheist hotheads weaned on Muscovite dogma. They were for the most part devout Catholics, dirt-poor peasants who had inherited from their parents' generation a profoundly patriotic sense that the 'real' revolution of 1898 (that of Andres Bonifacio, the true *anak pawis* or 'son of sweat') had still to be won. At the core of their motivation was the knowledge that they were still as landless, and hence as impotent, as they had been in the time of the Spanish. At the level of bare subsistence, remarkably little had changed for them. In 1969, the year of Marcos's re-election as President, the writer Alfredo Saulo – who during the war had taken part in the Huks' provisional government – had this to say about Communism in the Philippines:

> The CPP is a unique and durable party. It has been outlawed twice, first in 1932 and again in 1957, but it has taken all this in its stride. It is extremely doubtful if the CPP can be legislated out of existence. All the important Communist leaders have been placed behind bars, but there is no doubt that Communism continues to win adherents, especially from the ranks of the alienated: people disenchanted and disgusted with unfulfilled promises of public officials, fed up with government graft and corruption, impatient with police inability to curb the rising crime wave, furious with the growing unemployment and the widening gap between the rich and poor, and, finally, distraught with the failure of priests and laity alike to live up to the teachings of Christianity.[11]

This hardly sounds like a sinister organization controlled from abroad whose atheistic threat could bring about the collapse of either civilization itself or that of the Philippine domino. The awful irony is that Saulo's list of the sources of people's alienation is still just as valid today, thirty years on. (It must be added that, like most of Bonifacio's and Aguinaldo's revolutionaries of 1898, Filipino Communists of the period were often better on strategies for seizing power than on giving detailed descriptions of what they would actually do with that power.)

Back in the thirties the first President of the Commonwealth, Manuel Quezon (who nowadays looks to have been as sane and statesmanlike as was possible in the circumstances), had recognized the origin of peasant unrest in Central Luzon and knew perfectly well that some sort of land reform lay at the heart of any solution. He would go and cajole landowners to treat their farm workers better, then address peasant rallies in areas where there had been unrest and exhort them to patience. ('I beseech you to have more patience! I ask you to desist from resorting to the worst – by burning the sugar-cane fields and harvesting the *palay* [rice] at your will and then seizing all, including that which does not belong to you. You must not do that! It takes time to help you improve your condition . . .'[12])

Shortly after this the war intervened and the more actively motivated of these peasants joined the Huks. The land reform issue was shelved, effectively remaining unaddressed until 1954. In that year President Magsaysay passed his Agricultural Tenancy Act, which increased rice and corn tenants' share of the crop to 70 percent but otherwise achieved little. (In 1963 President Macapagal enacted proposals for a far more sweeping series of reforms that gave the government greater powers to expropriate landed estates. But the programme was hopelessly underfunded, and dawdled until Marcos himself initiated a genuine if uncompleted land reform programme that earned him a good deal of popularity at the grassroots level of Kansulay's folk.) At the end of the war the Huks' betrayal by the liberating American forces was nothing short of grotesque. American commanders, having used the Huk guerrillas to mop up the Japanese in Central Luzon while complimenting them on their organization and fighting skills, promptly turned around and ordered them disarmed. The Huks could not believe their ears. Their leaders were rounded up by the same CIC (Counter Intelligence Corps) to which the brilliant agent Richard Sakakida had belonged. Part of the CIC's brief was to 'detect and investigate all matters pertaining to espionage, sabotage, treason, sedition, disaffection and subversive activity'.[13] They arrested, jailed and interrogated men who, a few weeks earlier, had been their bravest allies, accusing them of being Communists and rebels. Their orders might not have come directly from MacArthur, but he no doubt applauded the motivation; his own wealthy patrician's horror of Communism was notorious.

The CPP had kept a low ideological profile during the war in order not to complicate the straightforward issue of organizing the Huk resistance. The Party's reaction to the Huks' sudden betrayal by its American allies – who to compound the insult were re-arming and commissioning the very USAFFE guerrillas the Huks had disdained as '*tulisaffe*' – was to form the PKM (*Pambansang Kaisahan ng mga Magbubukid*, or National Peasants' Union) which absorbed nearly all those former Huk guerrillas who in civilian garb were ordinary landless sharecroppers. It was hardly a typically Communist act when the PKM urged its members to take part in the post-war democratic process and support the Democratic Alliance and Nacionalista parties in the 1946 elections. Six peasant-backed DA Congressmen were duly voted into Central Luzon seats, but the Liberal Party which won the election refused to allow them to take their seats in Congress and eventually had them disbarred on trumped-up charges of 'fraud and terrorism' at the polls. Nothing could have more stupidly guaranteed trouble. From that moment on, the peasants' faith and confidence in the democratic process evaporated. Despite President Roxas's hasty and inept attempts at pacification, agrarian unrest became more and more widespread in Central Luzon.

What finally drove the CPP out of reformism and into active struggle were the elections of 1949 in which Marcos first won a seat. These were widely acknowledged as the bloodiest and most corrupt in Philippine history. Hundreds of people were done to death in inventive, headline-grabbing ways. The CPP and the Huks were obliged to support the candidacy of Senator Jose Laurel, ironically the ex-President of the wartime Second Republic whom MacArthur had later jailed in Japan for collaboration. This gave his rival, Vice-President Elpidio Quirino, all the excuse he needed to send in the military. Armed goons terrorized the polling stations, but even so Quirino only won by a small margin. The defeated Laurel angrily cried fraud. The entire election's grotesque nature so enraged the electorate that there were open demands for armed revolt. Laurel only called off his own plans for an uprising after a stern warning from the US Embassy. Quirino was currently their 'boy' and Laurel might as well accept it with as good grace as he could muster. In 1950 the CPP leadership foolishly decided that 'a revolutionary situation' now existed, and formulated a two-year plan for seizing power. They were able to field some 15,000 guerrillas and believed they had at least another million sympathizers. As a show of strength and in the hopes of winning over more peasants to their cause, several thousand Huks carried out damaging raids on towns all over Luzon. Some towns actually did fall into Huk control for several days at a stretch, but nothing was consolidated because nobody had worked out in advance what to do next. Another series of raids was planned for targets in Manila, but in the meantime the new Defence Secretary, Magsaysay, intervened. With the intelligence resources of Edward Lansdale's CIA as well as his own network of informers, he learned enough to carry out pre-emptive raids himself and arrest 105 Communist and Huk suspects, including the CPP's entire politburo.

Such, in brief, is the story of how landless peasants were driven further and further into marginalization and finally into outright rebellion and subversion. Leaving aside questions of social justice, it does seem immensely stupid and recalcitrant of Presidents Roxas and Quirino to have allowed things to degenerate to this extent. Yet there was probably nothing men like that could have done. Themselves members of the élite, they were in the grip of a historical reluctance to side with anyone other than rich landowners and their own American 'advisers'. This was as much an ingrained social reaction as a conscious defence of business and property (so much of the Philippines' business was American owned). It was a pattern that would be repeated endlessly all over the 'Free World' in the next decades, both elsewhere in Asia (Indonesia, for example) and in practically the whole of Latin and Central America. Beneath it lay a kind of insane logic that grew out of the United States' hysteria about a global Communist conspiracy. According to this logic it was easier to drive masses of marginalized peasants into the black-hatted ranks of 'international Communism' than it was to grant their elementary demands for a reasonable living. That way, none of the unpalatable and difficult social questions needed to be addressed and the issue simply became a crusade. That way, too, it could all be subsumed under the general heading of the Cold War. It became hugely profitable for American armaments industries which, in addition to supplying their domestic armed forces, were supplying those of a dozen or more 'friendly' foreign countries. This specialized economy lay at the heart of the rapidly growing 'military-industrial complex' which so alarmed President Eisenhower (himself, of course, a distinguished ex-soldier) that he took to referring to it in speeches in the late fifties and most notably in his Farewell Address in January 1961, warning that its rapidly growing power could reach the point when it, and not the President, determined the United States' foreign policy. His prophetic misgivings were amply confirmed within a few years as men, weapons and materiel were poured into South Vietnam in ever-increasing quantities after the CIA itself had concluded the war was probably unwinnable. Thus in the Philippines, the needs of America's domestic economy led in a straight line to numberless bloody encounters between the US-armed and -trained Philippine Constabulary and peasant guerrillas.

However, it would be naive and wrong to give the impression that the United States' strategy in Asia was based on a malevolent self-interest, that it was simply acting quite cynically to acquire a network of new colonies to satisfy the capitalists of Wall Street. This, of course, was the interpretation that Communists and Socialists favoured and which, by the time of serious student protests against the Vietnam war, even radical Americans found all too plausible. Such an interpretation did indeed seem obvious, but only if one ignored the status which Communism held in the American psyche. To successive US administrations Communism was not a joke or just one of those quaint foreign beliefs that a sophisticate might shrug off as *autre pays, autres moeurs*. It was a virulent political and moral cancer that so threatened the world as to make necessary heroic surgery even if some of that surgery's local effects were regrettable. These 'local effects' in the Philippines, in Vietnam and in a dozen Latin American countries were frequently so abominable that it is hard to recount them without becoming polemical. One has to cling manfully to the idea that American intentions were never in origin wicked, and it is this alone that gives the subsequent events their status of genuine tragedy. Neil Sheehan, the Vietnam war correspondent who won the Pulitzer Prize for bringing the Pentagon Papers to light, gives a balanced reading of his country's strategic thinking:

> The men who ran the American imperial system – men like Dean Acheson, who had been Truman's principal secretary of state, and the Dulles brothers in the Eisenhower administration, John Foster at the State Department and Allen at the CIA – were not

naive enough to think they could export democracy to every nation on earth. The United States had established democratic governments in occupied West Germany and Japan and in its former colony of the Philippines. If American statesmen saw a choice and high strategy did not rule otherwise, they favoured a democratic state or a reformist-minded dictatorship. Their high strategy was to organize the entire non-Communist world into a network of countries allied with or dependent on the United States. They wanted a tranquil array of nations protected by American military power, recognizing American leadership in international affairs, and integrated into an economic order where the dollar was the main currency of exchange and American business was pre-eminent.

The United States did not seek colonies as such. Having overt colonies was not acceptable to the American political conscience. Americans were convinced that their imperial system did not victimize foreign peoples. 'Enlightened self-interest' was the sole national egotism to which Americans would admit. The fashionable political commentators of the day intended more than a mere harkening back to the imperial grandeur of Britain and Rome when they minted the term 'Pax Americana'. Americans perceived their order as a new and benevolent form of international guidance. It was thought to be neither exploitative, like the nineteenth-century-style colonialism of the European empires, nor destructive of personal freedom and other worthy human values, like the totalitarianism of the Soviet Union and China and their Communist allies. Instead of formal colonies, the United States sought local governments amenable to American wishes and, where possible, subject to indirect control from behind the scenes. Washington wanted native regimes that would act as surrogates for American power. The goal was to achieve the sway over allies and dependencies which every imperial nation needs to work its will in world affairs without the structure of old-fashioned colonialism.[14]

One of the fatal flaws in this ambition is, of course, that it is quite impossible from a dependency's point of view to tell the difference between enlightened self-interest and old-style colonialism. It is also naive not to foresee how, with the borrowed strength of this American imperium behind them, local élites would hasten to increase their own power and upset delicate social equilibria by pursuing ancient tribal agendas: all manner of revenge, land-grabbing and victimization. But an imperium does not bother itself with such native trivia – not, that is, until brought face to face with their untrivial consequences as the United States was in Vietnam. That war may be long over, but its fall-out of unrest continues to this day all over what used to be Indochina, and with particular virulence in Cambodia.

The Philippines was the obvious place in which to base efforts to win over Asia to the American fold after the Second World War. The United States had done at least two important deals with the Philippines in exchange for its long-promised independence: a trade pact (the Bell Act and the Parity Agreement that gave American businesses huge trading advantages) and the ninety-nine-year lease on twenty-three military bases on Philippine soil, including Clark Air Base and the immense naval dockyard of Subic Bay. These bases were not yet even nominally under the control of Filipino officers, and there was never the slightest question that the United States ran them, just as it ran the Philippines' military and intelligence services.

With all this in place and with the CIA's limitless support behind him, the charismatic Edward Lansdale took Magsaysay under his wing to show him how to break the Huks and the Communist menace. Together they made a remarkable team. With Lansdale's coaching Magsaysay did achieve some notable reforms. He re-organized the military and turned the Philippine Constabulary into a paramilitary service, firing the lazy and corrupt and promoting men with a sense of mission. Yet he also understood Lansdale's insistence that no matter how efficient the armed forces were, it would never be possible to win hearts and minds unless the men in uniform were firmly disciplined. Filipinos needed to break the dis-trust of centuries (like that for the old *guardia civil*, for instance) before they could look on the military as their allies rather than as the enemy.

The eminent good sense of the theory behind this reformism has lent Magsaysay's rule an air of radical achievement. It is largely for this that some older Filipinos still look back to his time with respect and a certain longing, as at a golden age when the old

American–Filipino alliance really worked and the anarchy left over from the end of the Second World War was at last brought under control. After all, by 1953 the Communist 'insurgency' had dwindled to practically nothing and the time when Huk guerrillas could take over entire towns was long gone. What could be a greater testament to Magsaysay's bona fides and sincerity than the Huk supremo, Luis Taruc, coming down from the hills in voluntary surrender to the President? This particular incident was a tribute to Magsaysay's quite genuine nationalism that existed independently of his usefulness to the United States. Magsaysay's championing of agrarian reform reflected his conviction that things would never improve for ordinary Filipinos until they were liberated from that feudal and sterile cycle of oppression, armed struggle and more repression. Even so, to cite his nobler motivations is to side with the optimists. Others, including hard-headed people like Ferdinand Marcos, had very different memories of Magsaysay's reign.

Among the things they remembered were the so-called 'Nenita' death squads organized by Colonel Napoleon Valeriano of the Philippine Constabulary. Valeriano's ruthless efficiency confirmed Lansdale's observations and the CIA man took a fatherly interest in this handsome young killer. Valeriano and Marcos went all the way back to high school, where they had been classmates. Like Ferdinand, he had been interned by the Japanese after the Fall of Bataan, but unlike his friend he had escaped from the camp. He managed to reach Australia and join up with MacArthur's command, where he fell under the spell of the General's rabid anti-Communism. Half a dozen years later his 'Nenita' squads specialized in meting out to suspected Communists the sort of memorable deaths calculated to encourage others to desert the ideological fold. With the Philippine Constabulary's CIA-supported intelligence they terrorized much of Central Luzon and were frequently dispatched to other parts of the archipelago to pacify trouble-spots and instil some righteous fear. On Lansdale's advice these death squads were upgraded to death battalions, trained by JUSMAG (Joint US Military Advisory Group) and given a virtually free hand to wage whatever war they felt like against whomever they wished. In Central Luzon, especially, Valeriano's 'Nenita' battalions held peasants in the grip of a terror they had not known even under the Japanese. This was one prong of the Lansdale–Magsaysay strategy.

The other prong was image-building the Quirino regime for the benefit of all those outside the Philippines who knew nothing of terror in remote provinces. The CIA was determined to ensure that the 1951 congressional elections would not be a repeat of 1949, which had been widely seen as a complete travesty of the democratic process. This led to the importing of an early version of a professional spin-doctor in the person of a New York lawyer and PR man named Gabe Kaplan. Under the cover of such CIA fronts as the Asia Foundation, and aided by a team of young Filipino CIA recruits, Kaplan went around the nation's Rotary Clubs preaching the absolute necessity for free and fair elections. Like Lansdale, he was a character straight out of a novel: a likely model for one of those sixties' Ross Thomas heroes like Clinton Shartelle in *The Seersucker Whipsaw* who were always being sent off by 'Langley' to some steamy country to 'pull a shitty' in the presidential election. (Thomas had served in the Philippines during the war and retained a keen interest in the country, as his later novel *Out on the Rim* showed.) Certainly Kaplan was good at his job, and with the middle-class support he was building up all over the Philippines Lansdale and the CIA set up NAMFREL (National Movement for Free Elections), the organization that was to play such a vital role in the snap election of 1986 and the ousting of the Marcoses. Colonel Valeriano himself was in command of one of the NAMFREL detachments sent to watch the polling in 1951. The outcome was, as intended, adjudged a masterpiece of democratic fair play and was prominently billed as such by the US press. The whole election with its appearance of scrupulousness had the equally calculated effect of winning over people of centrist and middle-class politics who had recently been wavering leftwards in sympathy for the Huks and peasants on the receiving end of 'Nenita' tactics.

By 1953 the CIA–Magsaysay alliance was such that the outcome of the November presidential election was guaranteed. The Magsaysay-for-President Movement had been bolstered by the traditional official US blessing of laudatory articles in *Time, Collier's Magazine* and *Reader's Digest* about the one man who could maintain American-style democracy in the Philippines. Raul Manglapus (who went on to become Magsaysay's Foreign Secretary and, more than three decades later, Cory Aquino's too) composed a hugely popular 'Magsaysay Mambo' to whose catchy beat voters might dance to the polls. (It was to be resurrected as one of the anthems of the 1986 'EDSA Revolution'.) The CIA, meanwhile, had a fall-back position in case Quirino's Liberals resorted to their 1949 tactics of murder and mayhem. They arranged for military com-pounds and radio stations throughout the country to be occupied by teams of Lansdale's Filipinos. In addition, a few days before polling began some US destroyers and a small aircraft carrier casu-ally hove up over the horizon and dropped anchor in Manila Bay as a reminder of what might happen unless things went the way Lansdale had organized. It was pure Ross Thomas. Magsaysay won in a landslide.

The CIA's ability to ensure the election of their anointed candi-date in a strategically vital 'independent' Asian country was impressive. More revealing, though, was the way they tailored their aims to coincide uncannily with those of the most powerful families in the country. The old *ilustrado* class, for the most part, saw absolutely eye to eye with these new Americans, as so many of them had back in 1898. It was perfectly predictable that Lansdale, like MacArthur before him, should have used a Del Monte pine-apple estate as one of the retreats where he formulated his various plans and carried out briefing sessions. One of the journalists who had been co-opted onto the Magsaysay campaign had been Ninoy Aquino himself, who was currently dating the Cojuangco family's daughter Corazon, whom he had known since they were both nine years old. (They married a year later in October 1954, the same year the Marcoses were wed.) Soon after the election Ninoy pro-posed to Magsaysay that he could do with a publicity boost to cement his victory and show that it had not been founded entirely on skilfully manipulated (and foreign-backed) hot air, as some cynics were suggesting. Aquino volunteered to track down the legendary Huk leader, Luis Taruc, and talk him into coming down out of hiding and surrendering to Magsaysay in person. If it could be done it would be a great propaganda victory for the President, as well as the final straw for Taruc's remaining followers. (Nor would it do much harm to the enterprising young Ninoy's own fame and fortune.) Against all expectations, and greatly helped by his personal credentials as the man who had so courageously reported on the Philippine battalion in Korea and become an Asian nationalist, Ninoy made contact with Taruc. The Huk leader's dignified response to the proposition proved as nothing else that he was a Filipino to the core, a constitutionalist second, and a Communist a very long way third. 'I am a Filipino first and last,' he said, while admitting he hadn't supported Magsaysay's candidacy because he thought the man was 'dangerously inclined to the American imperialists'. But since the people had voted for him, *vox populi* had to be respected. 'It is for us to accept their verdict.'[15] After elaborate arrangements, Taruc agreed to surrender to Magsaysay. At the last moment, though, Ninoy's personal coup was thwarted when Colonel Valeriano popped up out of the undergrowth and arrested Taruc so that for publicity purposes this much-wanted man could be brought in by the Armed Forces of the Philippines instead of by a cocky young journalist. Ninoy was understandably mortified. He went home, wrote his scoop and burst into tears. He need not have worried. Everybody of any consequence knew Taruc's surrender had been all his work.

If this interweaving of American post-war global strategy with Philippine domestic politics makes for a complicated story, it does explain how by 1953 it could have brought together such disparate characters as Edward Lansdale, Ramon Magsaysay, Napoleon Valeriano, Ferdinand Marcos and Ninoy Aquino. This is not to imply that a single conspiracy connected them, nor even that they necessarily liked one another. The unifying factor was the American cause, which was broad enough for each to maintain a private agenda on the side. Whatever else, it hints at a feature of Filipino society that remains as significant today as it was in 1953: the sheer interconnectedness of the comparatively small circle of oligarchs who ran – and still run – the Philippines. Through marriage, through contiguity of business and social interests and through the unspoken knowledge that they swim or sink together, they have everything in common.

It is quite possible that Marcos already knew Lansdale before Jose Laurel (who before the war had acquitted Ferdinand of the Nalundasan murder) called in the debt and asked him to represent his old schoolmate Valeriano. This came about because of some temporary rejigging of alliances during the 1949 elections.

Valeriano had found himself in Negros Province trying to oppose Governor Rafael Lacson's private army. The Governor was using his forces to ensure victory for the Lopez–Quirino faction in his province, and Valeriano's men had agreed to a midnight meeting with an opponent of the Governor's. Unprepared for trouble, the Nenita squad was jumped by the Governor's men and trounced. Although Valeriano himself was not in personal command of the squad, he was held responsible, considerably embarrassing the Nacionalista cause when he was charged with sedition. The Nacionalista party chief, Jose Laurel, called on Ferdinand Marcos to defend Valeriano against the charges. Marcos won the case.[16] From that moment there is no question that Ferdinand had a first-hand link with Asia's most powerful CIA officer. As we know, he had already been to Washington in 1947 to negotiate the veterans' back-pay, and through his wartime alliances would have had serviceable contacts with both the Pentagon and the State Department. Adding the CIA to this would have made him a man with connections to the highest places in the US Government. In the next dozen or so years he took good care to cement these relationships and to ensure he put the right people in his debt. This led to his tacit endorsement as 'America's boy' in the 1965 election. And that, in turn, produced an interesting dilemma for Marcos when President Lyndon Johnson called on him to send a token fighting force to help the US cause in Vietnam. The demands of Philippine nationalism required him to distance himself from all appearance of being the White House's lap dog; on the other hand he owed his presidency at least indirectly to the White House and now these debts, too, were being called in. Apart from that, he was close to the two men who had probably done more than anyone else to shape the present strategic entity of South Vietnam: Edward Lansdale and Napoleon Valeriano. For this pair had gone on to greater things.

To describe Lansdale as a character out of a book was strictly correct. Well before the sixties Edward G. Lansdale had become a myth, having appeared in Graham Greene's 1955 Saigon novel, *The Quiet American* and then (perfunctorily disguised as 'Edwin B. Hillandale') in the best-selling novel *The Ugly American*.[17] This last was essentially a political tract designed to convince Americans that they could wrest Asia from Communism if only they could find a way of getting Asians to co-operate. Asians were only superficially wily; they were highly susceptible through the Achilles' heel of their hopeless superstitiousness. To bend Asians to the American will, therefore, would require learning their local language well enough to convince the natives that Americans were essentially decent and their intentions honourable. This rapport could then be followed up with some harmless deception here and there, accompanied by judicious handouts of candy. Forty years on, the book still makes fascinating reading with the tragic retrospective light of Vietnam flickering across its pages. For in its study of Hillandale/Lansdale it emphasizes precisely those 'psy-war' tactics that were the real man's trademark. Having just helped Magsaysay overcome Huk Communism in the Philippines and install Pax Americana in the form of a paragon of Asian democracy, Hillandale is posted to Sarkhan (clearly Vietnam). He has a diploma from the 'Chungking School of Occult Sciences' – referred to now and then as the 'Occult Sciences School', whose initials ought to have struck any reader. Once in Sarkhan he discerns how political decisions there depend to a large extent on augury and superstition. He uses his own skills in fortune-telling to convince the Prime Minister that he is the world's greatest astrologer, duly influencing him in day-to-day decisions and thereby imperceptibly taking charge of the country's political direction.

This, in essence, is what actually happened. As soon as Magsaysay was safely installed in Malacañang, Lansdale returned to Washington to a hero's welcome in acknowledgement of the mystique that now surrounded him. He was seen as having single-handedly turned back the tide of Communism in an Asian country and brought an ally firmly back into the fold. One down and a long list to go; but it was a splendid start. As the CIA's expert on counter-terrorism and guerrilla warfare, Lansdale was next dispatched hurriedly to Vietnam in 1954 when the French defeat at Dien Bien Phu had set 'alarm bells ringing all over Washington', as he himself put it. Historians like Neil Sheehan believe that South Vietnam was really Lansdale's own creation, since the action he took in his first two years in Saigon prevented Ho Chi Minh from following up the French collapse with a sweeping victory throughout the country. By any standards Lansdale was a remarkable man, extremely likeable and warm. (He is remembered fondly by a celebrated Filipino leftist and Marcos opponent who, as a child, lived near Lansdale's compound in Quezon City. This man recalls Lansdale's generosity with lemonade and the sort of American delicacies that brightened up the lean post-war years: Babe Ruths and all-day suckers.) Lansdale was also oddly free of Foggy Bottom theory and dogma in that he artlessly and sincerely believed that Communism was doomed in Asia as long as it was opposed by a mixture of counter-intelligence and enlightened government – dirty tricks and Babe Ruths, in other words. Once he had decided that America should back the Vietnamese Prime Minister, Ngo Dinh Diem, Lansdale flew to Manila and talked Magsaysay into letting him have Colonel Valeriano as his security adviser in Vietnam. In this way Valeriano began his international career as a killer.

> Through Lansdale, Valeriano became a favourite of CIA covert operations specialists William Colby and Theodore Shackley, moved on from Saigon to train Shackley's Cuban Brigade for the Bay of Pigs, then back to Indochina as chief 'gook-zapper' in Colby's Operation Phoenix.[18]

(The Phoenix Programme was set up in 1969 in South Vietnam as an instrument of terror. 'The programme in effect eliminated the cumbersome category of "civilian"; it gave the GVN [Government of (South) Vietnam], and initially the American troops as well, licence and justification for the arrest, torture or killing of anyone in the country, whether or not the person was carrying a gun.'[19] It was simply an extension of the old 'Nenita' tactics.) By then, what was seen as the magic formula Lansdale had invented and pioneered in the Philippines had become the CIA's standard operating procedure elsewhere in the Third World – not merely in Vietnam but in Indonesia, Cuba and Chile. In each case the operations were carried out by the same team of Americans and Filipinos who had created Magsaysay.

Magsaysay's identification with the CIA's pragmatic approach to a global crusade that transcended mere national politics was shared by his successor, Carlos Garcia, despite Garcia's famous 'Filipino First Policy' favouring Filipino business. In 1957 the 'Permesta' rebellion against President Sukarno was under way in Indonesia. Sukarno's increasingly virulent anti-Western stance was inevitably labelled 'Red-leaning', and a group of Indonesian colonels defected to the Philippines. Once there they sought refuge, and according to Ninoy Aquino President Garcia asked him if the exiles could be accommodated at the Hacienda Luisita, the huge estate in Tarlac which Ninoy's in-laws, the Cojuangcos, had lately acquired. He arranged for the renegade Indonesians to have sanctuary there as well as a training camp for anti-Sukarno subversion (American arms were already being supplied from the Philippines to rebels in Indonesia). 'We even set up an elaborate radio network so the colonels could contact their own people,' Ninoy testified.[20]

To look back now at this period from the century's end is a deeply melancholy business, and all the more so because the collapse of 'world Communism' did not come about through the agency of a latter-day Lansdale. It was less that good triumphed than that evil fizzled. What strikes one about the great crusade, then, is its awesome waste. By 1969, when the war in Vietnam had become deeply unpopular in the United States itself, one answer to the question *What was it all for?* was supplied by the US Senate in an Armed Services Committee Report signed by Senators Stuart Symington, Stephen M. Young and Daniel K. Inouye:

> The American people have lived with fears of a Soviet attack for some quarter of a century, ever since World War II, and have expended a thousand billion dollars on defence in recognition of this possible danger. These gigantic expenditures have been detrimental to many other plans, programmes and policies which now also appear vitally important to the security and well-being of this Nation. The American people now know that many billions of these dollars spent on defence have been wasted.

Commenting on this document, the independent investigative reporter I. F. Stone wrote in *I. F. Stone's Weekly*:

> The truth is that we have spent a trillion dollars since World War II on a gigantic hoax. The US emerged from World War II, as from World War I, virtually unscathed, enormously enriched and – with the atom bomb – immeasurably more powerful than any nation on the earth had ever been. The notion that it was in

danger of attack from a devastated Soviet Union with 25 million war dead, a generation behind it in industrial development, was a wicked fantasy. But this myth has been the mainstay of the military and the war machine.[21]

It all seemed to confirm Eisenhower's gloomy forebodings about the autonomous nature of the military–industrial complex. Yet as little as eight years earlier, when Lansdale's highly secret stick-and-carrot attempts to win over Vietnam had not yet degenerated into full-scale war, the 'wicked fantasy' had probably not been that clear to anyone in the United States. In his recent memoir Gore Vidal, who once referred to himself with belligerent modesty as 'America's biographer', wrote that when he checked the notes he had taken in 1962 while hobnobbing with his old family acquaintance, John F. Kennedy, he was surprised to discover 'how little understanding any of us had of what was actually going on at the time':

> We had been carefully conditioned to believe that the gallant, lonely USA was, on every side, beleaguered by the Soviet Union, a monolithic Omnipotency; we now know that they were weak and reactive while we were strong and provocative. Once Jack [JFK] had inherited the make-believe war against Communism in general and the Soviet in particular, he proceeded, unknown to all but a few, to change the rules of the game. He was about to turn Truman's pseudo-war into a real war. He was going to fight, somewhere, anywhere. Cuba had gone wrong. At Vienna, Laos had been marginalized as a place of no essential interest to us or to the Soviet. Yet in June and July of 1961, Jack had called for a $3.5 billion military appropriation to deal with what he termed the 'Berlin Crisis'.[22]

Three months earlier, in Arthur Schlesinger's account, Kennedy 'saw [Soviet diplomat] Gromyko . . . took him to a bench in the Rose Garden, and observing that too many wars had arisen from miscalculation said that Moscow must not misjudge the American determination to stop aggression in Southeast Asia.'[23] But as Mirsky and Stonefield pointed out, 'What Kennedy could never grasp was that the United States was playing the aggressive role.

American policy makers, then as now, habitually used American "defensive" rhetoric to disguise intervention.'[24]

Such was the power of the United States' own thought-control it is likely that few Americans ever quite grasped why, for example, much of the rest of the world perceived the ring of US bases on 'friendly' soil surrounding the USSR as an aggressive deployment. From these were dispatched daily flights by Strategic Air Command bombers loaded with nuclear weapons targeted on Soviet sites and cities, missions that were always – mercifully – aborted before it was too late. The introduction to the 1955 film starring James Stewart, *Strategic Air Command*, hopes to disguise this military aggressiveness by pretending that nuclear bombers are *defensive* aircraft. Against logos of screaming eagles clutching thunderbolts and serried ranks of vast, gleaming B-36s the text scrolls: 'In these skies of peace, the nation is building its defence . . .'

Secrets and *realpolitik* notwithstanding, the United States' source of public moral capital has always been as the defender of freedoms and the champion of ethical governance (as witness a current pre-occupation with its own interpretation of what human rights should be, especially in Asian countries like China). And yet the American Revolution was the first great anti-colonial movement, which casts an ironic pall over US foreign policy in the Philippines and elsewhere. As Albert Kahn noted, 'The very concept of defend-ing a Free World that included a fascist Spain, military dictatorships in Latin America, and a feudal oligarchy on Formosa [Taiwan] placed a certain strain on credulity.'[25]

The Marcos era fell squarely into this squalid moral gulf between good intentions in the White House and peasant-hunting in Central Luzon. One of the side effects of this was that disillusionment with Marcos, when it finally came, provoked Washington and much of the American press to cries of outrage. Marcos had been a 'fake' from the first, a greedy self-seeker who beneath the guise of . . . (but we have heard all this before). Yet the United States cannot reason-ably have it both ways. From the time of President Magsaysay in the early fifties, Marcos had espoused America's broad strategic aims as perfectly as he later fulfilled US requirements for an accept-ably reformist and basically amenable Filipino President. If then, like Diem in Vietnam (who had to be assassinated, probably by Valeriano), Marcos turned out to be his own man after all, that was the Americans' look-out. It was pure hypocrisy to meddle in another nation's internal affairs while protesting benevolence, and then to complain when what they mistook for a loyal puppet turned around and bit them in the leg while dextrously removing their wallet.

All this goes to show that when his more judgemental biographers referred to Marcos as having 'plotted his way to the presidency', the image of Machiavellian cunning and unprincipled opportunism is the least interesting aspect of the story. By the year of his marriage, sheer chance, his own forensic skill and a foreign power's global intentions had given him access to the centre of a stage on which, over the next thirty years, the fortunes of the whole of Asia would be played out. This was surely what Imelda Marcos meant when she was overheard in the mid-fifties saying of her husband 'he is already a statesman, you know', at a time when he was a mere Congressman. Thanks to his Washington connections, he was already *thinking* like a statesman.

This is not to deny that cunning and opportunism – even ruthlessness – played a part in his ascent, just as they inevitably would in anyone else's winning the presidency of the Philippines. But his main ploy had been to make his own ambitions mesh with those of the United States. If the United States, as we have been assured, had the entirely praiseworthy and unsinister purpose of resisting the global spread of Communism, then Marcos can hardly be blamed for having supported this aim. Perhaps after all he did show a streak of political genius in never having been fooled by the granting of Philippine independence into thinking the United States would now withdraw from active interference with its former colony's domestic politics, so long as they did not conflict with American business and strategic interests. It is likely, for instance, that President Quirino never understood why, after his despicable 1949 campaign, he was going to have to be dumped; that the United States had bigger fish to fry in Asia than keeping him in power after he had outlived his usefulness. It was precisely this that Marcos perceived. Far from being newly independent, the Philippines was about to become freshly dependent, this time for global strategic reasons. The US bases would become increasingly important. This was the new post-war *realpolitik*. Thereafter in his quest for the presidency, Marcos was artful in knowing how to play off this knowledge against the prevailing spirit of Asian nationalism. Of course he was seduced by his proximity to the real power of a man like Lansdale; anyone would have been who could feel the erotic charge that drives all politicians towards its source. Against this he had to balance the fact that in his innermost self he was still less America's boy than he was an *anak ti Batac*, a son of Batac, a dissenting Ilocano brought up on stories of heroic patriotism. Eros was destined to win, as it generally does; but the struggle made for a lively and inventive career. When in 1957 President Magsaysay was killed in a plane crash with his reputation intact as 'the champion of the masses', Marcos would have known that with luck and pluck it was only a matter of time before he became the next 'America's boy'.

8

The Marcoses of Malacañang

While waiting to present his credentials to President Macapagal in Manila on 1 September 1963, the newly appointed British ambassador, John Addis, wrote one of his regular weekly letters home to his sister Robina. Then forty-nine, he was a career diplomat and China specialist who had spent the post-war years in Nanjing and Beijing. He was posted to Manila after two years as ambassador to Laos from 1960–2. One wonders how he felt about leaving the Asian mainland where his main interests lay. He was a fluent Chinese speaker and had got to grips with Lao, besides which his private passion was for Chinese porcelain, on which he was an authority. As it turned out, he was destined to remain ambassador in Manila until 1969 when, to round off his career, he was given the one posting he had always coveted: that of ambassador to Beijing (1970–4). Addis's presence in Manila thus overlapped the transition from Macapagal's presidency to that of Marcos, and he was there throughout Ferdinand's first term of office. By that time he had acquired many emotional ties with the Philippines and went on maintaining cordial – if diplomatic – relations with Marcos until 1983, the year of Addis's death. Long after he had been posted away, he kept visiting his friends in Manila and writing astute letters about the political scene there. From a historian's point of view his occasional private conversations with Marcos – the last was in 1982 – provide some idea of the diplomatic world's attitudes towards the President and his administration.

Sir John Mansfield Addis KCMG was very much a man of his class and time (born 1914, Rugby and Oxford). Neither he nor his sister Robina married. He wrote to her at their family home outside Tunbridge Wells informative, mildly witty letters whose tone seldom varied from an affectionate urbanity. 'Dear Bina . . . love from John' they went, week after week (at moments of excitement twice a week). They were a prolongation of the sort of Sunday letter home he would have been obliged to write when he was first sent off to boarding school, the dutifulness long since become a discipline and softened still further into a reassuring habit. They gave little away about the private John Addis: occasionally a light, mellow homesickness for Tunbridge Wells, nothing whatever about his own erotic affections. For those, one has to read between the lines or talk to people who remember him. For a description of his physical presence one can rely on the man himself, touchingly under few illusions:

> I have seen myself on television. It was a shattering experience, and I had to go away after less than a minute. The long face and heavy head, quite bald except for some touches of white, the bad posture, and most odious of all the rich fruity voice, affectedly upper-class. Oh dear! Never again! People must love me very much for my inner qualities![1]

The letter he was writing to Robina in September 1963 contained the sharp observations of a travelled man with alert political and social antennae. Manila was still strange to him. So far, he had been unimpressed by the leafy and exclusive enclave of Forbes Park, which was full of grandees and his diplomatic kith and kin: 'First impressions of the rich upper class are that they have exhausted all their natural appetites, bored, artificial, craving novelty.'[2] In those days his own house was safely far from Forbes Park (where the current residence is). It was downtown on Manila Bay, on the border between the old residential districts of Ermita and Malate which were classy in a quite different way. Even then there were still some ageing Ermiteños who could recall the local Spanish dialect once peculiar to those few blocks bordering the bay. Addis's house was pretty and stood in a lovely garden with (again, in those days) a view of the sea. If his first impressions of Manila's élite had been lukewarm, Addis was more enthusiastic about the ebullient freedom (many would say licence) of the national press.

One good thing that goes on here is the lively debate in the newspapers on matters of current importance, often critical of the Government. One of the issues discussed is the attendance of the Philippines at the 'Games of the Newly Emerged Forces' organized by Indonesia. One commentator urged the Government to refuse to attend on the ground that attendance would be a departure from the Government's 'hard anti-red line of no dealings with the Communists' – i.e. they would be compromised politically by playing basketball against North Vietnam or by racing against North Korea! I feel as baffled as I would be in arguing about apartheid with a South African – where does one begin when the gulf is so wide and there is no visible point of contact? I feel a vague uneasiness over this 'hard line' – hard lines which have no give may break suddenly. But there are no signs of any cracks. The two political parties stand for nothing except the organization of power and its benefits. The labour unions, as in the US, are non-political welfare organizations. Even such issues as land reform and the Philippines' relations with other Asian nations are not matters for political debate. They seem a very immature people, not yet emerged, spiritually, from their colonial status, less aware even than the Lao . . .[3]

Addis's bafflement at Filipino/American attitudes to Communism was, of course, very much a European's reaction. In addition, as a scholarly man who knew and loved China, he was fascinated by that vast country's painful political evolution as it tried to reconstruct itself into a modern state. In 1947 he had been First Secretary and Head of Chancery in Nanjing, the Nationalist capital city so brutally sacked by the Japanese in 1937, and had moved to Beijing in 1949 when Mao's Communists took over. The period in which he was now writing fell roughly midway between the Great Leap Forward and the Cultural Revolution and was one of intense ideological debate. Addis, though of course not himself a Communist, watched avidly and sympathetically from Manila as best he could.

His comment on the lack of newspaper debate concerning the Philippines' relations with the rest of Asia is odd, for he had arrived at a tense political moment in this respect, and particularly from the point of view of a British diplomat. The Philippines had an out-standing territorial claim on North Borneo based on a historical family link between the Sultan of Sulu (in the extreme south of the archipelago) and the Sultan of Brunei. According to this the Sultan of Brunei, back in the late seventeenth century, had either leased or ceded North Borneo to his relative in Sulu, and the latter's pre-sumed – but highly doubtful – allegiance to the Spanish Philippines allegedly made this territory part of the modern Philippine Republic. Until 1963 North Borneo was part of the remaining British Empire then rapidly being dismantled. In that year it was renamed Sabah and, together with Sarawak, incorporated into the new state of Malaysia. This did not prevent the Philippines from prosecuting its claim, however, and President Macapagal formed an unlikely alliance with President Sukarno of Indonesia. Together they pro-posed that, instead of the new country of Malaysia, a sort of super-confederation of states should be formed. Comprising Malaya, the Philippines and Indonesia, it was to be called 'Maphilindo'. By the time John Addis arrived in Manila this grandiose fantasy was already beginning to founder, and Britain was seen as largely to blame because it was siding quite unashamedly with Malaysia, its former colony. This was not mere caprice on Britain's part. The for-mation of Malaysia presented an acute problem of demography. With Singapore, but without Sabah and its Malay population, there would have been a large overall Chinese majority in the new nation. Britain was unwilling to grant independence to a union quite so obviously foredoomed to racial unrest, so it took Malaysia's part. His country's sudden unpopularity with Filipinos who supported the Sabah claim was brought home to Addis when his residence was picketed by furious protesters. As he wrote to Robina:

We now have photographs of the little demonstration outside my gate the other evening. Two of the placards read 'Britishers we shall ax and hammer you' and 'White monkeys go home'. I particularly treasure the latter.[4]

A fortnight later he wrote:

> There is a very puzzling political situation here, and I don't see
> my way through it at all. Politically, the Philippine leaders are
> very immature. They have preferred not to leave the nursery in
> which the Americans brought them up. The President,
> Macapagal, has, I think, some inclinations to be a demagogue
> and an autocrat, though not the strength of personality of
> Soekarno. Most Philippinos [sic] assume so strongly that they
> belong to the West that it is a pleasing adventure for them, no
> more, to make a little excursion with fraternization with Asian
> neighbours – like the little rich boy who plays with the children
> in the street and finds it exciting just because he doesn't belong to
> them and has the security of the mansion behind him. I think it
> was in this spirit that Macapagal entered into his flirtation with
> Soekarno, perhaps also envying Soekarno's autocracy and cer-
> tainly seeing his new role in Asian affairs as a valuable addition
> to his persona in internal politics, which is what matters most to
> him. But I don't think he has realized how far his behaviour over
> Malaysia has in fact committed him to his new friends and fur-
> thered their interests and separated him from his old position in
> the lap of the Americans. Until last week there was a chance that
> he would pull back before it was too late. But on Friday, with his
> full approval, the Foreign Secretary made a statement of policy
> which commits them further to the pro-Indonesian anti-
> Malaysian line. It was incidentally crudely and clumsily
> anti-British. It is a measure of their immaturity and irresponsi-
> bility that when I went through the text of the Foreign Secretary's
> speech with him yesterday morning pointing out where it was
> untrue and unjust, his reaction was to laugh and say genially
> 'Yes, of course you're right, it wasn't so, don't pay attention to
> that, this was just for internal consumption, to meet criticisms, it
> was just journalism!' I feel there is nothing to get hold of. With
> General Phoumi I at least knew I was dealing with a snake . . .*

* 6 October 1963. General Phoumi Nosavan led the CIA-backed faction that
seized control from the neutralist Laotian head of state, Prince Souvanna
Phouma, in order to achieve Washington's policy of 'polarization'. General
Phoumi was frequently described by CIA officers as 'our boy'.

(A footnote to the Sabah claim – which is still alive today – is Imelda Marcos's assertion that some years later 'Ferdinand offered the United States a base on Sabah for as long as they wanted, in exchange for their help in getting Sabah.'[5] If so, Marcos may have intended renegotiating the open-ended status of this proposed lien on Filipino territory once the deal was safely in the bag. Yet by then the whole scheme was surely quite unrealistic.)

It is interesting to watch a middle-aged career diplomat settle somewhat wearily into a new posting, especially when he does not yet realize he will come to love the country deeply. By 10 November Addis had begun Tagalog lessons, which in those days must have been a rarity for any diplomat, especially an ambassador. He reported that 'the mental effort is terrible' after Chinese and Lao. Inevitably, his cultural comparisons were with those Asian countries he knew well and he found himself shocked by the living conditions of the poor in Manila and began an informal archive of newspaper cuttings of various horror stories he came across. He was particularly distressed by the tale of a poor mad mother of three children whose charred skeleton was found, still chained, in the remains of her house. (He was probably unaware that in 1912, referring to Spanish colonial times, an American doctor had reported: 'There was no governmental provision for the insane, and it was no uncommon sight to see these unfortunates tied to a stake under a house or in a yard with a dog-chain, and it often happened that during fires, which are so frequent in towns built of *nipa*, they were burned because no one thought to release them . . .'[6])

Addis's judgement that the two main political parties of the day (Liberals and Nacionalistas) stood for nothing 'except the organization of power and its benefits' was not far wrong. This had an acute bearing on domestic political events that were unfolding in Manila beneath his eyes and which were about to take Ferdinand Marcos from being a Liberal Senate President to winning the presidency of the Philippines as a Nacionalista. Even before the 1961 presidential campaign Macapagal and Marcos, both Liberals, had come to a working verbal agreement. This was that in exchange for Ferdinand's support and that of the Ilocano bloc (the so-called Solid North) which he could muster, Macapagal promised to limit his presidency (if he won) to a single term of office and then in 1965 to throw his own weight behind Ferdinand's candidacy.

As early as 1964 Marcos was making it clear he had not forgotten this quid pro quo. 'Of course I want to be President of the Philippines,' he told an interviewer. Yet it soon became obvious that Macapagal was going to renege on his promise and stand again. In a memorable political coup Marcos deserted the Liberals and joined the Nacionalistas as their Opposition candidate, and as such he subsequently fought and won the 1965 campaign. This 'defection' was something else his foreign biographers seized on later as evidence for a radical lack of principle on his part, for self-interested turncoatism. That was not only unjust, it was wrong. Once again it was an assessment made on the basis of a cultural misconception. The fact is that principle (in the sense of a party ideology as opposed to an individual's sense of honour) is indeed rare in Filipino politics. The reason is not that Filipinos are inherently less honourable than anyone else, but because the political system they have inherited from their peculiar history of mongrel cultural influences does not depend on party loyalty in the way a European or even an American might understand it. Political parties in the Philippines are loose agglomerations of men and women interested in their own preferment. The party is seldom more than a convenient horse to carry a candidate on to personal glory. If it looks like weakening or becomes suddenly lame, the animal is swapped without more ado for one that looks sturdier. If this changeover takes place in mid-stream, so much the better for the delighted spectators.

This state of affairs is possible because so little Philippine politics is fought on the basis of a coherent platform of issues. It is far more about personalities, which is why so many showbiz people wind up in positions of power. (As of writing, the country's current Vice-President is Joseph 'Erap' Estrada, an ex-action-movie star.) If a candidate adopts a particular issue it will usually be because he or she thinks it will be a vote-winner rather than because it stems from a deeply held conviction. Much of the real emotion of an election campaign, and most of whatever wit or originality a candidate can muster, will go into assassinating the characters of the other candidates – even occasionally the candidates themselves. In this respect the model for the Filipino electoral process is more the

American than the European style. It is not an electorate that would hold still for the lengthy disquisitions on ideology and policy that, for example, characterize a French campaign. In the local context, therefore, Ferdinand's swapping parties was not dishonourable. Quite the contrary: once he had seen that Macapagal was not going to honour his own promise he had little choice but to become the Opposition candidate. It was a gamble, of course. To desert the incumbent's majority party for that of the minority was obviously risky. He was no stranger to taking risks, but he was quite as shrewd as he was brave. His reckoning of his chances included the fact that the Nacionalista Speaker *pro tempore* of the House was now his cousin-by-marriage, Danieling Romualdez, the very man who had once escorted the Rose of Tacloban back to Manila from her penurious exile in wartime Leyte. Danieling was his bridge to the Opposition whose candidate he was about to become. Imelda was overjoyed. 'He has come home,' she said of her husband, implying that his being a Liberal had always been a bone of contention between them. At last he was part of her family in politics as well. She now threw all her energies into campaigning for him.

The 1965 presidential campaign was the first in the Philippines to rely on up-to-date techniques, especially radio and TV. In order for the Marcos camp to ensure the blanket coverage it wanted it was decided to recruit Fernando Lopez as Ferdinand's running mate. Lopez was a member of one of the most powerful families in the country: a typical oligarch of the kind Marcos would turn on and savage some years later. In 1965, though, he needed the exposure the Lopez family's nationwide TV and radio network could give him. Initially, all attempts to cajole Lopez into running for Vice-President failed. So Ferdinand sent Imelda.

Imelda did not rely on up-to-date techniques to get Lopez to change his mind. Just as she had years before in Mayor Lacson's office, she wept, she pleaded. And just as it had worked then, it worked now. Lopez agreed. Thereafter, Imelda Marcos became probably the hardest-working campaigner in any election in the nation's history. She had already gathered around her a nucleus of personal aides: twenty-five young women from the wealthiest families, all dressed in blue. They had started by being known as the 'Friends of Imelda' but they soon became famous as the 'Blue Ladies'. It was one of her private triumphs that she managed to turn these elegant members of the seigneurial class into gofers who vied with each other for her favours and periodically smarted beneath her slights. The Rose of Tacloban was well on her way to recouping her pound of flesh and deciding that a mere pound wouldn't quite cover the debt.

There was scarcely a town in the archipelago she did not visit in the company of hand-picked teams of these courtiers. She travelled by helicopter, by leaky boat, in jeeps bouncing over rutted tracks, even by ox cart. She gave the same speech twenty times a day. She shook hands until her own was numb; she kissed babies until her lips bled. And, of course, she sang. She sang herself hoarse. She took the trouble to learn songs in the appropriate dialect, and the locals were spellbound at the sight of this astoundingly glamorous apparition who seemed to have descended from another world, belting out Ilocano love songs or Waray ballads or Tagalog ditties. (On one visit she passed close to Kansulay, and several villagers went to the rally. 'She was very . . . *feminine,*' said one judiciously towards the end of the Marcos era.) She went on campaigning even when so exhausted she was barely conscious. Yet she always contrived to look radiant, as the press faithfully kept pointing out. Ferdinand had coached her well, but something else was taking over – something he had perhaps not bargained for: a natural politician's instinct as well as a genuine warmth in her touch to which people responded. In many ways it was she who set the tone of the Marcos campaign, and there are still people who swear it was she who won him the presidency. (They say three I's won in 1965: Iglesia, Imelda and Ilocanos.) Nothing could better illustrate the distance she had come in the last half-dozen years or so since her nervous breakdown. She was a person who had found her *métier*.

Macapagal replied with jingles and slogans. Marcos followed suit. By present-day standards 'Forward the Filipino!' and 'Let this Nation be Great Again!' may seem anodyne enough, but at the time they struck a chord and at least the sentiments expressed made the name of Ferdinand's Nacionalista party sound plausible. He had stolen a march by commissioning Hartzell Spence to write *For Every Tear a Victory*. Macapagal, dogged by bad luck (one of his authors died) came up very late with a biography of himself modestly called *The Incorruptible*. On the grounds that any publicity is good publicity Marcos seemed not to mind that Spence's book was savaged by several critics. It had served its purpose.

> In tone, the Spence book 'offended and antagonized, was rude, (defaming) a people to glorify one man.' It painted the Filipinos 'smaller and blacker to make Marcos look bigger and whiter.' Many were antagonized by its patently patronizing air, with Marcos praised not for being a 'good Filipino' but for being 'almost like an American'. (In a candid moment, much later, Imelda would confess to a trauma induced by Spence's book.)[7]

The book was turned into a film, *Iginuhit ng Tadhana* ['Fated by Destiny'], which was popular enough in the weepy tradition of Tagalog films to add up to 'at least 300,000 non-intellectual votes', as one estimate put it. The love scenes between the actors playing Ferdinand and Imelda were chaste and gooey, in conformity with popular taste, and probably did much to set a precedent for the couple's recurring public protestations of love which made Filipinos feel like children overhearing their parents' bedroom talk. Some were deeply reassured and touched; the more sophisticated reeled with nausea.

The campaign progressed inevitably into its dirty tricks phase. The Macapagal camp revived memories of the Nalundasan case by asking Filipinos if they wanted a murderer as president ('What else would be new?' one newspaper replied tartly). Campaigners went around handing out black toothbrushes – a not unwitty reminder that Nalundasan had been shot while cleaning his teeth. The Marcos camp countered 'The Incorruptible' with allegations of corruption and sleaze and Macapagal's links with Harry Stonehill. They also wondered loudly what Macapagal had done in the war that could match their man's bemedalled heroism. Imelda herself fell victim to a worse trauma even than that occasioned by Spence's book. She discovered that a faked picture was being widely circulated with her head superimposed on the body of a lubricious nude. She locked herself in her bedroom in San Juan, pulled down the blinds, and gave herself up to 'anger and pain'. But she recovered by recalling that the Liberal Party had to be running scared if it needed to resort to such tactics. On election day she stayed in San Juan to vote while Ferdinand flew up to Laoag to cast his ballot in his home territory, the Solid North. He was piloted by a curious Swiss-Filipino industrialist, Hans Menzi, who would remain a faithful and increasingly powerful Marcos loyalist until his death. It so happened that some relatives of Imelda's had once tried to pair her off with Menzi, an idea that would have caused hilarity in knowing circles. Menzi and John Addis were already friends and would relax from the cares of office by cruising the seafront at sundown in Addis's ambassadorial Rolls.

As must be clear by now, anyone becoming President of the Philippines would need the full approval of the United States. Ever since the convention at which Ferdinand topped the ballot and was nominated as the Nacionalistas' presidential candidate, he had had the backing of the CIA's machine. He of course had his own influential connections; but in any case Jaime Ferrer, the Lansdale protégé who had helped set up NAMFREL for the 1951 congressional elections and had made sure of Magsaysay's victory in 1953, had independently thrown his weight behind Marcos from the moment it was clear he could run, and had conveyed this choice to the US Embassy in Manila in person.

> Many on the [Marcos] campaign team were old Lansdale men. One of them, Jose Aspiras, an Ilocano from La Union and former president of the National Press Club, headed the Marcos press campaign. Rafael Salas, a professorial-looking bachelor of thirty-seven, one-time head of the National Economic Council, served as the campaign co-ordinator and legal counsel. He had been president of Lansdale's National Student Movement when it launched Magsaysay's presidential bid in 1953. Blas Ople, Ferdinand's propaganda chief, was a former newspaperman and assistant to Magsaysay. Jose Crisol was a CIA-trained secret policeman who joined the Marcos team to gather political intelligence. He had been chief of Magsaysay's bogus land reform programme intended to undercut the Huks. The Agency's fingerprints were everywhere.[8]

Once again the hallmark of CIA backing was the official imprimatur of laudatory coverage in the American press for the anointed. Dozens of articles about Marcos were published in the United States, nearly all of which drew heavily on Spence's recent biography. This was the first time that a wider international public became acquainted with him, and they knew him from the start in that book's histrionic version. The myth was not for denting for at least the next decade, and at the level of White House rhetoric it was still intact twenty years on. In 1965 there could have been no doubt in any American reader's mind who the blue-eyed boy was in the forthcoming election in the Philippines. It was anyway widely rumoured that the US State Department was no longer happy with Macapagal who, himself infuriated by Foggy Bottom, had changed the day on which the Philippines celebrated its independence from 4 July (the same as the United States') to the more meaningful 12 June (12 June 1898 being the day on which General Aguinaldo had proclaimed Philippine independence from Spain from his balcony in Kawit). Washington never forgave Macapagal; and it is probable that he was the first Filipino President never to be invited to the US. It arguably remains his one act as President for which he is fondly remembered by his countrymen, but it was nothing like enough to win him a second term of office. (This is not to suggest that his presidency was particularly dishonourable. Indeed, it could be argued that of all Filipino Presidents, Macapagal had the clearest idea of what he wanted to do when he first arrived in Malacañang. He at least had a plan, which was basically the doctoral thesis he wrote at the University of Santo Tomas rejigged as a five-year socio-economic programme. But it was all too academic, too inflexible, and its failure only made him the more stubborn.)

In the event Marcos won by nearly three-quarters of a million votes. 'I never had any doubts,' remarked an exhausted Imelda, even though the uncountable sacks of money that had constantly arrived at their San Juan campaign headquarters must have greatly bolstered her natural confidence. She then went and stood in front of the mirror in her bedroom and began practising a variety of stiff salutes and casual waves. She was watched curiously by the new Vice-President's niece, Presy Lopez. 'How does she do it?' Imelda wondered aloud. 'How does the Queen of England wave?'[9]

By the time of her husband's inauguration she had perfected a suitably regal gesture. The parade was a grand affair. The White House was represented by Vice-President Hubert Humphrey. The

CIA's 'chief gook-zapper', Ferdinand's friend and ex-client Napoleon Valeriano, trotted along on horseback. By then the Marcoses had taken up residence in Malacañang Palace and the first signs of the Camelot-on-the-Pasig it would become were already evident. Yet there was still a certain innocence in the glittery shenanigans. Nothing yet prefigured the vulgarity of the victory celebrations in Luneta Park for Marcos's 1969 re-election, when massed choirs sang the Hallelujah Chorus and people swapped horrified glances at the menacing phrase 'And he shall reign for ever and ever'. Ferdinand's inaugural speech strove for the Churchillian note: 'Come, then, let us march together toward the dream of greatness . . .' Even the press and Manila's sophisticates who could see beyond the filmic aspects of the new First Couple's glamour and who understood the political realities behind their victory were prepared to be faintly impressed as the hero called for heroes to match him:

> The Filipino has lost his soul and his courage. Our people have come to the point of despair. Justice and security are as myths. Our government is gripped in the iron hand of venality, its treasury is barren, its resources are wasted, its civil service slothful and indifferent. Not one hero alone do I ask, but many.

There was cautious optimism among the less cynical. During the campaign, the issue of the US bases had been raised once more, chiefly because of the American Embassy's mishandling of an allegation that two Filipinos had tried to bomb a school on Clark Air Base. Since over thirty Filipinos had already died around the perimeters of American bases in incidents mostly involving ragged scavengers and jittery guards, it was an emotional issue. Marcos had made appropriately nationalist noises. While nobody seriously believed he would, or could, do anything radical about the Americans' presence on Philippine soil (the bases agreement still had over seventy-five of its ninety-nine years to run), there were hopes that this dashing and youthful politician whose valour had been so widely touted might yet have both the courage and skill at last to plot a more independent course for his country.

It would be a mistake to read Marcos's victory in the election as proof of his overwhelming popularity with the electorate as a whole. Leaving aside the Solid North, which would have backed a donkey provided it was an Ilocano donkey, much of the country probably did think he presented a plausibly dynamic image, while his beautiful and charismatic wife's glamour and warmth would have tipped the balance of tens of thousands of waverers. But in Manila, in areas of cultural or ideological dissent (the Moslem south and Central Luzon), and in generally well-informed and educated circles, there was a good deal of scepticism about Marcos. It was no secret that he was already a prodigiously rich man, and everyone knew perfectly well how politicians became prodigiously rich in the Philippines. There was a lot of gossip about his 'Mr Ten Percent' methods, as about his deep involvement with Harry Stonehill. His CIA connections – and especially his closeness to Valeriano – were also common knowledge. It all added up to a picture of someone who was just a little too much the complete Filipino politician for comfort. Nothing succeeded like success, and so on; but there definitely were widespread misgivings among the intelligentsia about Marcos becoming President. Contemporary newspaper and magazine articles provide ample evidence of this to counter the picture his propagandists later airbrushed into a glowing retrospective portrait of popular acclaim and trust. It is inherent in the Filipino electoral system that a village like Kansulay can be presented as having overwhelmingly backed a particular candidate when all that has happened is that voters have been given fifty pesos to put their cross against that name on the ballot, and the presence of muscular men with bulges in their hip pockets has suggested that it would be foolish to do otherwise. To try to infer an electorate's sentiments from such a voting system is as much bogus psephology as the system itself is sham democracy.

It was now 1966. The build-up of American troops in South Vietnam was proceeding at a hectic rate. By June the previous year there were 75,000 US military there; the Pentagon was foreseeing a total of half a million by 1967. President Lyndon Johnson's long and agonizing battle for public credibility over the non-existent war in Vietnam (war never was officially declared) was already lost, if a speech by the TV anchorman Walter Cronkite was anything to go by:

The political lie has become a way of bureaucratic life. It has been called by the more genteel name of 'news management'. I say here now, let's call it what it is – lying.[10]

Vice-President Humphrey had come to Manila for Marcos's inauguration saying 'The tide of battle has turned.' This was the year LBJ was to call on Congress for $9 billion more in military spending on the war. It was an extraordinary spectacle: the world's most massive and sophisticated war machine ranged against a tiny nation peopled largely by villagers who were simply Vietnamese versions of Kansulay's. Yet this aggressive campaign was somehow still perceived by the US administration as being primarily *defensive*. There was no shred of irony on his part when the US Joint Chief of Staff's former chairman, General Nathan Twining, said that same year:

Red China under its present leadership seems to me at this writing to be practically a hopeless case. Naked force seems to be the only logic which the leadership of that unfortunate nation can comprehend . . .[11]

It was China's thought rather than any 'naked force' that was about to have a considerable effect on Filipino politics and, indeed, on Marcos's future, although at the time nobody knew it. Even as the Cultural Revolution began to hit the world's headlines with stories of the Red Guards' excesses, few realized that at least part of its ideology would strike a chord in peasant societies the world over, and not least in the Philippines. The British writer James Kirkup, passing through Manila in this period, singled out the *Manila Times* columnist J. V. Cruz (former President Magsaysay's press secretary and destined to become a Marcos ambassador to Great Britain) for his courage in praising Felix Greene's book about China, *A Curtain of Ignorance*. Cruz also warmly recommended Greene's *Awakened China: The Country Americans Don't Know*. 'In the American-dominated Philippines,' Kirkup remarked, 'it takes guts to write such things.'[12] It is a vivid reminder of the climate of public discourse in the Philippines that it actually required courage to review favourably a scholarly book about the huge and ancient nation on the Philippines' very doorstep.

At the least, Cruz's review would surely have gladdened John Addis, who continued to be depressed and angry at what seemed to him a wilful lack of understanding in Whitehall and Washington of Chinese history and China's current motives. He had been Ambassador in Vientiane at a critical moment for Laos, watching sadly as the CIA's 'polarization' doctrine (which had been launched with President Eisenhower's blessing) destroyed Prince Souvanna's delicately balanced neutrality in order for his feudal people to be labelled as either Communists or non-Communists. (These were Lao and other tribes who mostly lived so remote from politics they had not even heard of Laos, let alone the United States. Without warning they suddenly found themselves herded off their land and into camps while bombs fell in a steady rain from B-52s on the archaeological splendour of the Plain of Jars.) As Ambassador, Addis had naturally known all about the CIA's backing of General Phoumi's faction, just as he knew about China's own policy of strict neutrality towards Laos. The Chinese were in little position to meddle in foreign adventures: it was as much as they could do to feed themselves, reconstruct, and contain the ideological ferment that Chairman Mao was unleashing.

As the Vietnam war escalated and engulfed neighbouring countries, Addis clearly found himself at odds with official British policy, which was basically one of abject support for the US position. In 1967 he was to write gloomily to his sister about his suspicion that he would never now be offered a 'better' post than Manila (meaning, of course, Beijing):

> I realize that my views on China and on Vietnam are not palatable in the Foreign Office. This has been made clear recently. I am not greatly concerned. I have a sense of duty, even of vocation, about the interests to be pursued and also about the time to speak out. I am set on a course, which I must follow, and which will continue to lead me on even if I do not get a new appointment after Manila . . .[13]

At the time of James Kirkup's visit in early 1966 another *Manila Times* columnist, Alfredo Roces (the future author of *Culture Shock! Philippines*), was expressing deep misgivings about the way the Vietnam war was beginning to spill over into the Philippines in the form of battle-weary and often traumatized GIs on R & R rampaging through Manila, Olongapo and San Fernando. He then began to wonder if the war might not begin to involve the Philippines at a more sinister level. He asked exactly what Marcos's election portended where the country's relations with the United States were concerned: precisely the question that was on many intelligent Filipinos' minds, only most lacked the courage or opportunity to put it into print:

> Just what is the significance of the Marcos administration in Philippine–US relations? The first obvious point is that the Philippines under Marcos will shift to the right, bound and committed deeper towards the American sphere of influence . . . To our mind the indications that the Marcos administration will lean over backwards towards pro-Americanism are his choice of men, the fact that the sugar bloc is most vulnerable to US pressure, his statements of military commitment to Vietnam, and, lastly, the persistent shadow of the CIA – in Mindanao during the critical period of election tallying, and at the inauguration, according to our sources. There is also the presence (for the inauguration) of US Vice-President Humphrey, and the [de facto] conversion of Manila and other areas into a rest centre for the American GIs fighting in Vietnam . . .[14]

Whatever the start of the Marcos era signified politically, it undoubtedly marked the creation of some potent public fantasies. If Ferdinand took office in the guise of a populist reformer, Imelda Marcos took up residence in Malacañang with cries of horror at the state of the place, a reaction that is almost *de rigueur* for the wives of heads of state the world over. It is at once a comment on their predecessor's atrocious lack of taste and on the run-down nature of his regime. It serves notice that things are going to change, that fresh blood is about to flow in the sclerotic arteries of government, that things will even *look* new. Accordingly, the state palace has to set a tone and image of rejuvenation. Where Imelda was concerned, it was not just the old garage in which she had lived as a child on nearby General Solano Street that would have to go. Reminders of the Philippines' own unhappy past equally needed purging from Malacañang. The sombre décor and dreary state rooms were grim enough; far worse was the whole pervasive Third World aura of cockroach bait behind potted palms, door handles with one screw-hole jammed with matchsticks, lights that wouldn't work when it rained and grinning footmen crouching to stuff paper wedges under wobbling table-legs during state receptions.

Her immediate inspiration was probably Lady Bird Johnson, who had had her own ideas of what to do with the deserted set of Camelot she had inherited from the Kennedys. Yet Jackie Kennedy's own famous redecoration of the White House was undoubtedly a greater influence on her for its ethos. The *idea* of a Palace was what intrigued Imelda: part national showcase (Filipino craftsmanship and Filipino materials) in the carpet-and-chandelier areas to be seen by the world's dignitaries, and part fantasy land in the private zones. The Marcoses' version of The House Beautiful was every bit as metaphorical as Bunyan's in *Pilgrim's Progress*, though to somewhat different effect. Imelda took her cue from her husband:

As the President said, a government is like building a house. And he told me he would build the structure, I was to take care of the refinements, the trimmings, the details – like curtains, for instance. What kind of people will live in the house? Cultured people, good people. So then the President said: 'That is the house I would like to put up.'[15]

In at least one respect she was unerring. She singled out a national characteristic that has always dogged the Philippines but was so obvious almost nobody ever noticed it: the habit of thinking small and building temporarily. This was no doubt partly the re-action to constant termites and regular typhoons of a predominantly rural people constructing in wood. She ascribed it to her country having been colonized and subjected to so many changing regimes and wars (one has to remember it was still barely twenty years after Manila's almost complete destruction in 1945). The effect on the people of this constant unsettling, she said, was dispiriting,

so much so that Filipinos say: So what? Tomorrow maybe this house will not be mine because some foreigner will come to these shores and take it. There's no incentive, especially in the barrios.

There they say: *Para que?* What for? So what? It's a total attitude of 'It won't be there tomorrow so why bother?'.[16]

To have shown this level of awareness of how people in the *barrios* thought was most unusual then for a Filipina First Lady, a testament to all that unprecedented campaigning out in the sticks. It was also at least partly the impetus behind her grand building projects (concert halls, hospitals, a university, convention centres, palaces) that characterized her incumbency and which became derided as mere pathological symptoms of her 'Edifice complex'.*

The Marcoses began their first term of office in an amazing burst of energy and with long lists of ambitious projects. One says 'their' advisedly. Although at this stage there was no doubt as to who was the President, Imelda's role was from the first portioned out as having complementary status to his. She had already drawn up a checklist of her own social projects. Among those which began to take shape were nutrition schemes, self-help projects, a nationwide home garden movement for using waste ground to grow vegetables, and an Integrated Social Welfare Programme which included the building of five welfare villages. Several of these replaced an appalling Manila sub-division called Welfareville which was a national disgrace. This was where many of the country's handicapped, orphans, delinquents, mentally ill and otherwise alienated and deprived citizens were herded in subhuman conditions. Voteless, they had never been on any politician's list of priorities. On new sites, often in the countryside surrounding the city, Imelda built brand-new institutions: a training school for delinquent boys, the Marillac Home for abused girls, 'Golden Acres' for the elderly. These were proper, even worthy, ventures for a First Lady; nor was it hard to see why someone with an artistic bent like hers might also have begun various civic beautification schemes. But ordinary people began to shed some of their scepticism when she tackled an unphotogenic oubliette like the mental hospital in Mandaluyong. The newspaper story about the charred and chained madwoman which had so upset John

---

* The pun on 'Oedipus' is far clearer in Filipino pronunciation, with 'p' for 'f'.

Addis faithfully reflected a mediaeval casualness on the part of the health authorities towards the mentally ill.

It must have taken courage for the erstwhile Rose of Tacloban not only to do something about the problem, but to visit the place in person – which she did, looking her usual fragrant self and wearing a restrained polka-dotted suit and sensible shoes.

> What she saw was repulsive . . . The inhuman conditions at the mental hospital were a disgrace, reminiscent of slave labour camps. The patients were neglected and abandoned. Many of them were emaciated and disease-ridden. Most were in some degree of nakedness.
>
> Most of the pavilions were filthy. The stench was unbearable. The patients were crowded into the pavilions like animals herded into a corral and left to endure the wretched conditions. Most of the wards did not have beds. The sick slept on the cold bare floor. Many of them became chronic tubercular patients . . . There were not enough knives and forks. Many ate like animals from rusty pails . . .[17]

The booklet from which this description comes notes that Mrs Marcos made 'her own private investigations into the ineptitude and maladministration of the hospital officials, and took action immediately'. There is a hint here of draconian measures being carried out behind the scenes. But while it was easy to sack and discipline individuals, it was another matter to change a culture's ingrained attitudes and habits. Still, such social projects were greatly to her credit. As to how zealously they were maintained is another issue, but many of them survive to this day although her connection with them is scrupulously suppressed. Senators' wives and actresses pitching for a political career drop by Boys Town and the home for the aged for their photo-op appearances, or go out to Muntinlupa to visit Marillac Hills, nowadays described as 'the Department of Social Welfare and Development's centre for abused children'; but with never a mention of Imelda Marcos. They will even pay a call on the mental hospital in Mandaluyong, these days quite salubrious and progressive, but nobody speaks of her long-overdue act of rescue that brought it into the twentieth century. Official discredit dares leave no Brownie points.

While Imelda was busy being motherly (as she put it), Ferdinand was occupied with the country's infrastructure, organizing schemes for building roads, schools, hospitals, waterworks and the like, as well as drafting policies such as a new labour code and agricultural reforms. In his *Manila Times* article Alfredo Roces had cited Marcos's 'choice of men' as evidence of his right-wing pro-Americanism. This may have been true, but it was also a fact that a reformer like Ferdinand had very little option when it came to picking a Cabinet. He didn't want *trapo** types – the usual bench-warmers fatly rewarded for doing nothing. He needed technocrats, and the best young Filipino technocrats mostly had degrees from American universities. A compromise had also to be reached with older and respected figures whose names would lend credibility. This is how the historian O. D. Corpuz described the circumstances surrounding the formation of Marcos's first Cabinet:

> During the 1964–5 campaign I worked with my group, Rafael Salas, Johnny Ponce [Enrile] and myself – they were my juniors at Harvard – on top strategy. That's to say, we were working on what Marcos's broad campaign should be rather than on the political relationships between us all as individuals. After the Election, when we'd all been successful, the first chance we had to meet we decided to make one last contribution and form his Cabinet for him. So we did, nominating only people we knew to be first-rate and spotless: [Carlos P.] Romulo, [Alfonso] Calalang, Maitan [Clemente Gatmaitan, Sr.] etc. They were all appointed. We also nominated ourselves (except for Salas) as under-secre-taries – you know, as a way of keeping in touch without onerous duties. For example, I chose to be Under-Secretary of Education. Fine; except that we ought to have anticipated that because our chosen Cabinet members were mostly elderly, they were sooner or later going to retire or pass on and we ourselves would be stepping up into their posts as they left the scene . . .[18]

---

* A formulation that felicitously combines the first few letters of 'tradi-tional *politician*' to make the Spanish word for 'rag', which has the same overtones as the English concept of 'dirty linen'. The epithet suggests a pri-vate army, sundry mistresses, ill-gotten gains and dubious connections.

This was exactly what happened, and 'O. D.' duly became Marcos's Education Minister, a post he held twice (with a resignation in the middle) until 1983 when he finally left to write *The Roots of the Filipino Nation*.

Corpuz's group was not the only 'think-tank' to provide intellectual backing for Marcos's presidency. In today's climate of opinion, when the tendency is to dismiss him as simply one more of the world's corrupt dictators, it is important to remember that from the beginning he had attracted honourable and intelligent people. He unquestionably did make foolish and scoundrelly appointments in his time, yet it remains one of the sadder aspects of his regime that right until the end he had some of the most talented and qualified people in the country working for him. Back in 1966, such 'think-tank' members were his core strategists. One such loose association of journalists, academics and artists was the Medis Group (named after the Medis building in Intramuros, where it met). This had started in 1964, when Ferdinand was still Senate President, with the express purpose of writing speeches for him and doing propaganda work for the forthcoming National Convention. The Group's leader was Blas Ople (later to become Marcos's best-known Labour Secretary and a senator). Other members included the journalist Adrian Cristobal, Amado Gat Insiong (another future Labour Secretary), Rony V. Diaz (today Senator Ople's chief-of-staff) and the noted artist 'Malang' (Mauro Malang Santos). 'I think it was Ople's idea. Macapagal was a great disappointment and Marcos was the only possible choice then. Can you imagine a President announcing "I am the best qualified intellectually for the Presidency"? That was Macapagal's line. He'd easily beaten [his predecessor, President] Garcia, but he was still useless. The Group folded in 1969, I think, when our Government jobs became too demanding. Eventually everyone in the Group got appointed.'[19] This also explains how the steady stream of publications put out under Marcos's name – of which he personally wrote scarcely a word – were often neither stupid nor badly written. In particular, those which provided a rationale for his declaration of martial law were argued by professional journalists like Adrian Cristobal and Florentino Dauz. Even today, well after the awful denouement, their polemics make plausible cases and fairly interesting reading, surviving as rather more than trash propaganda.

In early 1966 Marcos appointed Rafael Salas as Chairman of the Rice and Corn Producers' Council, briefed to make the country self-sufficient in basic grains. The new 'miracle' high-yield varieties of rice were just becoming available from IRRI, the International Rice Research Institute at Los Baños, outside Manila. Bypassing regional offices and using direct governmental intervention, Salas imposed technocratic methods that did in fact bring about self-sufficiency by the 1970s. It was an impressive turnaround. Simultaneously, Marcos introduced the most incisive measure towards general land reform yet enacted.[20] This specifically concerned only rice and corn farmers. 'Critics said it was too limited, but actually it was a wise move because such land is the most heavily tenanted of all agricultural land. Marcos was highly enthusiastic about the scheme, personally involved. His original idea had been to let farmers pay a nominal rent for 15 years, and after that the land would revert to them. But it didn't happen.'[21]

It didn't happen partly because of difficulties with the Land Bank that had been set up expressly for the purpose, but mostly because Marcos came up against a predictable and perennial problem. Many of the Philippines' most powerful oligarchs were themselves landowners and they didn't want their estates sequestered, parcelled up and given away to their tenants, not even with compensation. Marcos, of course, was not himself from a landowning background – neither in a family nor in a regional sense – and it may be he simply miscalculated the degree of opposition his policies would arouse. If so, he was naive, especially since the landowners employed the very same legal delaying tactics of which he himself was such a master. But there was another aspect to it, which in the long run probably proved more dangerous to him than if he had reneged on his promises for agrarian reform altogether. For, once having started so radically and in such a blaze of publicity, he aroused greater hopes in the country's peasants than he or anyone else could possibly have fulfilled. This was true above all in the so-called 'Rice Bowl' of Central Luzon: the very territory which, since the days of the Huks, was the most radicalized of the entire archipelago. It was to backfire badly on him, as he was to discover as the sixties wore on and the time of his re-election campaign approached. By then the increasingly vociferous opposition of the student and intellectual left, while undoubtedly influenced by similar movements throughout Europe and the United States protesting against the Vietnam war, in the Philippines also had roots in the discontent of small farmers and peasants in Central Luzon. It was an indication of the extent to which the Maoist theory of China's Cultural Revolution had caught the imagination of the youth of other Asian countries.

Even so, a good deal of the reforming legislation that Marcos enacted as President is on the books to this day, much of it still ahead of its time (given the context) and remarkably enlightened. The Labour Code,[22] authored principally by Blas Ople, is not only still in force (with some minor amendments) but was considered by the UN's International Labour Organization as a model for the developing world. Likewise the 1975 laws governing fisheries[23] remain progressive and sensible. This is one of the reasons why ageing technocrats often look back to the Marcos administration with a wistful mixture of pride and sadness. Not only had there been so much promise, but a great deal was actually achieved. That other things collapsed in scandal and disarray, eclipsing the achievements, was a tragedy of a kind and probably accounts for much of the anger still directed at Marcos's memory. The feeling is that had he not become weakened by moral blindness and illness, he could have been the greatest President the Philippines ever had.

> Marcos cared deeply for the public interest. He had a real streak of idealism in him. He built the physical structure of our present development, there's no doubt about that. All the highways, bridges and electrification were his. In 1965 only ten percent of the Philippines had electricity. By 1986 eighty-five percent did. Lenin himself would have been proud of such an achievement. And it was all done at a time when we had very much less money than is available now.[24]

In September 1966 Ferdinand and Imelda, the developing world's dynamic duo, flew to Washington for a state visit to the court of Lyndon Baines Johnson. According to Beatriz Francia, Ferdinand had put his wife through a stiff preparatory course before they left, making her read 'the biographies of several key presidents, and especially of Johnson himself'.[25] From the inestimable tedium of this exercise she had gleaned two useful facts: LBJ's favourite brand of scent and his fondness for the colour yellow. The research paid off. At their first White House dinner she wore a brilliant Texas-yellow *terno* (the formal Filipino dress with stiff, high sleeves) and periodically fanned herself so that her perfume wafted enticingly across the American President's plate. No doubt a drudge in the lower echelons of the White House's protocol corps had been doing similar research and discovered that she had a notoriously sweet tooth, for lo! on the menu card was a special dessert named 'Imelda'. In any case her feminine wiles worked only too well. After dinner LBJ had several dances with her, and then several more. Other revellers affected not to notice the huge Texan hands straying intimately over the yellow *terno*'s salient features. When Ferdinand drifted by within earshot, Imelda said to him in Tagalog over LBJ's shoulder: 'I'm being groped by this guy, darling,' to which her husband replied, also in Tagalog, 'Ignore it, Meldy. It's in a good cause.'[26] Life at the top.

The visit was a dazzling success. Its high point came when Ferdinand addressed a joint session of Congress in a speech brilliantly crafted to mesh with the Spence version of himself as war hero, which his audience would already have known. He gave a dramatic and solemn account of the death of an American GI just before the Fall of Bataan. 'Yes, my American comrade died in my arms. We were surrounded and we had to break out. He fell and, as he tried to crawl to safety, I returned to him to fall at his side – Filipino and American blood commingling in Philippine soil.'[27] *Commingling?* To judge from the twenty-two occasions when he was obliged to stop for spontaneous applause, this terrible hokum went straight to Congress's collective heart. There was not a dry eye in the house. Up in the gallery Imelda was weeping too and, when she was spotted, was herself given a three-minute standing ovation. She went on to wow New York, singing 'Strangers in the Night' to Mayor John Lindsay in Manhattan, going to the Met in a white gown and diamond tiara with Lady Bird Johnson and being assured by Senator Jacob Javits that she had taken New York by storm. A Washington newspaper described Mrs Marcos as 'a blessing not only to her country but to the world'.

Her husband, meanwhile, was doing equally well with a sheaf of speeches, addressing the National Press Club in Washington, the

Philippine–American Chamber of Commerce in New York and the UN General Assembly. To read them now, more than thirty years later, is to be stunned by the ironies they contain. The sermonesque tone of statespeople's speeches is in any case depressing since it irresistibly suggests to the global public that our lives are in the hands of people whose thought processes are probably every bit as banal as their self-expression. Yet often behind the ritual sententiousness are statements of ironic clarity. As Ferdinand told the National Press Club:

> . . . if democratic institutions cannot grow in the soil of under-development, then the Americans and the Vietnamese are fighting and dying for a hollow illusion in South Vietnam – in effect, an unattainable dream for the developing nations in Asia, Africa and Latin America. Then Americans are not fighting in Vietnam to keep open the option for liberty of the Vietnamese people, but for a mirage of their own making.[28]

The anti-Communist stance of his own nation, he went on to explain, was rooted in its history; though where recent history was concerned he was evidently the victim of a discretionary attack of amnesia. The Colonel Lansdales of the world of *realpolitik* might never have existed:

> The Philippines is the first developing country in the whole world, to the best of my knowledge, that has overcome a full-fledged Communist rebellion without the aid of a single foreign soldier . . .[29]

Vietnam, of course, was a major topic in all his speeches. Curiously, the one address he gave that may have most accurately reflected his own personal views was that to the Chamber of Commerce. Perhaps because it was aimed at businessmen it was the least bombastic, and he was more pungent than he had yet been about the US presence in Vietnam:

> But to remain the leader nation of the Free World, the United States has neither the right nor the duty to maintain in Vietnam *or anywhere else* the posture of imperialist domination and control.

The last thing Americans should do is to give any impression that
they are in Vietnam to pick up the fallen sceptre of French imperialism. They should make it absolutely crystal clear that they are
in South Vietnam only to help the people defend their freedom,
and that they will stay there only so long as their presence is
needed *and wanted*. Only in this way can Americans avoid the
odium that attaches to the conduct of any state that attempts to
pursue at this late day the ancient goals of imperialism under a
neo-colonialist disguise.[30]

Given the number of fellow Asians in his audience, this was
judiciously pitched. The Filipinos among them would certainly
have picked up on the veiled hint that the Americans might not
necessarily be wanted in places they had unilaterally decided were
front-line zones in their global crusade. Unlike his other speeches,
this revealed a Marcos suffering post-operatively, as it were, from
some heroic feat of plastic surgery that had provided him with two
faces: that of America's Boy and that of the Asian Nationalist. He
had already succumbed before the state visit to Johnson's heavy
insistence and had reluctantly been obliged to send a Filipino battalion to Vietnam. Unlike the one that went to Korea, however, it
was (at least nominally) non-combatant. The Philcag (Philippine
Civic Action Group) was a unit of a mere 2,000 men, mostly engineers. It was rumoured that LBJ had been extremely disappointed
and put out by Marcos's refusal to send a fighting force, and
Ferdinand must have needed to call on his considerable resources
of plausible cajolery to resist the Texan's pressure. What better way
was there, LBJ had wanted to know, of showing that the Filipinos'
foxhole spirit – so movingly described by Marcos to Congress –
was still flourishing, than by sending troops to new foxholes to
fight in the crusade with their good American buddies? But the
Philippine President had his domestic situation to consider. Grand
verbal gestures in the UN General Assembly were all very well;
back home it would have been political suicide for him after all the
nationalist rhetoric of his election campaign to have sent Filipinos
abroad to help fight Uncle Sam's battles for him elsewhere in Asia.
So he had held out for the Philcag engineers and LBJ had to be content with fondling his wife at a White House function. Marcos had
told Johnson that it would be far more efficient if the Philippines

sent money rather than men to Vietnam. Years later, Imelda added a footnote to this:

> After the fall of Vietnam [Soviet Premier, Leonid] Brezhnev told me that if Ferdinand had sent a combat group to Vietnam as Johnson demanded it would have drawn us into total disaster. 'As long as Marcos is President, we will never invade the Philippines!' Brezhnev said . . . Then Pham Van Dong [Hanoi's Prime Minister] came here on his first visit abroad. I asked him, 'Why did you choose the Philippines for your first mission?' And he said, 'Because we were so impressed by your husband offering to send *money* to Vietnam rather than combat troops.'[31]

In any case the whole production of a weeping Congress and a President Johnson greeting Marcos as a war hero took place on a level of discourse that was pure fantasy. The sheer absurdity of the public posturing became evident years later. Sterling Seagrave, who had access to the relevant CIA documents, put it simply: 'President Johnson knew that the Marcos war record was a total sham, but endorsed it publicly to gain support for his Vietnam policy.'[32]

Overall, the trip was a huge success. Ferdinand had managed to talk LBJ into shortening the US lease on its Philippine bases from ninety-nine to twenty-five years, which greatly helped to appease his opponents at home. The quid pro quo was that the 'Philcag' would be replaced by five new construction battalions for Vietnam, to equip which the US would pay $20 million. LBJ also leaned on the World Bank to open new lines of credit to Manila. Some knowing glances were exchanged when the Philippine Finance Secretary, Eduardo Romualdez (who happened to be Imelda's cousin) announced that the Philippines was looking forward to receiving $125 million. Meanwhile, quieter things were afoot as more and more agreements were signed for the training of Filipino police as well as army officers at military schools like Fort Bragg and Fort Benning in the United States. Counter-insurgency, an issue never far from the minds of post-war Philippine presidents and their American advisers, was predicted to be a growth industry back in the archipelago's expanding cities and still-extensive jungles. Also included was the deployment of Filipino CIA and combat personnel in Vietnam, most of whom had been trained in the Huk-killing fields of Central Luzon and were skilled in the use of advanced interrogation techniques. The man who did most to institute these methods was Frank Walton, who had already retrained the police in South Vietnam for a counter-insurgency role and who afterwards went on to reorganize the Shah of Iran's secret police, SAVAK. Little of these dark manoeuvres showed on the surface; yet there were '[a]s many as ten thousand counter-insurgency jobs in Indochina . . . under Walton's guidance'.[33]

Marcos's first term of office poses several linked questions, none of which can be answered definitively – or rather, asking them yields nothing but conflicting opinions. The questions are: What *really* were his intentions when he became President? Was the necessary taint, without which he could never have come to power, decisively outweighed by his reformist, even patriotic, intentions for his country? In which case, precisely when did things begin to go wrong? Or, conversely, had he always considered the presidency as nothing more than an Ali Baba's cave of loot to be cleaned out as efficiently as possible – which is what everyone asserted after 1986?

Many thoughtful people who had known and worked with him from the beginning of the 'think-tank' era when he was Senate President remain to this day convinced that his intentions began by being fairly honourable. He made it quite clear on numerous occasions, both public and private, that he wanted to be remembered as a great President, even the greatest of all – as the man who had finally turned around the Philippines' chronic social and economic stagnation. 'Marcos did have a vision,' Senator Ople confirmed. 'He was going to transform the Philippines into a modern state by industrialization. He was much agitated by the backwardness of the country regions. As an Ilocano, he was always jealous of the Tagalog regions, which were richer. He was extremely proud of the history of the Ilocos. He knew that in Manila the Tagalogs looked down on Ilocanos and he felt socially inferior.'[34]

It is no doubt a fantasy shared by most incoming heads of state, that of radically transforming their country into a New Jerusalem of sweetness and light and plenty. History is littered with the empty names of these wishful endeavours which lie like last year's cartridge cases around a huntsman's abandoned hide. Lion

Kingdoms, Great Republics, New Deals, Thousand-Year Reichs, Great Societies and – Ferdinand's own – the New Society: ceaselessly trodden down by their successors armed with the same powerful ambition and fresh hopes. These infantile fantasies of personal greatness are for the most part grotesquely at variance with the true wishes of electorates, who would happily settle for nothing more grandiose than affordable food, decent health and education services, telephones that worked and policemen who didn't moonlight as members of kidnapping syndicates. Be that as it may, it is safe to assume that the triumphant reception Lyndon Johnson painstakingly laid on for the Marcoses in Washington would have fired both Presidents with appropriate dreams of greatness.

Where Imelda was concerned, it must have seemed there was now nothing she might not dare. What must it have been like for the ex-Rose of Tacloban, at the age of thirty-seven, to be escorted to the opera by the wife of the President of the United States and to be given a standing ovation by Congress? One effect would surely have been to endow her own fantasies with the one missing ingredient: omnipotence. Mrs Francia renders down her aunt's character with a succinct accuracy: 'The world Imelda inhabited was a composite of the Visayan [Leyte] and Hispanic ways of life: a world of feasting and a dream of aristocratic grandeur.'[35] Anyone who had taken New York and Washington by storm, and had been fondled by the American President into the bargain, had nothing to fear at home. Part of her, at least, was free to play the greedy queen to the point of surfeit.

Her husband must have been left with more complex residues. On the one hand he, too, had had the treatment. But although it was calculated to turn anyone's head a little, he was enough the professional politician to know that these accolades were both discretionary and temporary. He did not need to be a student of history to grasp the concept of expediency. At the same time President Johnson, whose own dreams of social reform had not yet been broken by the sheer economic drain of the war in Vietnam, would have been lyrical – even piously so – about his 'all-out war on poverty and hunger' at home. LBJ's vision of a Great Society was still undented. In 1966 he was able to boast about 'the American economic miracle' (as he did in his economic report to

Congress of that year) and be backed up by men like Sargent Shriver, Director of the Office of Economic Opportunity, who stated reassuringly: 'Our country is big enough to support a war in Vietnam and a successful war on poverty at home.'[36] This was the sort of hubris that seldom goes unpunished, and in due course the distant mirage of Johnson's Great Society thinned and disappeared. But in late 1966 Ferdinand would have flown back to Manila fired by LBJ's ambition to wage war on poverty and hunger, as well as by the American President's various earnests of aid and support.

On another level, though, it may not be fanciful to imagine that despite the triumph, there would have been an aspect of Ferdinand that responded to LBJ with an increased passivity. Like all Filipinos of his generation, he had grown up with a self-image of submissiveness and deference where Americans were concerned. He might have gone to Washington as the President of the Philippines, but he knew he was massively outranked by this Texan who also physically towered over him. LBJ was notorious for using his size and macho aura to induce feelings of inferiority in other men. The unwary who were invited to spend informal time with the President often found themselves firmly invited to swim with him, only discovering too late that they were expected to swim naked, as he did. The reason for this became all too monstrously apparent as the President stripped off, leaving his shrinking guests to face a hopeless dilemma. Either they risked mocking remarks about how only 'pansies' or 'pantywaists' wore swimming trunks, or they braved the tape-measure stare of those shrewdly dismissive eyes. One trusts that Ferdinand was never subjected to this ordeal; for although he himself cultivated a macho image (he had an athletic, even beautiful body in those days, beside which the naked LBJ would have looked like an ogre) and wore Brut aftershave into the bargain, the fact was he was in no position to indulge in locker-room competitiveness.

But of course there were other ways than mere physical dominance for LBJ to ensure that Marcos knew exactly where he stood. The Filipino had, after all, grown up with the American missionaries' description of his people as 'little brown brothers' inherent in, and defining, the entire relationship between the two countries. The situation where an American President could with impunity run his hands over a Filipino President's wife in public was simply a logical extension of this relationship. It spoke well of the Marcoses – and, indeed, of the Filipino character – that they could make a joke of it in their own language right under LBJ's nose. 'Never mind – it's in a good cause' is the Asian pragmatism that refuses to waste energy by taking offence. (After all, Ferdinand had his revenge. LBJ was merely the first of four American Presidents he saw come and go while he held unbroken office.) He must have felt far more compromised by the way in which Johnson had made such enormous play with the story of his heroic war exploits. An actor himself, like all politicians, he would have perceived that LBJ also knew it was blarney, yet at the same time a part of him must have come to believe it was true. The image had been over twenty years in the making; it had been written down for posterity in Spence's book; a presidential campaign had been successfully fought on the basis of its constant repetition. In some sense the story had actually *happened*. Now this account had been publicly endorsed by the American President. (It went on being believed almost to the end by Ronald Reagan. The wonderful irony is that Reagan himself was afflicted by an exactly similar inability to separate fantasy from actuality in his own stories of the Second World War. It was well known that Reagan had never left the United States during the war; yet on 29 November 1983 he told the Israeli Prime Minister Yitzhak Shamir that he had been given the task of filming the Nazi death camps for the US Signal Corps. The White House tied itself into semantic knots trying to wriggle out of this awesome gaffe.[37] Marcos was by no means alone in being saddled with a mythic past.) And yet . . . at any time they chose, the Americans could pull the rug out from under him. Not merely by exposing his war record, of course; that would be deeply embarrassing but not necessarily fatal. But it was a perpetual reminder of all those files buried away on the other side of the Pacific: OSS, CIA, CIC. They would contain some very detailed information about the past, about deals done and corners cut.

So he returned to Manila both glowing with triumph and freshly convinced that whatever else he wanted to do with his presidency, he needed to stay on the right side of Washington. At the very least he wanted to retain American support so that he could win a second term of office. If we allow Marcos his ideals, then, at what point did things begin to go wrong? Those who assert that even his fancy to go down in history as a great President had always taken second place to ordinary greed would point to the documents which Cory Aquino's PCGG (Presidential Commission on Good Government) agents confiscated from the Marcoses' private quarters in Malacañang after they had fled in 1986. These revealed they had both begun building up dollar accounts abroad under the names 'William Saunders' and 'Jane Ryan' as early as 1967. There were certainly Swiss accounts by 1968, with cash deposits of sums like $1.5m not unusual. So where was all this cash coming from that needed constant siphoning off abroad like a safety valve relieving pressure? One thinks all the time of that claim of Mrs Marcos's: 'By 1949 [he] already had 4,000 tons of gold. Then in 1957 with the Bretton Woods Agreement, the US came off the gold standard and we bought another 3,000 tons at $35 per ounce. So at a time when the world total of gold was 17,000 tons, we had 7,000 of them.'[38] What does this mean? Is it true, or is it 'true'? For one thing, it is plainly incorrect in certain details. The Bretton Woods Agreement was reached after a conference in 1944 at which the International Monetary Fund was established. But does this mistake of historical fact suggest the other figures are wrong? Maybe this story has the same status as that of Ferdinand's war as he related it to Hartzell Spence. Perhaps it is designed to reduce the hearer either to utter credulity or to utter disbelief. Any further investigation is discouraged by a smokescreen of the improbable. (Even the current Central Bank Governor talks of 1,231 tons of 'missing Marcos gold'.)

The corruption of the Marcos presidency was being acknowledged within two years of Ferdinand's taking office. Even a foreign diplomat like John Addis commented on it, although with his usual weary sharpness he did put it into context:

I dined with the Macapagals on Thursday, the first time since he ceased to be President. They have built an enormous house overlooking a golf-course in the grandest area – with 'her money' of course. She was wearing large diamonds in her ears and in a ring, and even her daughter, much prettier now, had great pearls set in diamonds. And his administration was much less corrupt than the previous and present ones.[39]

Should the implications of all this invalidate any further claims for a Marcos idealism? The diary Ferdinand kept might be expected to throw some light on his true motivation, but unfortunately its precise standing remains a vexed problem. By his own family's account he wrote this more frequently than John Addis did his letters home. His son said he would usually write it in the evenings after dinner, and could often be heard chuckling evilly. When asked what he was laughing about, the President would say only that he was setting the record straight in a way that would one day bring extreme discomfort to his enemies (or words to that effect). He handwrote it, mostly on loose sheets of Palace stationery which built up into a substantial collection of boxes containing many thousands of pages. He often told his family and close aides that this diary was to be his true legacy: a blow-by-blow account of political realities that would form the centrepiece of the archive he would bequeath the nation. Accordingly, it was very precious to him, which makes it all the more surprising that when he left in a hurry for Hawaii in 1986 some of the boxes were reportedly abandoned and found only later in a dark corner of Malacañang. So far as one can tell, these fell into the hands of the PCGG. Meanwhile, US Customs impounded some, if not all, of the documents the Marcos family took with them into exile; but they must not have returned the diary since according to Bong Bong Marcos it has vanished and the family would dearly like it back. There is a version on CD-Rom which can be obtained with some difficulty, but the text is highly corrupt and has substantial gaps. (This may, however, be down to incompatibility with the Unix operating system that was apparently used for the huge archive.) In the first issue of *Smart File*, Ricardo Manapat (the author of the scholarly exposé of Marcos's 'crony capitalism', *Some Are Smarter Than Others*) gave an account that suggested he had the entire work, which started on 31 December 1969, and was intending to publish it in instalments in each issue of *Smart File*. What is more, he quoted 'a foreign diplomat' who was shown the diaries in Hawaii and who commented favourably on Marcos's industriousness. Thus one is left with a clear impression that the entire text does exist. Given Mr Manapat's friendly connections with the National Intelligence Co-ordinating Agency, it seems highly likely that the Marcos diaries – assuming they are genuine – will have been sanitized along the way by both

Americans and Filipinos so that anything truly embarrassing or revelatory remains suppressed.

There is an outside possibility that what has been suppressed included entries that showed Ferdinand's intentions to have been entirely honourable from start to finish. There is no question that the Manichaean dynamics of the 1986 'revolution' demanded that the Marcoses should be allowed not a single redeeming feature, and it is conceivable (though not very likely) that the unedited diaries would have revealed a version of Ferdinand that flatly contradicted the image of a thieving and criminal dictator which so suited people's purposes. As they stand, they convey an impression of someone with a watchful eye on posterity's gaze: a man giving himself some careful dictation as he had once given it to Hartzell Spence. There are many entries whose assertions are later flatly contradicted by evidence that turned up in the wake of 1986 – for example, those dealing with the Dovie Beams affair which we shall come to shortly. Apart from that, one takes the liberty to doubt the tone of such self-conscious loftiness as can be found as early as the second entry:

> Yesterday I finally transferred all of my worldly possessions to the Filipino people through the Ferdinand E. Marcos Foundation. I have been planning this for many years but I felt that the beginning of my second term was the most propitious time. This was a decision arrived at after a long deliberation and was not the result of pique, anger, despair or emotions. Nor is it due to a sense of guilt because some of the funds came from the Yamashita treasure. Nor is it just a political stunt. And it seems a burden has been lifted from my shoulders. The surprising thing is that the reaction of people seems to be of no consequence to me. It was a noble act waiting to be done. I feel I am above all the pettiness of men and I look down on them with some contempt but with a counter-balance of understanding.[40]

These are not the words or expressions of a man communing with a private diary ('I have been planning this for many years'), but an exercise in image-building. It does make one suspect that no matter what may eventually come to light in US archives, it is unlikely to show this man in a radically different light. On the other hand, it would undoubtedly furnish some extremely interesting detail from which to make informed deductions. As his son remarked, 'He knew *all* the gossip in town. At the dinner table the rest of us would be chattering away and he would be reading a book down at one end and now and again he'd look up when someone said something that caught his attention. Then he'd say, "For you it's gossip; but for me it's intelligence."'[41] The complete Filipino politician.

As the Marcoses' first term of office proceeded it was noticeable that Imelda began to acquire a considerable degree of autonomy. She, too, was the complete Filipina politician, not least in her remarkable ability to extract funds from people. This talent became abundantly apparent with her huge project to build the Cultural Centre of the Philippines on a stretch of newly reclaimed land on the foreshore of Manila Bay, not far from John Addis's residence. She had successfully wheedled some money out of LBJ during the state visit but it was nothing like enough and she cast her net wider, generally cajoling and twisting arms until a cascade of money was wrung out. 'I'm like Robin Hood,' she observed, 'I rob the rich. It's not difficult; you just have to smile. You can terrorize the rich, you see. The poor have nothing to lose.' Mrs 'King' Kasilag, her former music teacher, confirmed her extraordinary ability as a fund-raiser. 'Whenever she needed funding for a major project she would call her friends. Imelda Marcos was our professional beggar.'[42]

The Cultural Centre was in effect a large concert hall with a complex of administrative offices, built to a design by the Philippines' most distinguished architect of the day, Leandro ('Lindy') Locsin. It was roundly criticized from the pouring of the first concrete for being a white elephant, an absurdity, a grotesque waste of precious resources in a Third World nation where people were dying of hunger and disease. It was also accused of being a Western-style temple for Western-style arts, an accusation many felt was validated when classical concert pianists like Van Cliburn and ballet dancers like Dame Margot Fonteyn came to perform at Imelda's behest. Naturally, these charges carried a large component of self-righteousness and begged several questions. When exactly is a nation to be considered rich enough to be able to construct such a building without a blush? Are we really expected to believe that all Europe's and America's great public art buildings were only built once all their hungry had been fed and their sick tended? The clear implication is that the only aspect of a nation worth worrying about is that of the purely material. As Dr Kasilag suggested in an official report, the Philippines in those days was something of a cultural desert, at least in terms of public recognition of the arts:

> In the early sixties the whole issue of art and culture had not yet entered into the public mind . . . The issue of total human development . . . was an idea whose time had not yet come. The emergence of the Cultural Centre under the leadership of the First Lady focused public and national attention on the arts.[43]

Nothing if not artistic herself, Imelda recognized from the start the crudeness of the assumption that the sole yardstick of a nation was its economy and material development. She had been aware of her own cultural insecurity even as she observed the deep effect she had produced by singing well-loved songs to audiences who ranged from Irving Berlin in person to Kalinga tribespeople on her campaign trail. This conviction of hers that everyone needed culture as much as they needed cash because 'the heart, too, knows starvation' was not a pose, and was made plain in the speech she gave at her Cultural Centre's opening:

> Today, we too are people of courage and faith in the future. We are young and struggling to understand ourselves, trying to construct the nobler meaning of our race. Our greatest strength lies in being truly what we are; by nature and by grace, one people; by fortune and by fate, Filipinos. Yet so long as we know not ourselves, we face the dangers that face the very young; a lack of soul, a vagueness of values. It is the purpose of this Centre to enrich the minds and spirit of our people and to foster among other people a true understanding of the Filipino self . . .[44]

Mrs Marcos's CCP remains to this day one of Asia's best auditoriums, with excellent seating and acoustics, while its programmes are carefully even-handed in their choice of Western and Filipino music, theatre and dance. There are times when the CCP seems the most unarguable of her various legacies to the country, and it is one of which any of the world's other First Ladies might be proud.

This is not to say that while its building progressed and she was exploring the thrilling bounds of her omnipotence Imelda was not also acquiring a reputation for arrogance and grandeur. As a foreign diplomat and friend of the Locsin family, Ambassador John Addis was often required to attend various functions of hers. One week he wrote despondently to his sister: 'On Friday I have to fly down to Tacloban for 3 days' celebration of the First Lady's birthday. My heart sinks.'[45] Six days later he followed this more cheerfully: 'To my immense relief the trip to Tacloban to celebrate the First Lady's birthday was cancelled because of press criticism. Several times a day I have been calling out aloud: "How *glad* I am that I am not there!" Three days of festivities in the company of my diplomatic colleagues would have been a terrible ordeal.'[46] (Never let it be thought that an ambassador's life is one of untrammelled, gracious ease. 'Yesterday [with a stomach upset] I stood for 80 minutes while a bank was inaugurated and then after an hour more standing before dinner was faced with shrimp cocktail followed by poulet à la Kiev. How does one survive? . . .'[47])

However, John Addis was from the start an admirer of Imelda Marcos's Cultural Centre, whose progress he followed keenly. Shortly before its opening he attended a concert at the Meralco Theatre out in Quezon City and, although he couldn't guess its outcome, he did catch a strong whiff of anti-Marcos political rivalry that in Ferdinand's next term was to have dire consequences for many of the 'oligarch' families, and in particular the Lopezes:

The concert a week ago needs some background explanation. Don Eugenio Lopez, a dry saurian figure, is the head of one of the great sugar-growing families. He has extended into business and owns the Manila Electric Company [Meralco] which he has expanded from a lucrative utility company into a vast financial and holding company. He must be many times a millionaire but is said to be insatiable for ever more power. Earlier this year he opened his new office block, which has a complete theatre at the back. This is in deliberate rivalry to the First Lady's Cultural Centre, which is to open this week. For Don Eugenio's opening he had over some 'stars' from the Bolshoi Ballet, quite a good girl but three third-class men who could hardly move off the ground. To steal some of the First Lady's limelight, he had over, a week before her opening, Beverley [sic] Sills, the new star of the New York Opera. Her first night was by invitation only – a glittering audience and I know so many of them now. As I walked through the glass doors of the entrance, there was a 'Good evening, Mr Ambassador' behind me – the Locsins!, so we sat together. Beverley [sic] Sills is *superb*, one of the very great artists of all times . . .[48]

In these letters Addis does hint at various events which suggest that, somewhere in the political background, things were becoming seriously unglued after the initial honeymoon period of Marcos's first term of office. Both he and Marcos were approaching the end of a period: Addis as Ambassador in Manila and Ferdinand as a first-term President. Addis's comment that it was newspaper criticism that had caused the cancellation of Imelda's birthday celebrations in 1967 indicated a growing opposition to her extravagant style, if not a personal unpopularity (although she was indeed strongly disliked in many quarters). The reference to the Lopez family's Meralco Theatre having been planned as a deliberate rival to Imelda's CCP shows how things had changed since the days when she had so brilliantly wooed Fernando Lopez as Marcos's running-mate in the 1965 election. By now, her husband had come to view the Lopez family as the prime exemplars of the oligarchs he was determined to crush just as soon as he could get himself re-elected. When Blas Ople remarked that Marcos, as an Ilocano, had been made to feel socially inferior in Manila, he was simply voicing the widely held theory that revenge played a large part in the Marcoses' joint attack on the old-money upper class.

John Addis left Manila just at the moment when he sensed things were coming to a head. Unlike probably every other ambassador in Manila at the time, and always the China specialist, he had taken the trouble to go out personally into the wilds of Central Luzon to discover for himself the extent to which Mao Zedong Thought had infiltrated the growing leftist opposition to Marcos. Earlier in the year he had already alluded to 'demonstrations' at the University of the Philippines, and he plainly saw trouble in store for whoever won the election (he was betting on Marcos). Despite his close ties and one particular private affection he had built up, John Addis gives the impression of a certain weariness:

It will be a relief when the elections are over. The politicians are campaigning 20 and more hours a day. Money is being poured out in millions. It is like a wild party and everyone will wake up with a headache . . .[49]

Then, six days later:

Marcos has won, as I predicted. It is a good thing for the country to have broken at last out of the cycle of a 4-year Presidency which has done it so much harm. And Marcos is stronger and abler than anyone else. For us there is the advantage that we do not have to make a new set of friends again, as I had to when the Macapagals went, but can carry straight on. I am pleased. It would have broken the First Lady to have lost.[50]

Shortly after this, John Addis was posted home.

9

Villagers and élites

Mrs del Rosario's jeepney is held up by a knot of villagers standing on the track and staring down at Kansulay's river in its eroded bed a dozen feet below. The vehicle is long and battered and of the private kind with a little door at the back with 'The del Rosario Family' painted across it in red for the benefit of anyone mistaking it for public transport. It is full of sacks of this and that, plus some trussed hens panting on their sides. Mrs del Rosario is sitting up front next to the driver with a silk *panyo* pressed to her nose and mouth against the dust, for the windscreen has been hinged upwards like a visor to allow the wind of their passage to stream through.

'What's all this, then?' she says through the scarf.

'A death, Mam. Last night.'

'A death? Who?'

'Si Kulas, Mam. Obrero.'

'Who? Oh, that drunk? Well, what happened?'

'He was drunk, Mam. We think he fell over the edge here in the dark and hit his head on the rocks. Pasing found him at first light.'

'Didn't I tell you what would happen?' said Mrs del Rosario crossly. 'I don't know how many times I told him. It was a waste of breath, obviously. *These people.*' She added this to herself, much as Imelda Marcos was once overheard saying 'Poor fools' *sotto voce* in

Waray dialect when being cheered by a rapturous crowd. She began fanning herself where she sat with a heart-shaped fan woven from *nipa* fronds. Sensing a vibration from the jeep's rear she glanced up at the long mirror stretching above the windscreen and stencilled with the phrase 'God Bless Our Trip'. In it she caught sight of two inquisitive dark eyes atop a row of fingers (the tiny nails white with effort) as a child chinned itself to see inside. *'Totoy! Alis ka diyan!'* she barked and the jeep gave a jerk as the boy dropped off the rear step and scuttled back among the onlookers.

Her driver had got out and was also looking down at the bend in the stream. Around his neck he wore the Filipino driver's insignia, a flimsy little towel with 'Good Morning' printed at either end in English and Chinese. His name was Bert, and he was an expert in every known illegal fishing method as well as being a healer who was especially good with teeth. We all stared down but there was nothing to see other than the scatter of boulders at the water's edge and two of Kulas's sons looking for some money his fellow drinkers had said was in his pocket when he had staggered off. Kulas was yet one more victim in Kansulay of drink's steady attrition. Sometimes they fell and hit their heads; sometimes they inhaled their own vomit in their stupor; sometimes they died with their livers eaten to sponge by the worms and flukes which seemed to go with heavy *tuba* drinking, as though this naturally fermented pure palm sap had betrayed them by containing rather too much nature. We would miss Kulas because, when sober, he had been a kindly soul who could do a consummate imitation of a cat-fight that would set the village dogs barking for hours.

Born, bred, married and dead in the village he had never left, he now feels to have been only the latest in a long chain of Kulas incarnations stretching back to pre-Hispanic days to the groups of early settlers who left their fire-blackened pottery beside this same river. The country poet Macario Pineda, who died in 1950, has a verse in his *Talambuhay ng Aming Nayon* ('Biography of our Village') that places all the remaining Kansulays of the world at the still centre of these immemorial processes. The quiet internal rhythms of the Tagalog exhale the deep reassurance of such continuity. The 'we' does not include the reader:

Sa silangan daw ay kabuhayan . . .
sa kanluran daw ay kamatayan . . .
at sa pagitan nito ang aming nayon.
Dito kami ipinanganak,
dito kami nabubuhay,
dito kami mamamatay . . .
at dito kami muling mabubuhay.

They say life is eastward
and death is westward
and our village lies in between.
Here we were born,
here we live,
here we will die –
and here we will live once again.

'Bert!' calls Mrs del Rosario, fanning herself with petulant vigour. Her driver nods briefly at the crinkled water as it glints its way seaward, then climbs back behind the wheel. The crowd edges aside to let the jeep jolt away up the track in a blare of carbon fumes.

Mrs del Rosario is not going far. For vehicles, the track ends a few hundred yards away where a raw earth bank carved by the bulldozers twelve years ago has slumped, blocking it with soil and boulders and several trees growing at odd angles, their roots half exposed. This matters not at all to Mrs del Rosario, since fortunately her land is not affected, lying as it does on the near side of the blockage. If today she appears sorely tried it is probably because she has been obliged to come slumming to Kansulay. Her husband is unwell, lying at home up near the town hall on the far side of the provincial capital. Some zealous official in the plywood office in town (which Kulas used to call 'the *aglaryan*') representing the local branch of the Department of Agrarian Reform has a quota to achieve if he hopes to keep intact his dream of promotion. Ominous suggestions have been made recently to the del Rosarios that certain of their tenants might be in a position to buy some land of their own: not just any old land, either, but the three-hectare patch their families have been working since the Japanese left fifty years ago. It appears that two families have decided to club together to buy this land (*where* did they get the money?) and it is Mrs del Rosario's mission to talk them out of such foolishness. She will do it by explaining in that special 'you know it makes sense' tone of hers that two families – *big* families (she will raise an eyebrow at all the toddlers crawling around on the packed earth surrounding the hut) – cannot hope to be self-sufficient on three hectares. It is quite impossible nowadays. It is simply a friendly warning; she has only their best interests at heart. Have their families not known each other for years and years? Good times and bad? So they never had to starve if a typhoon ruined the crops or rats ate next year's seed? Well, it wouldn't be like that once they were on their own. They could hardly expect to turn to the del Rosarios for help after that, could they?

The del Rosarios are not major landowners. They have fifty hectares of coconuts here, half a dozen of rice there, the bald flank of a hill on the far side of the river which was slashed-and-burned some years ago to yield a couple of good crops of sweet potato and cassava. They also have much the same again in a similar area about fifteen miles away. Apart from that they have a small residential lot in distant Quezon City, not far from the UP campus, on which their dentist son has built a modest house for his family. One of their daughters is married in San Diego, California, and Mrs del Rosario's house in town looks like a PX store with its megajars of Yuban coffee and weird packets of cake-mix and exploding breakfast cereal. The del Rosarios are sitting pretty.

It is all relative, of course. It is all relative to rock-bottom Kansulay, to this backward province. Just as occasional no-hope Westerners drift along these coasts – riff-raff from Europe and Australia, mostly – and take away biddable young brides of a dewiness they could never hope to lay hands on in their own countries, so the del Rosarios and others like them would be unable to lord it anywhere outside the Philippines. For lord it they do; not in the sense of wielding major political clout in the province but in being paid deference, in having servants, and in being able to get inconveniences fixed in their favour. All this can be read from the body-language of the people they talk to in Kansulay. The villagers do not quite stand as José Rizal depicted the folk of his lakeside town in *Noli Me Tangere* standing when spoken to by Spaniards, priests, policemen or anyone with the slightest authority: head bared and bowed, struck dumb. The posture they adopt in Kansulay is more casual, as befits a democratic age. They hold themselves in a carefully calculated slouch, neither too respectful nor too insolent, their eyes skidded off slightly to one side of the face talking at them. The very young are beginning to show some welcome signs of cockiness, of a direct gaze; but the older and more uneducated the villager, the more his or her posture suggests by its tense embarrassment an inheritance of ingrained obedience.

The greatest mistake foreign strangers to these parts can make is to think they can intervene with impunity in any aspect of social or economic life. Visitors from almost classless, urbanized societies seldom understand or even imagine how the entire fabric of Philippine society, from top to bottom, is structured by a class or caste system, as well as by an invisible network of private indebtedness and the tiny local pecking-orders based on it. It is extremely hard for a Filipino to drop out of this system other than by becoming a pariah or else a member of an entirely separate social order, such as a nun or a monk. It is a constantly flexing yet remarkably stable and *inclusive* system (everyday speech uses the same word, *malungkot*, to mean both 'lonely' and 'sad'. This is not a society of cheerful loners.) As already described, it is a social order held together by interlocking structures of great complexity: the *compadre* or baptismal sponsor system, the *padrino* or 'godfather'/boss system, and that of *utang na loob* indebtedness which can place entire families in a state of scarcely perceptible subordination.

   This last system is the one Mrs del Rosario is trying to play on by reminding her uppity tenants that they owe her: not merely half of whatever they produce on her land but also loyalty for her magnanimity in not allowing them to starve in bad times. To avail themselves of their rights under the provisions of agrarian reform is hence a kind of treason, a brutal tearing of the web that binds them all in this relationship. If it goes through, and the tenants succeed in buying the land, it will probably feel a Pyrrhic victory, leaving hollow residues and an obscure sense of damage and awkwardness which will likely persist for the best part of a generation. The families concerned will almost certainly have jokes made about them behind their backs by the more merciless of Kansulay's wits ('Ah, the new *landowner* . . . Excuse my not getting up'), especially if they fail to make a go of it and find after all the upheaval that they cannot live off this patch of land. So a foreigner who blunders in from outside with straightforward notions full of rectitude about human rights and liberation and breaking the bonds of feudal servitude will never be able to guess the depths of unhappiness, upset, even ostracism which may actually be entailed. People in the Philippines, particularly in small communities, seldom if ever stand in purely economic relation to one another (e.g. employer/employee), but are enmeshed as well in sticky familial and emotional threads.

It is fashionable on the part of young, highly urbanized Filipinos and the internationally mobile élite either to decry this social system as a sort of mediaeval hangover or else to deny it as being much exaggerated by anthropologists. Far from feeling it can be dismissed as a last-gasp relic of bad old feudal days, one becomes convinced that it is precisely this which has enabled the Philippines to survive as a nation with something collective intact. For all sorts of good reasons commentators and journalists like James Fallows, a contributing editor of *Atlantic Monthly*, have notoriously summed up the country with apodictic phrases such as 'a damaged culture'. These have not always been respectfully received, some Filipinos resenting Mr Fallows's tone and the implied presumption that he is speaking from a correspondingly sound cultural standpoint. Yet 'damaged' or not, this Filipino principle of a nationwide, subtle, hermetic tangle of interpersonal tensions and relationships has survived four centuries of assault by foreign cultures, and it is hard to imagine a more unifying, non-religious, social cement – at least, in default of more traditional nation-building continuities.

However, this is not to say that such a system does not also have its drawbacks and may even be reaching the end of its usefulness. In its essentially rural nature it is probably too much at odds with the democratic urban values of a modern industrialized society which the current Philippines' leadership is keen to foster. And yet it is hard to see how the instinctive and ubiquitous polarization of society into diffuse layers of élites and underlings can soon disappear, above all because it is coded into the political process. It is amazing to watch it manifest at all levels, sometimes merely through a tone of voice that can be switched on or off at will. Thus a bonhomous and charming dinner party in a private room of one of the grandest hotels in Manila can be punctuated by utterly chilling asides to men who come scuttling in, slightly bent at the waist so as not to obtrude on the diners' line of vision, in response to an imperious double-click on a little radio gadget (bells are old hat). These moments exist as though in parentheses, ignored or no longer seen by others at the table, when warm and jovial discourse freezes on the instant into a series of glacial questions and commands ('*Why* haven't you? Get him. Who gave him permission to go home?') delivered with a killer's flat stare. Immediately the wretched man has sped from the room (he might be an *alalay*, a factotum or even a bodyguard of twenty years' devoted service whose children are having a proper high school education thanks to this relationship), the warmth and geniality are switched back on in the eyes and manner as though they had never been absent. One feels terror by proxy, the effect little softened by the knowledge that, once outside, the bodyguard will pass it all on with a vengeance to *his* underlings, and so on down to the wretched driver whose job is nothing more complex than to ensure the limousine is somehow waiting – despite impos-sible traffic and no-parking zones – exactly at the door and at the precise instant for the mellowed diners to step right into it without breaking their conversation. Nor is it ever quite enough to remind oneself that this is indeed a dangerous society, and people often pay with their lives for negligence, be they a humble bodyguard or a multi-millionaire tycoon.

Westerners are usually profoundly shocked by these reminders of the social realities underlying the charm and generosity of the Filipino wealthy and sophisticated. Even John Addis revealed his own distress at this discovery, despite the fact that as an ambas-sador from an élite social background he was himself very much a member of a class accustomed to giving orders. But his social edu-cation had been rather different, with the relaxed gentility proper to a secure and unviolent society by whose codes a real gentleman was *never* rude to servants or shopkeepers, above all not in public. In his letters from Manila to his sister he constantly agonized about his cook, Leonarda, who was evidently a lady given to grand emotional states:

After almost 2 years, Leonarda had one of her tantrums recently. I thought we had finished with them. Even the next day her face was black and transformed. She is all right again now. I know better now how to deal with these scenes, but how I hate all violence! I feel sick and want to run away. There was a smile when I saw her this morning, so we may be all right again now. I should hate to lose the cook who suits me so well, and she is such a sweet person when these terrible storms are not brewing. But her moods never spoil her cooking and this week I have had four small lunch-parties.[1]

'I feel sick and want to run away' is not the voice of a Filipino confronting a servant problem, and is evidence of a very different kind of cultural sensibility. After a weekend away from Manila at the private beach retreat of two of his closest grandee friends, Addis observes of his hostess:

Luisa has sacked the good maid who had actually survived some months, and all the staff were new. So sweet and gentle a person to be so arrogantly tyrannical! Every word and deed to the domestics calls for The Revolution. I understand those terrible stories in the newspapers when a mistress is hacked to death by her maid.[2]

When a British ambassador is moved to call for The Revolution, particularly in the heyday of Chairman Mao, it shows considerable depth of feeling. The 'tyrannical' behaviour he noted is by no means confined to the wealthy élite, however. Nearly everyone in Manila seems to have servants in one form or another. The middle classes have servants, and even quite lowly people turn out to have dogsbodies living out at the back somewhere. 'Here, maids have maids,' as someone wryly observed, and the *padrino* mentality extends to the grubbiest urchin boss of a gang of glue-sniffing waifs. The streets of residential subdivisions at seven or eight o'clock at night become a blaring hubbub of car horns as breadwinners return and sit outside, hooting imperiously until some skivvy runs to open the tall, blank metal gates which form the only breach in high cement-block walls topped with barbed wire and broken glass. The idea that any of these white-collar workers might actually get out of his car to walk five yards across the street and ring the bell (or even use his mobile phone) is as ludicrous as the notion that he might consider the peace of the neighbourhood. On the contrary, the horn is the naked proclamation of the *arriviste*, and the more people that hear it the better.

Needless to say, certain people look after their servants exceedingly well, with thoughtfulness and civility, but they tend to be the 'older' families. They very often have strong links to a particular province, so the servants will tend to come from the same village or neighbouring town, all speaking the same dialect and with constant news of home. Usually the family will ensure that such long-term retainers will have a house to retire to on their provincial estate and that their children will have an education and are decently looked after. This, of course, is what paternalism properly is. Exactly the same system was once common among more enlightened families in Europe, until it was virtually ended by the First World War. The interesting thing is that there still has not been a 'First World War' in the Philippines, in the sense of a cataclysmic event that overturns an entire social order. The Second World War was cataclysmic indeed, but it did not radically change overall social relationships. Some now think that, in default of John Addis's 'Revolution', the class structure will simply erode gradually and patchily under the democratizing influences of urbanization, mobility and increasing financial independence. Others are more pessimistic. The distinguished writer Frank Sionil José, who almost alone among those of his generation writing in English never forgets his roots in an obscure village like Kansulay, made a sad admission recently: 'I know now that the revolution I am hoping for will not come in my lifetime. The young people who were fired by such ideas in the sixties and seventies are no longer with us.'[3] And the ex-journalist and ex-ambassador J. V. Cruz has made a similarly resigned assessment: 'I don't think there'll be any change unless and until a truly, genuinely *political* movement rooted in ideological and even class distinctions takes hold in this country. And I don't see that coming.'[4]

Meanwhile, it is sometimes hard to resist glimpsing behind life in the Philippines the shadowy outlines of a social structure as recorded by the earliest Spanish priests. This had three tiers. At the top were the ruling class, the aristocrats who, when they had followers, were known as *datu*. They were the heads of *barangays*. Their supporters and followers were called *maharlika*, a word most often translated as 'noble' and which betrays the ancient Indian influence in these islands since it derives from Sanskrit. (No doubt it was this meaning Ferdinand Marcos had in mind when he gave it to his shadowy wartime guerrilla group – he presumably being the *datu*.) Everyone else fell into the broad category of *alipin*, which the Spanish translated as 'slave' even as they noted that the group was further subdivided and included bondsmen and debt peons. The thing that characterized these *alipin* was that they were beholden to a master or his family by one or other form of indebtedness, but that there were ways of buying their freedom and cancelling the debt. The Spanish scholar-priest, Pedro de San Buenavista, who produced a Tagalog dictionary as early as 1613, commented that the idea of the *nouveau riche* was perfectly current at the time and a scornful phrase existed to describe 'jumped-up people with a lot of gold'.[5] This, of course, was exactly what Manila's élite were calling the Marcoses in the 1960s.

The Filipino ruling élite is a fascinating mixture of 'old' money and new, and delicate snobberies still exist between the two. When the Marcoses were married in the fifties the phrase 'the 400' or 'Manila's 400' was taken to refer to the little *'prinsipalya'* class of intermarried families who effectively owned and ran the entire country. (This dated phrase has been widely misunderstood as literally meaning four hundred families, whereas it is simply an expression for an exclusive social set. It was originally supposed to have referred to the number of people who could fit into Caroline Astor's ballroom at the end of the nineteenth century.) One of the tensions and resentments Imelda Marcos in particular must have harboured was her equivocal social position as an impoverished, 'country cousin' member of a well-established clan. The behaviour of even the most sophisticated and enlightened ruling-class Filipino is often a mixture of utter charm and stone arrogance which may alternate so rapidly as to be homogenous, like the apparently steady glow of a domestic light bulb, and it is not surprising that this characteristic should have been detected by her critics in Imelda. But while foreigners singled it out after her 'downfall' as evidence of, variously, immaturity or insecurity or else a fundamentally black heart, they overlooked that her behaviour was actually no different in kind from that of most others of her class. Many of the élite who themselves decried her behaviour did so from a very shaky position, the gap between their own general behaviour and Mrs Marcos's being evidence not so much of their better breeding and finer feeling as of the First Lady's having a good deal more power, so that her gestures were correspondingly larger and more eye-catching. In fact somebody – and it may have been Imelda's own niece, Mrs Francia herself – coined the phrase 'datuism' to describe the First Lady's manner and her steady gathering of a dedicated band of followers: the Blue Ladies, political allies, and people back in Leyte whom she owed. 'Nobles' though these groupies might have been in the ancient sense, it was made plain to all of them at one time or another that they were minions, and her gratitude and favour could change in an instant to the freezing imperiousness that characterizes her class.

Outside the Palace, of course, each of those minions would be a smaller edition of their *datu*, very powerful by extension, with minions of her or his own – and so on down the pecking order to the lowliest scullions sleeping in lofts and cupboards. Such dependency has a pyramidal, Christmas-tree structure, with money and favours percolating down from the top.

By the time Mrs del Rosario's jeep comes bumping back down the track, now noisier and heavier by two trussed pigs, the knot of onlookers gazing at the place of Kulas's death has dispersed. Many will have gone to his house for the wake. There, sponged, shaved and dressed in his newest shirt, he is the centrepiece lit with candles, serenaded by chanted prayers and restored to the continuity of life by the half-naked toddlers mumbling biscuits under the table on which he lies. The shouts of older children playing outside pierce his unhearing ears and are then briefly drowned by the noise of Mrs del Rosario's jeep crashing past, towing a tail of porcine squeals and barefoot boys racing to keep up. The jeep stops outside Rading's house, through whose bamboo-framed window a grey-haired lady can be seen at a venerable Singer sewing machine. The house itself is in sad disrepair, the cheap coconut-frond thatch having weathered from a sun-bleached mane to ash-grey stubs so thin in parts that the bamboo lattice that supports it is visible. There has been an attempt to patch the worst of these holes with plastic bags and a flattened tin which once held 'Nido' milk powder.

If Rading's house is in no great shape, Conrado himself is a disaster. Or rather, he is one of those people who goes his own sweet way leaving a series of disasters behind him. He vanished from Kansulay nearly three years ago, abandoning five children, the eldest twelve years old and the youngest two. A few months later his 'live-in' wife disappeared too, some said to work in a bar in Manila (everyone knew what *that* meant). Meanwhile the children became loosely attached to an 'aunt', the grey-haired woman. She is a distant cousin of Rading's, a spinster who is actually fortyish rather than the seventy she looks. In effect, the children were thrown onto village charity which, in a subsistence economy, is less than munificent. In another culture they would have been classified as deprived, and the youngest as disturbed – as well they might be, once the grapevine had yielded up the gossip that Conrado was thought to have at least three other families in neighbouring provinces, totalling twenty-two children. Where he was nobody knew. Some said he had a job in Saudi Arabia, others that he was doing piecework in the Mindoro rice fields; still others claimed he had died in a bus that went over a gorge in Isabela where he was an NPA guerrilla. All his children know is that they are hungry, have no mother or father, and that their aunt whips them with a piece of flex tied to a bamboo handle. The sound of this little quirt, accompanied by pitiful screams, sometimes punctuates the nightly drinking-sessions in neighbouring huts, making the drinkers stir uneasily. The people of Kansulay do not like to hear children cry and are not given to corporal punishment. The uneasiness comes from knowing it is not the unmarried aunt's fault that she does not understand how to manage small children. Nor is it unreasonable that, poor enough herself, she should resent having to act as a foster parent to this unruly and perpetually hungry brood. She is not an unkind person, simply out of her depth in despair. Now and then the *barangay* captain's wife (who, like Mrs del Rosario, owns some land) is moved to give her a kilo of rice, a few small fish or a can of 'Alaska' condensed milk. It is noticed that these sudden bursts of generosity mostly coincide with the local priest's pastoral visits to the village. And so it goes on.

Today, Mrs del Rosario has stopped in order to negotiate with the grey-haired 'auntie'. She is in the market for a kitchen maid, and none of her other tenants has a suitably aged girl they will part with. Rading's eldest daughter Epdi, who is twelve, seems to fit the bill. (Her name has a curious origin. For whimsical reasons best known to himself her father had her christened Flower Drum Song, which was understandably shortened. But instead of her being known as Flower, she became FDS or FD, hence 'Epdi'.) Epdi is one of those children who, despite skimpy nourishment, reach puberty early. She is already a busty child, not pretty but handsome, one might say, with strong and even slightly mannish features. The sheer violence of rapid adolescence has left her momentarily with an ungainly body, dumpy rather than willowy like most of her peers. She is submissive, downcast when addressed by the village adults, as though she knows she is near the bottom of Kansulay's poor social heap, with just a set of initials for a Christian name. But when unaware of being observed, her eyes alight on things and people with such a blaze of intelligence it is a wonder they do not scorch and shrivel them. Epdi more or less fell out of the little village school a year or more ago because, as the eldest of Rading's daughters, it increasingly became her task to look after her younger siblings. For a while her teachers mildly scolded her when they found her squatting in the stream washing clothes; but because they recognized the reason for it they eventually gave up. She already fetches the *barangay* captain's water from the pump morning and evening in the never-repayable repayment of those occasional plastic bags of fish and rice and the candles by whose light her 'aunt' can work at her sewing machine in the evenings, mending the clothes of the captain's own children.

There has been some talk recently that Epdi might go to Manila as a maid, or else to look for her mother and maybe get a job through her. In this way she could become a remittance-girl, sending back what little she could save to help the family she has inherited from her father's blithe truancy. This proposal is treated with a mixture of opposition and fatalism, as though everyone knew perfectly well that it was quite wrong to allow a country child of twelve to go wandering alone through the slime-pits of Manila, while at the same time accepting that such things happen to the orphans of the feckless. It is not part of social expression here to give vent to moral outrage. People must eat. It is much better to be a child prostitute than it is to starve. Better still to become a maid, of course, preferably in the house of someone with relatives back home in Kansulay so that her employer's behaviour stands some chance of modification by shame if need be. Heads are being scratched without much urgency when Mrs del Rosario turns up and wants to know if the 'aunt' would let Epdi live in town with them and skivvy there for her keep. Nobody is about to consult Epdi herself, of course; chattels have their lives arranged for them, as is inevitable if they are financially unable to say otherwise. Word soon gets back that the 'aunt' is overjoyed. One less mouth to feed, and a dependency with one of the local élite. Things are definitely looking up.

For her part, Mrs del Rosario knows that by taking on Epdi she is also, in a distant and informal sort of way, adding that family to her tenant list, which means she will be more or less obliged to ensure they do not starve. 'Auntie' is understandably happy with a deal that simultaneously gets rid of one child and provides a minimal safety net for the rest, a situation she never enjoyed as the recipient of irregular and capricious tokens of village charity. Epdi does not climb straight into the jeep among the sacks and pigs, but the bargain is struck in her absence (she is off somewhere at the time, probably down on the shore with the smallest children). And in a day or two she duly stops one of the jeepneys that roar along the coastal road and is borne off to the little capital town a few kilometres away. Thereafter, she returns very seldom to Kansulay, partly because Mrs del Rosario keeps her so busy sweeping and cleaning and fetching and carrying, and partly because even the jeep fare represents a significant slice of her wages, which are anyway paid more in board and lodging than they are in cash. Also, it may be that she is glad to be free of Kansulay. Then after six months, news of a miracle. She has caught someone's attention in town (an inquisitive priest doing his rounds? a teacher from the provincial board of education?) and is going to high school. Epdi in school? Wonders will never cease. Thereafter, reports filter back to the village that she has become a star pupil, maybe the brightest in the school, making up for lost time with an effortless speed that leaves people astounded and predicting scholarships, college degrees, even careers in government. It is early days yet to envisage Epdi as representing the Philippines at the UN, but who knows what of life's oysters she might not open one day?

So that naked flare behind her glances had not lied, and the memory of them carries with it a profound relief, the sense of a rare occasion when justice is done. Not everyone in Kansulay agrees, apparently. Other families with girls of Epdi's age whom they judge much worthier to be singled out for a lucky break are distinctly miffed even as they pretend to rejoice at her good fortune. (What is the point of being a virtuous and conscientious parent, they imply, if a wastrel's half-starved brat gets all the chances?) And of course it is this recognition of how arbitrary it all was that blunts the pleasure, that reminds one of how many others are destined not to have a similar opportunity. For one does not look out across Kansulay's emerald green paddies at dusk, across the swerving carpet of dragonflies to the smoke of evening fires drifting up from among the palms opposite, and see an idyll. One has to hold out against too much enticement, too much lulling. The ocean murmurs to itself in the background; the men are crouched outside their huts to light battered pressure-lamps for a night's fishing; their children sing as they play, dashing about in the twilight on sandy soil among palm stumps and clothes-props. A sow in a cement-block sty roofed with dry fronds slurps and chomps her swill from a halved motor tyre with grunts of pleasure. These are the immemorial sounds of evening, and they carry with them a great calm:

> *Here we were born,*
> *here we live,*
> *here we will die –*
> *and here we will live once again.*

But no; too much has happened in this century for it to be that simple any longer. Something uneasy has happened to villages everywhere since Pineda wrote his poem. The truth is, those evening sounds are now the sounds of underdevelopment, and the ache to hold on to them encodes a denial of the right of lesser Epdis to escape the grip of unchanging history. There are moments when it is all too clear that the people of Kansulay have, by a mere accident of birth, been obliged to act out their only lives disguised as villagers on an obscure stage in one of the world's backwaters. It may be that the priest, Father Demetrio, really does see in all their several faces that of Christ, as he claims. But the secular see doctors and executives and TV actresses and bureaucrats and musicians and poets and scientists. They see ordinary layabouts and drunks too, of course, as well as plain housewives and car park attendants. But the creak and slither of the buffalo sled returning at dusk, the hollow grating bounce on the track of the flexing tips of heavy bamboos being shouldered down from the forest by tired youths, the screech of Carding's absurd child's bicycle as he collects *tuba* for the night's drinking sessions: all these are the sounds of *waste*, of people who know from magazines and TV that it might have turned out very differently for them. The scientist and teacher, Stephen Jay Gould, became sharp when overmuch attention was paid to the vulgar quantification of genius and its alleged ability to surface infallibly:

> I am, somehow, less interested in the weight and convolutions of Einstein's brain than in the near certainty that people of equal talent have lived and died in cotton fields and sweatshops.[6]

To those cotton fields add the paddies and forests of Kansulay.

For this is precisely the point about the Filipino village: that even as the urban middle classes affect to idealize and sentimentalize it as the last repository of true family values, it is treated not as a fund of individual talent but as a pool of anonymous cheap labour. For reasons of administrative blindness as well as of fashionable economics, the rural Philippines has to a large extent been abandoned by central government – at least, if Kansulay is anything to go by. In the last ten years the contagious hysteria of 'tiger' economics has swept through Southeast Asia, belatedly infecting the Philippines (which well within living memory, back in the fifties, was the region's strongest and best-developed economy, barring only Japan). In place of a steady and rational development that ought to have been spread over the last forty years, there is now a sudden manic rush accompanied by silly slogans as though to meet some imaginary deadline represented by that fictitious date, the year 2000 AD. Why then? What then? Nobody knows. It represents a national government in the grip of an advertising agency's fantasy.

Nor does looking around at other nations in the region inspire confidence. It is not so much a view of fluctuating economic fortunes while the region's currencies totter and slump, as a vision of social upheaval brought about by completely untheorized 'development'.

The gnomes of the World Bank and the IMF must be profoundly stupid if they have been dazzled and seduced by the prestige buildings and gleaming towers of Kuala Lumpur and Jakarta and Bangkok and the rest, but do not also wonder who will be left in this erstwhile Asian rice bowl to grow the food the expanding urban populations will need in twenty years' time. For the moment, the vision of the future is that of the same endless shopping malls and temples of finance and multinational computer factories, with the sun flashing off anodized aluminium and stainless steel cladding to the horizon beneath a buff pall of pollution.

Meanwhile, no government help comes to Kansulay in the form of a single tractor to make ploughing the paddies easier and more efficient, or to convince the village youths that there might be a future here rather than in Manila's slums. No provincial government agency has yet decided that the people of Kansulay are even worth a proper supply of drinkable water. Because of the social system that deeply underlies all forms of the country's administration, any funding for such projects remains largely dependent on the 'pork barrel' allocations of local politicians, from the Provincial Governor downwards. Thus a *barangay* captain competes, cap in hand, to beg money for his community which – should it magnanimously be granted – carries with it the implied obligation of the entire village's voting for the donor in the next election. So funding trickles down to Kansulay, at the bottom of the Christmas tree, as from a *datu*. One does not even bother to enquire what has happened to the inconceivable sums of aid money that have poured into the Philippines over the last thirty years, much of it earmarked for the nation's Kansulays. 'Gone abroad,' people say without rancour but with the smile that hides resignation in the face of the inevitable. Most of it barely stayed in the country's coffers long enough even for an outer layer to rub off before it was hastily funnelled out again into those Australian ranches and Los Angeles condos and Swiss accounts. Gone abroad.

'*Na sa abrod*' is the phrase also sometimes used locally to describe the great migrant army of people who have flooded out of towns and villages all over the Philippines to scatter themselves overseas. There are all sorts of reasonable excuses for governments that make dire economic blunders through inexperience, or for a particular regime that falls victim to a passing ideological fad such as supply-side Reaganomics. But if one wanted a single yardstick by which to measure the abject failure of successive Philippine governments, it would surely be provided by this business of Overseas Contract Workers (OCWs). The Philippines is probably the only nation in the world whose entire economy rests to such an extent on the export of its own citizens, many of whom are the country's best-qualified men and women. (Currently they remit over $7 billion each year.) It is not just the lunacy of a developing nation electing to do without its better-educated people that amazes, but the very idea of an economic system so inept that people are obliged to leave their homeland *en masse* for the deserts of the Middle East, the hospitals of the United Kingdom, the kitchens and hotels of the world. Moreover, when they do leave as a valuable economic resource, they are generally accorded so little protection by their own government that many of them arrive home again in coffins: girls and women, mostly, raped and abused and murdered or else the suicidal victims of terminal depression and homesickness. Their families are generally paid off with a few thousand pesos so that they make no fuss and demand no tiresome enquiries.

This overseas contract work began under Marcos, but in a very limited fashion. Then, Filipino construction companies started winning contracts for projects abroad, typically in the Middle East, and workers were hired for them and repatriated as soon as they were finished. The major outflow of OCWs took place during Cory Aquino's presidency in the mid- to late eighties with the expansion of the domestics market. Very few OCWs went abroad as domestics under Marcos. It is predicted that the market will dry up in the next five to ten years, leaving the government to cope with a corresponding rise in unemployment at home and a great shortfall in revenue to make up.

There is a case for saying that such a situation is a direct consequence of an underlying ethos of *datu*ism. It is simply the same principle of the élites and their servants, but writ on an international scale. Like goods and chattels, these Filipino citizens are simply disposable sources of labour to be shunted about as necessary, but now without even the protection of a paternalist concern for their welfare since they are in essence sold into the ownership of overseas employers. The system's defenders habitually make three points in its favour. They say that not only do a worker's remittances enable his family to survive, but when his contract expires he ought (if he has been properly thrifty and conscientious) to be able to return with a nest-egg. With this he can buy a motorcycle and sidecar and set up as a tricycle driver, or else invest in a dozen pigs and become a hog-breeder. What is more, they say, the effect of someone returning to a small village who has for the last few years become accustomed to the things the developed world takes for granted (clean water at the turn of a tap, lights that come on at the click of a switch, hospitals that treat gravely injured casualties without first checking their ability to pay) is to raise the locals' consciousness and increase the pressure for political change.

On the evidence Kansulay offers this is pious wishfulness. Hopes that returning OCWs will help 'modernize' their villages are as naively futile as the identical hopes of Don Crisostomo Ibarra in *Noli Me Tangere* proved to be when he returned from a long educational trip to Europe fired with enthusiasm for modernizing his home town. For a start, OCWs are not generally paid large salaries, although they might seem munificent by Philippine standards. The cost of living overseas is proportionally higher, and the majority of OCWs do not return to their village with nest-eggs to buy hogs and taxis: they come home with TVs and karaoke systems powerful enough to blast the frogs out of the paddies (this being the rural *arriviste*'s equivalent of leaning on a car horn). They come home as semi-strangers, black with sun and laden with presents for children they can scarcely recognize. And as for their raised expectations helping in turn to raise the standards of local amenities, the effect is usually the polar opposite. After a week spent wandering around the village with a beaming smile, renewing old friendships and letting everyone admire their shoes and crested Zippo lighter, a strange restlessness creeps in. A gulf (maybe even the Gulf) has opened up between the OCW and his stay-at-home friends. He has acquired a Johnny Walker habit and will now only drink *tuba* under the duress of bonhomie. He is impatient with the busted communal Jetmatic water pump held together with wire and bound around with tourniquets of black rubber cut from an inner tube. He cannot believe that the last electricity pole is forty yards short of his house so that the microwave oven he has bizarrely brought all the way from Bahrain cannot be used but sits in its box in a prominent position as a talking-point and talisman of the far-off world of consumerism. Bit by bit he grows dismissive and critical. His wife looks older than he remembers and moans as constantly as she ever did about cash for the children's clothes, graduations, school projects and the rest. He disappears with his cronies to the local town for longer and longer each day. And then one day he has gone again. There is no work here. The hired hand has signed a fresh contract, knowing that nothing here is going to change in the foreseeable future, and certainly not as the result of any pressure he could ever bring. Worse, the recognition of his own impotence to influence things has led him to feel faintly contemptuous of those who continue to put up with it, something not lost on his family and the rest of the village. And so Kansulay acquires another molecule-thick layer of humility to add to its inchoate sense of failure.

Thanks to news press reports about the tragic fate of so many OCWs, and thanks also to so many returning contract workers describing the harsh or disgusting living conditions they have endured, few Filipinos now really believe the streets of 'abroad' are paved with gold. If despite the loss of such naivety they are still anxious to go there, it is an indication of how impossible it is to make a living at home: itself scarcely a mark of administrative success on the part of the government. That people should *want* to leave their own country, should be resigned to spending so much time and energy queuing for US Green Cards or EU visas (because once you're in you can vanish), makes concepts like loyalty and patriotism less clear. Is a Filipino patriot one who doggedly remains? Is a truly loyal father or mother someone who goes abroad for their family's sake? Such things are discussed with resigned bitterness in Kansulay.

Interestingly, this philosophical crux extends beyond the impoverished denizens of the rural labour pool. The fact that the del Rosarios' married daughter living in San Diego is now an American citizen does something to the rest of her family. It gives them a toehold in the promised land, and by so doing maybe casts a faint shadow over their unqualified commitment to their province, their bit of land, their tenants. The same principle applies to the élite who run the country. Luckily for them, there has never

been a moment over this last century when a Communist-style revolution of the kind envisaged by John Addis looked seriously likely
to sweep the Philippines, although there were some uneasy
moments at the start of Marcos's second term of office in the early
seventies. However, if worse ever did come to the worst, most of
the élite could scamper abroad where they have property, money
and very often children with professional qualifications and foreign
citizenship. This is not to say they would, only that they could;
and the constant knowledge of this safety net places them always at
one remove from the consequences of their own governance.

These days, fewer of the political élite are major landowners and
more are rich businessmen and entrepreneurs. ('About eighty to
ninety percent of the House of Representatives and of the Senate
are millionaires,' a newspaper pointed out. 'With such a member-
ship how can we expect the two chambers to vote for measures that
would benefit the poor?'[7]) This decreasing incidence of land ownership probably makes it more likely for a politician to consider
cutting his or her losses and fleeing abroad in the case of emergency. No doubt a large proportion of the entire governing class of
the Philippines has access to boltholes overseas, and it must have a
real effect on politicians if they know they can escape accountabil-
ity. This was notoriously the case with many of the so-called
'Marcos cronies' who absconded with huge sums of money or fled,
leaving banks collapsing beneath the weight of debts they never
intended to pay. They went off and bought castles in Austria or
entire city blocks in Vancouver.

Predictably, it is often members of the 'old money' élite who
retain the greatest sense of duty and responsibility to their country,
and who in a quiet way behind the scenes do what they can to promote social causes and obstruct the worst of the self-seeking
legislation proposed by the uncaring. To that extent they do indeed
act in a paternal fashion towards the country as a whole, individuals as enlightened and principled as one could hope to meet
anywhere. But it is still not a democratic *system*, and shows few
signs of becoming one. Because it is no longer principally landowning, much of the governing class now seems quite divorced from
the people it is supposed to represent. By and large, it makes and
breaks laws for its own benefit and economic advantage, goes junk-
eting around the globe on buying sprees and freebies, attends each

other's showbiz parties and first nights, marries into each other's family and complains endlessly about the problem of finding reliable cooks, *yayas* (wet nurses) and drivers nowadays. 'The servant problem' is a constant subject of conversation in these circles, but of course it is – or has been – an age-old lament almost everywhere.

Sometimes around dawn a light breeze blows off the sea, pressing thin cotton against the backs of early risers heading for the forest. They walk up the track whistling, long knives at their waists rattling against pails of swill. A boy carries a pole with an arm sticking out at right angles. The arm has a pinkish coating of *dagtâ*, a birdlime made of sticky saps and resins. They walk up beside Kansulay's shrinking river past Turing's patch, over the earthfall that prevented Mrs del Rosario's jeep from going any further, up to their forest plots. Their bare feet trace out that ancient axis of life in these islands: *sa ilaya*, upstream, into the interior. Where the coconut palms are sparse enough to allow a view, the strengthening sunlight can be seen thinning the mists layer by layer to reveal distant steep hills, whose hunched shoulders of dark forest hide a holy mountain, a sacred cave. High grassfields emerge into light, far off, as slabs of textureless green; but the dawn wind will be running through them in mysterious wavering corridors. Here and there in the hills trickles of smoke mark the presence of people taking up the rhythms of the day, cooking or lighting fires in shallow pits to roast coconut shells for charcoal. Into a sky the colour of steam leak cautious birds'-egg blues.

Something distils itself from the air that is not the wind, not the villagers' whistling, not the smoke. It is like a reagent that permits an etching to emerge, dissolving whatever is not wind and whistles and smoke. Of great and invisible power, it eats away at theorizings of every kind, causing sociologies to collapse in silence like clouds. The people walking away from the shore, where the sea's rumpled tinfoil still retains some of night's darkness, are in a narrative off at a tangent to our own plain tales. On the path which would once have formed part of the river bed they are moving along a boundary which has nothing to do with past or present. From time to time dapples of sunlight fall through the leaves to pick out a brown curve of shoulder here, an ear or ankle there, brilliant tokens of beings more generally elusive as they fade among the trees.

10

Love-nests, leftists and riots

There is a tendency for Marcos loyalists nowadays to speak of his first term of office as though he had been a remarkable reforming President, having placed all sorts of modernizing legislation on the statute books, to say nothing of building a tally of infrastructural projects that far exceeded anything achieved by any of his predecessors. Roads, bridges, airports, schools, hospitals and clinics: there was scarcely a part of the archipelago that had not felt some impact of central government – in many areas for the first time. To a certain extent this is still a tenable opinion; but only if one records that it was not universally shared at the time, especially by foreigners. Somewhere towards the middle of this first term, for example, John Addis sent a typewritten dispatch to the British Foreign Office marked 'Confidential':

I know that many American officials concerned with the Philippines are disappointed with Marcos's performance, and he is also being more widely criticized by his own people. This is partly a normal feature of the second year of a Presidency. Marcos has in fact done quite well in his roadbuilding programme and in his drive for increased rice production. He has, however, failed to throw his weight behind land reform, while ostensibly conserving the main lines of Macapagal's programme. I think that too much has been expected of Marcos and that, particularly at the time of his State Visit to the United States last October [*sic*. It was in fact September], hopes were expressed which it was not in his capacity to fulfil. He is not a reformer, as Macapagal was. The best hope is that because he is ambitious and wants to be a success, he will for this reason strive to have some solid achievements on the record.[1]

When assessing Marcos's record in this first term, his wife and her own social projects must not be left out of the equation since her influence was equally felt up and down the country. And if certain of those welfare campaigns (her 'Happy Christmas' scheme, for example, which by 1968 was sending out half a million bags of presents to 66 out of 73 provinces) smacked of Lady Bountiful, one needs to remember that this was no more than in accordance with prevailing cultural norms. The destitute beneficiaries of these seasonal goodies would have been touched and thankful to have been remembered just the same. Nearly thirty years later she was to remark of her own generosity with innocent high camp, 'I do not just give: I give until it is *beautifully* given . . .'[2]

For a more interesting and down-to-earth assessment of Marcos's first term one can turn to his celebrated opponent, Ninoy Aquino himself, who in early 1969 was interviewed by De La Salle College's student magazine *Horizons* and gave the following opinion:

[Marcos] is a blend of the practical and the theoretical, [having] always grounded himself on the practical side. He will not tell you that he is an honest man; he is not going to waste time trying to prove that. Because he is not. So maybe you say: '*Terible naman si Marcos*, he is crooked.' A Marcos man will never answer you, 'That's just not true.' What do they say? 'Could be, but he certainly gets things done.' In other words they [exonerate] him. Marcos is practical. You attack him. Guilty. But this is what he says: 'Say what you may, but I've built roads, I've built schools, I've built this, I've built that. Say what you may, but I've exported rice.' . . . And this is where I think Marcos might just succeed himself. I am convinced that he might be the only person who will break the tradition wherein every president has been toppled by the common denominator of corruption. No recent president has actually *done* anything – other than corruption. Every president tried to prove that they were not corrupt and they fell. Marcos no longer tries to prove that. 'Accepted I am corrupt. I am nothing new. Everybody has been corrupt anyway, but judge me by my achievements. How many before me have been able to do this?'

But this was before the 1969 election campaign began, marking something of a watershed in Philippine political history as also in the career of Ferdinand Marcos. He was determined at all costs to have a second term in office, no matter how he might have glossed it as being necessary to complete his 'grand plan' for dragging the Philippines into the modern world. The result was an election that surpassed even that of 1949 for fraud and violence, while in terms of spending it was in a new league altogether. Back in the forties, Philippine presidential candidates and national parties had spent something of the order of $1.5–2.5m on campaigning. In 1969 it cost Marcos $168m to be re-elected. This reflected what in effect was the institutionalizing of the traditional patronage system. At some point he must have made the leap in logic, realizing that long chains of indebtedness based on small favours would become more controllable and more accountable if based on hard cash. The effect of this was to 'up the ante' in two immediate ways. One was to ensure that from now on, the supposedly democratic Filipino political system became a game for only the wealthiest players (in this sense little different from the American system). The other effect was to begin turning Marcos as much as possible into the personal *datu* of the entire electorate. From now on his autocratic streak – common to virtually anybody reaching the top in such a society – became more pronounced.

While planning his 1969 campaign he remembered that the film (*Iginuhit ng Tadhana*) made from Hartzell Spence's book for his previous campaign had paid dividends. It was a pity to let such a dramatic story go to waste, so he decided to have it rewritten and use it again. This time, though, it would be less of a documentary with Tagalog weepie episodes and more of a full-scale Hollywood epic. It was to be called *Ang mga Maharlika* or 'The Nobles'. He turned over the task of having it made to a group of trusted business friends, among whom were his golfing cronies Potenciano

('Nanoy') Ilusorio, Honorio ('Nori') Poblador, and the manager of Wack Wack Golf and Country Club, Diosdado Bote. (Ilusorio and Poblador, together with the Chinese millionaire Jose Y. Campos who had helped Marcos in the 1965 election campaign, constituted a triumvirate known jocularly as 'XYZ'. They acted as front men for Marcos, investing in companies and negotiating takeovers on his behalf. Mining companies were their speciality.) Nanoy Ilusorio now got in touch with Paul Mason, a producer at Universal Studios, and together they discussed the crucial casting of the film's 'Evelyn', the Fil-American lady guerrilla with whom Ferdinand had had a fling in the heat of battle during the Second World War. At Christmas 1968 Mason sent over two possible candidates to Manila to audition for this role: Joyce Reese and Dovie Beams. With Dovie Beams Ferdinand was to have an affair that hit the headlines and arguably had far-reaching political consequences.

Since one of the threads running through Marcos's biography is his much-cited womanizing it seems useful – although far from easy – to acquire some perspective on the matter. As has been mentioned already, rumours of philandering probably never yet hurt a male Filipino politician and, despite pious editorializing, might actually do him good. This strange public double-act of appearing simultaneously to be a man famously wed (like Marcos or Ninoy Aquino) and a celebrated philanderer (like Marcos or Ninoy Aquino) would seem impossible to bring off without public double-think, much as it was in the case of John F. Kennedy. There is little doubt that, despite a brave (and occasionally furious) face, Mrs Marcos, like many another Filipino politician's wife, suffered a good deal from her husband's dalliances. She had, after all, been brought up in the demure, pre-war traditions of Spanish Catholicism. Until martial law in 1972 there was plenty of gossip and vulgar speculation in the tabloids about the nature of their private relationship, but she always made it staunchly plain that, as First Couple, they were indivisible in their love for one another.

Strangely enough (in view of every possible opprobrium that was to be heaped on Imelda), the charge of unfaithfulness, though frequently hinted at, never stuck to her and was never seriously believed. Apart from anything else she was so clearly one of those people whose phenomenal energy seemed possible only if supplemented by erotic reserves. In the scandal sheets a sexual relationship was suggested with her known close friends such as the actor George Hamilton and the wife of Henry Ford II, Cristina; but not even the malicious set much store by such rumours. Nobody doubted she was exceedingly generous to her friends (in 1982 Hamilton bought Charlie Chaplin's Beverly Hills mansion for a sum that included $1.2m allegedly given by Mrs Marcos), but they did not necessarily assume there had been a carnal quid pro quo. In fact, Mrs Marcos herself tackled such rumours head-on in a magazine interview:

> 'I have many weaknesses, *pero kati* [but itching] is not one of them.' [*laughter*] . . . 'I have many weaknesses, but to be a, to be a hotsie-patotsie is not one of them.' [*laughter*]. . . . Do these criticisms or rumours affect the President? 'He's so macho he doesn't bother. He and Hamilton? What a choice! *Wawa naman* [poor thing!].'[3]

It was left to the Marcoses' oldest daughter, Imee, to voice clearly what most people had long recognized:

> 'I'm a fag-hag. And so is my mother. Homosexuals just adore her, and me, as well.'[4]

By contrast, there is no doubt that Ferdinand, to put it vulgarly, screwed around. In this, he was really only doing what was expected of any Filipino with great power and wealth. Several of his closest aides and associates would on occasion double as pimps, discreetly ensuring that the President might have relief from the cares of office whenever he felt so inclined. Yet he was by no means as undiscriminating and insatiable as his reputation (which he did little to discourage) suggested, and there was always the high moral tone of Catholic petty-bourgeois public opinion to take into account. One of his oldest friends from pre-war UP days, Leonilo Ocampo, said:

> About his women – a quarter of it is true. One-fourth. He was *mapili* [able to be choosy]. And all the other things his regime was accused of, probably thirty to forty percent is true. The rest is exaggerated by sheer jealousy and pure hatred.[5]

In fact, there is reason for thinking that mere sexual encounters were not by any means the only thing he wanted, and it was the emotional seriousness of his unexpected relationship with Dovie Beams that caused all the problems.

Various press reports and interviews survive of the affair, but for the fullest account one is obliged to rely on a book entitled *Marcos' Lovey Dovie* by a journalist, Hermie Rotea. Although this has been much quoted, nobody has raised certain obvious points – not so much about the book's factual accuracy as about its author's motivation. It was published in the US in 1984, fully fifteen years after the scandal. Why then? Why there? It was scarcely fortuitous that it should have been published on the West Coast, which by then was full of vociferous Filipino exiles from martial law, and at a time when the anti-Marcos campaign was reaching its climax, encouraged by large sections of the American media and government with almost the sole exception of the White House itself. That Rotea's book is written with malicious intent is obvious from his Prologue ('[Marcos] violated his own oath of office and lost the value of his leadership as clearly shown in the Dovie Beams story. As a result, he is the most hated man in the Philippines today.'[6] Would that everybody else who has written about Marcos had come as clean). What is interesting about the book is how the author, in taking pains to reveal Ferdinand in as ridiculous and un-presidential light as possible, often unwittingly makes the man so vulnerable as to be touching.

Dovie Beams was born Dovie Osborne, and enters the story when she was thirty-six, though looking younger. She was formerly a piano teacher from Tennessee, just as she was formerly married to Edward Boehms, who had successfully sued her for divorce in 1962. The judge in the case found that 'Dovie Osborne Boehms was guilty of such cruel and inhuman treatment or conduct toward [her husband] as renders cohabitation unsafe and improper.'[7] A tough nut, this lady, cruising the minor reaches of Hollywood in search of the main chance and now in the Philippines to audition for a vital role in the President's electoral propaganda film. She struck lucky her first evening in Manila. Invited to a party by Nanoy Ilusorio in a house that was still being renovated (the swimming pool was a raw pit with a bulldozer parked at the bottom of it), Dovie was introduced to a very personable man named Fred. Fred was hospitality itself, and showed her over the house until they reached its deserted recesses, when after some humming and hawing he made the immortal admission: 'I have something to do with the legal profession – I am President of the Philippines. I am in love with you.' It was an auspicious start. To employ the smutty delicacy of the tabloids, 'intimacy took place' only the following evening in more private circumstances, but it was not long before it was obvious that Ferdinand really had fallen in love with her to some extent. Dovie Beams's role as Evelyn was clinched, and she was set up in the house in Greenhills, now fully renovated, where they had first met.

No matter how much of an optimist, she must have found it hard to believe the luck that had taken her from LA and into a President's bed within two days of landing in a strange country. Her account gains from her complete ignorance of Philippine culture and politics; only much later did the tape recordings and conversations from which Rotea worked reflect a slightly more savvy awareness of the secrets that Marcos let drop in the course of their affair. However, it should not be forgotten that Rotea's book was published long after the event and with a definite political purpose. So one is inclined to believe her assertion that Ferdinand confessed early on to being impotent with his wife and that he and Imelda had been 'sexually estranged' from one another for some years. Maybe this is what all men say to their mistresses; but there again, maybe it is what many men experience after nearly fifteen years of marriage. At any rate, the importance here lies in the revelation that he was prepared to confide in Dovie from the first, to the point of indiscretion and frequently beyond.

The film got slowly under way, with Marcos coaching her in her lines during languorous afternoons spent in the large double bed up in Greenhills. Nanoy Ilusorio might well have been pleased by the evident success of his talent for casting and matchmaking, but as he realized with each passing day that this was no casual romance for his President he began to worry about how Imelda might react when she found out. On several occasions Ilusorio confided in Dovie that he was frankly afraid Mrs Marcos would have him shot. In the meantime they had cast Stephen Boyd to play the lead role as Ferdinand Marcos, but he backed out and was replaced by Paul Burke. (It might well be wondered why Marcos was to be played by a white American actor in a film whose primary purpose was as a propaganda vehicle in a Filipino election, for viewing by a domestic audience. It says something about cultural confusion when an incumbent Filipino President tries to broaden his appeal by turning himself into an American onscreen. Maybe he thought that, like Hartzell Spence's original book, the film might have an image-making impact on Americans if they could *see* him – and not merely intuit him – as one of them.)

Dovie likewise claimed to be 'hopelessly in love' with Ferdinand, and certainly there were domestic scenes of remarkable ease and familiarity up there on Northwestern St, Greenhills. The President would work naked on his state papers while she played the piano to him in the nude. He even allowed her to see him shitting, which is probably too indelicate a detail for a biographer like Rotea to have invented. We may take this as presumptive evidence for the likely validity of at least some of the political chit-chat she later reports as the elections draw closer. A man whose trust extends to that degree might also have been quite capable of leaving state papers around for her beady gaze to light on.

It was inevitable that sooner or later the press would catch up with the affair, which it did at the end of April 1969. From then on, it became a major topic of public mirth and gossip. Imelda was reputed to go 'black in the face with rage' at the mere mention of Dovie Beams's name. At some point Ilusorio and Poblador accused the actress of taking advantage of the situation and of monopolizing too much of the President's attention. They threatened to sack her as Evelyn and have her replaced with Suzanne Pleshette; but nobody really believed that a Dovie personally coached by Marcos could suddenly be dropped at this late stage for someone completely new to the role. In any case, Ilusorio was hardly in much of a position himself to make remarks about people taking advantage because there came a day when he had to go to the President and confess that the money Marcos had given him to make *Ang mga Maharlika* had, well, become substantively downsized. He claimed that he had prudently 'invested it in stocks, but that the stock had gone down rather than up'. These things happen. This was not the first time, and nothing like the last, that Marcos was to hear such a story from a crony to whom he had made a large cash advance. But he was always strangely incautious about such things, proving yet again that his interest in money was really limited to the political, rather than to the purchasing, power it represented. Provided the friendship was close enough, he seemed unwilling to insist on good accounting. One day this was to prove a large element in his undoing. Meanwhile, he explained to Dovie that he and Ilusorio had once smuggled gold together, so it was all right about the money. More funds miraculously replaced those lost.

It is at this point that an inner sadness first leaks onto the page.

> Marcos started talking about his father, and how he could have saved him from the Japanese soldiers who killed him, but his own cowardice kept him from going to his father's rescue. He expressed a very profound feeling and a deep sense of guilt about it.[8]

It is difficult to judge to what degree Ferdinand, in true Ronald Reagan fashion, now believed his own stories. But a note of authenticity is struck by this self-accusation of cowardice, an admission quite unthinkable in terms of his usual public image. Saying that the Japanese had killed Mariano is surely what any son might do when confronting the alternative of acknowledging that his father had been quartered by buffaloes by his own side for collaboration. Though the *modus vivendi* Marcos and Washington had tacitly worked out as regards his war exploits is always presented as having been a straightforwardly cynical political ploy, the suspicion is that it may well have cost him dear, and that the war's real residues had gone on being unresolved and causing him a distress he could only hint at in moments of unguarded intimacy like those with Dovie Beams. Rehearsing her in bed as she did her best to impersonate his wartime lover, Evelyn, must have awakened painful memories or at least made him thoughtful about the way he had allowed a fictionalized account of his war to stand for him. As his old friend Leonilo Ocampo remarked, 'He never enjoyed his life. You know who enjoyed it? Imelda.'[9]

By September the affair had become notorious and Dovie was herself nervous about its future, as about her own. When she flew to the US for studio dubbing sessions she took with her a cache of things to put in a safe against the rainy day she sensed might be coming. Among them were some cassettes she had secretly made of their love-making, including recordings of the President singing Ilocano folk songs to her post-coitally as they lay in bed. He had taken some Polaroid pictures of her and they had exchanged tufts of each other's pubic hair. By now Ferdinand was begging her to have his baby, a love-child that seemed to have considerable significance for him. He talked about it obsessively, and had even decided it was to be a son named Lawin (Tagalog for 'eagle', which seems more likely than its alternative dialect meaning of 'flying fish'). Yet Dovie did not conceive. When one day he discovered her birth-control pills, he seemed more mortified and downcast than angry.

Away from their bed in Greenhills, Marcos was preoccupied with his efforts to win a second term of office. He told Dovie that no Philippine President had ever served out a full second term, and he was determined to win regardless of the means. This included being prepared to use the Communist threat as an excuse to declare martial law if need be. (In the event, he did not declare martial law until 1972, so this provides at least circumstantial evidence that it was an option he had been toying with for some years.) Campaigning had now started in earnest. Marcos was up against the Liberal, Sergio Osmeña Jr. and his running-mate Genaro Magsaysay, the late President's brother. (How the old names perpetually recur in Philippine politics as a testament to the clannish mentality of *datu*ism!) Sergio Osmeña, a former Mayor of Cebu and son of the President of the old Commonwealth whom MacArthur had replaced with Manuel Roxas in 1948, had himself been accused of collaboration with the Japanese during the war. Specifically, he was alleged to have made a killing by selling scrap metal to the occupiers, though like most of the others he had been granted a blanket amnesty. With a fair degree of chutzpah, given his own wartime activities, Marcos now raked up these old charges of treason against him, while Osmeña and Magsaysay brought out the old black toothbrushes once more.

In July 1969 the American President Richard Nixon, who had replaced LBJ the previous year, came to Manila on the first leg of a swing through Asia and made a show of impartiality by spending time with both contenders. There was never any doubt where US support lay, however. Washington judged Osmeña as weak and, with his past, not a man who could be guaranteed to react infallibly as America's Boy. Nixon's tour of Asia came at a critical time for the American President. Having seen what the Vietnam war had done to his own predecessor, as well as what it was doing to the United States, Nixon was determined to find a way out of Vietnam as quickly as was consistent with honour, an expression that in practical terms meant incurring a minimum of American casualties and a maximum of face saved.

The speech Marcos gave at the state dinner he threw for the Nixons was, in its way, a small masterpiece of political juggling. He started easily with fulsome praise for the day's hot topic, the Apollo Moon landing which had taken place only six days before, but moved discreetly onto the offensive to hint that, no matter how great US technological prowess, America was by no means sitting pretty:

> Ladies and gentlemen, we have as our honoured guest tonight a man who has assumed the leadership of a nation in crisis, a nation confused by overwhelming internal problems . . .[10]

He then made an almost casual transition to the question of Communist subversion in Asia, thus bearing out what he had told Dovie Beams about not hesitating to use this gambit:

> The greatest threat to almost all Asian countries today is not external aggression but internal subversion, either by indigenous forces alone or with support from outside. This is true in the Philippines today. We are fighting, and will continue to fight, all attempts to subvert our free institutions with Filipino troops alone as we have done in the past. We are confident we can overwhelm efforts to destroy our Republic through subversion. But we do expect fulfilment of American commitments of assistance embodied in formal treaties between the two countries. The pledged assistance takes the form of equipment, armaments and material, but not ground troops.[11]

Gradually he elides from a grateful acknowledgement of American help, through reminders and veiled threats, to an assertion of Philippine nationalism:

In return for American assistance and friendship, we have allowed the United States certain concessions, including the lease of bases for the use of its armed forces and the grant of certain economic privileges.[12]

Basically, Marcos's demand was for maximum US aid with minimum US interference. 'Such regional arrangements would operate for as long as necessary under the American nuclear umbrella but without the involvement of American troops.' It was as much a crafty campaigning speech as one statesman's toast to another, delivered from an actual position of comparative weakness but pitched to sound as though Marcos were dictating terms to Washington. Its patriotic cheek would not have been lost on the voters (for the speech was widely reprinted) and would have sounded good taken in conjunction with stories of Osmeña's alleged wartime collaboration. As he sat there, Nixon must have mused about this man LBJ had privately referred to as 'that son-ofabitch' when it appeared to him that Marcos had approached Washington's milch cow, jauntily swinging an enormous pail, once too often.

But when Nixon had left, and away from this comparatively urbane level of politicking, the 1969 election campaign degenerated into atrocious violence in which whole villages were burned to the ground by local warlords acting for one or other candidate. Philippine Constabulary murder squads known as 'the Monkees' capitalized on all those exchange training visits to the US. Other military gangs such as the Suzuki Boys and the Barracudas terrorized provincial electorates. In the end, Marcos won by almost two million votes, an absurd margin that made humiliatingly obvious the level of fraud. It was a victory for the 'three G's' of Filipino politics: goons, guns and gold. As news filtered back to the capital of ballot boxes in the provinces vanishing *en masse* to be replaced by carefully stuffed boxes that had been stored in military safe houses, Eduardo Lachica of the *Philippines Herald* observed: 'The Liberals were outspent, outshouted, and outgunned,' while Serging Osmeña refused to concede defeat, a position he never altered, maintaining ever after that Marcos had not by any stretch of terminology won the 1969 election.

Curiously, this outcome appeared to have a profoundly depressing effect on Ferdinand. Far from exulting in the victory he had always planned on winning 'by whatever means', he now found himself unexpectedly affected by the public outcry. Dovie Beams thought him 'withdrawn' and said her lover had lost his usual self-confidence, as though he feared that the people might not have preferred him after all. The problem was that, like many a Filipino politician before him, he had been utterly unable to resist overkill. After all, too much democratic process merely increases one's chances of losing, so the thing to aim for is 99 percent of the vote, leaving a generous 1 percent up for grabs. Given an incumbent President's almost unlimited power to fix things in his own favour, he in fact had no need to win by such a ludicrous margin (a temptation he would again fail to resist in the snap election of February 1986). By indulging in such gross manipulation he lost all way of gauging what true support he had. Having taken this fatal electoral step, it was impossible for him to retreat. From here on he had to rely on his own propaganda machine and *hakot* (bussed) crowds to guarantee an impression of mass approval no matter what he did. For a man of Marcos's unexpected insecurity and need for reassurance it was doubly regrettable because in fact he could still count on a good deal of unforced grassroots support right to the end.

It was probably to counter the charges of having won the election by simply flattening the opposition with a golden steamroller that he made his curious, uneasy pledge at the Oath of Office ceremony at Luneta Park:

> Moved by the strongest desire and the purest will to set the example of self-denial and self-sacrifice for all our people, I have today decided to give away all my worldly possessions so that they may serve the greater needs of the greater number of our people through a foundation to be organized and to be known as the Ferdinand E. Marcos Foundation.[13]

Whereupon massed choirs sang the Hallelujah Chorus. It is interesting to compare this text with his diary entry the following day (quoted on p. 222). The care he takes in his diary to assert that the decision was 'not the result of pique, anger, despair or emotions' almost certainly indicates that these were precisely the reasons for it. After all, why would anyone think that pique or despair might be the hidden motives for a decision he goes on to describe as 'a noble act waiting to be done'? It makes no sense, except as an unconscious admission of how much his self-esteem had been shaken by the consequences of his own ruthless tactics. It was yet another demonstration of how little good could be expected of a political system which made such things possible and hence, in a winner-takes-all atmosphere where no unethical holds are barred, inevitable. It was not Marcos's fault that politics practically anywhere on earth guarantee that Mr Nice Guy loses; but it was his fault that his own anxiety led him to allow the Philippines' electoral process to sink to indiscriminate depths of terrorism and fraud. He was, after all, the President; and the President sets the tone of a campaign. (But as O. D. Corpuz so wisely remarked, 'in every Filipino President beats the heart of a tribal chief'.)

His affair with Dovie Beams survived throughout most of 1970 even as it became more and more a pretext for public mockery. The election had served to polarize all sorts of dissent and opposition to Marcos's continued presidency; and the affair with Dovie Beams was targeted as his Achilles' heel the more that threats grew to the stability of his regime, particularly from the student left and the New People's Army (the NPA, which was the military wing of the Communist Party of the Philippines and of the National Democratic Front, had been established on 29 March 1969, exactly twenty-seven years after the founding of the Hukbalahap). In October 1970 the *Philippines Free Press* – the country's oldest and most respected weekly news magazine – led with a cover story about Dovie Beams which was very damaging to the President, partly because it made him look ridiculous but also because it hinted at a serious rift between him and Imelda whose consequences went far beyond the merely marital.

For some time Filipino observers had been getting wind of an increasing polarization in Malacañang Palace between what they identified as the Ilocano and Leyteño factions of, respectively, the President and Mrs Marcos. This, too, was a consequence of *datu*ism, since each relied on his or her own network of political patronage, and the two sets of appointees did not necessarily get on with each other. Gossip leaked out of monster feuds and constant bickering, of disagreements about projects and countermanded orders. Mrs

Marcos's own political power had been steadily growing the more she acquired confidence and her welfare and building programmes acquired funding. To her already considerable ambitiousness was now added the goad of humiliation over her husband's much-publicized unfaithfulness. It is hard not to feel for her. Through no fault of her own she had been made to look like a failed wife by a Hollywood third-ranker who was herself, as it happened, a failed wife. There is some reason for believing that for a while Imelda felt herself wounded to the point of seriously considering separation, and her confidantes attest to her utter mortification and rage. She reacted as many a scorned woman before her, with venom. She was, after all, no stranger to the notion of getting even. Her first act was to have *Ang mga Maharlika* banned for starring Dovie Beams, ordering banks to foreclose on the Filipino production company to make the point quite clear. She then gave orders to Edmundo Reyes, the Commissioner of Immigration and Deportation, to go to Greenhills in person and serve a deportation order on her. The actress frustrated him by the simple expedient of slamming the door in Munding's face. When shortly afterwards she fell ill, he had a second chance.

> She was in Manila Medical – I served the deportation order on her there. She was very thin and did not strike me as at all attractive; but still, there was no doubt about [her and the President's] relationship. Marcos was a womanizer, no question.[14]

But this was not about womanizing so much as a love affair that had got out of hand. Via the US Embassy Dovie Beams received an offer that they assured her came from Imelda of $100,000 in cash in exchange for all her tape recordings and other evidence. Now seriously scared, Dovie put herself under the protection of her Embassy and Ambassador Henry Byroade. She then called a press conference where she confirmed the existence of the tapes she had made of her love-making sessions. In the Bay View Hotel across the road from the Embassy she backed her claim by playing to reporters some of the recordings of the President, drowsy with erotic contentment, crooning in the double bed up in Greenhills. Unknown to her, two of the reporters made copies of the recordings which they promptly sold to several prominent people including

Benigno Aquino, who was said to have cheerfully paid $500 for his cassette.

> Student protesters at the University of the Philippines comman-
> deered the campus radio station and broadcast a looped tape;
> soon the entire nation was listening in astonishment to President
> Marcos begging Dovie Beams to perform oral sex. For over a
> week the President's hoarse injunctions boomed out over uni-
> versity loudspeakers. Special forces troopers sent to recapture
> the radio station crumpled with laughter. Barely able to keep a
> straight face, Ninoy Aquino called for a Senate investigation.[15]

On 11 November 1970 Dovie Beams was whisked to Hong Kong, escorted by the US Consul, Lawrence Harris. At the airport she was immediately arrested by British intelligence as much for her own safety as for the debriefing they presently conducted. They told her that a man named Delfin Cueto, who had been sitting near her on the plane, might well have been hired by Mrs Marcos to kill her in Hong Kong (Cueto was believed by some to be Ferdinand's half-brother). When they arrested Cueto he reportedly told the British officers that his name was Fred, that Dovie Beams was his mistress and that there was no connection with Ferdinand Marcos. Dovie Beams eventually made it back home to Los Angeles where she made copies of everything and stored them in different safes as her security. Apparently she was never entirely happy with Rotea's book and allegedly wrote her own, copies of which she also stashed in various vaults. She lived for some years in circumstances that suggested her two-year affair with the President of the Philippines had not gone unrewarded, occasionally fending off emissaries from Imelda who offered her various inducements to part with her hidden material. She was recently reported as having died, after earning for herself a special niche in post-war Philippine history.

Given all the evidence, it would seem pointless for either the President or his wife to have attempted to deny the basic fact of the Dovie Beams affair. One excellent reason for doubting that Ferdinand ever intended his diary to be more than a highly sani-tized version of his Presidency with posterity in mind is supplied by an entry where he affects to treat the whole affair as though it had no connection with him. He had been impersonated by 'Fred' as part of an elaborate attempt by a mentally unstable Dovie Boehms [sic] to blackmail him:

> Called in Ambassador Byroade [. . .] to find out what the participation of the American government is in the Boehms blackmail conspiracy. They denied any such participation and claimed that the presence of Consul Harris was merely to guarantee her departure. [. . .] There is an indication that the Fred whom she talks about is Federico Delfin Cueto. He is also known for having been introducing himself as President Marcos. And he may have done so to Boehms. He is now in Hongkong in the same Ambassador Hotel in which the Boehms woman is staying. [. . .] She (Boehms) was treated for a brain injury in a hospital some time ago. We are now checking Memphis, Tennessee, Los Angeles and New York hospitals and asylums. She is a psychiatry case.[16]

That the 'Boehms woman' did not drop out of the President's mind is suggested by a postscript to this tale. According to Rotea, in 1972 Marcos's trusty lieutenant Nanoy Ilusorio was sent to find Dovie in Beverly Hills and the following conversation allegedly took place:

> *Ilusorio*:   He [Marcos] loves you very much . . . And he wants
>   you to come back as the First Lady.
> *Dovie*:   What about the First Lady [Imelda]?
> *Ilusorio*:   Well, she is going to die.
> *Dovie*:   How is she going to die?
> *Ilusorio*:   Just wait and see.[17]

A few months later, on 7 December 1972, Mrs Marcos was presenting awards at a televized ceremony at the Nayong Pilipino pavilion near Manila International Airport. Suddenly a man wearing a formal suit lunged at her with a knife in full view of the cameras. Her security guards wrestled him to the ground and shot him to death, but not before he had deeply gashed an arm that Imelda had instinctively thrown up to defend herself (she bears the scar to this day). His name was later given variously as Carlito Dimaali or Limailig, believed to be either a Moslem from the south with a grievance or a resident of Batangas with no personal motivation.

No more was ever heard of him. Imelda was widely praised for her dignified behaviour, it being considered that few people survived an assassination attempt with such composure. Thereafter she bore her wound proudly and not long afterwards appeared at the Nixon inaugural with her injured arm in a sling made of a double strand of pearls. (It should be stressed that the circumstantial linking of this event with Ilusorio's alleged 'prediction' of Mrs Marcos's death rests entirely on Hermie Rotea's account which, as has already been noted, had its own political axe to grind at a time when no rumour about either of the Marcoses was too perverse or grotesque to be published as gospel by the exiled opposition in the US.)

In the immediate aftermath of the Dovie Beams scandal Marcos went on the attack, using a Manila newspaper he owned, the *Republic Weekly*. Between February and April 1971 the paper published ten articles calculated to discredit the actress as 'an obscure Hollywood bit-player who had come to Manila to extort money from President Marcos and from certain Filipino businessmen who claim to be close to the President. When she failed to get the thousands that she wanted, Miss Beams rocked the nation by involving the President in a lurid sex scandal with herself.'[18] Her psychiatric record was dredged up from among those of her divorce proceedings. Her therapist had described her as 'a latent schizophrenic' and noted her 'pursuit of erotic self-satisfaction [sic] through romance'. Better still was the account Dovie had given reporters of her own amatory career:

> According to her in her various conversations with media representatives, she had had carnal relations with the late President John F. Kennedy and his brother, Ted. She was intimate with the Canadian Prime Minister Trudeau. She went to bed with the former Prime Minister of England, Harold Wilson. She had sexual relations with the present Prime Minister of West Germany, the former Mayor of Berlin, the President of France, the Sheikh of Kuwait, Baron Ernst Valentine von Wendel, Prince Hohenhow, Howard Hughes, Senator [Albert] Gore of Tennessee . . .

(*Harold Wilson?* Can it be that we journalists of the late sixties actually missed finding a love-nest in Hampstead Garden Suburb?)

This demolition of Dovie Beams was countered by another magazine, the *Graphic*, which had initially published all her material, such as the transcripts of her tapes. This was shortly to earn the *Graphic* summary closure – one of Marcos's early acts under martial law. The passage quoted immediately above was included in Imelda's private dossier of the scandal which was found in the Palace after the Marcoses' flight in 1986. Also in the file was painful evidence of what it had signified for her: Ferdinand's Polaroid snapshots of the naked Dovie Beams, in one of which the actress's vagina had been obliterated by furious ballpoint scrawls.

Many people considered that the Dovie Beams affair gave Imelda Marcos the impetus she needed to acquire emotional, even political, dominance over her husband:

> Imelda had caught him philandering, and that weakened his hold over her. Marcos had been cast as a bumbling Casanova [. . .]. To Imelda, who had so carefully nurtured the image of a perfect marriage – and her image of Marcos as a superhero – his public humiliation was unforgivable. Marcos had squandered his side of the partnership, and now the scales of power tipped in Imelda's favour.[19]

It is believed that the reparations exacted from Ferdinand by his wife included the Benguet gold mines that he was stealthily trying to acquire via the good offices of 'XYZ'. These now passed to the Romualdez family by means of a takeover conducted by similar methods. (Specifically, it was fronted by the Ayala Corporation, through Enrique Zobel, who took over the Benguet board on behalf of Imelda's favourite brother, Kokoy Romualdez.) Some believe this acquisition should be viewed differently, however. 'After the Dovie business Kokoy knew he could get away with whatever his imagination – or that of the Wall Street types who advised him in his takeovers – suggested. Thus he didn't get Benguet as Ferdinand's expiation to Imelda but through the President's general disinclination to stop him. It was almost as if Marcos was suddenly weary. From then on, Kokoy's clout grew.'

An interesting after-effect of the Dovie Beams affair was that of making amends by public works. Ferdinand had already claimed to have built the San Juanico Bridge between Samar and Leyte

(Imelda's home province) for his wife. Certainly the public billet-doux Ferdinand attached to it was 'A Birthday Gift to Imelda the Fabulous by the President', even though such a road link was a vital part of the nation's Pan-Pacific Highway running the length of the archipelago. From now on the Marcoses began to play out their marital tiffs by means of public monuments. Not only that, but the longer martial law dragged on, the more frequently the controlled press printed 'intimate' poems from one of the First Couple to the other, generally couched in embarrassing terms, on birthdays and anniversaries. Their ingenuous tastelessness embraced the Philippine nation as an extension of the First Family, assuring the children that Daddy and Mommy loved each other very, very much, and this was one family that would *never* break up. (In February 1997 Senator Gloria Macapagal, the daughter of the late President, published her own Valentine message to the nation in Tagalog which translated as 'I treasure true love. I want you to be part of my dream.' Some commentators saw this as a new low in Philippine politics in the use of cloying intimacy as part of a steely campaign of self-promotion, for the Senator was making no secret of her plans to stand as a Presidential candidate in 1998. Yet it was really nothing new. The Senator understood to a nicety that while most Filipinos would not remember the Marcos era clearly enough to draw that politically risky parallel, they would paradoxically recall that her own political capital ultimately derived from her connection to Marcos's immediate predecessor.) *Datus* again.

By now, in the initial days of his second term, Marcos was in trouble. The intense public disquiet that his tactics for winning the election had caused was a separate issue from the growing opposition of the left, but the left certainly capitalized on it in the early months of 1970. The rioting and demonstrations of the so-called 'First Quarter Storm' were so serious that for a while Malacañang Palace was under siege and the gates had to be welded shut. And this came about despite the deployment of the anti-riot squads of the dreaded Metropolitan Command. (METROCOM had been set up in July 1967 with American security technology supplied under USAID. This permitted complete nationwide co-ordination with the National Bureau of Investigation's computerized intelligence network at Camps Crame and Aguinaldo, the military bases on

Manila's main ring road, E. de los Santos Avenue [EDSA]. In command of this entire network was the Philippines' chief of secret police, Fabian Ver, a fellow Ilocano and relative of Ferdinand's as well as his most loyal *maharlika*.)

It is now a part of received wisdom that these demonstrations of the First Quarter Storm were really instigated by Marcos himself in order to give him a pretext for the martial law he had long been planning. Dovie Beams claimed to have heard him say as much, though this was towards the end of the affair when she had acquired enough knowledge of local politics to know how to interest the journalists who interviewed her. There is no question that Marcos – both as the man he was and in the political tradition he was operating from – had the requisite craftiness to use the tactics of *agent provocateur* when it suited him. (The faked 'assassination attempt' on Juan Ponce Enrile which was supposed to have provided the final straw for precipitating the declaration of martial law in September 1972 was a case in point.) But the evidence is now overwhelming that the First Quarter Storm was quite spontaneous. Indeed, it was the very genuineness of the protesters' rage that took Marcos completely by surprise and occasioned his severe post-election depression. (Not least among the contributory reasons for this was the indignity of having been mocked over the campus loudspeaker system of his own beloved Alma Mater, UP.) On 26 January 1970, he emerged from having opened Congress to be greeted by 'The Battle of Burgos Drive': 40,000 demonstrators demanding a stop to such things as subservience to Washington and the widespread form of corruption involving 'grease money' or *tong*. Everywhere placards denounced 'Senatongs', 'Tongressmen', 'Fixcals' and the 'House of Representathieves', as well as 'US Puppets'. There were also jocular references to 'Ferdie & Meldy: Bonnie & Clyde'. A large coffin entitled 'Death of Democracy' was paraded in front of the security forces, and before he could reach the safety of his car the President was attacked by a papier-mâché crocodile labelled 'The Administration' that bit his pompadour. (*Buwaya*, crocodile, is everyday slang for someone on the take, being most commonly used to describe the police.)

It was precisely because of the enormous power he wielded through his American-trained security network that Marcos would have found it almost impossible to have organized the very sort of riots METROCOM was expressly designed to prevent. It is anyway highly doubtful if he could have arranged disruption on such a scale, nor would he have risked rioting so severe it actually caused Palace aides to decamp to the safety of Baguio, taking with them crates of money and state papers.

> I recalled that night in January 1970, when, at the height of the so-called First Quarter Storm, a mob had gathered outside Gate 4 of the Palace. They rammed the gate with a commandeered fire truck they had set on fire, throwing Molotov cocktails and shouting, 'Dante! Dante!' [Bernabe Buscayno, aka Kumander Dante, Commander-in-Chief of the New People's Army – NPA]. We had repulsed them with water cannons. It was bedlam but we put that down. That same night, a convoy of trucks prepared to leave the Palace loaded with papers, guns, ammunition and money, all headed for Baguio, where it had long been decided the seat of government would be set up if the Palace fell to the mob.
>
> The convoy was leaving the Palace grounds when Col. Fabian Ver called me and ordered me to ride in the lead truck. [. . .] We made Baguio in good time with our load, and set up the place in case the President and his party arrived . . .[20]

As it happened, METROCOM prevailed and the Marcoses did not have to flee to Baguio; but for a moment it had been a close thing.

The University of the Philippines (UP) out in Quezon City was the radical students' focal point – so much so that it was frequently and disparagingly referred to as 'The Diliman Republic' or 'The People's Republic of Diliman'. ('Diliman' is the name of the University's main campus. *Dilim* means 'dark' in Tagalog; *diliman* is therefore a place of darkness or shade, and commemorates the forest that stood there before the campus was built after the Second World War. It is a lovely name, with its pleasing irony that a seat of enlightenment should be named for obfuscation.)

Student radicalism was, of course, much in the air at the time, and not only in the Philippines. As one might expect, the Filipino movement had close links with the revolutionary as well as with the ideological left. To show how the latter was still predicated on nothing more (but nothing less) revolutionary than the old question of land reform, the General Secretary of the new Communist Party of the Philippines, Luis Taruc, had written to the *Manila Times* from his prison cell in Camp Crame a few years earlier:

> In assessing the Huk problem today we need to study the cen-turies-old background of feudal landlordism, of the virtual slavery of the masses of our people. For social justice's sake let us not forget that the Huks are the living symbol of resistance and rebellion against the status quo, and as such must be looked upon with understanding and sympathy by the privileged class whose long-range selfish interest is on the side of non-communist genuine Huks. We must reform and change according to the Christian democratic way, as called upon by Pope Paul VI in His Holiness' encyclical 'On the Development of People': *There is no other way, and we cannot delay, for time is running out on us.* Otherwise, godless totalitarianism will do it for us at the cost of so much bitterness, hate, and destruction of lives, property and time-respected human values, human freedom and spiritual expression.[21]

This is interesting not only for its reasonableness (the jailed General Secretary of the CPP invoking a Papal encyclical about social justice, no less) but for its anxious premonition of martial law, then still five years in the future. Far from indulging in alarmist special pleading, Taruc was by no means alone. The *Manila Times* had already noted that foreign observers were making the same point, while Raul S. Manglapus (an Opposition senator) in a speech to the Rotary Club in October 1967 said that 'the outgoing Apostolic Nuncio to the Philippines whose former post was in Latin America said publicly in Manila [. . .] that he found in this country's disparity of wealth and in the conditions of society, the same symptoms of revolution as those in pre-Castro Cuba.'[22] Meanwhile, it is instructive to let someone who was intimately involved with events on the left put them into perspective, if only to show once and for all the absurdity of the widely held belief that 'the left' was a mere tail which the old dog Marcos could wag at will.

The new party [CPP] grew phenomenally among the young. I was Chairman of the Philippine Committee for Freedom in

South Vietnam. There were huge anti-war demos in front of the
US Embassy in 1964 and 1965 – much earlier in the Philippines
than elsewhere. I was going on Leftist conferences abroad when
I was a student at UP between 1960 and 1965. For example, I
went to Indonesia with Nur Misuari [the founder in 1968 of the
Moslem MNLF – Moro National Liberation Front] and Adrian
Cristobal, who was then a starving Leftist. In 1966 I went to
China with [now Senator] Heherson Alvarez as guests of the
Chinese Youth Federation, the Red Guard organization, so we
saw the Cultural Revolution at close range. I came away definitely thinking it could be duplicated here. They were seductive
concepts for young people then: egalitarianism, a classless society, the dictatorship of the proletariat . . . You wanted a cause to
embrace and Maoism filled the void. So we returned to the
Philippines preaching Maoism – or at least some of us did.
Sonny Alvarez didn't.

In 1969/70, at the beginning of his second term, Marcos had
become very unpopular. The Party's strategy was to hasten the
victory of the Maoist revolution in the Philippines. The plan was
for there to be increasingly violent disturbances in the city as the
guerrilla movement spread throughout the countryside. In 1969
China had agreed to send material help to the Filipino revolution. We had highly secret contacts with Beijing. Marcos certainly
had no idea of these preparations. As a journalist [with the
Manila Chronicle], one of my tasks was to act as liaison between
[the Party and] our representatives in Beijing. I was a courier. I
went twice to Hong Kong with important documents and
instructions to our man in Beijing.

Meanwhile, Marcos was becoming a despised tyrant. There
were bloody demonstrations, including the First Quarter Storm,
in which many students died – manna from heaven, as far as the
Party was concerned. All we lacked were weapons. The NPA
[New People's Army] already existed under Kumander Dante,
but it too had virtually no guns. We badly needed arms, so in
1971 the Party decided the time was ripe for a quantum leap in
the struggle. So we sent a delegation to China to negotiate aid in
the form of heavy weapons. Our first task was to arrange an
arms shipment to Isabela. A ship was bought here in the
Philippines and a shipping 'company' established. The Chinese

agreed to ship us M-14s, the Chinese copy with wooden stocks. JoMa Sison [Jose Maria Sison, who had 're-established' the CPP along Maoist lines in 1968 after its break with the PKP] had a long shopping list and was demanding anti-aircraft guns and other sophisticated weapons, but the Chinese told him to settle for M-14s. That initial shipment was 1200 M-14s, 5 bazookas, several pairs of binoculars and plenty of ammunition. The plan called for the ship to go to the Fujien coast for loading, and then to head for the east coast of Isabela province where it would be unloaded by a waiting detachment of NPAs.

This first project was a failure. The ship, the *Karagatan*, was spotted by a logging company's plane as it was being unloaded. The PC [Philippine Constabulary, the paramilitary police force] were tipped off and there was a firefight. The NPA saved only about 200 rifles. The rest went to the PC. It was bad luck; but to be frank JoMa Sison had botched it. There had been far too little planning. Marcos was convinced that the shipment had been sent by the Chinese but he kept quiet because he didn't dare speak out. With the exception of a few stray pens whom no-one believed, the Marcos-controlled media blamed everyone except the Chinese.[23]

It is particularly ironic that post-1986 anti-Marcos historians such as Sterling Seagrave should have sided with these journalists of the 'Marcos-controlled media' in their accounts of this famous *Karagatan* incident. Compare, for example, Seagrave's version:

Ferdinand soon proved that when his enemies closed in on him he was a close student of Lyndon Johnson's Tonkin Gulf manoeuvre [the incident in August 1964, in which an 'unprovoked attack' on the US destroyer *Maddox* gave LBJ the pretext he needed to bomb North Vietnamese oil refineries and naval bases, plans for which had long been laid down. The *Maddox* was in fact on a spying mission in North Vietnamese waters, and the North Vietnamese attack on it was consequently a legitimate defensive act against a hostile power]. That summer of 1972, the fishing trawler M/V *Karagatan* went aground off the northeast coast of Luzon and was boarded by the military, who reported to headquarters that they found nothing suspicious, only some food supplies. The crew had vanished. Ferdinand made a great issue over the *Karagatan*, claiming it was running guns to the Communists. [. . .] According to Malacañang, the trawler had aboard 3,500 M-15 rifles, 30 rocket launchers, and 160,000 rounds of ammunition – completely contradicting the original military report. [. . .] Journalists confirmed that the gun-running shipment was a sham. The real owner of the trawler was the Karagatan Fishing Corporation [and the ship] apparently had been engaged in nothing more sinister than cigarette smuggling for an Ilocano syndicate.[24]

As it happened, Seagrave was perfectly correct as to the 'real owner' of the *Karagatan*; but in every other respect he fell easy victim to the anti-Marcos mania which, in the late eighties, had reached such a proportion that practically any incident in the preceding two decades was credulously attributed to his evil hand. This was partly due to such writers' disinclination to talk to anybody on the left (and vice versa). But it also betrayed a radical naivety about the way in which a country like the Philippines is actually governed, in which the writ of the President – no matter how powerful he or she is – does not infallibly run even twenty miles outside Metro Manila. To view everything that happened in Marcos's Philippines as evidence of his sinister control reveals a misunderstanding of the country's social dynamics, as well as a highly optimistic notion of the state of communications in its remoter regions in the 1970s. At the time of the *Karagatan* incident, many of the country's provinces (regardless of how during elections they might be bought with money filtering through the hierarchical Christmas tree) remained highly autonomous, ruled by infinitely complex arrangements of warlords, élite landowners and politicians, each with their own contacts with the local military and crime syndicates. While a good deal of what happened in the country between 1965 and 1986 took place as a consequence of, or was facilitated by, Marcos's Presidency, it did not necessarily mean that he had either planned it or could control it. One of the reasons why he 'Ilocanized' the Army at officer level was precisely to give him some degree of unified military control throughout the archipelago; but in practice the further south from Manila one went the more this seemingly unified control frayed into areas of intricate anarchy.

Indeed, even today the writ of a Filipino President is not guaranteed to run within Malacañang Palace itself, let alone outside it. One indication of this is the frequent spectacle of the Philippines' Chief Executive having to give the National Police, the National Bureau of Investigation or other government agencies his personal orders to carry out the duties they are already charged with. Often, too, the presumably valuable time of the head of state is taken up by trivial matters that apparently cannot be entrusted to his staff. Thus in 1993 President Ramos was himself obliged to warn the public about a fake Palace 'aide' in his own presidential office. 'I do not know him. I have not authorized him and he is not a member of this office. He is not a member of my staff and any authority given him is unauthorized and illegal . . .' Ramos then vowed to investigate his own presidential assistant who had issued the bogus aide with a siren-equipped white Nissan Sentra with government plates. 'We'll have him investigated,' the President said. Two weeks previously, President Ramos had ordered his Executive Secretary to look into the case, but nothing had happened.[25]

The real story of incidents like the *Karagatan* comes better from someone on the inside.

In 1974 there was a second attempt, which our group in Beijing also negotiated. This time the arms were to be dropped into the sea in airtight, vacuum-packed containers which were to be retrieved by scuba divers off the coast of La Union. Another boat was bought; but this time the tragedy that befell the attempt was far greater since more people and resources were involved. It was of course much more complicated, what with selecting and training scuba diving teams unobserved by the PC. But it was another disaster. The ship – the *Doña Andrea* – ran aground on the way to China on an atoll between Hainan and Taiwan called Pratas Island [Dongsha Qundao]. It was pure inexperience. The crew were NPAs, not professional seamen. They were spotted by a ship out of Hong Kong. Our NPA crew offered them the *Doña Andrea* in return for a passage to China. The other ship refused the offer and took them to Hong Kong, where their identity was obvious.

They were rescued by the Chinese Government interceding through the Chinese Red Cross. The Hong Kong authorities didn't want to antagonize Beijing by deporting the NPAs to the Philippines, so they were quietly transferred to China. So for the second time Marcos became aware of China trying to destabilize the Philippines. Again he kept quiet. But then he tried a *coup* of his own in the shape of Kissinger-style diplomacy. That year he sent Imelda on a state visit to charm Mao and break the ground for formal diplomatic relations, which came when Marcos appointed her brother Kokoy Romualdez to Beijing as the first Philippine Ambassador, another concession to her. Then he sent his son Bong Bong, and finally he went himself. He wanted to undercut the Left by offering China diplomatic recognition in exchange for their dropping support for the NPA and the CPP. Imelda went to Beijing and actually swept Mao and the rest off their feet. Mao kissed her hand and embraced her. It was unheard-of. ['My greatest-ever compliment came from Mao Zedong: "I like Mrs Marcos because she is so natural, and that is perfection."'[26]]

We felt betrayed by the Chinese. We never imagined they would privilege State relations over Party revolutionary ideals. Really, they were very disappointed by JoMa Sison's performance, and they characterized us as amateurs, as 'infantile Leftists'. Deng Xiao Ping [the Chinese vice-premier] himself said 'The Filipino comrades are very clumsy' – as it was relayed to us by one of the interpreters.

By now it was the mid-seventies. Our CPP delegation in China found itself jobless once Marcos and the Beijing Government had established diplomatic relations. The Chinese refused to take any further part in our struggle. I and some other comrades had gone into exile in China as fugitives from martial law. We couldn't return to the Philippines since we were facing charges there of subversion following the *Karagatan* and *Doña Andrea* débâcles. We were in deep shit. So we went to the countryside, to the depths of Hunan province, and there we all stayed for four long years. The Chinese there were very sympathetic to us. They built us a nice compound and we planted chestnuts, oranges, pears, figs, vegetables and water melons. This rustic exile came to an end because of a split in our ranks over the leadership of the CPP. Some accused JoMa Sison of revisionism, while we others defended him. So we parted ways. [Our group] went back to

Beijing and stayed for two more years near Democracy Wall. By then there was growing liberalization in China and it was an interesting period.[27]

As it turned out, the left never did come close to toppling Marcos, although there were some anxious moments. However, its underground resistance to martial law did have a salutary and radicalizing effect on many middle-class students and professionals who had been targeted by the security forces. This made them far more sympathetic to the oppressed lives of ordinary Filipinos in the countryside than they would ordinarily have been and, for a brief decade or so, gave them a common cause. That the popular reaction to Marcos's election victory in 1969 was more a windfall for the left than a conspiracy by student hotheads is borne out by another of the participants:

The First Quarter Storm was spontaneous, but it turned into the first flexing of the Left's muscles. The idea was not to instigate an urban uprising. Rather, it was the classic Maoist policy of spreading the ideology of revolution to the countryside. It was more a matter of consciousness-raising. Concepts such as imperialism, feudalism and fascism were just beginning to be understood in their Filipino context. It took the declaration of martial law to polarize things urgently and get the Left organized underground.[28]

It is important not to underestimate the fear created by student and Maoist factional unrest in the Philippines in the late sixties and early seventies. When Mao Zedong implemented his 'Cultural Revolution' between 1966 and 1969, excesses by the Red Guards shocked much of the world. The spectacle of a formal education system being abolished and students publicly accusing, assaulting and sometimes executing their own teachers provided potent images of fanaticism and anarchy. In the Philippines, a metaphorical stone's throw from mainland China, these social forces were deeply alarming, especially given the largely unreconstructed feudalism that still held sway over enough areas of the rural Philippines as to make the country as a whole feel ideologically vulnerable. Complex political tensions were set up. Old CPP members were none too happy about the Maoist cadres of the NPA.

Ordinary leftist intellectuals found themselves caught between calling for radical change and rejecting the violence and horror the Maoist model seemed to promise. For a large number of thinking Filipinos neither alternative – Marcos or Mao – was in any way ideal. Plenty of people considered some form of forcible expropriation of land for landless peasants might be made acceptable; but no grade-school teachers cared to picture themselves being forced to kneel in the local marketplace, wearing a placard and 'confessing' to awesome ideological crimes before being subjected to the mercy of their crazed pupils. Among the many conundrums posed to ordinary Filipinos was, what sort of a government would these Maoist NPAs institute if ever they did come to power? The answer was never made clear. As always, revolutionary leftism seemed to deal more with how to seize power than with explaining the precise policies a successful regime would adopt if Marcos were overthrown. At best, student rhetoric that wasn't violently anarchic hinted vaguely at a sort of peasant utopia with nationalist trimmings (the US bases would, of course, be the first things to go). Most Filipinos found all this quite unsatisfactory as a sensible blueprint for their future.

By 1969, of course, Mao Zedong and Zhou Enlai had realized what a disaster the 'Cultural Revolution' had been for China, which had temporarily collapsed as a coherent economic and social unit. By 1970 a desperate national reconstruction was in hand. So when the Communist Party of the Philippines made its bid to import arms from China in 1971, it was already late in the day. China's ideas of exporting the Revolution to the rest of Asia had been seriously revised under the pressures of domestic *realpolitik*. By the time the CPP made its request for assistance, it was unlikely they would ever have got much even had Beijing trusted the Filipino revolutionary leadership. The thoroughness of Mao's about-face in foreign policy was cheerfully summed up in 1972 when he told Nixon 'I like Rightists!' So when Imelda Marcos herself went to Beijing in September 1974 and alternately dazzled and charmed Mao and a whole series of silk-jacketed ancients, the writing was indeed on Democracy Wall as far as the CPP was concerned.

In 1971, before the continued social upheaval led Marcos to declare martial law, there was a particular terrorist incident that has echoed to this day: the bombing of a political meeting at Plaza

Miranda in downtown Manila. On 21 August 1971 the opposition Liberal Party was holding a large public rally there when two grenades were thrown, killing ten and wounding sixty-six. All the Liberals' senatorial candidates present were wounded, including Marcos's defeated opponent, Serging Osmeña; his nephew John Osmeña; Sen. Gerardo Roxas (the late President's son); Sen. Genaro Magsaysay (the late President's brother); Sen. Jovito Salonga; Sen. Eva Kalaw and Ramon Mitra. The only member of the Liberal leadership to escape death or injury was Sen. Ninoy Aquino, by then the chief opposition contender for the 1973 presidential election. He was absent from the platform because, according to one version, he had been delayed at a party. He had caught the start of the rally on his car radio on the way to Plaza Miranda. His absence was later seen as conclusive evidence that the bombing had been the work of Communist terrorists, a charge Marcos immediately made. It was assumed that Aquino's many NPA friends had tipped him off in advance to stay at home. Marcos at once suspended the writ of habeas corpus, which duly gave his opponents all the proof they needed that the outrage, far from being the work of Communists, had simply been arranged by him much as the Nazis had arranged the Reichstag fire. According to this version, its function was to prepare the way for a declaration of martial law, and it had clearly been bad luck for him that he had failed to kill Aquino, his only serious political opponent.

The reason why Plaza Miranda still echoes is not just because the injured still bear their scars, nor even that it was seen as a signal moment in the Marcos Presidency, but because like many another incident in Philippine politics (including the assassination of Ninoy Aquino himself twelve years later) it is still not unequivocally agreed who bombed the rally and why. The view that it was the work of Marcos himself has naturally been favoured by later historians because it fits with their picture of a boundlessly cynical tyrant. Sterling Seagrave is himself breezily self-assured on the subject, backed up by journalistic hints of being privy to the definitive story:

Palace insiders eventually confirmed it was all a set-up, carried out by Ver's agents. According to Primitivo Mijares, chief press spokesman for Marcos at the time, orders for the bombing came from the Presidential Security Command, which made all the arrangements with the grenade throwers, including the pay-off. Mijares discussed the bombing immediately afterward with members of the Command, and was told that the men who threw the grenades were murdered when they tried to collect their fee, apparently standard procedure for Ver.[29]

Leaving aside whether or not one thinks it likely that US-trained military of the crack Presidential Security Command would be likely to chat about such a highly sensitive operation to a Palace press man, one has also to bear in mind that Mijares was far from being an impartial witness. He was shortly to become the most celebrated Marcos turncoat when he defected to the United States and wrote a book (catchily titled *The Conjugal Dictatorship of Ferdinandimelda Marcos*) which became an early bible for the exiled opponents of the regime.

As Seagrave and others ought to have recognized, there are inside stories and there are inside stories, and nowhere more so than in the Philippines. Here, for example, is what Senator Blas Ople had to say sixteen years after Plaza Miranda (he was a member of Marcos's cabinet at the time):

Marcos was quite daunted by the NPA threat. The Plaza Miranda incident was, they now say, an intention by the Communists to split the ruling class. JoMa Sison was later denounced by one of the conspirators – the head of the Kalookan City chapter of the CPP. Marcos was extremely worried by the incident, I remember. His instincts were sound, though, and he immediately suspected the Communists. [As to Ninoy Aquino's alleged part in it being made the more glaring by his fortunate absence]: In private conversations with Marcos the name of Aquino did come up now and again, but he really did not consider him seriously as a suspect. He thought Ninoy was a major player [i.e. with political ambitions for high office] and also had a conscience.[30]

Yet another insider is Ricardo Malay who, as we have seen, knew the politburo from within:

Plaza Miranda was JoMa Sison's attempt to dare Marcos to impose martial law so that oppression would breed resistance, and more struggle in turn, and so on to victory . . . What Marcos did was suspend the writ of habeas corpus. He only began to be seriously alarmed the following year with the proof of Chinese interference following the capture of the [M/V] *Karagatan*.[31]

The violent incidents climaxed in the 'assassination attempt' on the new Defence Minister, Marcos's personal lawyer Juan Ponce Enrile (which in 1986 Enrile admitted had been faked). This was wholly pointless, given that the President had already fixed the date for martial law; but the Thespian in him never could resist staginess. It was part of his innate belief in overkill. He finally declared martial law on 21 September 1972. What strikes one incongruously but forcefully is how it can be read as having been almost an *erotic* event for him. This is at least partly due to its long drawn-out anticipation, and his own description of it as leading to 'the birth of a New Society'. The anticipation had certainly pre-dated his double-bedded conversations with Dovie Beams, when she later reported him as having mentioned martial law as one of the options open to him as an increasingly beleaguered President. He had been toying with the idea for years (as any President might) as a possible way of sidestepping the constitutional obligation to stand down after two terms of office. He must have spent a long time researching the legal aspects, let alone stealthily laying the military foundations for its nationwide implementation. For well over a year the topic had been discussed openly by his political opponents and by the press as a possible recourse, which is why the Plaza Miranda bombing was instantly suspected in many quarters as being his work. In mid-July of 1972 Senator Jose Diokno, who was to become famous as the Philippines' foremost human rights advocate, had made a speech in the Senate entitled 'A Throne of Bayonets' in which he warned the nation about the likelihood of a summary declaration of martial law. When it actually happened a couple of months later few were surprised – least of all Diokno, who found himself arrested and held in a military stockade until the Supreme Court had ruled in favour of the legitimacy of Marcos's *diktat*.

The eroticism of Marcos's political move can be glimpsed not only in his breathless but painstaking preparations but equally in his pride in it afterwards, when he constantly harked back to the date of its declaration as to a moment of triumphant personal conquest. This date, 21/9/72, was of private significance to him in that it undoubtedly reflected his concern with numerology. His lucky number was seven, and he had already renamed the Presidential yacht 777. The digits of the date of his proclamation of martial law add up to twenty-one, divisible by seven.* Far from wanting it hushed up as a painful reminder of a piece of *realpolitik* made necessary, many would say, by his mishandling of land reform as well as of his country's affairs in general, he even emblazoned this precious date next to his head on five-*piso* coins minted from 1975 onwards. (Ten years after he had declared martial law and already weakened by terminal illness, he was still commemorating this proudest, most macho moment on his coinage.) It was undoubtedly this virile self-image that Ninoy Aquino had intuited in his 1969 interview with De La Salle students quoted on p. 251–2. Marcos was content to let people accuse him of ordinary corruption provided they allowed him extraordinary machismo as a 'can-do' achiever. Nor is it beyond speculation that the act of declaring martial law contained an element of rebound from the confusions and depressions of the affair with Dovie Beams, a way of making amends by a sudden regaining of his old energy and decisiveness that Imelda had always found attractive. Meanwhile, in an almost obsessive desire to stress the constitutional legitimacy of his action, books and pamphlets flooded off the presses either under his own name or that of a government information agency. *The Democratic Revolution in the Philippines*; *Guiding Principles of the New Society*; *Notes on the New Society*; *Today's Revolution, Democracy*; *An Ideology for Filipinos*; *Marcos and Humanism* . . . The list goes on and on.

The actual Proclamation, as Presidential Decree no. 1081, is a lengthy document published in a fifty-six-page booklet, the bulk of which consists of possibly the best contender for the longest sentence ever written. This is because it is drafted as a legal document

---

* 'Don't imagine it was chance that he was President for 21 years: 7–7–7. You see? His number was 7. Mine is 8.' – Imelda Marcos, in conversation, 2 February 1997.

beginning 'Whereas . . .' which, after numerous paragraphs also beginning 'Whereas . . .' and ending in a temporizing semi-colon, concludes only on p. 54 with 'Now, therefore, I, Ferdinand E. Marcos . . .' with an acute syntactical sense of release.

These legalistic terms are not only typical of Filipino politics in general, and Marcos in particular (how can we ever forget the 'Bar top-notcher' of 1940?). They are central to his passionate insistence that this was an entirely legitimate move sanctioned by the existing Constitution and even by the historical precedent of Abraham Lincoln himself, who during the American Civil War in 1863 had suspended the writ of habeas corpus, which in the US arguably amounted to a declaration of martial law. In the case of the Philippine Constitution, its article 7, section 10, paragraph 2 read:

> The President shall be commander-in-chief of all the armed forces of the Philippines and whenever it becomes necessary he may call out such armed forces to prevent or suppress lawless violence, invasion, insurrection or rebellion. [. . .] [W]hen the public safety requires it, he may suspend the privilege of the writ of habeas corpus or place the Philippines or any part thereof under martial law.

Pointing out the extreme danger that was currently posed to the country by Communists and Moslem secessionists in Mindanao, the President went on reassuringly:

> The proclamation of martial law is not a military takeover. [. . .] A republican and democratic form of government is not a helpless government. When it is imperilled by the danger of a violent overthrow, insurrection and rebellion, it has inherent and built-in powers wisely provided for under the Constitution . . .[32]

Martial law was not declared without Washington's prior approval, of course. President Nixon, Henry Kissinger and Ambassador Henry Byroade had all agreed to the plan well in advance. US foreign policy-makers at the time evidently had no quarrel with the idea in principle, as shown by a US Senate Staff Report dated five months after martial law was imposed:

We found few, if any, Americans who took the position that the demise in individual rights and democratic institutions would adversely affect US interests . . .[33]

This issue of why the US would approve the declaration of martial law is important because in the aftermath of the Marcoses' flight to Hawaii, when Filipinos were trying to take stock of the previous two decades, the more naive occasionally wondered aloud how it was that Washington had ever agreed to such an obvious intensification of the grip Marcos already had on the country, and assumed it really hadn't grasped what he was up to. The better-informed knew there was abundant evidence that long before 1972 the CIA had been perfectly well informed about the Philippine President's business activities. Once he had defected to the US Tibo Mijares, Malacañang's ex-press spokesman, had passed on in his 1976 book what John Marks had revealed. Marks was a former State Department assistant who had seen a psychological profile of Marcos prepared by the CIA. Mijares wrote:

The corruption of the Marcos Administrations [i.e. since 1965] even compelled the Central Intelligence Agency to revise its profile on Marcos to include therein an observation that Marcos was 'incredibly corrupt', having amassed as of the year 1969 a total asset of cash and other holdings in the Philippines and various foreign countries, including the United States and Switzerland, to the tune of TWO BILLION ($2,000,000,000) DOLLARS.[34]

It was hard for Filipinos to accept that their 'guiding brothers' in Washington should have been so indifferent to their fate, but it was all of a piece with what had happened in South Vietnam and elsewhere. The truth was that in the final analysis the United States was interested in the United States, and there matters ended. Also according to Mijares, Marcos had agreed a deal with Byroade and Nixon that in exchange for US support he would guarantee not to interfere with American business or investment in the Philippines. From any US point of view (including that of the 35,000 American servicemen stationed in the country) the Philippines under martial law would represent business as usual. The effects of the military regime would be strictly confined to the domestic scene. Part of the

private pleasure Ferdinand must have derived from the whole circumstances surrounding his momentous declaration must surely
have come from the strange intensification of his relations with
Washington. Half of this was due to his erotic assertion of raw
power (unlike LBJ, Nixon was not a man who ranked other men by
how they measured up to him in swimming-baths); Marcos was,
after all, conscious of making history. The other half stemmed from
an almost flirtatious challenging of the Americans to see how far he
could push them (a very Filipino trait, this). It would have given
him immense pleasure to discover how much they could be
induced to let him redefine democracy, to find out just what he
could get away with so long as they were allowed to make money
and keep their military bases – a pleasure that over the years would
have grown the further he went. Somewhat satirically, he referred
to his action as 'constitutional authoritarianism' and talked of 'the
revolution from the centre'.

The immediate reaction in the US was, needless to say, one of
firm approval – above all from the business community who had
been alarmed by the increasing violence and chaos in the
Philippines, in which they had well over $2 billion invested. A
telegram from the very same Philippine–American Chamber of
Commerce Ferdinand had so resoundingly addressed on his state
visit in 1966 read: '[We] wish you every success in your endeavours to restore peace and order, business confidence, economic
growth, and the well-being of the Filipino people and nation.' He
would have been quick to note how far ahead of the Filipinos'
well-being the Chamber ranked its business interests. The *New
York Times* confirmed that the American business community in
the Philippines had greeted the declaration of martial law 'with
relief'.

By now, most Filipinos were in favour of martial law. They had
had quite enough of violent demonstrations, bombings, street crime
and general unrest. Since martial law was by its very nature an
extreme emergency measure, people steeled themselves for a few
months' intervention by the military to bring the left and other law-
less elements under control, and otherwise to instil some discipline
in a society that often bordered on the anarchic. Senior politicians
were soon obliged to think more realistically in terms of its lasting a
couple of years. However, nobody in their worst nightmares could

seriously have dreamed that martial law would not finally be lifted until early 1981, nearly nine years later.

> Marcos had a deal with the leaders of Congress when martial law was first imposed that it would be lifted within two years or so. I was present when, after this period was up, Speaker of the House [Cornelio] Villareal told him, 'Sir, we had a solemn agreement that martial law should be lifted after two years,' and the President, who himself had had no idea martial law would last so long, told him, 'Just be patient a little longer.'[35]

This is yet another point at which one instinctively parts company with received opinion and resists the suggestion that throughout those first six years of his Presidency Marcos had been plotting and scheming towards this grand, climactic moment. There is undoubtedly a sense in which, as time went on, the much-predicted act became practically a self-fulfilling prophecy. But this is not the same thing as saying it had been a conscious conspiracy from the first. The more one examines the man, the more it becomes apparent that a good deal of his motivation remained quite unconscious; but because commentators and critics have so far only been able to make a narrative sense of his regime by applying cause-and-effect reasoning, they have always attributed to Marcos a conspiratorial genius and an ill-will that he never possessed, and which many of those closest to him also deny ever existed. Like his reputation for having been an outstanding intellectual and thinker, it is one of those misrepresentations designed to intimidate. He was certainly crafty, and like a good lawyer knew how to use or to gloss things to his advantage; but no calculating long-term planner would have committed so gross an error as to have allowed himself the Dovie Beams affair. Nor, once having done so, would he have let it run on for two years, getting ever more disastrously out of hand. There were many moments such as this and in money matters involving his friends when he became unguarded to the point of utter naivety, none of which squares with the picture of him as an ice-cold plotter of his own best interests. However, this latter image was naturally congenial to Filipino journalists and historians who wanted an excuse, an explanation for how he had got the better of his fellow countrymen for over two decades. It was some consolation to think they had been bamboozled by an evil genius who had been conspiring since at least the end of the war, backed by Washington, and who at last had fooled even the United States.

The charge against Marcos that must inevitably follow one of 'conspiracy' is that he deliberately allowed civil disorder and crime to increase so as to have an excuse to declare martial law. This is utterly absurd. No head of state – especially one in Southeast Asia with a cherished 'macho' image and 35,000 US troops garrisoned on his own soil – is going to permit unrest if he can help it. On the contrary, what we have here is an old-style Filipino ruler finding himself at a loss when confronted by a new political sophistication on the part of the nation's youth. People nowadays tend to forget the educational aspects of the worldwide anti-Vietnam protests of the sixties, especially in developing nations like the Philippines. It was not just the spectacle of a little Asian country like Vietnam besting the mighty United States – though that was indeed a remarkable boost to fledgling nationalisms everywhere. The real effect of the war was to make ordinary people reconsider the ethics of government, think about the limits of power and, particularly in democracies, increasingly to hold authorities liable for their abuses.

Vietnam was a parable whose global moral message was most clearly stated in May 1970 – just after the Philippines' First Quarter Storm – when in the United States the Ohio National Guard opened fire on an anti-war demonstration at Kent State University. Four students, two of them women, were killed outright and at least eight others were wounded. The incident provoked a national outcry and intensified debate in democracies everywhere about the right of conscientious people to protest their country's foreign policy. Such was the climate in which Marcos tried to deal with his own problems of student unrest. In his case he really did have a 'Communist menace' to contend with as the ethos of Mao's Cultural Revolution spilled over from China and spread into the Philippine countryside. His reactions were instinctively those of Nixon, Spiro Agnew and Reagan; but initially he was both savvy enough as a politician and too imbued with his own First Family fantasies about wanting to be a popular father to his people to risk exacerbating things further with full-scale troop deployments and curbs on democratic freedoms such as those of assembly and speech. Instead, he relied on METROCOM to break a few heads and on the Philippine Constabulary in the provinces to be as violent as they saw fit in order to contain things. Manila was, after all, to some extent isolated from the rest of the country and it was possible to keep news of much that went on in the provinces from ever reaching the capital.

But none of this was enough. It was not so much the students who couldn't be controlled, but the *ideas* that were unstoppable. The discontent with a governmental system that was corrupt in the blood; the anger at the unrestrained violence of the security forces deployed against crowds of young Filipino citizens; the disgust with Malacañang's constant siding with the White House – all these were things Marcos was simply not equipped to deal with. He was of the wrong generation, speaking the wrong political vocabulary. When he declared martial law, it was as an act of last recourse. Still, this did not exclude the promptings of more private motives. He was now fifty-five. His inability to tame his opponents argued frustration and even impotence of a kind. He may well have yielded to nostalgia: a yearning for the clarities and youthful headiness of thirty years ago when Japanese martial law had proved so advantageous to him, when he had so cheekily flirted with adventure and wrung profit out of apparent anarchy.

All this being said, once he had declared martial law he undoubtedly milked it for all it was worth, both in financial terms and in order to settle several purely domestic scores. This was the *datu* able at last to sort out some irksome tribal matters, such as breaking the oligarchy that had been so disdainful towards him and his wife. To that extent it is maybe possible to maintain that his plot had been to so arrange things with Washington that he had carte blanche to indulge in some private politicking of his own. Martial law did, in fact, buy him all the time he needed. It effectively freed him from a good deal of day-to-day governance and the sheer mechanics of the democratic process. He could simply turn over the running of the country to his Ilocano-dominated military. The rejuvenated *datu* sat back and rubbed his hands.

11

Martial law

It has been suggested that, in the nearly three years that elapsed between the brutal 1969 elections and the declaration of martial law, Washington could have arranged for Marcos's dismissal or even demise. It was all too clear that the law and order situation in the Philippines had become progressively worse between 1969 and 1972 despite unprecedented amounts of US military and other aid, to say nothing of personnel training and the various security and intelligence networks that had been so expensively installed. It would not have been difficult for Washington to make a convincing public argument that Ferdinand Marcos had allowed matters to deteriorate to an extent that justified intervention.

The crucial difference between, say, Chile and the Philippines was that Marcos was not threatening US business interests. At that time, too, Washington was in no mood to change horses in mid-stream in a Southeast Asian country whose military bases were a crucial part of the strategic logistics of the Vietnam war. Ever since the night of 31 January 1968, when the Communist forces in South Vietnam had launched a nationwide offensive to coincide with the Vietnamese New Year holiday, Tet, it had become obvious to every-one – except maybe to 'hang-tough' elements in the Pentagon – that the war in Vietnam was lost. ('What the hell is going on?' Walter Cronkite exclaimed in his CBS news studio as the Tet Offensive began. 'I thought we were *winning* this war.') The sudden co-ordinated upsurge of a supposedly defeated enemy, captured in painful detail on TV screens around the world, was not a military defeat for the United States, contrary to general belief at the time. It was, though, a psychological blow from which there could be no recovery short of the expedient being urged by one or two Strangelovian generals of using tactical nuclear weapons against Hanoi. ('I don't say we wouldn't get our hair mussed,' as George C. Scott, playing an insane USAF general, had said in the 1963 film; 'but I do say no more than ten to twenty million people killed.') Nixon's more reasonable strategy was to sue for 'peace with honour', steadily withdrawing US forces and turning over the running of the war to the South Vietnamese. The more US forces that withdrew, the more exposed the remaining troops would become, since withdrawal under fire is probably the most delicate of all military manoeuvres. It was not, in short, the moment to organize a *coup* against the President of a friendly nation in the vicinity, still less against a man who had been anointed 'America's Boy'.

Another, even more convincing, aspect to the matter was the question of who could have been installed in Malacañang in place of Marcos. There was only one plausible candidate, and that was Ninoy Aquino, the leader of the opposition Liberal Party. The Senator's reputation had grown the more he attacked Marcos's actions and policies. He was an excellent speaker and produced some memorable challenges and exposés, as befitted the crusading journalist he had lately been. An instance of the first was his attack on Mrs Marcos's pet Cultural Centre of the Philippines (the concert hall that had so entranced John Addis) as 'Imelda's Pantheon'. A good example of the second was the story of the so-called 'Jabidah Massacre'.

From his predecessor, Macapagal, Marcos had inherited the revived plan to establish the Philippines' historic but shaky claim to Sabah (see p. 191). The idea of the 'Maphilindo' confederation was obviously dead by now, but he was disinclined to drop the Sabah claim altogether because it would be a useful nationalist card to play if ever he was accused of being too much Washington's lap-dog. (That on his wife's evidence he managed to combine *both* interests by promising the United States a base there in return for their help in prising Sabah loose from Malaysia is vintage Marcos.) In 1967/8, under cover of a civil programme, Moslem Filipino recruits began secret training for possible deployment as guerrilla fighters in Sabah. A group of these recruits was brought up from Sulu and Mindanao to a base on Corregidor Island in Manila Bay. The training was conducted under the auspices of the Army's Civil Affairs Office (CAO), headed by an eccentric air force major, Eddie Martelino, who had renounced Christianity to embrace Islam. The recruits wore black commando outfits and death's-head rings. Altogether, they were a curious gang to be selected to man civic action projects in provincial areas of Sulu and the south. The whole 'Jabidah' operation, as it was code-named, was top secret, its command linked directly by radio to Malacañang and Camp Aguinaldo. If news of it were to leak out it would at the very least have caused the Philippines severe problems in its relations with Malaysia, and most likely with the rest of the Islamic world. Then one day a Jabidah recruit crawled onto the shore in Cavite, dripping and exhausted, having swum all the way from Corregidor Island. According to him the recruits in the training camp had mutinied because they had never been paid or properly fed and, worse, had got wind of their real mission to carry out special operations in a foreign country. The CAO had tried to defuse the resulting uprising by flying most of the trainees back home to Mindanao, but a remaining hard-core group of twelve had allegedly been massacred by their two Christian officers, who were themselves later found dead. (This is yet another piece of recent Philippine history destined to remain cloudy because the people who knew the details of what really happened are dead.)

Ninoy Aquino exposed the story in a brilliant speech. He began with the embarrassing allegation that the heirs of the Sulu sultanate had secretly promised Marcos an enormous cash reward if he could restore Sabah to them, and went on to point out that the Jabidah recruits had not by any means all been Moslems but had included ex-convicts, ex-Huks and ex-Monkees (the Philippine Constabulary's terror squads about to be deployed to great effect in Central Luzon during the 1969 election campaign). The real point of these highly trained Jabidah commandos, said Aquino, was less for use against Sabah than against Liberal Party leaders such as himself and any other opponents of Marcos's administration.

This caused uproar and the President was furious. He and Aquino had known each other since the fifties and, indeed, were Upsilon Sigma Phi fraternity brothers at UP (Aquino being some fourteen years Ferdinand's junior). Neither man was under many illusions about the other's capability, and there is little question that Aquino was the politician most likely to succeed Marcos. Yet a considerable degree of affection as well as respect lay behind the public sparring. Evidence of this is supplied by Marcos's old friend and sometime employee, Roquito Ablan (whose father had been Governor of Ilocos Norte before the war when Ferdinand was jailed in Laoag for the Nalundasan murder, and who had converted the young convict's cell into a library for his law studies and bought him a ping-pong table for his diversion). Roque Ablan sheds new light on Ninoy's speech about 'Imelda's Pantheon' that had so enraged the First Lady:

> Ninoy and Marcos were very close in private. All three of us were frat. brothers. When Ferdinand was campaigning in 1969 Ninoy gave a speech condemning Imelda for the wastefulness of her new CCP project. The joke is, it was *Marcos* who edited the speech for him, writing his comments on Ninoy's draft like 'More!', 'Nothing like strong enough!' and 'Sock it to her!' Imelda was furious enough after Ninoy gave the speech even without knowing her own husband had made it still worse. All innocence, Marcos pacified her by saying 'Don't worry, sweetheart, we'll get even.' But it was all a joke. In return, Ninoy supplied Ferdinand during the same campaign with ammunition to score off Osmeña.[1]

Certainly Ninoy Aquino was by no means universally popular. Even today, long after his canonization as a national martyr, he can still arouse strong feelings among those who knew and worked with him. (Among various reactions are: 'He was an arrogant s.o.b..' 'He was a dedicated womanizer.' 'Every bit as ambitious as Marcos – hell, they knew each other like brothers and had got each other's measure.' 'Couldn't string two decent English sentences together.' 'Played both ends against the middle . . .') These are the judgements of journalists, ex-ministers and senators.

For the judgement of a foreign VIP one can turn to an account

Caroline Kennedy gave of a visit she made in late 1968 or early 1969 to Ninoy Aquino's estate. (It was actually his wife Cory's estate, but he failed to mention that.) 'She reported that she had been shown the Seven Wonders of Tarlac, including a $160,000 Arab stallion ("the best stud in the Orient") owned by the Senator. The tour had ended at the estate swimming pool. "Naturally the Senator and his ego were the first to take the plunge, still clutching his, now water-resistant, walkie-talkie. It never left his ample grip all weekend. [. . .] He is obviously under the distinct impression that he is the 'Now Sound', the only voice that dares challenge Marcos and thus, in his own opinion, the Saviour of the Philippines. But heaven help the Philippines if the Senator, his ego and his walkie-talkie – along with his $160,000 Arab stallion – ever move into Malacañang."'[2] From this it is at least clear that Aquino was being talked about (or was talking about himself) as a future President.

The accusation that Ninoy had played both ends against the middle refers to an admission he made in a television interview with Ronnie Nathanielsz that was conducted in Aquino's cell during martial law. At the time, Aquino was refusing to co-operate with the military tribunal hearing his case, or even to enter a plea. He told Nathanielsz that when he was in Indonesia in the early 1960s he 'did a project for' the CIA. This confirmed long-established rumours to match equally venerable stories that he also had Communist sympathies dating back to his immediate post-Korea days when he knew and was trusted by Huk leaders like Luis Taruc, whom he had induced to surrender. Being a big landowning family in Central Luzon, it was argued, the Aquinos could hardly have coexisted with the Huks and NPA guerrillas in their midst without some close and sympathetic relations with them, not to say political accommodation from time to time, above all when Ninoy was an opposition Governor of Tarlac in the first two years of the Marcos Presidency.

In the event, Washington no doubt decided to stick with the status quo. Marcos might be turning out to be more of a bastard than they had predicted but he was – in Foggy Bottom's weathered cliché – *their* bastard. As Aquino himself put it in a speech, 'The Philippines is still important in the overall global strategy of the Americans, and they find in Marcos a trustworthy ally because he belongs to the generation that fought side by side with them in Bataan and sang the "Star-Spangled Banner" with tears in their eyes.'[3]

One of the terms under which Washington had approved Marcos's martial law plans was that prominent opposition figures should be given the option of leaving the country beforehand. Serging Osmeña left for the US a day or two before the declaration; so did the brother of Marcos's own Vice-President Fernando Lopez, Eugenio, who was widely believed to have encouraged Dovie Beams in her damaging revelations. Others, including Ninoy Aquino himself, stayed. He was almost the first person to be arrested. Other celebrated thorns in the Administration's side such as former Justice Minister Senator Jose Diokno, Ramon Mitra, Joaquin ('Chino') Roces (publisher of the most influential daily newspaper, *Manila Times*), Teodoro ('Teddy') Locsin (owner-editor of the *Philippines Free Press*) and Hernando Abaya of the Civil Liberties Union, were also carted off in the dead of that same night to the stockade at Camp Crame. There they assembled in a dimly lit gymnasium, blinking at one another, not altogether sure whether they were asleep or awake.

One of the many casualties of those first weeks of martial law was the Café Los Indios Bravos in Malate, not far from John Addis's former residence. Los Indios Bravos was started in the sixties by Imelda's niece, Beatriz Romualdez Francia (who later wrote the biography of her aunt). It was a 'themed' café: the décor was turn-of-the-century and the name itself adopted from the society of émigré Filipino artists José Rizal had organized during the Paris Exhibition of 1889 (their use of the derogatory name *'indio'*, which was applied by the Spanish to Filipinos, was a deliberate attempt at nationalist pride). The café had quickly become a louche water-ing-hole for artists, intellectuals, journalists, film-makers, musicians, revolutionaries, con-men and diplomats. As Ms Francia herself said, 'Indios was one of those places where East and West had truly met. So many foreign correspondents and embassy employees liked to drop by, in fact, that people suggested we rename the place "Los Indios Bravos Y Cia", the last a pun on the Spanish abbreviation for *compañia* and the Central Intelligence Agency.'

John Addis, Don Luis Araneta and Hans Menzi used to drift down what was then Dewey Boulevard (it was re-named Roxas Boulevard in the Seventies, I think) in Addis's silver Rolls and pick up street trade along the seafront, taking them off to 'Indios'. John was very discreet, though. Menzi, of course, was very close to Marcos.[4]

At 10 p.m. on 14 October 1972 Los Indios Bravos was raided by forty METROCOM troops armed with M-16s ostensibly looking for drugs, and nineteen people were hauled off in trucks to Camp Crame. It was the beginning of the end for the café, which with its eclectic mix of leftists and Marcos loyalists belonged firmly to the liberal sixties and could hardly be tolerated by the New Society. The raid was typical of Marcos's tactics in that he was at some pains to show no favouritism. That the café was owned by his wife's niece was proof that a new era had dawned in which all those who had despaired of government corruption would clearly see how earnest he was. It did not matter that Indios had been patron-ized by intellectuals on his own staff such as Adrian Cristobal; it was a moment for showing that martial law was to be completely even-handed. One of the people the President had arrested was his old friend, fraternity brother and colleague, Roquito Ablan:

That was the point. Marcos was supposed to show himself scrupulously fair, and I was one of his trusted lieutenants. I was arrested just after martial law was declared, just after Ninoy him-self. I was charged with maintaining a private army, giving guns to Ninoy, giving guns to the NPA. I was photographed behind bars at [Camp] Crame, and the next day Ambassador [Carlos P.] Romulo went into the UN in New York and held up this huge picture of two Filipino Congressmen behind bars – Aquino and me – and said that Marcos had just declared martial law and to prove how serious he was, here was a picture of one of his most trusted henchmen in jail for being a warlord.[5]

The President was certainly not above window-dressing his martial law, which often led to bizarre scenes that did much to lend the entire period its extraordinary mixture of the draconian and the zany.

In the first few months he imposed a curfew. As one drove into town from Quezon City and Makati in the morning rush hour one would see men wearing shirts and ties and women in evening gowns weeding the central dividers along EDSA and Roxas Boulevard. At 8 a.m.! Everybody assumed they were curfew-breaking victims from the night before, the punishment evidently falling impartially on the social élite. Long afterwards we learned they were phony, just rent-a-crowd who'd been given a bath and loaned some 'proper' clothes . . . Also in these first few months there was a campaign of arresting people for failing to stand in cinemas when the National Anthem was played before and after the programme. This contributed to a deep feeling of popular support for Marcos, of a restoration of order and nationalistic sentiment. After his recent unpopularity public opinion swung ninety percent behind him . . . I still think his will to change things for the better was totally genuine in the first two years of martial law. You look at the Presidential Decrees from that period and you'll see he meant business and that his heart was in the right place.[6]

In fact, Marcos's desire to give martial law legitimacy by being even-handed was not only very popular, it gave him a perfect excuse to get rid of government officials who had become a liability.

The Commissioner of Internal Revenue, Misael Vera, was famously on-the-take as well as famously on-the-give to Marcos. There was a standing joke that at the end of Marcos's presidency someone would be able to set up shop selling briefcases, because at the end of each month Vera would arrive at the Palace with a briefcase stuffed with BIR [Bureau of Internal Revenue] money and leave it there. After the declaration of martial law, Marcos announced he was dismissing Vera. Things like that made people sit up. If he could dump Vera, where might his new broom not sweep?[7]

(This was the same Misael Vera who in 1965, as the newly appointed Commissioner of the BIR, had addressed the annual convention of the Philippine Institute of Certified Public Accountants:

Perhaps I can better explain myself by asking you this question: what makes a BIR agent harass a taxpayer? Some of you will, perhaps, say 'Grease money' . . . This is where the accounting profession comes in, by exercising *moral* influence on your clients. I refuse to believe that a CPA worth his calling would consciously allow himself to be used as a tool by crooked businessmen in their scheme to deprive the government of fair and just taxes.[8])

At some point, however, the President must have felt he needed a really attention-grabbing *coup de théâtre* that would leave nobody in any doubt about his determination to end crime and corruption. The arrest of Lim Seng presented him with the opportunity. Lim was a drug baron who had been buying morphine base from the Golden Triangle and turning out 100 kilos of refined heroin a month in his own laboratories. In this way (in Sterling Seagrave's estimate) 1.2 tons or ten percent of America's annual heroin supply was coming from the Philippines. Filipino narcotics agents of CANU (Constabulary Anti-Narcotics Unit) working with DEA ((US) Drug Enforcement Agency) agents arrested a couple of ex-GIs boarding a flight to Okinawa with six ounces of heroin and zealously traced it back, uncovering two of Lim's laboratories in Manila and incontrovertible evidence of his entire operation. Given that Lim was used to receiving his consignments of morphine base in his Manila Hotel suite, it was obvious he could not possibly be in business without pay-offs to people in the highest places.

At his trial, Lim pleaded guilty and was sentenced to life imprisonment. The case was given a good deal of attention by Malacañang's newly controlled broadcast media and press, and Marcos must have felt it needed an extra touch. He did something quite out of character, both as a man and as a lawyer, by overruling Lim's life sentence and ordering him to be publicly executed 'by musketry'. A man of Lim's wealth and powerful contacts did not for a moment take this seriously. This was, after all, a country where the rich never saw the inside of a jail for even a week. He understood it was part of the *palabas* or show of martial law, and that cunning old Marcos was planning to gain still further popularity by an equal show of clemency at the last minute. His fellow prisoner, Roque Ablan, takes up the story:

Lim Seng was in Crame with us, due to be shot. We told him that of course if the 'execution' went ahead it would be mock, for *palabas* only, and that the firing squad would just use blanks. When the day came they took him over to Fort Bonifacio and everything was televized. He was so confident he wouldn't be shot he didn't even want to be blindfolded. He was joking about it until they put the blindfold on. Then they shot him, *bam!*, just like that. We were a bit subdued the next two or three days. Poor fellow, may he rest in peace.[9]

Lim's execution did more than subdue Roque Ablan and his fellow inmates. Marcos never did such a thing again; but as a dire warning to other criminals enjoying high-level protection its shock value was dramatic and his popularity soared still further, especially among parents worried about the availability of drugs (which the Indochina war had greatly increased). It was out of character for Ferdinand, who was not *madugo* or bloodthirsty – most certainly not by prevailing standards of Asian strongmen. His Filipino instinct was essentially non-confrontational: an inclination to outwit or come to terms with those he arrested rather than to obliterate them. (Bong Bong Marcos once quoted his father's advice: 'Neutralize people – *never* humiliate them. Always give them a way out. Otherwise they'll come back and kill your children.'[10]) Maybe his comparative mildness stemmed also from an inchoate desire to be loved as a father by his people, something that might equally explain his peculiar indulgence towards friends who abused their position to steal money and otherwise endanger his Administration – an indifference, almost, as though he were abstractedly thinking of something quite else and couldn't bring himself to care about such details. In the end, this amounted to culpable weakness. Like Pontius Pilate, he managed to preserve a comparative innocence by keeping his own hands clean of violence through delegation. Malacañang kept aloof from what was happening in the country's jails and detention centres, all of which were now under military control. He left the really dirty work to others.

It would be grotesquely apologist, as well as immoral, to play down what actually did go on under martial law. 'I regret the violence. That I regret,' Ferdinand's own son was to say years later when asked what, if anything, of his father's years he felt uneasy about.[11] A Filipina journalist who was in active opposition from 1970 onwards put the matter into some perspective:

> There is one explanatory remark I would like to make regarding Marcos and his depredations, particularly against people. True, they do not equal the scale of Latin America or the bestiality of Africa, but there is enough of a record not to dismiss it. The Japanese and the Americans did much worse in their time, but this was a home-grown tyrant who took advantage of our good-will. In true Filipino fashion of valuing interpersonal relations in everything he let his minions – i.e. [Gen. Fabian] Ver, [Col. Rolando] Abadilla, [Col. Hernani] Figueroa, [Col. Gregorio] Gringo Honasan (in his time) do the torturing and *their* minions do the unspeakable, while the President appeared, posed, and acted statesmanlike. The ultimate tragedy for us was that he could have been a great agent of change for the better, but chose to keep to the same pattern of our leadership tradition.

This is surely right; and it would be unseemly indeed for a foreigner to tell Filipinos that the tortures and killings they endured under martial law hadn't really been all that bad, and they should stop making a fuss. But in all fairness to history – never mind to Ferdinand Marcos – it must also be said that it is necessary to pre-serve a pragmatic sense of proportion. Seen in ideal terms, Marcos's regime in the 1970s was indeed horrible. But ideal conditions have never prevailed in the world of *realpolitik*, and least of all did they do so in that hapless decade. A certain rueful balance can be restored by comparing Marcos's with a dozen other regimes operating at the time with Washington's blessing or backing – throughout Latin America, certainly, but also not forgetting South Vietnam, Cambodia and Laos, nor yet Franco's Spain or Salazar's and Gaetano's Portugal. There is simply no way to present Marcos's atrocities as having exceeded or even equalled those of the worst of the dictator-ships in the American orbit that occasionally masqueraded as democratic: Batista in Cuba, 'Papa Doc' Duvalier in Haiti, Pinochet in post-Allende Chile, Somoza in Nicaragua, Trujillo in the Dominican Republic, Diem's (or Thieu's) South Vietnam, Syngman Rhee in South Korea, the Shah of Iran, Argentina . . . (the list seems endless).

The Filipino 'leadership tradition' mentioned at the end of the letter quoted above was only half the problem. The other half was in the equally Filipino social tradition that constantly militates against forms of impersonal, centralized authority. Terrible violence went on, especially in the provinces. But terrible violence had *always* gone on in the provinces, as José Rizal documented in *Noli me Tangere*. Given *carte blanche* to use their own methods, martial law's police and army units simply took their lead from local commanders who, as we have already seen, were generally in league with local élites and warlords and often used Armed Forces of the Philippines troops as virtual mercenaries to settle private feuds or protect their illegal mining and logging operations. To say they were under the control of Marcos as Commander-in-Chief of all the Armed Forces of the Philippines is true only on paper. On the ground – at the end of logging trails, in the jungles and ravines and poor *barrios* of the interior – it was another world. The broad hacienda flatlands of Central Luzon were frequently killing fields during martial law's anti-NPA operations; but they were no more so then than they had been in the late forties and early fifties when Napoleon Valeriano's 'Nenita' battalions were on the rampage and his interrogation squads were giving peasants petrol enemas while men stood around joking and flicking their lighters.

What one can say is that under Marcos's martial law the lot of the ordinary folk in the countryside, the common *tao*, was mostly little different from what it had always been. Local policing methods had been brutal since the time of the Spanish *guardia civíl*. But provided they did not indulge in any sort of protest or form alliances with local guerrillas, most people's lives kept on going at the same subsistence level, remote from national politics as from the capital itself. Otherwise, if they noticed much change, it would have been less in quality than in intensity: there was more military visibility in most provinces.

In 1973 three Huey helicopters painted black landed at the little civil airstrip some miles from Kansulay. One of them carried a pair of high-ranking officers who had come for a conference with the Commander of the provincial forces. The officers were met by a jeep and disappeared for the best part of the day. They came back to the airfield at about 4 p.m. in time for the daylight hop back to Manila only to find that two of the helicopters had developed technical problems severe enough to ground them. The officers flew off in the remaining chopper, leaving the two aircraft stranded with their pilots and skeleton crews to look after them. It turned out that 'technical problems' was a reference to neither aircraft having enough fuel left to fill a hurricane lamp. This had come about because during the morning the pilots had sold their fuel to a local entrepreneur who – in those pre-electrification days – was always in the market for kerosene. Since Hueys hold 200 gallons, or just over half a ton, the store owner had made an excellent deal on a bulk purchase which had taken quite some time to siphon off into drums. The choppers were now stuck for as long as it might take for some more fuel to be flown in from Manila. Meanwhile, the pilots had been abandoned to shift for themselves.

At dawn the next day they turned up on the beach at Kansulay, hungry and mean-tempered. When a fisherman was unwilling to turn over his night's catch to them they shot up his boat with an M-16, reducing it to matchwood. Suitably cowed, other villagers wisely produced some fish and cooked the fliers a large breakfast. Somewhat mollified, the military men went off and returned with a couple of dozen fragmentation grenades which they turned over to three fishermen with instructions to use them for fishing in order to keep the stranded airmen in food, the surplus to be sold and the cash split. This was done, and after a few days the two black helicopters, refuelled, took off and disappeared for good. The village still talks about the incident, which in its way was minor and commonplace enough even as it had marked the first known use of dynamite fishing on Kansulay's reefs. Nevertheless, the military's high-handed methods were not forgotten, least of all by the fisherman whose livelihood had been temporarily ruined (and who grouses about the loss of his boat to this day). Yet people also still say how lucky Kansulay was; that had the men been drunk they might well have gone on a shooting spree, as so often happened, causing wholesale slaughter until their ammunition gave out or they collapsed in stupor. That sort of thing might occur at any time with the military or the Philippine Constabulary, whether before, during, or after martial law.

It is still argued that Marcos, by his strict control of the media, could always make martial law appear as though it were working.

Newspapers had been silenced, emasculated or closed down altogether. Radio and TV stations had passed into his hands by the dozen. However, there is little doubt from the accounts of people with every reason to remember the period in detail that, in the first two years at any rate, martial law really did lessen the crime rate dramatically and raise standards of public and even governmental behaviour. The wretched Lim Seng had served his purpose. Indeed, so marked was the sudden improvement that it is one of the reasons why older people even today look back on the early martial law years with genuine nostalgia, as at a time which reminded them of their childhoods when there were 'still some standards in public life'. It is this image of Marcos that lingers: of a purposeful man with the political will as well as the power to call a halt to the slide, to punish offenders irrespective of their rank and connections, to restore a sense of national pride. Marcos the doer; Marcos the nation's disciplinarian father.

Martial law effectively signalled the moment when the First Couple got down to some serious settling of old scores, and many people were happy to see them take on the social and economic status quo that existed under the hegemony of the '400'. Open season was declared on the oligarchs who had needled the Marcoses ever since 1965 with disdainful remarks about parvenus from the sticks with suspiciously gotten wealth. The Lopez family, in particular, became a chief target. This, given that Ferdinand's own Vice-President was a Lopez, perfectly illustrates that peculiarly Filipino intertwining of the personal with the political as well as of private wealth with state power.

In June 1972, Eugenio Lopez, Sr. (whom John Addis had memorably described as a 'dry, saurian figure . . . insatiable for ever more power') stood at the apex of Philippine public and social life. He was chairman of the country's largest media conglomerate (ABS-CBN) and president of its leading electricity utility, Meralco. His brother had been Vice-President since 1965. His clan dominated the sugar industry, the country's most profitable agricultural sector. But a sudden reversal of the Lopez fortunes was in the offing:

> Only three months later, President Marcos declared martial law and destroyed Eugenio Lopez. After imprisoning his eldest son on capital charges, Marcos forced Lopez to sign over his shares in

the Manila Electric Company [Meralco] and to watch silently while a presidential crony plundered his media conglomerate. Forced into exile, stripped of his wealth, and tortured by the threat of his son's execution, Lopez died of cancer in 1975 in a San Francisco hospital – a death ignored by Filipinos who had once sipped his champagne and celebrated his achievements.[12]

This certainly makes him sound something of a tragic figure; but before we lose sleep grieving for him it would be well to remember that no clan builds an empire in the Philippines without acquiring a good few skeletons in its cupboard (and in the case of the Lopezes the cupboard was more like an ossuary). It is not the substance but the tone of the above quotation that subtly misrepresents things to favour Eugenio Lopez. His family were actually no better and no worse than the Marcoses, there being really only two differences. The Lopezes had been at it for longer, so their fortune could pass as 'old' money; whereas Marcos was the President and had more raw power. Other than that, as McCoy's next quotation indeed confirms, they had everything in common. The Lopez clan was intimately allied to, and intermarried with, the Ledesma clan and the Montelibano clan (archetypal warlords of Negros province who controlled the sugar bloc that Marcos had always considered the strongest oligarchy in the country). Ferdinand had been put out that the Lopezes had got their hands on Meralco, a utility he himself coveted, and they scarcely helped matters by keeping up a barrage of editorials and cartoons in newspapers they owned (such as the *Manila Chronicle*) about how rich the Marcoses were allegedly growing from kickbacks. Marcos struck back by holding the price of the capital's electricity down while increasing the cost of the fuel oil Meralco's generators needed. The 'Meralco Theatre' that Eugenio Sr. built to rival Imelda Marcos's Cultural Centre of the Philippines has already been referred to (see p. 225); but the annoyance this caused the First Lady was nothing compared to an incident that occurred when she unwisely accepted an invitation to a grand party at a Montelibano hacienda. Unbeknown to her, a two-way mirror had been let into the wall of the bathroom especially for the occasion. When she used the lavatory Alfredo Montelibano took photographs of her which were gleefully circulated (Ninoy Aquino was said to have carried one in his wallet to his dying day).[13] On learning of this crude juvenile prank Imelda took briefly to her room, just as she did when the faked 'nude' photograph of her was circulated during the first election campaign. When she emerged the Montelibano clan, so far as she was concerned, was as good as dead.

What Marcos did to families like the Lopezes in terms of sequestering, appropriating, or otherwise buying out their assets for ludicrously small sums can be interpreted in two distinct ways, depending on one's view of his ulterior motives. The investigative academic Alfred McCoy is in no doubt about what Ferdinand Marcos and Eugenio Lopez Sr. had in common:

> Despite their deep personal enmity, Lopez and Marcos were in some respects more similar than either might have imagined. Putting aside their rhetoric, both acted in the apparent belief that the state should reward a self-selecting economic élite instead of using its resources to strengthen the public sector or uplift the country's poor. Both used their political influence to benefit private corporations controlled by their families.[14]

In this view, Marcos simply used his state powers to demolish Lopez conglomerates and 'transfer their assets to a new economic élite composed of his own kin and courtiers'. But there is another interpretation of his actions still held by many technocrats who worked for him. This is that initially, at any rate, he sincerely believed that the stranglehold such oligarch families held on the Philippines' economy was deeply damaging to the country's interests. They were, he argued, so used to their monopoly of vital sectors of the economy that they had become inefficient and uncompetitive. Not one of the clans seemed interested in building the future. For example, the Lopezes had decided that large-scale electrification schemes would need a vast investment before they would ever see any returns, so they showed no inclination to expand the Meralco grid, still less to set up similar utilities nationwide. It is possible to argue that Marcos's wanting to create an 'alternative' oligarchy by breaking up the business empires of the Lopezes, (or the Madrigals, or the Osmeñas) was in order to kill two birds with one stone. Yes, he could himself cream off some assets in the time-honoured fashion of any other *datu*; but he could also free the economy to start it moving forward, to attract foreign investment and bring a degree of dynamism to an otherwise congealed system. As Kerima Polotan Tuvera observed, 'In one sense cronyism was intended to build up a national *Filipino* entrepreneurial class, an idea that dated back to Quezon, as a way of counteracting the pervasive Chinese influence.'[15]

It was arguably this that pushed Marcos towards his 'crony capitalism', which started out from the fact that once the clans were broken, he had to rely on small entrepreneurs who were willing to work hard and take risks in order to bid for large-scale infrastructural projects. One of his priorities was the Pan-Pacific Highway – a great network of roads connecting as many of the islands as possible. He threw this project open to international bidding, and initially the bidders were all from elsewhere in Southeast Asia, from Taiwan and Japan. The natural, 'home-grown' choice would have been a company like Atlantic Gulf and Pacific, which never even bothered to bid. The reason seems to have been that the oligarchs who owned companies like AG&P were not really interested in government projects because such contracts were notorious for delayed payments and suddenly changing specifications. The sheer size of the Pan-Pacific Highway project implied there was a considerable fortune waiting to be made, but there were no bidders from among the oligarchs.

Enter Rodolfo ('Rudi') Cuenca, who had known Marcos from the fifties when Cuenca was just one of twenty-five contractors who had banded together to form Filipinas Cement, buying their equipment with Japanese reparations money.

> The challenge to the President's strategy of building up the infrastructure was that the government he'd inherited from Macapagal in 1965 was stony broke. They had no money, period. They couldn't even complete the North Expressway [the main road north to Bulacan Province from Manila]. By now I'd reformed Filipinas Cement as CDCP [Construction and Development Company of the Philippines] with myself as president. We were awarded the contract to finish it in about May of 1967. Six months later Ninoy Aquino filed a complaint that I'd bribed Marcos to get undue advantage in the terms of the contract. Actually, what I did was wangle funding with short-term

loans and this enabled us to complete the road. The President was impressed enough to push more work our way.[16]

To Ferdinand, Rudi Cuenca was just the sort of Filipino entrepreneur he needed to help build the country; and if giving him government contracts also undercut the effete oligarchs who had done so little of national benefit with their great wealth, so much the better. CDCP quickly became the Philippines' leading construction company, involved not only with large-scale projects at home, such as the Pan-Pacific Highway and Manila International Airport, but also abroad (the Borobudur Temple in Indonesia and multiple sites in Saudi Arabia). In 1983 the *Wall Street Journal* was to quote Cuenca as saying 'I never figured crony to be a bad word,'[17] but by the time he made the remark it most certainly was. By then the Philippines was not only deeply upset by Ninoy Aquino's assassination in August, it was sliding inexorably into a desperate economic and financial crisis brought on to a large degree by the activities of Marcos's cronies as well as by international lack of confidence in his ability to do anything about them. It is depressing now to read a documented exposé of the cronies' activities, such as Ricardo Manapat's painstaking and valuable *Some Are Smarter Than Others* (the title is a quotation from Imelda explaining how certain people became very rich under the Marcoses). The list of names that come under Manapat's scrutiny comprises half the most renowned families and personalities of the entire era, from oligarchs to nobodies: Benedicto, Floirendo, Enrile, Cojuangco, Elizalde, Silverio, Velasco, Disini, Lucio Tan, Yao, Gapud, Roman Cruz, the Enriquez and Panlilio families, Bienvenido and Gliceria Tantoco – apart from the Romualdezes and Marcoses themselves. One suspects, however, that few business fortunes anywhere in the world would bear such detailed investigation. Sharp practice and the favouritism of old college chums is hardly restricted to the Philippines; and there are many who believe that Mrs Marcos's acquittal in her 1990 New York federal racketeering trial was judiciously (and judicially) engineered for fear of what might be revealed about Wall Street, the real estate business, high-ranking US politicians, various intelligence agencies and even the White House itself had the trial been fought all the way. Here was a lady who knew entirely too much. *Her own lawyer,*

Gerald Spence, argued in court 'that the CIA was aware of every transaction Marcos made and that then-Vice President George Bush had even encouraged Imelda to bring money out of the Philippines and invest it in the US'.[18] This was the George Bush who in his Vice-Presidential capacity had gone to Manila in July 1981 to represent the White House in the ceremonies attendant on Marcos's winning a new six-year term of office. At the inauguration Bush stood and toasted the President in terms that the Filipino people, newly emerged from nearly nine years of martial law, never forgot or forgave: 'We love your adherence to democratic principles and to democratic processes. . . . We will not leave you in isolation. . . . It would be turning our backs on history if we did.' This short speech was received with incredulity, even in the US ('Where Has Bush Been?' as the editorial of 2 July's *Los Angeles Times* was headed).

Rather than go into further sordid details – which anyway are better documented in books like Manapat's – one can quote something that perfectly conveys the flavour as much as the substance of cronyism under Marcos's martial law. It concerns the sugar industry, which had been so spectacularly wrested from the hands of the Montelibanos and the Lopezes and their ilk and turned over to Roberto Benedicto. Benedicto was exactly the same age as Marcos as well as having been his classmate and fraternity brother at UP Law School. As soon as he became President in 1965, Ferdinand appointed him Chairman of the principal state bank, the Philippine National Bank, a post he held through 1970. Thereafter, he became Ambassador to Japan before being further rewarded by being presented with the sugar industry. Thanks to a series of Presidential Decrees, Benedicto acquired complete monopoly of an industry that accounted for 27 percent of the country's entire yearly dollar earnings. Through a series of inept speculations and corrupt practices, Benedicto effectively ruined it and brought thousands of peasant families in Negros – already among the poorest and most exploited agricultural workers to be found anywhere in the Philippines – to the point of starvation. (It was no accident that Negros was traditionally fertile territory for NPA recruitment and guerrilla activity.) In 1980 Benedicto's authority, Philsucom (Philippine Sugar Commission), committed itself to a disastrous speculative deal to sell two million tons of sugar on the world market over the following four years at an average price of $0.235 cents a pound, when the market price was $0.40. Desperate *hacenderos* and millers filed a suit in the Supreme Court to halt the deal and Benedicto countered it with a massive publicity campaign, using Marcos-controlled newspapers. In December the following announcement appeared under the title 'Prayer and Thanksgiving':

ALMIGHTY GOD OUR FATHER:

At a time when the price of sugar in the world market was at its lowest while the price of crude oil, gasoline and the other factors affecting cost of sugar production continuously rose, with banking institutions so strict in granting crop loans to the planters, our Beloved President Ferdinand E. Marcos thought it best that the government establish support for the sugar industry. This he did by first organizing the Philippine Sugar Commission and designating Ambassador Roberto S. Benedicto as head thereof, giving him full authority to save the sugar industry from total collapse.

PHILSUCOM then organized the National Sugar Trading Corporation or NASUTRA, a subsidiary corporation which handles the marketing of Philippine sugar both within the country and abroad. PHILSUCOM also established the Republic Planters Bank which provides funding of much-needed crop loans by the sugar planters, as well as the operational loans needed by the sugar centrals.

The policies and programs of President Marcos and Ambassador Benedicto of giving price support for the sugar industry enabled most planters to continue their farm operations despite high cost of production and low sugar price in the world market, so that the workers, both in the plantations and in the millsites, were provided with much-needed jobs.

However, Lord, in spite of the government's and PHILSUCOM's programs that all workers may stay on their jobs during the sugar crisis, there were those unlucky few who were laid off. Most of them though were later assisted by the Ministry of Labour and Employment.

Great God, our Father, during those times of trial in the sugar industry, we the labourers were patient and suffered quietly even when we did not receive any additional benefits according to existing laws despite the fact that prices of basic goods and services continued to increase because we understood the position of the government as far as the sugar industry was concerned.

Now, Lord, with the rising price of sugar in the world market, our President Marcos has also gradually increased the composite price, that amount which is paid by the NASUTRA to the planters and the sugar centrals. President Marcos, Minister Ople and Ambassador Benedicto are now of one accord that the workers in the industry be given additional allowances as contained in Letter of Instruction No. 1016, Presidential Decree No. 1713 and Ministry Order No. 5.

So now, Great God, Creator and Lord of our lives:

We, the workers in the sugar industry and our families do raise our voices in thanksgiving for all the guidance you have given to President Marcos, Minister Ople and Ambassador Benedicto.

We also thank President Marcos, Minister Ople and Ambassador Benedicto that through their efficient and effective management of the sugar industry in crisis, most of us workers were kept on our jobs – and now we are blessed with additional fringe benefits.

We, the workers and our families also thank the planters, as well as the sugar mill managements, who have complied with government laws, rules and regulations. And we earnestly pray for those who have not yet complied with such laws, rules and regulations that you may grant them the heart and mind to give their workers and employees their dues.

Oh, God Almighty, we know that if it were not for your ever-guiding providence upon our leaders in the sugar industry many of us workers would have lost our employment – our only source of livelihood.

So now we beseech you, our God, that you will continue to, and at all times, grant upon President Marcos, Minister Ople and Ambassador Benedicto good health, strength and wisdom. Amen.

National Sugar Trade Union[19]

There is hardly a single text that better encapsulates everything that was wrong with Philippine politics of the period. The grotesque trope that pretends to have shoeless and half-starved sugar workers giving public thanks; the bogus prayer-book syntax; the slavish cult of personalities; the use of religion to underwrite politics . . . The very worst of it all is that although the *device* of such an announcement was pure martial law, its *tone* was by no means peculiar to that period alone, being one that generations of priests had used to instil obedience to the status quo. It was simply a matter of business and politics donning canonicals and briefly ascending the pulpit.

It is not the least of the strange – and sad – aspects of Marcos's martial law that, side-by-side with the absurdities of such crony monopolism, serious and gifted young technocrats were working for him to produce an economic policy that would turn around the country's chronic stagnation. For a while the President seemed smitten with the *zaibatsu* model of development which Japan had employed before the Second World War as part of its modernization programme. The idea was to delegate industries to small groups of businessmen who would be given government incentives and facilities such as favourable banking and help with exports. This was attractive to Marcos since in the context of martial law's sweeping powers it could in theory give him a controlled and burgeoning economy.

*Zaibatsu*s had worked sensationally well in Japan, producing the huge exporting corporations familiar today, and were successfully cloned in South Korea with *chaebol*s like Samsung. It does have to be noted, however, that neither Japan nor South Korea nor Taiwan has escaped scandal and corruption. On the other hand, all might have been forgiven Marcos had any of his cronies produced a single conglomerate only half as successful as Sony. But a revealing thing happened. When Filipino family businesses which had not been dispossessed for being 'oligarchs' and were not part of the 'crony' system were admitted into the central group of companies trying to export – the San Miguel Corporation, for example – the difference immediately became apparent. Legitimate businesses soon made their way on the world market, whereas cronies like Benedicto proved to be uncompetitive since they were dependent on preferential treatment such as 'behest loans' from government banks to bail them out whenever their inefficiencies caught up with them. They inevitably began collapsing, and by 1983–4 were dragging the entire economy down with them.

It is impossible to say with absolute certainty whether Marcos's flirtation with the *zaibatsu* idea was a primary motive or a later rationalization for turning over industries such as sugar to cronies like Benedicto whose formal training was as a lawyer and not as a businessman. For example, when Danding Cojuangco (cousin of future President Cory Cojuangco Aquino) similarly took over the coconut industry, which was equally major, it could have been (and was) explained as a way of taking on the American multinationals. Palm oil was promoted as a natural and environmentally friendly alternative to Western substitutes, and patriotic to boot.

Early in martial law Marcos imposed tariffs on imported luxury items, annoying foreigners by seeming to renege on his promise not to interfere with business. More importantly, he never had the slightest intention of renewing the 'parity rights' agreement, due to lapse in 1974, despite pressure from Washington. Suddenly, Americans found themselves obliged to reduce their equity in strategic Philippine companies from 60% to 40% at most, yielding control to Filipinos. Once again, was this nationalism or cronyism on his part? Were his 'real' motives in economic matters patriotic, selfish, or both? Three different opinions may be quoted. The first is from a leftist position:

> The Left tried to paint Marcos as a puppet of US imperialism, but he showed real signs of independence. For instance, industrializing along the *zaibatsu* concept was anathema to the US since it meant we would no longer be dependent on their products. At least, that is the classic nationalist line. But as history showed, the US also thought it was good for Asian societies to industrialize because it would defuse the agrarian unrest endemic in the region. Well, if they actively disapproved of his behaviour they certainly did nothing to make him modify it.[20]

A second opinion comes from the man called in from the private sector (very much against his own will) by Marcos in 1979 to help save the Philippine economy. This was the talented Harvard Business School graduate, accountant and investment banker Roberto Ongpin:

I don't think the zaibatsu idea lasted very long. It was just one
more notion that swam into his ken. I associated it more with
someone like Mahathir [Mohamad, of Malaysia] as part of his
'look East' agenda. Cronies like Cuenca and Disini – they
brought him all sorts of far-fetched schemes, and if Marcos could
spot an angle that would help fill his political war-chest then
he'd just give them the go-ahead. It was all very simple. He
wanted to be rid of his political enemies so he labelled them 'oligarchs' for popular consumption. In this way he could be
appearing to wage a righteous ideological war. All he actually
was interested in was schemes for making a buck. He needed a
war-chest. It's quite straightforward. Forget zaibatsus.[21]

A third voice is that of Enrique Zobel de Ayala, whose family
never became cronies and for whom Marcos had considerable
respect. 'Enzo' broke his neck in a polo accident a few years ago,
which has left him arguably the world's wealthiest paraplegic, an
irony not lost on him. He and Marcos were intimate enough to
have discussed the ex-President's provisions for his will shortly
before his death in Hawaii:

Marcos felt that to control politics you had to control business.
He wanted – number one – to stay in power. But at least while he
did so he built more infrastructure in this country than any other
president. He used his cronies. He got them to invest in companies on his behalf, and a lot of his shares were put in their names.
He trusted them, you see. He trusted people too much, especially his UP classmates and co-frats. So they've wound up with
all this money of his, and the Marcos family knows damn well
these cronies still have his shares in their names but they can't
say anything because the government will only get it. They're
stymied. But when people like myself warned him about the
cronies, he just said to me: 'Better that someone steals ten percent
and accomplishes something than someone who is super-honest
like "Ting" Paterno and never gets anything done.' It was just a
pity they stole so much more than ten percent and did so little.[22]

Meanwhile, as martial law dragged on Senator Ninoy Aquino
stayed penned in his dark, solitary cell in Fort Bonifacio (from

which he had heard the shots that killed Lim Seng). Many others remained in jail, including the Vice-President's own nephew, Eugenio Lopez, Jr., and Sergio Osmeña III. Years were going by. Once the novelty had worn off and the immediate and obvious gains in public order had been taken for granted, opposition to martial law began hardening steadily. By the mid-seventies it did not seem as though the superficial stability visible in Manila was paying off in terms of a newly flourishing economy. The Communist Party's and the New People's Army's ranks continued to grow. According to figures in the *Washington Post* (12 August 1982) the estimated strength of armed guerrillas in 1972 was 950–1,300. By 1983 Western analysts were putting their numbers at 7,000–12,000. It was perfectly clear that the ostensible motive for declaring martial law had never been translated into tactics equal to the task.

The reasons were classic. The chronic neglect of rural areas, the abuses of the military, the patchiness of the land reform programme which Marcos had launched with such high ideals on taking office – none of these was being remedied. In a sense, the very declaration of emergency had polarized things still further. It had the effect of making yet more glaring the situation whereby an ineffective government now required all its forces to be on an armed footing just to protect that very ineffectiveness, let alone to start righting basic wrongs. It was a fertile period for NPA recruitment from among students and even among seminarians. These were not Communists but idealistic, principled and often devoutly Christian members of the middle class who swapped their comfortable lives in leafy campuses for often grim and dangerous living in the provinces, under constant harassment by the Philippine Constabulary. For most of them it was an astonishing revelation of the conditions which ninety percent of their countrymen had always endured.

In fact, concerted opposition to martial law on the basis of human rights violations only really began when its rigours impinged on intellectuals, journalists, students and other members of the gentility. It was the moment when Manila's erstwhile chattering classes were silenced by the sudden glimpse of what the mass of provincial Filipinos had been experiencing for the past century or two: arbitrary arrest, casual beatings, stinking cells and fear. To that extent the experience often produced strong feelings of solidarity with the peasants, although these largely wore off with the lifting of martial law and the restoration of middle-class norms and rights (and today they are virtually as extinct as they had been before 1972).

In the mid-seventies the principal men in charge of the security forces included General Fabian Ver, Ferdinand's devoted *maharlika*, who headed the Presidential Security Command and sat at the centre of several interlocking intelligence webs which effectively made him the nation's secret policeman. Next came the Chief-of-Staff of the Armed Forces, Romeo Espino. Ferdinand's friend and legal counsel, Juan Ponce Enrile, was Secretary of Defence and Chairman of the Executive Committee of the National Security Council. And in charge of the paramilitary Philippine Constabulary and the civilian Integrated National Police as well as being the Vice Chief-of-Staff of the Armed Forces was Lt.-Gen. Fidel V. Ramos, the son of Ferdinand's uncle Narciso, and thus his own cousin. (As of writing Fidel Ramos is the current President of the Philippines, approaching the end of his term of office.) It was these men who, next to Marcos himself, bore responsibility for the conduct of martial law, for its excesses and horrors. It is safe to say that all of them knew perfectly well what was going on.

It is hard to write about this period without offending someone either by exaggerating the violence or else by playing it down. At one level, out in the sticks where the PC or the special forces met the NPA, the brutality was often grotesque in a quite literal sense. An ex-PC officer told of a major in his unit who used to conduct 'interviews' with prisoners – which often proved terminal for the interviewee – while wearing Mickey Mouse ears. Sometimes he would don a large rubber nose covered in warts. On one occasion he greeted a handcuffed suspect with a smile that suddenly bared a gleaming pair of Dracula fangs, at the sight of which the hardened guerrilla fainted dead away. The major bought his props from a mail order firm in Fresno. ('Only in the Philippines,' his ex-comrade said, not without pride. This phrase, or just the letters 'OIP', is one many Filipinos are fond of quoting.)

On the other hand, with the exception of individuals like Ninoy Aquino who had earned personal attention for having crossed either or both of the Marcoses, many detainees were not maltreated. Even Ninoy was allowed to stand in the 1978 elections from his prison cell. He ran – unsuccessfully, of course – against Imelda herself. The well-known leftist Satur Ocampo was imprisoned for nine years from 1976 until his escape in 1985 (and he and his wife were both imprisoned again under Cory Aquino from 1989 until 1992 and 1991 respectively). Consequently, he has earned more right than most to venture an opinion on Marcos's prison system.

No matter that there were extensive cases of human rights violations, Marcos did make certain accommodations. Some say his training as a lawyer accounted for that, but I think it was due to his political sense that, as much as possible, he ought to give a democratic, legalist foundation to his dictatorship. He therefore aligned his government with internationally recognized human rights principles. For example, with regard to political detainees he acceded to certain policies:

1   Those not charged with actual crimes should be released.
2   When couples were arrested, one person (usually the wife) should be released.
3   Pregnant women and nursing mothers should be released.
4   Sick people should be released.

These were policies we took advantage of when I was in detention. Every six months new batches of detainees were brought into the detention centre in Bicutan and we would categorize them and make provisions for their release.

After a number of hunger strikes, etcetera, we were allowed the right to manage our own affairs in prison. I was elected leader of the Association of Political Prisoners in Bicutan – a post I held for nine years – a sort of 'mayor'.

Groups of people such as students, nuns, seminarians and student lawyers would be allowed to visit us in jail. We would meet them and hold impromptu seminars. These were classified by us as 'exposure trips', as when people's organizations and NGOs went on excursions to the countryside and to detention centres such as ours. We were just another trip destination. We had [visits from] human rights groups from Asia: the Malaysians and Indonesians especially were amazed, making the comparison with their own prison islands. They couldn't believe we were allowed to manage our own affairs in detention.

The press, too, was in a strange position. While Marcos took over and controlled the media on declaration of martial law, he also to a great degree tolerated oppositionist press when it managed to re-assert itself. Even we prisoners had access to the media. Letters and articles I wrote were printed in newspapers and magazines.[23]

Satur Ocampo also estimated the number of *desaparecidos* – those who 'disappeared' during the eight and a half years of martial law – as 'probably around 2,000' (compare this figure with that on p. 401).

On the subject of media censorship, it seemed that the more martial law bore on the *haut bourgeois* end of things such as films and the arts generally, the less repressive and generally amenable it tended to be. This was largely because it involved people who, given the Filipino system of extended families, often had all sorts of connections with Malacañang but who tended not to be powerful in a business or political sense. There is little doubt that Imelda Marcos's own strong sympathy for, and patronage of, the arts accounted for much of this comparatively liberal climate. The following account, which might otherwise be lost in a welter of far less palatable revelations, comes from Raffy Guerrero, who worked for years in the Mass Media Affairs Office.

It's universally stated that the Marcos regime was very repressive. In foreign books, for example, whenever they deal with the martial law era they say *Sakada* was banned by the military. This film [directed by Ben Cervantes] was based on a play by a leftist intellectual, Mauro Avena. Yet if you look at the newspaper ads for the film's release, they carried above them an endorsement by Maria de Vega, who was then head of the Board of Censors. She was also the widow of Guillermo de Vega, special assistant – with Cabinet rank – to Marcos himself. Guillermo had been assassinated in his office in Malacañang by a deranged attacker a year or two earlier. Now it's true, *Sakada* was confiscated; but only after it had been showing for a month to packed houses in Manila. It's hard to see this as evidence of an iron-fisted military dictatorship in, say, the context of Iran's SAVAK or Chile's DINA.

Even stranger was the case of *Batch 81*. This was by Mike de

Leon, a member of one of the oligarch families deeply opposed to Marcos. It was a story about fraternities and their use of torture during 'hazing' initiation ceremonies. Well, of course it was an allegory, a thinly veiled protest against fascism and the military. The film's producer was Marichu Maceda, the daughter of the head of the second-largest film studio, Sampaguita. Now, Marichu was the woman who later went to Honolulu with the Marcoses in exile and stayed with them as a factotum, rather like Sol Vanzi who was happy to cook for them out of loyalty and because she knew how to make Ilocano dishes for Marcos . . . So here is this lady, so close to the Marcoses, who produces *Batch 81* with their full knowledge and consent. And who plays the fraternity's Grand Vizier who oversees the electro-shock torturing of initiates? Why, the brother of Minister of Defence Juan Ponce Enrile, Chito Ponce Enrile. OIP [Only in the Philippines], right? The film ran to critical acclaim. There was no attempt by the military to censor or remove it, despite the electro-shock scene which horrified audiences and created quite a stir.

One really has to keep a sense of proportion. What went on in the Fil-American war at the beginning of this century was infinitely worse than anything Marcos's martial law did. *Infinitely*. Martial law was nothing compared to that. Anyway, I remember watching an American TV series in the States in the late seventies. It was a three-part series about military regimes. The first was on Iran, the second on Chile, and the third on Marcos's Philippines. In the first two there were practically no interviews with political prisoners because the ones they wanted to talk to were either dead or had 'disappeared'. All they got were relatives shielding their faces so they couldn't be identified. In the Philippine film they came and filmed Ninoy and Diokno in jail – all very Filipino and cheery, and Ninoy got off a good speech about Marcos turning himself into a sort of Shah. I mean, some repressive regime! The Philippines isn't *like* anywhere else, that's what you need to remember. Our martial law just wasn't like anybody else's martial law.

Nor can one resist an insight into the opposition's plans for the violent overthrow of President Marcos. This time the informant is a property agent.

Just before martial law began there was an old-style politician, Eddie Figueras, who though never big-time had once run for something like Vice-Mayor of Metro Manila. Anyway, one day in 1971 Eddie Figueras shows up at our office and says he wants to rent a furnished flat, giving his name as Santos. We'd recognized him at once, of course, from his campaign posters which were up on every street. Naturally we assumed he wanted the flat for a mistress. So he rents the room and pays for it. But he never moves in, and nor does anybody else. Every day he would drop by the flat and stay for an hour or so before leaving. After two months he arrives with a big van and unloads dozens of boxes. He gives me instructions that the air-con. in the flat should never in any circumstances be turned off. After several such truckloads the flat's filling up with boxes. The unloading is only ever done at night. Every night he would pass by, driving a big American car, look the building over and just cruise away again. What Mr Figueras didn't know was that our room-boys had keys to the apartment because it was part of our leasing policy to clean all the rooms once a week, check the filters on air-con. units and that sort of thing. Anyway, one day our supervisor calls and reports that the boys had found some explosive caps in the flat. I hurried over, and indeed there was a box full of *banig* [sheets of caps] but the caps were very big and the paper was plasticized and stamped 'Danger!' I opened some more boxes and came on a Japanese-brand electronic detonator, complete with miniature plunger. Other boxes were packed with bottles of hard plastic with two chambers joined by a thick aluminium tube. In one half was what looked like coarse crystals of salt, in the other were sandy-coloured pebbles.

Well, the then-Secretary of Defence, Juan Ponce Enrile, was a friend of my uncle's – himself a veteran of Bataan. I got hold of my uncle and we went together to Camp Crame to report what we'd found. It was midnight. The guy there was incredulous but agreed to send somebody back with us to take a look. When this officer saw the stuff there was instant panic. Our flat apparently contained enough explosives and incendiaries to obliterate two city blocks. The military asked if they could do a stakeout. Figueras's sidekick was a Crisologo [an Ilocano warlord family, relatives of Marcos]. One night this Crisologo boy turns up at the

flat with a girl, obviously hoping for a quick screw among the
boxes. The military nabbed them and Crisologo fingered
Figueras, who in turn spilled the beans.

The guys Figueras fingers are Steve Psinakis and Eugenio
Lopez Jr. himself. [Psinakis was an American engineer who had
been working for Meralco when Eugenio Lopez Sr. took it over.
There he met Lopez's daughter Presy, whom he married and
who became one of Imelda's Blue Ladies.] Their plot was to float
a raft packed with incendiaries down the Pasig to the back of
Malacañang Palace and explode it by radio with that miniature
detonator I'd found. Psinakis, Geny Lopez and Sergio Osmeña
[III] were all jailed for this plot. Psinakis got out and in 1977 he
organized an incredibly daring jail break at Fort Bonifacio and
sprang his brother-in-law Geny and Osmeña. It was brilliant.
Anyway, cut to 1986 and the snap election rallies, and who is
escorting a tottery Marcos up onto the stage while going 'Marcos! Mar-cos! Marcos *pa rin!*' [again]? Why, none other than old
Eddie Figueras. OIP. Only in the Philippines.

The plot to blow up Malacañang signalled the start of various
bombing and arson campaigns. These seemed linked to the fortunes of Ninoy Aquino in that they reached some sort of climax
with his release from jail. The Senator had undoubtedly acquired
considerable stature during his long years of imprisonment, both
in the sense of his public image and in that of his own character. To
Filipinos in general he had become a symbol of resistance. He had
obviously matured, too, under that curious prison regime which
had mixed solitary confinement with TV interviews. In 1975 he
had gone on a prolonged hunger strike that induced profound
religious experiences. Meanwhile, his case dragged on. He had
been charged with subversion, murder and illegal possession of
firearms, and he finally refused even to enter a plea. In June 1977
he was brought before Marcos who asked him sadly why he
hadn't taken the opportunity he was given to leave the country
before martial law was declared. Ninoy replied that he was a
Senator of the Republic and his duty had been to stay. Ferdinand
and he addressed each other throughout their conversation as
'brod', like any two fraternity brothers planning a get-together or
chatting of old times. Friends, comrades, respected rivals, sworn

enemies? – their relationship is beyond simplistic resolution. Each man was mysteriously destined to cause the other's fall. Later that year a military tribunal found Ninoy guilty as charged and sentenced him to death by musketry but the execution was stayed, largely because of tireless representations from a newly elected President Carter who personally dispatched his Under-secretary of State for Human Rights, Patricia Derian, to Manila to plead with Marcos for clemency. Aquino was eventually freed in 1980, ill enough to need rushing to the US at a few hours' notice for triple heart bypass surgery.

Ninoy had always denied any connection with the organization of a group calling itself the Light-a-Fire Movement whose activities caused General Fabian Ver a good deal of trouble in Manila in 1979. It was allegedly masterminded from San Francisco by Steve Psinakis and funded by the Lopez family. After his daring escapade in releasing his brother-in-law and Osmeña from military jail in Manila, Psinakis became active in the Movement for a Free Philippines which had been gathering strength among Filipino exiles from martial law in the United States. In the latter half of the year several government buildings in Manila caught fire and burned down, as did a floating casino moored in the bay that was owned by Imelda Marcos's brother Alfredo. The spectacle drew crowds of ill-wishers who sat happily on the seawall spitting melon seeds and crunching *tsitsaron*. Once Ninoy was safely in America a plot was hatched calculated to cause Marcos maximum damage and embarrassment.

One of the President's oldest friends was the book-buying Commodore Santiago Nuval, whose daughter Doris had married an American. Doris Baffrey, as she now was, worked for Joe Aspiras's Department of Tourism which in 1980 sent her to the US as part of a high-powered campaign to attract tourists to the Philippines. She went despite strong objections from General Ver, whose intelligence services already had a file on her (as they would on any government employee married to an American and with the ability to travel abroad). Despite this she went, managing on her return to smuggle components for a bomb through Customs hidden among (splendid irony!) a consignment of metal detectors. She was able to do this by exploiting her father's name and closeness to Marcos. Once home in Manila, Doris assembled the bomb and hid it in a suitcase beneath her parents' bed, only slightly inconvenienced by the house being full of relatives celebrating her parents' ruby wedding.

General Ver's misgivings had been increased by rumours already circulating in the United States that an attempt would be made to bomb the forthcoming ASTA (American Society of Travel Agents) conference due to be held in Imelda's Philippine International Convention Centre in October. These rumours were deliberately floated by the Movement for a Free Philippines in order to discourage US travel agents from attending the conference, but they went anyway. The rumours turned out to have been correct.

The bomb was at the back of the hall. It was more designed to make an impressive noise than to do serious harm. It left no crater in the floor, in any case. Nobody was killed, but some people were seriously hurt. Marcos, who was up on the stage, was very shocked. He appeared to show courage under fire, but actually I think he was stunned and disorientated by the explosion. When he got back to the Palace he flew into a rage, or as much as he ever did. It was so damaging to his image. Looking back now, I think it was the beginning of the end for him because it so clearly showed that in spite of seven years of military security he was still very vulnerable. Doris was never supposed to do the actual bombing, only to bring in the parts; but things had got too hot for the chosen bombers and she'd been pressured into doing it herself. It had an amazing effect, no doubt about that. General Ver went completely ballistic. I myself was suspected for a while. Yet two or three days went by before Doris was arrested, despite being the number one suspect. Explain that, if you can. She wasn't in hiding. A typical member of her class, she went shopping, saw her friends, went to a party. There was nothing of the desperate suicide bomber about her. That sort of person, I think she really imagined she could get away with it – that it would soon blow over and all would be forgiven and forgotten. Then Ver pounced, and she ended up spending five or six years in Camp Crame despite her father being who he was. They say the incident led to a cooling of relations between Commodore Nuval and the President, but Nuval still went out to

Hawaii to be one of the pallbearers when Marcos died in 1989. Doris Baffrey's now designing bathrooms and is head of Public Affairs at Channel 4 TV. A funny life, really.

Whatever else, stories like this bear out that peculiarly Filipino intertwining of the personal with the political. Teodoro ('Teddy Boy') Locsin, Jr., Editor of the prestigious daily newspaper *Today*, reflected on this recently in print. His father is the Editor-in-Chief of the *Philippines Free Press* who was jailed during martial law and had his printing works stolen. When the *Free Press* was confiscated Marcos's agents had tried to get hold of the title as well. 'Over my dead body,' Locsin Sr. had told them. 'You're not going to pervert an honoured name for your own propaganda.' After he was freed he went to the States, where he was visited by Imelda Marcos in 1988. 'It was a tiny apartment he had, with just two chairs in it. Just imagine it! Going and calling on the man your husband had jailed and dispossessed of everything he had, as though it were a social visit! Imelda came and sat down in the only available chair and Teddy Sr. said to her, "You know we'll try to get the *Free Press* back." To which Imelda replied with a laugh, "Come on, Teddy, you know that's Imee's."' (Imee is the Marcoses' elder daughter. 'Get the *Free Press* back' referred to land in Makati, Manila, as well as to the printing presses.) All of which is necessary background to what 'Teddy Boy' Locsin Jr. wrote in his column early in 1997, looking back at the martial law era:

> In a manner of speaking, martial law and all its repercussions and resistances, murders included, were just an affair among friends. Imee Marcos attended my brother's wedding reception at home while my father was detained in *her* father's jail. Fantastic! As a foreign journalist at the wedding said, 'Who can take you people seriously?'[24]

Opposition from abroad was crucial to turning around Marcos's political fortunes and slowly giving him that indelible international image of a corrupt and bloody dictator. Opposition figures like Raul Manglapus (who had judiciously gone to the US on a speaking tour the day before martial law was declared) initially found themselves isolated and marginalized. For the next four years he and various other Filipino fugitives abroad stayed in touch with each other and gradually coalesced, but it was clearly going to be uphill work to try from within the United States to dent the reputation of a man who enjoyed the almost unreserved admiration and total support of successive US administrations. Many suffered considerable poverty and hardship.

In 1976 the anti-Marcos cause was greatly helped by the publication of Tibo Mijares' book, *The Conjugal Dictatorship*, which for the first time documented what was happening from inside the Palace (or at any rate, it gave Mijares' version). Malacañang's pressman had defected in February 1975 while on a visit to the US. In June he appeared before the US Congressional House Subcommittee on International Relations and testified to conditions in the Marcoses' Philippines. He also said that the Philippine Consul General, Ambassador Trinidad Alconcel, had offered him $50,000 not to appear before the sub-committee. Jack Anderson, the crusading investigative journalist who had done so much to expose corruption in the US Congress, took up this story in his syndicated column.[25] Mijares then swore a deposition that he had been offered a further $100,000 to recant, deny everything and retire in comfort to Australia: a temptation he nobly resisted. By the time Anderson printed that, too, and portions of the forthcoming book had been leaked, the damage to the Marcos image was substantial. Suddenly, Americans found themselves having seriously to reconsider what was going on in their ex-colony, especially now that, with the Vietnam war ended, the absolute need for the US bases on Philippine soil was much reduced. Sadly for him, Mijares did not have long to enjoy his celebrity. He was last seen alive in Guam in 1977. Five months later his fifteen-year-old son was found murdered.

The growing opposition in the US received a further boost from a more general change in attitude towards America's client states. In 1973–4 US Congress had banned military and developmental aid to countries that were notorious violators of human rights, although an escape clause making an exception in cases where US assistance was 'justified' rendered it largely toothless. While Gerald Ford was still President the Ninety-fourth Congress ruled that gross violators of human rights throughout the world should be punished for their acts and that the US would dissociate itself from repressive regimes, regardless of the cost. The idea was to introduce some overdue 'moral purpose and traditional values' into American foreign policy. When Jimmy Carter took over from Ford in 1976 he appointed Patricia Derian to the newly created post of Under-Secretary for Human Rights. Seen in retrospect, this was a brief interlude before Ronald Reagan became President in 1980 and appointed Jeane Kirkpatrick Ambassador to the UN. (Mrs Kirkpatrick soon became identified with tough US policies in Central America and with making an influential academic distinction between 'authoritarian' and 'totalitarian' governments that she advanced in an article in *Commentary* (November 1979) entitled 'Dictatorships and Double Stands'. She attacked Carter for 'destabilizing' the regimes of friends like the Shah of Iran and Anastasio Somoza of Nicaragua.)

Interlude or not, the change of intellectual climate in the White House in the latter half of the 1970s gave much-needed encouragement to the Filipino exile community. People began the serious documentation of aspects of Marcos's administration, as well as forming the Movement for a Free Philippines. The researches of Filipinos like Boni Gillego into the validity of Ferdinand's medals and war record were taken up by US investigative newsmen and gradually an image of him took shape that was grossly at variance with the one sedulously promoted by the US Government. This whole effort was greatly helped by Ninoy Aquino's arrival. Once he had recovered from his heart operation he and his family settled in Boston with a grant from Harvard University where he gave seminars and acted as the focal point for a resistance now dedicated to 'bringing Marcos to his knees'.

Any survey of Marcos's martial law – even one as cursory as this – would be incomplete without some mention of the Church in the Philippines and how it reacted. The fact is that Marcos and the Roman Catholic Church were equal players in an old game which they both understood perfectly. The Church had, of course, always thrived on maintaining the status quo. Marcos, as we know, had been born an Aglipayan – that is to say, into a dissenting church. Bishop Aglipay, close friend of the Marcos family, had himself baptized the infant Ferdinand. Yet Aglipay's dissent was not particularly radical: it had merely revolved around the local

Filipino Church wanting to be administratively rather than doctrinally independent. This was part of the general upsurge in
nationalism at the turn of the century. It was a reaction against
what it saw as the old, friar-dominated Catholic Church reporting
to Rome via Spain. (Bishops in Spain were appointed by the state,
being nominated by the Spanish Crown on advice, and the
appointments were rubber-stamped by Rome.) In some ways the
Aglipayans were more Catholic than the Catholics in that their
services were more 'traditional'. (There is, perhaps, a certain
parallel between Aglipayanism in the Philippines and Anglo-
Catholicism in Britain.) In any case Marcos had grown up
understanding that politicians needed to co-opt rather than oppose
the Church. When he came to power he set about courting
Cardinal Santos of Manila (the predecessor of Cardinal Sin who
was appointed in 1972, the year of martial law, and who was to
play such a major role in the 'EDSA revolution' of 1986). Santos
was described as being 'in much the same mould as Cardinal
Spellman of New York'. Not to be outdone, Imelda decided she
needed a tame Cardinal too, and chose a friend of her family's, a
Waray-speaker from Samar Province named Julio Rosales. Thus
the Marcoses between them organized a neat balance of religious
power. Neither Cardinal could ever oppose the First Couple's
actions because the dissent of one would be cancelled by the assent
of the other.

Nevertheless, the apparently conservative Church showed distinct signs of unease with Julio Cardinal Rosales in 1974, and since
he was in Imelda's ambit the hierarchy initially focused their misgivings on her rather than on Marcos himself. The Cardinal was a
curious figure, even by the oddball standards of the Philippines
under martial law. Nicknamed 'Julie', he was considered to have
the best collection of dolls in the country. The Archbishop's Palace
in Cebu was stuffed with glass cases of them, and people wishing
to get into Julie's good books did well to come armed with some
unusual *poupée*. His private secretary was his own nephew, a priest
who maintained a reasonably extensive harem of young boys
whom he liked to take with him on his travels.

None of these peccadilloes was of much importance, but the
Cardinal's ecclesiastical politics were. He was a considerable reac-
tionary, and the Church hierarchy felt that Mrs Marcos was siding

with 'Julie' at the expense of the more radical clergy and bishops who were becoming progressively unhappier with martial law. As early as January 1970 seven of the country's most radical bishops had signed a joint open letter to Marcos that was published under the title 'Message to the President'. It was clear they had been as upset as anyone by the violence of the recent election, and were now writing as the First Quarter Storm was gathering (their letter being published a mere sixteen days before Ferdinand's hairdo was publicly assaulted by the papier-mâché crocodile). Their 'urgent appeal' read in part:

> The Word of God is Truth, and Truth dictates that we call a dis-torted social order distorted, and a corrupt government corrupt. Our country cannot and will not enjoy God's prosperity and peace until our leaders are able to face this undeniable truth, and in a spirit of deep, personal conversion, start to lead public and private lives of disinterested service . . .
>
> We are at a moment of our nation's history when we crucially need a charismatic leader, a deeply moral person whose honesty and integrity are beyond reproach, a President who will inspire us to be really one in action and national consciousness. We need a leader who will not tolerate graft and corruption, self-enrich-ment, vote-buying and goon-hiring which make a mockery of democracy, nor almost unlimited over-spending for campaigns, a real social crime in a poor country like ours . . .[26]

This was an astonishingly radical letter for seven Catholic bish-ops to have published in a country as deeply conservative as the Philippines. It is an eloquent testimony to their profound disquiet at the direction Marcos's leadership was taking. (The clear hint that the President was in need of 'conversion' suggested they felt they were dealing not so much with an Aglipayan as with a man who hadn't a truly Christian bone in his body.) However, it should be said that in those pre-martial law days even the Church's radicals could be scoffed at by the politicized laity. The above quotation can be neatly balanced by an editorial 'Teddy Boy' Locsin Jr. wrote for the same news magazine a bare two months after it had pub-lished the bishops' open letter. A Jesuit, Fr. Jose Blanco, issued a denial that he had ever called for a revolution:

I said what we need is a change of heart to convert someone to real Christianity; that is the revolution I sell. The surgery of the Leftist is the violent revolution, that of the Christian is revolution of the heart.

The *Philippines Free Press* scoffed at Blanco's distinction. Saying the revolution of the heart was hogwash, the editorial continued:

Fr. Blanco thinks we don't need palliatives or temporary cures but major surgery to cure the ills of the country. And what does he consider surgery? A change of heart. That's not surgery but faith healing.

Are revolutionary Jesuits really revolutionaries? Not at all. They are the reserve forces of the Establishment. Reformist perhaps. Anti-imperialist, certainly not. Have they denounced the imperialist war in Vietnam or the slaughter of Filipinos like wild pigs in the US bases? Counter-revolutionary is more like it. They confuse the situation and serve ultimately the imperialist purpose or, to put it in another way, they apply cosmetics to make it look alive. (*Philippines Free Press*, 14 March 1970)[27]

As for 'Julie', Cardinal Rosales, he was privately dismissed by all sides as a sort of Imelda-within-the-Church. After he died Rosales was replaced as the Cardinal Archbishop of Cebu by Ricardo Vidal. Vidal also took over the role of Imelda's Cardinal, and the First Lady flew a huge party of his relatives to the Vatican for his ordination. (It was Cardinal Vidal whom she would summon from Hawaii in 1989 to hear her husband's confession on his deathbed and to carry a letter back to President Cory Aquino begging her to grant 'Ferdinand's dying wish to go home to his motherland, the Philippines'.[28])

There is no doubt that martial law did encourage members of the Church to take an increasingly radical position. At the beginning, the main objection to it from within the Church came predictably from the lower ranks – from the priests who experienced its impact on their poor parishioners. Out in the provinces it was not unknown for clergy and lay Church members to be detained, tortured and even killed by the military for 'fraternizing with the Communists'. Since the media were controlled, incidents of this sort were not widely known, so these first clashes of the Church with martial law were mainly confined to grass-roots level.

Another reason why at first religious protest was muted was that Marcos had done a deal with the hierarchy. At that time the Church's three major worries were the increasing public agitation for a divorce law, the pressure towards some form of national population strategy and birth control, and the suggestion that the Church ought to be subject to some form of taxation. These were all sizeable political worries for the bishops, who were also preoccupied in a more general way about the Church's losing its hold over a flock that showed a disturbing inclination to turn its attentions – always eclectic at the best of times – towards revivalist, charismatic and other Protestant sects based mainly in the United States. The deal that Marcos struck with the bishops in return for their silence on martial law was to promise that their three chief worries were groundless so far as any new legislation was concerned. The status quo would be preserved.

However, the Church hierarchy was by no means as homogenous as this suggests. Martial law had revealed that Marcos's real enemies in the Church were the Jesuits, who were very active in their social ministry and considerably influenced by the Liberation Theology being preached at that time in Latin America. If all seven of the bishops who signed the open letter to him in 1970 were progressive, at least two of them – Antonio Fortich of Bacolod and Julio Labayen of Infanta – were genuinely radical. Together with the bishops of Bukidnon and Cotabato City they had opposed Marcos almost from the first. This was not altogether surprising: it was no coincidence that all four were bishops of territories with active NPA guerrilla movements. (Bacolod City, for example, was the capital of Negros Occidental and the centre of the Philippines' principal sugar-producing region. This was the province that had always borne most heavily the abuses of the sugar centrals, abuses that intensified still further when the crony, Roberto Benedicto, beggared the entire industry through mismanagement.) These radical bishops headed the National Social Action Committee (NASA), which was essentially a Jesuit organization designed to oversee the Church's social pastorate. NASA was mostly composed of lay workers and Catholic missionaries and busied itself with programmes for fighting poverty, organizing labour unions, and the like. Nor was NASA alone in the field. There was also the Association of Major Religious Superiors of the Philippines (AMRSP), which consisted of all the heads of the religious congregations: Redemptorist missionaries, Belgian missionaries, Maryknoll missionaries and the Columbans, as well as Benedictine sisters and Assumption nuns. It was under AMRSP that a special group was formed to minister to political detainees. Task Force Detainees (which is still very much in existence under the Franciscan missionary, Sister Mariani Dimaranan) worked under the severest conditions of harassment, intimidation and often brutality. Many disappeared altogether.

The Church had always been the single most powerful influence in Philippine society, especially in the provinces, and in many areas that influence during martial law became two-way, with religious and peasants radicalizing one another. True, a good many priests remained deeply conservative and either sat on the fence or were openly supportive of the regime; but the hierarchy itself gradually became of one mind. By the time martial law was lifted in 1981 the Church's opposition had gone beyond it to include both Marcoses personally.

Matters reached a head with the papal visit of John Paul II that year. Imelda Marcos had always had a thing about the Vatican and was constantly in Rome, especially for great occasions like the funeral of Pope Paul VI and the inauguration of John Paul I. She had appointed the husband of Glecy Tantoco, one of her Blue Ladies, Ambassador to the Vatican and would throw big dinners at the Tantocos' villa on the Via Appia Antica – one of the most splendid private residences in Rome. (This was the house where, after the Marcoses' fall, Italian police discovered a stockpile of weapons that led to Bienvenido Tantoco's arrest and a sentence of three years in prison from which he was only saved by the intervention of old Vatican friends.)* Imelda developed close relations with Vatican grandees like Cardinal Egidio Vagnozzi, who had been Papal Nuncio to the Philippines in the 1950s and who eventually became

---

* It was at the Tantocos's villa in Makiki Heights Drive, Honolulu, that the Marcoses stayed during their Hawaiian exile (see Manapat, op. cit., p. 380).

head of the IOR (*L'Istituto per le Opere di Religione*) which acts as the Vatican's bank. 'I have no doubt, though I have no proof,' a high-ranking Italian priest observed, 'that Madame Marcos contributed substantially to the coffers of the Church through Vagnozzi. The Church would have known that her husband was also immensely rich, with large holdings around the world. He would have been a useful business connection.' This is indeed an unsubstantiated allegation, but it is certain that the First Lady did have excellent connections within the Vatican. Be that as it may, none of it prevented her from making a bad tactical error as regards John Paul II's visit to the Philippines in 1981. She turned what was planned as a pastoral visit into a grand state occasion.

> She meddled with everything, with all the arrangements, the entire itinerary. She built the Coconut Palace expressly for him to stay in, although he did what visiting popes always do and stayed at the Nuncio's residence. The Vatican had been planning this visit for a long time, since Wojtyla really wanted to get the world to see him, to make the Church visible. Imelda's hijacking his visit really rankled with the bishops, who were relegated to playing the chorus-line in her road show. He did manage to get to Bacolod in Negros and to visit the Vietnamese Boat People's camp in Bataan. He had wanted to visit Smoky Mountain here in Tondo, too, but Imelda arranged for it to be impossible. However, in Negros he did speak publicly about the evils of untrammelled capitalism and the oppression of the poor – almost the only moment of genuine social comment in his entire trip. After 1981, therefore, it was war between the Church and the Marcoses. It no longer bothered to consider Imelda and Ferdinand as separate people. Like 'marital law', the phrase 'conjugal dictatorship' had already been coined and it was altogether too apt. Apart from anything else, the bishops were terrified that Marcos would nominate Imelda as his successor. That would have been the end.

The position of the Marcoses by the end of 1981 could therefore be described as increasingly beleaguered. True, martial law had at last been lifted; but ranged against them at home they had a solid body of middle-class opinion, including many of the most influential academics and intellectuals, as well as the most visible and committed portion of the Church. Businessmen, too, were becoming increasingly jittery about Marcos's handling of the economy. Abroad, and especially in the United States, opposition had rallied around the figurehead of Benigno Aquino and was beginning a scholarly debunking of the Marcos myth. The tide of opinion (as they like to say in historiographical circles) was beginning to turn. And to cap it all, Ferdinand had secretly known for at least the past year that he was gravely – perhaps fatally – ill.

The journalistic cliché that was so often applied to Marcos, 'Asian strongman', seems never to have been less appropriate than when looking back at his martial law period. That such a measure was ever necessary had shown he was unable to maintain control by ordinary means. But in a thousand other gestures, in compromises, holdings-back, capitulations and decisions deferred, he could display a strange lack of forcefulness, especially when dealing with people face to face. Just as he was to prove incapable of curbing his cronies, so his wife and close family were increasingly allowed the upper hand. One of his brightest young technocrat ministers leaves us with a vignette which comes close to being endearing:

> His sister Elizabeth terrorized him. Despite all his orders to keep her out of Malacañang she always got past the guards somehow, bluffing her way in or just storming through. Sometimes he was warned in time and could take cover in the john. But she would sail into his office like a carriage pulled by her two little Pekingese dogs on strings. She used to smoke cigarettes in a long holder. The one thing he couldn't stand was anyone smoking in his presence. It was quite deliberate, of course. It was her technique for getting what she wanted without too much delay. She knew he would only get rid of her by agreeing. What did she want? Oh, funds for something, a job for someone; the usual, I expect.

12

The politics of fantasy

Was Ferdinand Marcos brought up on the Oz books? This is an item of research to which future scholars might profitably address themselves, and 'Glinda of Malacañang' may yet be the title of a sober study. Certainly his attitude to democracy turned out to show a remarkable resemblance to that of the Supreme Dictator in the last Oz book:

> I'm the Supreme Dictator of all, and I'm elected once a year. This is a democracy, you know, where people are allowed to vote for their rulers. A good many others would like to be Supreme Dictator, but as I made a law that I am always to count the votes myself, I am always elected.[1]

In its way, this was an uncanny foreshadowing of the nature of Philippine democracy for at least half a century.

When President Marcos lifted martial law after eight years and four months he did so without relaxing his control over the government's major institutions. Indeed, by 1981 the Philippines' entire political scene was either so rigged or so cowed that there was no 'democratic process' left to return to. The judiciary was his, while the media went on receiving peremptory phone calls from Malacañang telling them what they might or might not report. He continued to use his decree-making powers to arrest enemies and grant patronage to his friends (through behest loans, for example). Cesar Virata, the least 'political' of his Cabinet, became Prime Minister, but he had many more functions than actual power. Above all, he had in practice no jurisdiction over Imelda Marcos's prodigious Ministry of Human Settlements. Ferdinand had created this specifically for her in 1978, appointing her the first minister, and she had rapidly developed it into her own governmental fiefdom. In the final analysis there is no doubt that Marcos had prolonged martial law for one reason only: to retain power and to continue consolidating it by fair means or foul, like the Supreme Dictator.

Loyalists traditionally make two arguments to oppose this bald accusation. They say first that the security situation throughout the seventies made it impossible for any responsible President to risk calling an election, especially since the opposition could have fielded no candidate of any stature (Ninoy Aquino being in prison on capital charges and others having disqualified themselves on moral as well as on technical grounds by having chosen exile). Secondly, the claim is made that since there was no credible alternative, Marcos was justified in using a constitutionally sanctioned state of emergency (necessitated by Maoist elements plotting to destabilize the country) to push forward his New Society's agenda of social reforms. What can be said for both these arguments is that Ferdinand himself probably half believed them.

Whether he came to believe them the more it was expedient to do so can never be decided. What is interesting now is that as martial law dragged on, granting both Marcoses the absolute power of an imperial presidency, certain mystical and fantasy elements began to flavour their governance. At these elements' lowest level of manifestation Ferdinand began building an image of himself as a Filipino superman. As with Mao Zedong and any number of other 'strongmen', once rumours had started to circulate about his ill-health, pictures appeared of the President water-skiing or golfing or jogging. (In judicious deference to his countrymen's satirical sense of humour, Malacañang's image-makers did stop short of presenting Marcos as having strolled for an hour on a river-bed, as the ageing Chairman Mao was alleged to have done in the Yangtze during the Cultural Revolution. An hour's immersion in the effluent-rich Pasig River would have been roughly equivalent to a week in an acid bath.) For a while gossip circulated about an alleged resemblance someone had noticed in the outline of the Province of Kalinga-Apayao (between Ilocos Norte and Cagayan) to the President's own profile, complete with Presleyesque pompadour. Was this perhaps evidence that the country had been literally made in his image? In Marcos's defence it must be said that the more vulgar appurtenances of a personality cult never appealed to him. He was no Oriental in the mode of Mao or Kim Il Sung, with their prodigious public statuary of themselves. (The famous concrete bust visible from the road going to Baguio was built without his knowledge, apparently. His Tourism Minister, Joe Aspiras, commissioned it as an act of friendship. Ferdinand was said to have been 'embarrassed' when shown pictures of the finished sculpture and, indeed, it is a long way from Mount Rushmore. A few years ago treasure-hunters burrowed into its neck and nowadays, as moulds darken it and give it a quieter, more weathered look, it is turning into a genuine heritage curio.) On the other hand there is reason for thinking that he did consciously model himself on the lines of a pre-Hispanic *datu*, even to the extent of growing one of his thumbnails long. In fact, far from being a Mao-style ideologue, he was really one of nature's sultans.

A person who constructs a superman image for himself does need to have some degree of belief in it; either that or the kind of sense of humour which Marcos did not have (his ran to mild irony). There is much evidence for thinking that both he and Ninoy Aquino, until very late indeed, believed themselves immortal – or at any rate, not to be felled by anything as weakly pedestrian as mere illness. This probably explains Ferdinand's chronic refusal to name his successor, although his wife's hoping it would be her could have something to do with that. The exact point at which his deteriorating health really became a political issue is still a matter of widely varying opinion. Strangely, those closest to him managed to ignore it and it was never talked about in the Palace, as though from some superstitious belief that to discuss the possibility might precipitate the reality. Adrian Cristobal (who was very briefly Labour Secretary as well as more perennially one of Malacañang's chief scriptwriters) said, 'You may find it hard to believe, but I think I only noticed he was really ill as late as 1984. We were all so busy. Then one day I did notice a patch of fresh blood seeping out on the inner sleeve of his *barong*. I didn't know it then, but he'd obviously just come off the dialysis machine.'[2] Marcos's loyal aide, Art Aruiza, wrote that even in 1986 the exact nature of the President's illness was a closely guarded secret known only to his family and his doctors. Everybody seems to be in agreement with Aruiza's assertion that until 1979 Ferdinand appeared extraordinarily fit. At sixty-two he 'looked forty or younger . . . and was partial to figure-hugging "Fila" golf shirts that showed off his fine physique.'[3] Yet the possibility that he was seriously ill was being discussed in diplomatic circles within the year, as witness a report by the now-retired John Addis describing a tour he made of the Philippines in 1980 that culminated in a visit to Malacañang:

> The persistent rumour is that Marcos has lupus, a kind of skin-cancer. The treatment for lupus is cortisone, cortisone affects the kidneys and Marcos has only one kidney. It is therefore the side-effect of the treatment that is more likely to be fatal than the malady itself. So the story goes. I thought I noticed a slight coarsening of Marcos's features since a year ago, which would be consistent with cortisone treatment.[4]

A year later Addis returned and provided an interesting glimpse of the country six months after martial law had been lifted:

> I . . . was more depressed about the situation there than I have been on any previous visit. All circles view the future with gloom. . . . The communist New People's Army has spread widely from Luzon to the Visayas and Mindanao.
>
> The reasons for the bleak prospect are more political than economic. Marcos has tightened his stranglehold on the political life of the country. The banking crisis has enabled him and his cronies to monopolize even more power. My friends in the hereditary oligarchy tell me that hardly one of them has not been 'side-swiped'. It is now clear that Marcos's lust for power is insatiable. I once thought that he was statesman enough to set a course for the transition to democracy. But he has gone so far along the path of dictatorship that there can now be no turning back . . .
>
> The rumours of his skin cancer persist. I observed him closely during my half-hour meeting with him. His complexion is darker than last year, his face heavier and more puffy, the eyes now

mere slits . . . Mrs Marcos will certainly try to take over when
Marcos goes. No doubt she has loyal supporters. But, like Jiang
Qing [Chairman Mao's wife], she does not have the capacity to
rule. The army might take control for a time, but the exercise of
political power by the military is alien to the Philippine tradition.
The Filipinos are a sophisticated people, to whom politics is the
way of life. After a period of confusion some form of more or less
democratic system would probably emerge.

If my impressions of the situation are anywhere near the truth,
Vice-President Bush's recent blanket endorsement of Marcos and
his policies seems unwise. I do not know whether or not Bush
also put pressure on Marcos in private to relax his stranglehold of
power and give the people a little real democracy. But the public
approval must surely alienate the more moderate of Marcos's
critics and lead to further polarization. The Americans are no
doubt, as always, hypnotized by their bases in the Philippines, so
that they cannot see beyond the short-term advantage.[5]

It is an altogether sad assessment by a man who would not live to
see the outcome, for John Addis died less than two years later. The
wily old *datu*, though, lived on, concealing as best he might the
mortal disease he carried. Art Aruiza has said that he believed
Marcos had decided to come clean and make it official that he was a
sick man, but that Imelda had vetoed this. More oddly, there are
many informed Filipinos who think that he concealed the fact that he
had lupus (if, indeed, he did) because 'in eight out of ten cases it is a
women's disease, and it was not possible for someone as macho as
he was to admit he had been struck down by a women's disease. It
would have looked too *malas* [unlucky, with overtones of the evil
eye]'. In any case the chieftain went on planning years ahead with
the sublime egoism of one who has long come to believe in his own
mythology. In the first post-martial law election of June 1981 Marcos
of Oz had organized for himself a further six years in office, and at
the snap election of 1986 was fully prepared to do the same again, by
which time he was so weak he often had to be carried from the platform after public appearances. Likewise, Ninoy Aquino's doctors
were allegedly giving Ninoy only another two years when in 1983 he
elected to return from the US to challenge Marcos at the polls in, presumably, 1987. Surely this sort of hubris can only come as a vestigial

hangover from the tradition of the tribal leader on his deathbed passing on his magic to his anointed. There was a grotesque, even pitiful, moment during the 'EDSA Revolution' when Ferdinand appeared on television furiously protesting his unimpaired capacity as a warrior: 'They may say I'm sick, but I am just like an old war-horse, smelling powder and getting stronger. I have all the power in my hands to eliminate this rebellion at any time . . .'

The tribal leader, the *datu*, had been very much in evidence during martial law. Marcos had resurrected the pre-Hispanic unit of the *barangay* to replace the Spanish *barrio*. *Barangays* and their captains (a reminder that the original *balangays* were vessels in which migrants had first arrived in the archipelago) now formed the needles, as it were, on the lower branches of his administrative Christmas tree. The *datu* tone is readily apparent in the model questionnaire he had circulated to all 42,000 *barangay* captains before the January referendum in 1973.

> *Question 4:* Do you want to hold elections in November 1973 as provided for under the 1935 Constitution?
>
> *A:* No. We are sick and tired of too frequent elections. We are fed up with politics, of the many debates and so much expenses [sic].
>
> *Question 6:* Do you want martial law to continue?
>
> *A:* Yes. We want Pres. Marcos to exercise his powers with more authority. We want him to be strong and firm so that we can accomplish all his reform programmes.

This is also a reminder of Ferdinand's meticulousness in ensuring that all his acts – and particularly during martial law – had a basis in law, as it is of his deftness in combining this constitutionalism with the paternal and the autocratic.

At the height of their imperium, the Marcoses' Malacañang *was* the Halls of Maharlika, or Camelot, or Oz. For most Westerners its nearest likeness probably would be the court of some mediaeval European monarch. On nearly any day one could see vignettes of incredible extravagance as well as of penny-pinching; of outrageous arrogance and curious abasements; of Byzantine intrigues and scheming side by side with ringing professions of to-the-death loyalty; of high society in tiaras entering by the front door while men in plain clothes left on sinister missions by the back. There was even the odd assassination (the case of Guillermo de Vega was alluded to in the previous chapter).

For the constant stream of distinguished guests and delegations to be wined and dined the fare tended towards cordon bleu baronial. (It is too easy to make the virtuous point that within a few hundred yards of the Palace shanty-dwellers were living off rice and fish sauce.) There was in Malacañang menus a deliberate mixture of the nationalist Filipino and the imported Western. On 31 January 1975, for example, the Marcoses gave a dinner in honour of the delegates of an Afro-Asian writers' symposium. There was a printed programme of African, Indonesian, Chinese and Filipino songs, plus Philippine folk dances. The bill of fare, beautifully printed, did not offer much in the ethnic line, however. It ran as follows:

LE CONSOMMÉ DOUBLE A L'ESSENCE DE TOMATE

∽

LE FILET DE LAPU-LAPU AMANDINE

Chablis

∽

LE TENDRE COEUR DE BOEUF CORDON ROUGE
Les Pommes Chablis
Les Legumes Assortis
COEUR DE LAITUE
LA SALADE CAESAR

St.Emilion

∽

LES CRÊPES CHANTILLY AUX MANGUE FLAMBÉ

Moët Et Chandon

∽

LA DEMI TASSE

One can see Ferdinand managing the consommé and toying with the grouper fillet (even though his Ilocano sensibilities might have winced a little at the almonds) but he would have skipped the wines and even wondered why the entire menu needed to be in a foreign tongue – at that, one which had never had the least purchase in the Philippines. No doubt he comforted himself with the thought that his wife knew what she was doing – flaming mangoes and all – since by now she was a good deal more travelled than he.

A further similarity between a mediaeval monarch and both Marcoses was the peculiar mixture of unlimited power and impotence. The king-as-patron, keeping his nobles sweet with gold and preferment, would have closely resembled the Filipino President; yet in each case there was the constant possibility that orders might be disobeyed. Throughout the Marcoses' reign these strange limits to the chief executive's power were made constantly clear, as they still are in the Malacañang of today's incumbent. Nowadays this is most vividly seen when a much-publicized criminal escapes from jail and goes on the run. After a few days' fruitless nationwide search various police chiefs assure the embarrassed President that the fellow is definitely out of the country. He has a habit of resurfacing, however, months and sometimes years later, when it turns out he was lying low in the domain of some provincial governor or else in an oligarch's private fiefdom, having reached an understanding with his pursuers that lasted until the money ran out. But it is clear it was suspected all along, if not known for certain, where the fugitive was, and equally that neither the police nor the military had wanted to go up against a private army.

Even within the Palace itself there were divided loyalties. One of the more fascinating aspects of the whole Marcos era is the growth of his wife's personal power until it reached a point where it was not unknown for the First Couple to countermand each other's orders. (Ferdinand's temporary embargo that halted the breakneck construction of Imelda's notorious film theatre in late 1981 is a case in point.) At her peak – say between 1975 and 1983 – Imelda Marcos was formidable. She was the living proof that Tennyson had been only half right when he wrote that men may rise on steppingstones/Of their dead selves to higher things. Women may, too. The way she had triumphed over the traumas of her childhood and youth amounted to genius. She has often been seen disdainfully as little more than the Queen of Shopping, but she was infinitely more than that. From her early nervous breakdown on being first exposed to the rough edges of Filipino politics she had recovered to turn herself into a consummate politician in her own right, adroit enough in her way to act for a while as a roving ambassadress for the Philippines. Ferdinand did not like to travel, and whenever he could he avoided it. Imelda adored it, and whenever she could she availed herself of one or more of the aircraft she could commandeer by virtue of having taken over Philippine Airlines (PAL), and off she would whizz to the Vatican, or Paris, or Persepolis, or New York, or anywhere else that took her fancy. Together, she and her husband hatched a remarkable double-act that gave birth to a kind of counter-diplomacy. Whenever he wanted to open up relations with a notoriously difficult or unfashionable foreign power – especially one in Washington's bad books – he would send Imelda, perfectly briefed, to wedge one of her exquisitely shod feet in the door.

The usual line taken about her various trips as an emissary (to Russia, to China, to Iran, to Libya and elsewhere) is that Marcos never let her go until she was so thoroughly groomed that she had become his clone, diplomatically speaking. 'She was Frankensteined by him,' as someone observed. But this gives her no credit for her style, which was as much a part of her diplomacy as was her eidetic memory of the political line she needed to take. Ferdinand himself had about as much style as a British trade union leader of the sixties, except when water-skiing and able to display his trim little pectorals. Heavy plain men like Leonid Brezhnev could have taken him in their stride, but Imelda threw them completely. It was like having the Queen of Sheba come calling on the Kremlin. She reminded grim apparatchiks of sunnier climes and stimulated them to ponderous gallantries. Her mere physical presence brought atrophied libidos out of long hibernation, peeping shyly forth like rabbit noses in spring. Not surprisingly, Washington strongly disapproved of one of its client states showing such wilful independence in its foreign policy. The CIA sniffily dismissed her diplomacy as all a matter of publicity, the real negotiations having been accomplished in advance by men in suits – as though this were not true of all such foreign trips by heads of state, including those of any American President.

Mrs Marcos gives a memorable account of her two missions to Colonel Ghaddafi in Libya in 1976 and 1977. The nominal purpose of these visits was to induce Ghaddafi to stop funding and supplying Nur Misuari's Moro National Liberation Front (MNLF), which was fighting a kind of *jihad* in the Philippines' Moslem south. Back in the days of the Spanish, Manila had largely solved the problem of 'the Moors' by simply ignoring it; but during the American occupation a process was begun that involved resettling landless peasants from Luzon down in Mindanao. This was seen as a neat way of sidestepping land reform while diluting the Islamic population with a steady influx of Christians, and it continued under Marcos despite the Moslems' growing unrest at what they saw as a Christian plot to grab their lands and submerge their culture. In 1968 Nur Misuari, much influenced by the Islamic nationalist movements in Malaysia and Indonesia, founded the MNLF. He appealed successfully to various Arab states including Libya for funds and military aid and by 1974 his long-standing religious and demographic struggle had become a full-scale war. The MNLF was able to field nearly 60,000 guerrilla fighters, mostly armed by Libya via Malaysia.

By 1977 this war was tying down two-thirds of the Philippine Armed Forces' combat units and the situation seemed completely intractable. Acts of random terror by Moslems and Christians alike were exacerbated by fanaticism and by the behaviour of often ill-disciplined, badly supplied and frightened troops. The casualties on both sides of this much under-reported conflict were horrendous (Misuari was later to say that in the 1980s alone some 100,000 Moros were killed), and by 1977 tens of thousands of Filipino Moslems had sought temporary refuge across the Sulu Sea in Sabah and East Malaysia. It became clear that, no matter what extraordinary powers martial law might be giving Marcos in the Christian parts of the country, he was sooner or later going to be forced to come to a political deal with Misuari and the MNLF. Misuari was unimpressed by the tentative regional autonomy Marcos was offering. Instead, he was insisting on complete independence for an area comprising the whole of Mindanao, Sulu and Palawan (handily known as 'Minsupala'). In this impasse towards the end of 1976 Ferdinand sent Imelda to Libya to beard the West's *bête noire* in his famous bedouin tent.

Ferdy sent me to see Ghaddafi because thirty thousand Filipinos, both Christian and Moslem, were already dead. JUSMAG [Joint US Military Advisory Group] wouldn't arm us so we'd gone to Israel to get arms, which is why Israel gave us so many national honours and awards. I flew to Tripoli with Fidel Ramos [Vice Chief-of-Staff of the Armed Forces] and Enrile [Secretary of Defence]. But Ghaddafi wouldn't see us. We sat there for three days. Then Nur Misuari appeared and told us the Libyans were going to blow up our PAL plane that had brought us and which was sitting out there on the tarmac. At that point FVR and Enrile started to get really scared and itchy. They and the others panicked and decided to leave me there. So they bundled into the plane and flew off home and I was left stranded with Joe Aspiras [the Tourism Minister] and a few generals.

Once they had gone, Ghaddafi came to see me. I thanked him and he said, 'Mrs Marcos, I like you. Why don't you become a Moslem?' I replied, 'Mr President, I've been a Catholic all my life. It's hard for an old dog to learn new tricks.' You see, he had been sending me copies of the Koran in English with various passages underlined. So we sat down and I said, 'Mr President, it says in the Koran that Islam is peace, isn't that true?' 'Yes, yes,' he said. 'So let's have a cease-fire in Mindanao.' 'All right,' he said. That was number one. Next, I told him that as I understood it, Islam is generous, so let us have no more claims on Minsupala, those balkanization plans. He agreed to that. So that was number two. Number three was Palawan – I told him it was tiny and he agreed to leave it alone. Number four was the freedom of our OCWs to go to work on construction contracts in the Middle East. OK too. And last, we needed to buy his oil. No problem. You see? Everything that was on my list I got. I never failed in any of my diplomatic missions, just as I never failed in any of my domestic projects. Years later, during my [racketeering] trial in New York, Ghaddafi offered to pay my bail. He told a friend of mine, 'Imelda's a good woman. Even ten times that.'[6] (In the event, bail was paid by the late tobacco heiress, Doris Duke.)

This somewhat stagily naive account seems to conflate two separate visits. A preliminary accord for a 'Tripoli Agreement' was indeed signed at the end of December 1976 in which President Marcos undertook to give the Moros their own representative assembly and Islamic courts. Thereupon Marcos made one of those moves of his which suggested that the statesman in him was always at the mercy of the Bar top-notcher, unable to resist a kind of glaring canniness. He announced that there would be a conditional amnesty for the Moslem rebels while a referendum was held in the southern provinces to determine which merited autonomous status. Given that the demographic 'stuffing' by Christians of these traditionally Islamic areas was the war's pretext, it was hardly surprising that the provisional Tripoli Agreement promptly collapsed and in March 1977 the MNLF resumed fighting. It was as a result of this that Ferdinand sent Imelda back to Libya to renew her charm offensive.

There is little doubt that she played her part with considerable dexterity and probably did much to counteract the effects of the uniformly bad press that her husband had earned himself in the Islamic world. The outcome of this second visit was favourable, and Ghaddafi did indeed stop funding the Moros.[7] It would seem ungallant to suggest that anything other than Imelda Marcos's famous charisma might have tipped the balance, but the fact is that shifting political alliances far outside her control lay behind the change of mood in Tripoli. Under various pressures the MNLF was about to split into factions, with several nation-members of the Islamic Conference offering asylum to the various groups. Always mercurial in his enthusiasms, Ghaddafi must have perceived that the whole thing was getting out of hand. He appeared to lose interest, no doubt thinking that he had done his bit and the Islamic Conference could take over the Moros' cause. (When sections of the Moros allied themselves with the NPAs in the early eighties it would only have confirmed Ghaddafi in his judgement. Maoists, Communists and atheists were not fit comrades for Islamic warriors.)

Regardless of the underlying dynamics, however, Imelda Marcos and he had parted on the most amicable terms and he promised a return visit to the Philippines (which never took place) before she flew back to Manila to be debriefed personally by the head of the CIA, William Casey. Something undeniably concrete did come of her trips because she ordered the building of the Quiapo mosque in anticipation of Ghaddafi's visit and it has long since become a focus for Manila's Moslem community. In 1996 Juan Ponce Enrile uncivilly claimed she had 'acted like a houri' towards Ghaddafi when he had accompanied her to Tripoli. It is unclear how he knew this since by the time she and Ghaddafi met – at least, in her version of the visit – Enrile had already high-tailed it home to Manila in panic.

It does have to be said that Mrs Marcos's claim that she never failed in any of her domestic projects is open to qualification, though her list of such projects – to say nothing of her building programme – is so large it would be surprising had everything gone according to plan. In 1975 she became Governor of Metro Manila and three years later Ferdinand appointed her to head a newly created Ministry, that of Human Settlements. This new Ministry became the political seat of Imelda's private empire. There she held sway with her deputy and *éminence grise* Dr Jolly Benitez. Dr Benitez was a curious figure whom many began seeing as a Svengali who had acquired considerable influence over her and personal power to go with it. He was the nephew of Helena Benitez who, as recounted in Chapter 6, had once backed the Rose of Tacloban in her effort to become Miss Manila. All foreign funding for social developmental projects was theoretically routed through the Ministry of Human Settlements, which in practice meant through the hands of Dr Benitez.

All Imelda's troubles really stem from him. The Benitez family owns the Philippine Women's University, which is highly respectable, so you could say Jolly had a background in education. He got a doctorate in it from Stanford. Before that he was a dancer in his Aunt Helena's Bayanihan dance company. Somewhere in the mid-seventies he began convincing Imelda she had a mind and decided to give her an intellectual stamp. Only after he appeared on the scene did she start spouting all this technological jargon about habitats and cities, how to make cities more livable, stuff like that. He persuaded her she had an international role in this which led to her giving a speech in Vancouver to a UN conference on human habitations. I mean, she was up in front of people like Buckminster Fuller and Margaret Mead.

(But there again, why not? If the Rose of Tacloban could have sung to Irving Berlin, why mightn't a minister of a developing Asian nation talk to Margaret Mead?)

Before long, Imelda had built up her Ministry until it began functioning as practically a rival government, duplicating most of the Government's major functions, with comparable powers and the limitless funding which she alone seemed able to conjure up. It was not long before vehicles bearing her slogans became a commonplace in Manila's gridlocked traffic: DO NOT DELAY: ANOTHER PROJECT OF THE FIRST LADY. And projects there were. She had long since treated the reclaimed land on which she built the Cultural Centre as her personal site. She built the Folk Arts Theatre from scratch in an incredible seventy-seven days. In 1976 she completed the Philippine International Convention Centre (PICC), a building large enough that, should the occasion arise, it could accommodate the 5,500 delegates of the entire United Nations General Assembly. It could also serve a sit-down state dinner to 4,000. The Philippine Plaza Hotel right next to it, owned through fronts by Imelda herself, was largely built with $75m of Government Service Insurance System (GSIS) money – in other words, civil servants' pension funds. It was a sign of the power wielded by the Ministry she headed that she was able to poach GSIS funds for her own projects. Apart from this there were on the same site a fast food centre, the Philcite Trade Show Centre, the Coconut Palace which Pope John Paul II would disdain, and the Film Centre. This last was rushed into being in order that its theatre should be completed by early 1982 when her first Manila International Film Festival (designed to rival Cannes) was due to open. According to the architect, Froilan Hong, the speed of the project was so hectic that serious corners were cut in its construction. On the fateful night of 17 November 1981, the newly poured top floor collapsed onto shift workers sleeping below in the auditorium, burying them in tons of setting concrete. Such was the urgency of the project that security forces sealed off the site even before rescue teams were allowed in. Barely twenty-four hours later, while rescue operations were still going on, orders were given to have the rubble bulldozed down to the foreshore and for work to recommence. To this day nobody is certain how many workers died in the Film Theatre and it is said that many are still there, entombed in its walls and floors. The theatre (now closed owing to earthquake damage) is reputed to be the most haunted building in Manila.[8] Contrary to rumour, Mrs Marcos had nothing to do with giving the orders to bulldoze the debris regardless of the possibility of there still being survivors. The project was under the personal aegis of Dr Benitez's wife, Betty.

Apart from these buildings on the CCP complex, Imelda completed the Metropolitan Museum on nearby Roxas Avenue; dozens of hotels for the longed-for tourist boom; thirty-two palaces or rest-houses scattered at spectacular sites all over the country for guests and friends; the so-called 'innards hospitals' (medical centres specializing in heart, kidney, lung and other ailments); a University of Life; and the National Arts Centre which houses the Philippine High School for the Arts – one of her pet projects for gifted children. With the exception of the palaces, which were nationalized after 1986, the ravaged Film Theatre and the University of Life (whose deserted campus has been trapped in a species of time-warp or limbo ever since General Fabian Ver used it as an assembly-point for his tanks and forces during the 'EDSA Revolution'), all Imelda's major buildings are fully functional. But as to all of her domestic projects being as successful as she claimed, one would certainly have to make an exception for several of the schemes under her Ministry's programme known as *Sariling Sikap*.

Sariling Sikap (which translates literally as 'by one's own efforts') was so famous for its rigged tenders, kickbacks and crooked land deals it became known popularly as *Sariling Sikwat* ('by one's own theft') – precisely the difference between 'self-help' and 'help yourself'. Imelda's problem had always been a surfeit of ideas. She would awake one morning from a night of fertile dreams and minor visions with the germs of half a dozen new projects. A brief blast of oxygen from the cylinder beside her bed or a brainstorming session with Jolly Benitez might add several more. With the extraordinary power she commanded she had a habit of waving a jewelled hand and saying, 'Well, don't just stand there. We must get on!' and orders were given and out sped the fleets of trucks and vans with 'DO NOT DELAY: ANOTHER PROJECT OF THE FIRST LADY' on them, and men in hard hats with theodolites would break ground in some godforsaken patch of weeds way out in Rizal Province towards the mountains, and there matters would rest. The commands stopped coming and the money dried up and Imelda's dragonfly mind had darted away to some other priority scheme for tiling Manila's roofs or stripping the stucco off Spanish churches. No follow-through, that was the problem.

This was exactly what happened with one of *Sariling Sikap*'s housing schemes in about 1980. The first Minister of Human Settlements had laudably decided that the poor should be helped to buy proper houses of their own. Never at a loss for a neo-Platonic precept, she quoted 'The heart must be healthy for the body to grow strong,' which meant to her that a *house*'s heart must also be healthy. Thus she reasoned that the lavatory should be the focal (as indeed the fecal) point of any poor family's home. Forget the hearth, the literal focus; it was the bathroom that had to be healthy. So she ordered that even before the foundations were laid, the lavatory bowl must be installed and plumbed. In due course bulldozers and diggers arrived and soon on a Cavite lot arose the remarkable sight of hundreds of white lavatory bowls, all in precise rows, each gleaming on its little patch of fresh cement. But then, just as suddenly, the bulldozers vanished again and nobody came back to lay the foundations. Within a month or two the local poor decided to upgrade their existing shacks rather than start afresh and began stealing the bowls. Today they have vanished; but the site is forever known locally as '*Kubeta Siti*' or 'Toilet Town'. So for Imelda to have claimed that none of her domestic projects had failed is perhaps poetic licence.

It is noticeable that as the seventies gave way to the eighties the fantasy nature of Malacañang's world intensified, becoming positively mystical after Ninoy Aquino's assassination in 1983. Part of this was due to an interest the Palace shared with the rest of the nation in the supernatural and the occult. A popular manifestation of this was Johnny Midnite and 'toning'. Johnny Midnite was Johnny Joseph, a has-been DJ with a radio programme nobody listened to on DZBB called the 'Johnny Midnite Hour'. Something then moved Johnny Midnite to ascend the holy mountain of Banahaw some eighty kilometres south-east of Manila. This is famous for its cults and apparitions of Jose Rizal, Jesus Christ and – more recently – Ferdinand Marcos. There he spent several months communing with the *genii loci* and returned to Dee Zee Double-Bee a changed man. Thereafter the Johnny Midnite Hour was listened to by everyone within radio earshot, from Imelda Marcos to shanty-dwellers, from METROCOM goons sitting in their patrol cars with the lamplight gleaming off their reflecting sunglasses to child prostitutes resting between tricks on the roofs and stairwells of Ermita. For those months in the wilderness had turned Johnny Midnite into a healer. He could even heal over the radio. All one needed was a glass of ordinary water, and Johnny would recite his incantations over the airwaves and 'tone' the water until it had magic properties. Millions of folk sat in the dead of night with millions of glasses of water beside them as Johnny chanted his prayers. And what did he recite? Why, spells and charms indistinguishable from any one might collect in Kansulay. Whatever else, they gave the lie to all those who claimed nobody but ignorant peasants buried in the boondocks would still pay attention to such nonsense. Millions of devoted urbanites from Malacañang downwards paid it the raptest attention and drank their newly vibrant water.

> ACNO AMISIOTAM IPOCSO CAMAD
> HAPHAP ROCOB BAIO ICOB
> LEPUS NAPRAP
> ADONAI JEHOVA ELOIM SABAOTH[9]

Johnny Midnite held his audience in thrall, his powers vouched for by thousands of listeners who phoned in, testifying to miraculous cures. (The notion that occult powers are transmittable on broadcast frequencies had already been implanted by Uri Geller, who was alleged to be able to bend viewers' spoons at home.) Johnny Midnite was also keen on the curative powers of pyramids, like many others of the era. Then without warning he vanished from the scene, never to reappear. He left behind the memory of a strange phenomenon, doubly so in that he had operated no scam and had made no obvious profit. He had not even cultivated the great and the good in order to embark on a career in politics, unlike many another Filipino entertainer.

Closer to home, if one may thus describe Malacañang Palace, was 'Bionic Boy', whose nickname dates his advent to the seventies when the TV series *The Six Million Dollar Man* was on, starring Lee Majors as the 'bionic man' stuffed ('We can repair him!') with transistors. Of all the myriad occultists, mystics, gurus and psychic oddballs who drifted in and out of the Palace over the years to hold one or other of the Marcoses in temporary thrall, none lasted so long or became as celebrated as Bionic Boy. He was supposed to have been abandoned by his parents and appeared towards the end of the seventies as an overweight and somewhat ill-favoured teenager with remarkable powers. He had soon entranced the Marcoses with his abilities, which included reading aloud from the palm of his own hand a text someone else was looking at and being able to 'write' by miming the act on the top sheet of a stack of paper, the sentence then being discovered in visible handwriting on a sheet buried near the bottom of the pile. These phenomena were accompanied by a mysterious high buzzing or whining sound that was presumably the origin of his nickname. So taken were the Marcoses by his uncanny predictions and outlandish skills that they virtually adopted him and the boy took the name of Ronald (after Reagan) Marcos. He was given his own room in the Palace, called the Marcoses 'Mom' and 'Dad', and went everywhere with them, including trips to the 'Palace in the North' at Paoay, Ilocos Norte. He soon began giving demonstrations of his powers on television programmes such as that hosted by Julie Yap Daza, according to whom Bionic Boy had first been 'discovered' by Carmelo Barbero, then Under-secretary of Defence, before he graduated socially to Malacañang.

Having thus started out as a martial law foundling, Bionic Boy swiftly rose to occupy a position in Camelot-on-the-Pasig of a teenage Merlin or court wizard. The feat for which he became most celebrated (before, that is, removing a tumour from Ronald Reagan's rectum) was his ability to empower toy telephones to act like real ones. There is an enduring image of this, recounted by an eye-witness, of Ferdinand Marcos sitting on the floor of Bionic Boy's chaotic room chatting to Henry Kissinger 8,000 miles away in Washington by means of a plastic Mattel toy phone, its tiny handset connected with string ('You could be in the next room, Henry'). Bionic Boy must then have made the mistake of assuming that a medium was more important than his message. He fell from grace in 1985, apparently for having predicted the Marcoses' downfall (at first gladdening Imelda with the news that Ferdinand would be succeeded by the Philippines' first woman President, and then dashing her hopes by pointing out that it wasn't her he saw in the palm of his hand. Sorry, Mom). He went on to throw his psychic weight behind the 'EDSA revolution' with results that are, as they say, history.

Years later Mrs Marcos put her hand to her brow in an elegant gesture of perplexity. 'Bionic Boy?' she said, as though she had been asked to remember a cigarette brand from her childhood. '*Bionic* Boy? No, I rather think . . . I'm sorry, that name doesn't seem at all familiar.' For those interested to know what happens to ex-court wizards, the answer is they change their name to Ronnie Joaquin and move to LA where their talents are appreciated. According to a rare interview he is now 'doing special missions for the US Government', an activity that leads him to 'unimaginable places' – a description that would surely include an ex-President's fundament:

> Ronnie reportedly asked President Reagan to close his eyes as [he] snapped his fingers. At that same instant, Reagan reportedly felt something warm enter his body towards the rectal area. From then on, the US President was allegedly healed.[10]

In addition, he claims to be 400 years old and is predicting a catastrophic meteor strike in July 1999. Altogether he seems in excellent spirits and has clearly made good. He is a credit to his foster parents in their Palace on the banks of the Pasig long ago.

This was all innocent stuff, to be sure; but some more politically potent fantasies were hatched in or around Malacañang, two of the more pervasive being those of the Tasaday and Malakas and Maganda. Here we enter that contentious, quasi-anthropological territory that lies between folklore and 'fakelore' (as the UP anthropologist, Arnold Azurin, puts it[11]). The Tasaday first hit the world's headlines on 7 June 1971 when Manuel 'Manda' Elizalde announced that a hitherto undiscovered Stone Age tribe had been found living on a thickly jungled hill in South Cotabato Province down in southern Mindanao. Modestly, Manda called it 'the most important discovery in anthropology this century' and *National Geographic* (which devoted two issues to the Tasaday full of lyrical pictures of Tarzanic family cave-scenes) called him a 'visionary idealist' who cared more about 'the hard-pressed national minorities than about his family fortune'.

The Elizalde family fortune was not inconsiderable. One of the old élite families who supported rather than fell foul of Marcos, their interests included mining, sugar and distilling (in those days they owned Tanduay Distilleries, whose rum is as ubiquitous in the Philippines as Coca-Cola). At the time of his discovery Manda Elizalde was head of PANAMIN (Presidential Assistance on National Minorities), an organization charged with the protection of Philippine 'cultural minorities': some forty-four tribal groups making up sixteen percent of the population. (In *The Creation of a Cultural Minority* the late scholar William Henry Scott made the point that 'cultural minorities' in this context is less an anthropological definition than a political category since it refers to indigenous Filipinos who have so far resisted integration into the dominant political culture, whether Spanish, American or mainstream urban Filipino.) In any case Elizalde's news was greeted with great interest, later stimulated still further by the pictures in *National Geographic* and a coffee-table book by John Nance, *The Gentle Tasaday*. So pure and untouched were these *ur*-folk, these delicious remnants of Eden, they had at all costs to be kept safe from contamination and exploitation. A decree from the President (P.D. 1017) prohibited any unauthorized person from entering their newly created reservation. His wife used to chopper in with friends like Charles Lindbergh and Gina Lollobrigida. More than twenty years later, Imelda is still looking to the Tasaday for unspoiled wisdom:

> We watched a marriage ceremony. There was none of this 'to have and to hold' business. Do you know what their vow said? 'You and I will make a beautiful world together.' You see? *Beauty*. Nothing about ownership, about possession, about material things.[12]

Other than such VIP visits and those of highly selected journalists, the Tasaday remained closed to the world. No serious anthropologist was allowed to live and work with them, which made *National Geographic*'s credulity all the odder. Although rumours of a hoax had circulated since June 1971 it was not until 1986 that it at last became possible to examine these 'Stone Age' folk in any detail. It at once became apparent that they were T'bolis, their cave site being within easy walking distance of the nearest T'boli village and their language a local Manobo dialect. Their number was deemed far too small for them to have been a viable tribe in isolation, nor could the surrounding jungle have met all their dietary needs as hunter-gatherers. It was also unfortunate that in the fifteen years that had elapsed since their discovery they had become 'acculturated', and the dewy toddlers who had been filmed in a state of nature were now gum-chewing teenagers wearing jeans, T-shirts and wicked grins. It was not lost on sceptics that Manda had been running for the Senate when he made his 'discovery', and although he was unsuccessful then, Marcos later named him Presidential Assistant on National Minorities with ministerial status.

What was interesting about the Tasaday hoax was everybody's eagerness to believe it (*National Geographic* and John Nance being left looking particularly silly). Marcos undoubtedly seized on it as a public relations gift to martial law. Not only did it stimulate outsiders to non-political interest in the Philippines as a country, diverting attention away from his 'constitutional authoritarianism', but it supposedly showed a humane and responsible approach towards cultural minorities to counteract the effect of incidents like the execution of Lim Seng. But at another level the affair revealed itself as a potent piece of myth-making or wishful thinking that might be comparable with, for example, the discovery of a small tribe of Druids who had been miraculously overlooked and found skulking in some Celtic fastness in Ireland or Wales or Brittany. To that broad streak in Malacañang that was mystically attuned to Filipino nationalism the Tasaday spoke of the nation's very roots, showing the world how pre-history was alive and well in some yet unravaged Arcadia.

It should be added that there are still certain people (including, presumably, Imelda herself) who do not believe the Tasaday were fake; that the way in which Elizalde, Marcos and others made use of them did not itself make them any less genuine. However, those uses are what one chiefly remembers. Elizalde's exploitation of PANAMIN and the Tasaday was certainly profitable for someone. It was not just that the garden of Manda's Manila home was famously full of cultural minorities living in log cabins, tree-houses and similar ethnic hovels – among whom a preponderance of girls that seemed to defy demographic likelihood. It was also that 'when PANAMIN was finally audited after the downfall of Marcos, at least $17 million of government money earmarked for cultural minorities was missing'.[13]

The question that must be asked, but which remains for ever unanswerable, is, to what extent did the Marcoses themselves believe in the Tasaday? That is to say, did Ferdinand know from the start that it was a hoax and simply exploit it for what it was worth (did he, indeed, conspire with Elizalde?); or did he exploit it while also believing the fantasy that his country's pre-Hispanic past still existed in a living form? This is an area of discourse in which faith can co-exist with expediency, myth with *realpolitik* (as in the occult underpinnings of Nazism, or even in a concept like 'the Vatican bank'). It is not always possible to say with any certainty which aspect predominates at any one time. This crux was perfectly exemplified in the late seventies and early eighties with Imelda's rediscovery of the myth of Malakas and Maganda.

Malakas and Maganda (the male and female principle, alias strength and beauty) are Adam and Eve figures who appear in several Filipino regional mythologies. The central story has the Filipino race originating from this couple who are born within a single stem of bamboo that splits to reveal them nested together like spoons. Thus the bamboo itself has a certain mythic significance for Filipinos – or at least, it maybe does for those who know the myth – as the plant from which their race sprang. It seems likely that the person who introduced Imelda to the significance of this tale was her Svengali, Dr Jolly Benitez. If so, it was a stroke of genius because it supplied her with the perfect metaphor for her entire life: a *raison d'être*, a justification, an explanation, a political testament and an autobiography all in one. In 1980 *Si Malakas at Si Maganda* was published, and in many ways it stands as her central text.

It is an extraordinary book, written in a florid, 'deep' Tagalog, both verse and prose, and illustrated with original paintings. It is divided into three Books, the first dealing with the Malakas and Maganda story, the second with the legend of Talamuging and Sinagtala, two Filipino folk heroes, and the last with Ferdinand and Imelda, two heroes for the modern age. So closely did Imelda identify Malakas and Maganda with herself and her husband – the first couple turning into the First Couple – that the image practically became her trademark and appeared in many of her buildings as paintings or murals. In the musty foyer of the Film Theatre, for example, there is a large painting of Malakas and Maganda couched in their twin halves of split bamboo amid a sort of Douanier Rousseau jungle over which a ghostly deity spreads his protective arms. The same image was found in Malacañang Palace after the Marcoses' hurried departure in 1986, the rendition in 'their' bedroom (which they allegedly had not shared for years) being particularly mocked by Western journalists. Because the two figures had the Marcoses' faces it simply looked to these foreigners like Tarzan and Jane posing in a Disney forest and done in a naive, personality-cult style. All they could see was Kim Il Sung lyricism with Hollywood imagery, the muscular Jungle Boy of the picture grotesquely at odds with the bloated and terminally ill figure who had just flown off to Hawaii. Yet people close to the First Couple believed it had considerable psychic and even erotic significance for them, which does suggest that the whole use of the myth was much more than just an adroit exercise in propaganda. No cynical dictator of the sort Marcos was supposed to be hangs his regime's propaganda on his own bedroom wall unless he believes it expresses something close to him. This icon of himself as in some mystical way the nation's first *datu*, the macho embodiment of political as well as physical strength who was potent enough to bring his people to heel by means of martial law, certainly seems to bear out one's suspicions of an erotic component in his rule. This joint imagery of the Marcoses came to dominate the era. Manila only narrowly escaped acquiring a gigantic silhouette of Malakas and Maganda on its seafront, higher than the Empire State Building and doubling as a massive priapic lighthouse. The idea for this came to Imelda, like so many of her ideas, through a psychic who saw it as a testament to the resurgent Filipino spirit.

Book Two – the legend of Sinagtala and Talamuging (whose name in Ilokano means 'star-on-the-brow', as the mark of one chosen to be the noble chief and champion of the race) – provides the intermediate step in the Marcoses' metamorphosis. Here one makes a happy discovery. Looked at from a cultural tangent, and translated with only a little rhythmic licence, the verse is revealed as a natural parody of Longfellow. At any moment one expects to glimpse Old Nokomis fettling up his wigwam:

> From the highlands and the mountains,
> From the seas and golden flatlands,
> Each from lion's tooth endangered,
> Each from eagle's claw and serpent –
> Sinagtala with her children,
> Talamuging on his stallion
> Together with his faithful followers –
> Bore his hopes and dreams of freedom,
> Bore her prayers for rest and safety . . .[14]

Book Three is where the whole myth is given its modern significance or, as the Introduction puts it, 'reveals the continuing development of the new Malakas and Maganda in the country's harmony and progress, as shaped by the New Society: a noble nation, prosperous and peaceful, under the guidance of the True, the Good and the Beautiful, a humane community'. 'The True, the Good and the Beautiful' is Imelda Marcos's personal motto, her catchphrase, her credo, constantly invoked and alluded to. Whom she first heard it from is not certain. A typical piece of neo-Platonism such as influenced the New Testament writers (one thinks immediately of St Paul's Epistle to – who else? – the Philippians, chapter 4 verse 8, and its reference to things that are honest, just, pure and of good report), she might have acquired it from any mentor-priest. On the other hand she could as easily have caught it from the contagious epigrams ('Beauty is truth, truth beauty') of the Western classics. Come to that, she might have fallen beneath the spell of a classic Western, *The Good, the Bad and the Ugly*. Whatever the phrase's provenance, it has come to speak for her in a way that a more conventional expression of spirituality might no longer. (Outwardly, she remains the devout Catholic of her upbringing; but in private she confesses to being no longer at ease with such conventional Christian tenets as that of original sin. Imelda does not believe in burdens of guilt.)

This last Book of *Malakas at Maganda* also contains some highly autobiographical scenes from her life, notably the obviously traumatic attempted assassination by the knife-wielding stranger shortly after martial law was declared. The episode is narrated in the mythic style she so easily adopts when speaking of herself and which sounds so natural in the book's Tagalog. In her delirium following the attack she returns to her girlhood in Leyte with her mother and aunt at her bedside telling her folk tales. A white figure approaches her, a *babaylan* or native priestess leading a huge crowd in prayers for Imelda's recovery. She then has a vision of an Egyptian queen trying to raise her even as the *babaylan* chants a Manobo epic. Heartened by the crowd's affection and strengthened by her vision, Imelda gradually 'rejoins the stream of life'. The crisis is over; she regains consciousness to find herself in hospital with Ferdinand at her bedside holding her hand. The curious illustration that blends Imelda with a Nefertiti-like figure supposedly represents this delirium, the influence for which was doubtless the Indian mystic who had once told her she was a reincarnation of Semiramis. Never mind that Semiramis was Assyrian rather than Egyptian: even Hollywood could get things like that wrong. What surely mattered to her was that Semiramis, after her husband the King of Babylon's death, became ruler of a vast empire which stretched practically to India. (Mrs Marcos had never quite accepted the idea of being a queen without also being the sole ruler.) The vision of the *babaylan* might, conceivably, have been unconsciously suggested by the lurking theme of Babylon; but with such priestesses' links to a pre-Hispanic Filipino past they, too, were an authentic part of her fantasy. The original *babaylanes* were shamans who were believed to have crossed gender lines with impunity, something else she would approve of. Indeed, the leading gay and lesbian students' support group at UP today is called UP Babaylan on the grounds that 'modern-day *babaylanes* believe that fighting for lesbian and gay rights is merely regaining the exalted historical status of their forebears in Philippine society'.[15]

Much of the rest of the Book is devoted to recounting the triumphs and crises of the Marcoses' lives, interpreting everything from Ferdinand's war heroism to the First Quarter Storm and martial law in terms of Philippine mythology. In particular, it picks up on the way they had met, their whirlwind courtship and the conviction they shared that their union had been fated from the first. Their relationship is a perfect allegory in which, yin and yang, they complement one another. The Marcoses *are* Malakas and Maganda.

By mystically embodying the Filipino spirit they represent – in their psychic links with the prehistoric past – all Filipinos and all Filipinas in an epitomizing dyad. Like the Osiris legend of ancient Egypt it had the political function of uniting two kingdoms, that of the north (Ilocos) and that of the south (Leyte, the Visayas and, hopefully, Moslem Mindanao). In order to make manifest the First Couple's parental role it was easy to beef up the *datu*'s own 'mystical' aspects (such as the magic charm – a splinter of wood – which Bishop Aglipay had supposedly inserted in his back, and his skill in numerology), as it was to play up his wife's own maternality until she became the mother of her race. The fact that a dozen years after their downfall and nine years after Ferdinand's death Imelda still believes in the force of this allegory surely suggests that it always had been more than just a cynical exercise in window-dressing their regime:

> Ferdie had an ideology. I had a theology. The *barangay* was our extended family. It embodied participatory democracy. He had a personal vision for the average Filipino; he had a national vision for the Philippines; he had a global vision for . . . for all of us. *My natural role is to be the mother. My cultural role is to be beautiful. Our story is the story of the country.*[16]

It is an extraordinary feat of modern political mythologizing, but it does need to be remembered that it became an official myth at the very moment when Mrs Marcos made her bid for power. Nor should it be forgotten that one of the people who advised her on the Malakas and Maganda fable and helped her disseminate it was a certain Dr David Baradas, an anthropologist who had worked with Manda Elizalde at PANAMIN. The worlds of folklore and fakelore were indeed closely interwoven in Malacañang's official fantasies; but no matter how blurred their boundaries, some hard-edged political calculations lay beneath. Semiramis or no, Imelda was every inch a *datu* in her own right, and it showed. She was always blamed for the more obviously regal aspects of the fantasy-Palace that Malacañang became – for everything that seemed inappropriate to a developing nation where hunger and poverty were the everyday experience of the bulk of its citizens. She always justified her fabulous clothes and astonishing expenditures as a *datu* would, rather than in a way that satisfied Western moralism. From the very beginning of Ferdinand's Presidency Imelda had had a maxim that worked superbly in the outback she knew so well from her campaigning: 'Never dress down for the poor. They won't thank you for it.' When she said 'My cultural role is to be beautiful' she really meant it. To anything that was not beautiful, to the noisome realities of Third World existence, she grew increasingly impatient. There was a notorious incident in 1982 following increasing foreign publicity being given to the incidence of child prostitution in the Philippines. In one European magazine a feature appeared about a little girl in Ermita who catered to foreign tourists. When Imelda learned of this she ordered the police to find the girl and bring her to the Palace. They did so, and she scolded the child soundly and gave her a stern lecture about how she was 'dishonouring the country'. This story did not go down well in the West. What was overlooked was the Philippines' history of deference to white-skinned foreigners, with whom a *datu* might automatically side and who had rights over brown-skinned locals. Neither was it imagined that a *datu* like Imelda, who identified with her country, might feel that by causing unwelcome publicity, rather than by the nature of her profession, the child was giving her nation a bad name. In some ways her reaction was precisely that of an old-fashioned mother worried about what the neighbours would think.

By now we have reached a chronological point in the Marcoses' story where, if nothing else is clear, we at least have to recognize the centrality of *fantasy* to their regime. Onto Ferdinand's and Imelda's carefully edited pasts were grafted various myths and fragments of myths, ranging from the conquering hero to Cinderella, from cosmogony to Camelot, which in turn encapsulated snippets of the Abe Lincoln log-cabin-to-President mythology that Lyndon Baines Johnson also laid claim to.

Where Cinderella was concerned Mrs Marcos quite consciously drew the parallel herself on several occasions. No doubt the image she had in mind was a Disneyfied version of handsome princes and happy endings. The Ugly Sisters could stand for members of her own clan regardless of their actual gender (one thinks of her cousin Norberto Jr. whom she successfully broke by stopping him run for re-election as Governor of Leyte). They could also include all those of Manila's '400' who remained in any doubt as to whose foot the glass slipper fitted. (The Cinderella story as an original Asian folk tale has been traced to ninth-century China, where the heroine is treated cruelly by her step-family and helped by a supernatural agent, sometimes an animal and sometimes a fairy godmother, according to source. Imelda's conviction that she, like her nation, lived beneath a special hole in the sky through which a wand of divine fortune occasionally reached to single her out for special blessing could well fill the latter role.)

Among the above fantasies Malakas and Maganda manages to combine practically all of them, from cosmogony to nationalism to a *Reader's Digest* moral order. Here one is irresistibly reminded of President Ronald Reagan himself, with his beliefs, his superstitions and his own imaginary (yet somehow truthful) war experiences. Suddenly one finds oneself having to acknowledge the centrality of fantasy to heads of state the world over. All one can say is that if the Marcoses were fantasists they were in good company. For much of their first term of office LBJ was enmeshed in his fantasy that the war in Vietnam (that according to Washington never was a war) was both a crusade and winnable. Canny old Ferdinand Marcos had decided in private that it was neither; but plenty of Western nations including Britain supported Johnson in his delusion with varying degrees of eagerness, and even encouraged him (Australia, for example, sent combat troops). Two decades later, when the Marcoses left office, Ronald Reagan was equally deep in a fantasy that had come to him via Hollywood, his 'Star Wars' or Strategic Defence Initiative, whose profoundly bellicose nature was inadequately masked by the characteristic euphemism 'Peace Shield'. This was less futuristic than nostalgic, being at the same time a revival of H. G. Wells's notion of a death ray and a schoolboy's dream of omnipotence. The grandiose plan, had it been technically feasible, might have turned the entire globe and neighbouring space into a twinkling battlefield (remember 'smart pebbles'?). Beside it, the Marcoses' giving themselves Arthurian airs and graces in a Third World palace by a polluted river seems small beer, even quite touching.

Considering once again the private past of garage floors and humiliation that had moulded Imelda Marcos, no one need be a

Freudian to realize how there never can be any public version of events that does not also conceal something repressed, sometimes temporarily smudged and sometimes furiously denied but always *there*, threatening to return and upset the record. As Jacqueline Rose wrote recently,

> there is no way of understanding political identities and destinies without letting fantasy into the frame. More, that fantasy – far from being the antagonist of public, social being – plays a central, constitutive role in the modern world of states and nations.[17]

The fantasy element in the Marcoses' rule is the proof of this, all the more so because it was connived at for a while by so many other nation states, and hence to some extent became collective. It is fascinating to observe how even earthbound diplomats and technocrats who supposedly inhabit a hard-edged world of *realpolitik* find themselves willy-nilly drawn into such fantasies and obliged to devise policies to fit the fable, thereby acknowledging that in some sense it is indeed real. (An example of this is the American ambassador quoted on pages 92–3 trying to plan a medal-awarding ceremony for Ferdinand's state visit to Washington when both he and President Johnson had ample evidence that the Marcos claims to heroism were highly dubious.)

It should be added that the media play an essential role in maintaining political fantasy. In the Marcoses' early years in Malacañang nobody worked harder to ensure their fables' currency – especially those of Cinderella and Camelot-on-the-Pasig – than did the English language international press. Simultaneously, a thousand miles due west of Manila, what US pressmen used to call 'the Snow Machine' was cranking out a blizzard of stories of imminent victory in Vietnam, of prodigious body counts that mathematically showed the Viet Cong were down to their last few hundred men, of hearts and minds won over to the American cause, all to reassure the US public and bolster the President politically.

LBJ's tragedy was that the burgeoning war he had inherited and had been assured was winnable in a matter of months (yet more stories about troops being 'home by Christmas' – that optimistic trope of everybody's foreign adventures this century) finally killed off the funding he needed to implement his plans for a Great

Society at home. Yet for a while he was carried away by the myth of the US war machine's invincibility and by a private Texan dream about his righteous GI gunfighters saving the West. Johnson had, after all, invented a grandfather whom he claimed had died heroically at the Alamo.[18] It is extraordinary, in a century of technological marvels, how often the biography of a single individual can be glimpsed behind world events which otherwise appear to have a quite autonomous and logical life of their own. This was as true of LBJ as it was of Hitler. At a far more innocuous and local level it was popularly understood in Manila that Imelda's plans for her elder daughter, Imee, included her marrying Britain's Prince Charles. In her mind the perfect fairytale ending to her own Cinderella story involved the uniting of the Romualdez-Marcos dynasty with the House of Windsor. Such a union would doubtless have been fraught with interest, but sadly it was not to be. For its part, the ensuing unworkable marriage between Prince Charles and Lady Diana Spencer in 1981 was probably the object of more fantasy-making by the international media than any event before or since.

There are indeed moments when it seems that the world's affairs are transacted by dreamers. There is a sadness here in the spectacle of nations, no less than individuals, helping each other along with their delusions. In this way what is fondly thought to be clear-sighted pragmatism may actually be shoring up a regime's ideology whose hidden purpose is itself nothing more than to assuage the pain of a single person's unhappy past.

Beneath the fantasies, though, some most unwelcome realities had been seeping steadily into Malacañang Palace. In 1981 a Chinese businessman named Dewey Dee, a textile manufacturer and minor crony, had decamped suddenly, leaving debts of over $90 million. Marcos's bankers, under pressure of his friends, had so relaxed their lending policy to favoured individuals that huge loans were being made on hardly any collateral, and in the absence of any centrally kept records (shades of the Philippine National Bank in 1921!) nobody could determine the bank's total exposure until too late. Dee's defection left investors panicky; there was a rush to withdraw savings and several banks went swiftly out of business. To prevent the collapse of the entire Philippine banking system

Marcos raised large dollar loans from US banks, thereby increasing the foreign debt. The following year much the same thing happened again with a far closer crony of his, Herminio Disini, who made off with his millions intact but with companies collapsing in his wake. Again the government was obliged to shore these up, thereby assuming still further debts it could not possibly cover.

In October 1981 Marcos had attended the Cancun Summit in Mexico (the International Meeting on Cooperation and Development, a post-Brandt Commission conference on the economic and other problems of the North–South developmental divide). While there, he was invited to Washington for his second state visit to the US. At his first, sixteen years earlier in the days of LBJ, he had seemed to have everything going for him. Now, four American Presidents later, things were different. The visit did not take place for nearly a year, during which time several US Senators openly criticized him. Edward Kennedy in particular was to remind President Reagan that 'The security of the United States does not require our support for the repression of the Filipino people. [. . .] There is convincing evidence, confirmed by the Department of State, that the government of President Marcos [. . .] has engaged in persistent persecution of the press, labour, church, students, and business leaders.'[19] Added to that, the World Bank leaked a report that said the Philippines had already borrowed to its allowable maximum and was managing its finances in a most inefficient manner.

Marcos decided that a careful campaign would be necessary if his visit to Washington were to be a success. Somehow or other US investors would have to be induced to take the view that, the Cassandras of the World Bank notwithstanding, the Philippines still offered wonderful returns. US Senators would similarly need wooing and convincing that their negative views were founded on the propaganda of ingrates and political rivals like Ninoy Aquino, who was notorious for his impromptu seminars over at Harvard. Accordingly, the trip was meticulously planned, starting with the appointment of Imelda's favourite brother, Kokoy Romualdez, as Ambassador to the United States. It paid off. For all that Amnesty International had just released a report utterly at odds with the Marcos-and-Reagan version of Philippine democracy, the human rights issue was never on the agenda at the two Presidents' meetings.

On the contrary, Marcos received Reagan's assurance that the US would yet again help modernize the Philippines' armed forces. He also extracted a promise that the rent on the US bases could be renegotiated upwards.

Evidence of the degree to which Marcos still retained Washington's backing was supplied by the Movement for a Free Philippines, which had just obtained a copy of a classified US intelligence document dated 23 July 1982. This revealed that five named military attachés assigned to the Philippine Embassy in Washington had been sent by Malacañang purposely to spy on the operations of anti-Marcos activists in the US. These men were implicated in the abduction or deaths of several Filipinos on US soil, possibly including that of Tibo Mijares. The document showed that the Reagan Administration was perfectly aware of the presence of Philippine military agents in the United States, as also of their mission to undermine constitutionally guaranteed rights to free speech and free political assembly. At the very least it was evidence of double standards, since one of the US's allegations against Iran by which it justified (and still justifies) its condemnation is that Iran murders its enemies abroad. Though the Philippines was known to be doing the same, Washington remained silent. In any case the FBI had for years been passing on the names of underground anti-Marcos operatives in the US to General Ver back in Malacañang or to Fidel Ramos's PC headquarters at Camp Crame.

On the evening of the Marcoses' arrival in Washington the Reagans gave a grand and glittering dinner-reception at the White House. Everyone dined in the Rose Garden at tables lit by candles and with concealed fairy-lights in the shrubbery. The scene was later described as 'being somewhere between a Christmas image and a South Seas fantasy',[20] for the White House set-dressers had let their imaginations run riot. The only bad moment of the trip for Ferdinand came when he appeared on TV in 'Meet the Press'. The editorial staffers of the *Washington Post* and the *New York Times* were altogether tougher meat than the white-maned Senators he was confident he could charm and reassure. They asked him nasty questions about his human rights record to which he gave blustery answers. His performance aroused the suspicion that the previous twelve years of autocratic rule and a cowed press had dulled his reactions and done nothing to keep his intelligence sharp, though no doubt illness did not help. Apart from this, though, the overall public tone of the visit which he and Reagan managed to engineer was one of the warmest mutual regard, shot through with those abstract nouns that presidential rhetoric reaches for as instinctively as an alcoholic for a bottle: democracy, honour, liberty, equality, justice, fraternity ... Marcos left Washington still a war hero and as much 'America's right arm in Asia' as ever.

A courageous dissenting voice among many back in Manila was that of the Church. Jaime, Cardinal Sin reacted with open scepticism to Marcos's American speeches and interviews, to the whole fantasy world which the two Presidents had erected. To hear Marcos, the Cardinal said, was to experience the yawning gulf between his words in Washington and social realities known to everyone in the Philippines.

> I should not believe there is malnutrition in the Philippines even if, in the centres run by the Archdiocese of Manila, children are daily snatched from the jaws of death because of starvation. . . . I should not believe that there are political detainees held for months and years without charges even if the families of these detainees regularly come to me for help. . . . I should not believe that there are military abuses even if the victims themselves – or the widows of the victims – related to me what they saw with their own eyes.[21]

Back home in the Palace the Marcoses, though still unified in public fantasy, were increasingly divided by political machinations. The rival Ilocano and Leyteño factions were jockeying for advantage and trying to second-guess the President's next move. Ferdinand was by now seriously ill and about to undergo a kidney transplant. He was no longer able to maintain his previous control over day-to-day decisions. His cronies were virtually free to do as they chose, while reliable technocrats such as Bobby Ongpin had their hands full, trying to prevent the total collapse of both the banking system and the economy. Much of the divisiveness was due to the fact that the closest Marcos had yet come to designating his successor was to nominate a fifteen-member Executive Commission. His wife's own political power had increased to a level close to that of his, with the all-important distinction that she had no armed forces at her disposal and scarcely a fraction of the popular support which even then Ferdinand could still patchily command. One of the great fears of the Ilocano faction in the Palace – one shared by General Ver and the armed forces he headed – was that Marcos might suddenly die and Imelda attempt to slide into his throne with a gesture of 'sa wakas!': At last! Vivat Semiramis! Even more feared by Palace intellectuals was the possibility that in this case Imelda and Ver might make an alliance.

It was reportedly the thought of this last scenario that finally made up Ninoy Aquino's mind for him to return to the Philippines. Some claim his own health was worsening to the point where it was by no means certain whether he or his Harvard Fellowship would expire first. He made no secret of the contention that he was the only Filipino politician left of a stature equal to Marcos's and capable of talking power with him as a fraternity brother. In this he was probably right. After ending martial law in 1981 the President had cobbled together a token Opposition, largely for foreign consumption. Called UNIDO (United Nationalist Democratic Organization), it was a coalition of pre-martial law trapos headed by Salvador Laurel (whose elder brother, the former Speaker of the old Congress, had helped Marcos get the Presidential nomination in 1965). But no Opposition of ruling-class politicos was going to appease the left; and NPA activity was once again alarmingly on the increase, especially in the canefields of Negros in the aftermath of Roberto Benedicto's mishandling of the sugar industry.

The question is, did Marcos share Ninoy's view of himself as the man likely to succeed? It is by no means certain exactly how close the two men still were or had ever been, leaving aside the effects of the eight years Ninoy had recently spent in his fraternity brother's jail. Even people who knew them disagree on this fundamental point. Representative Roque Ablan, for example, who shared the same fraternity, swears Ninoy and Ferdinand were very close in private. 'Ninoy and Ver used to stay here in this house. When FVR [Fidel Ramos] was promoted to General, Ninoy got Marcos to delay his approval until Ver's own promotion had come through. That's how close they were.'[22] In strong disagreement is Kerima Polotan Tuvera, the writer and widow of Ferdinand's senior Presidential Assistant and right-hand man, Johnny Tuvera. 'They weren't that close at all. Marcos most certainly did not see Aquino as his successor. Not at all. He was actually looking at Enrile.'[23]

In any case, close or not, Ninoy Aquino made arrangements for his return to the Philippines. Roque Ablan gives the following account:

> April 22nd is my birthday, and Ninoy called me and my wife over to New York to celebrate it there with him in 1983. I went and he said, 'US Immigration wants me out of here. They won't renew my visa. They said I lied on my application form to conceal my connections with the Communists – as if they didn't know perfectly well about those when they allowed me in in the first place. Can you help fix me a residence with either France or the USSR?'
>
> Marcos was now really worried about the succession. There was no one close to him he wanted to succeed him, nobody he thought was ready and capable except Ninoy. So he had the Filipino Consul in New Orleans, Joey Ampeso, issue Ninoy a full and valid passport. He got onto Ninoy and asked him to delay his return for a while because he couldn't guarantee his safety. As for the Americans, well, they frankly told Ninoy to go home because Marcos was dying.[24]

In the event Aquino decided to return on Sunday, 21 August 1983, in a series of flights broken by TV interviews in San Francisco, Hong Kong, Singapore, Bangkok, Taipei, and in the aircraft itself. He made a point of being unafraid to die. In the Grand Hotel in Taipei he held up a Kevlar bullet-proof waistcoat and is quoted as having said 'I just got a report from Manila. I may get hit at the airport when I land, and then they will hit the hit man. That's why I'm going to wear this vest. But, you know, if they get me in the head, I'm a goner.' From Manila the journalist Rod Dula followed the journey throughout:

> I was working for Joe Aspiras [the Tourism Minister]. Fidel Ramos's father Narciso was representing the Philippines in Taiwan at the time – we had no Ambassador, of course, since having recognized China we were not recognizing Taiwan. Joe was trying to persuade Ninoy to call it off, not to return. He had

already sent two people privately to Hong Kong to intercept him and head him off. I was acting as his [Aspiras's] private secretary and I read Narciso's cables as they came in, detailing exactly where Ninoy was and which flights he took. We monitored him all the way home, since Aspiras was also chairman of the Civil Aeronautics Board. The garrison Commander saw Ninoy at Taipeh airport when he left. Ninoy seemed both melancholy and egotistical, pretty much as he always did.[25]

There was a huge turn-out of spectators waiting at Manila International Airport to greet Aquino, plus a large contingent of AVSECOM (Aviation Security Command) and other forces. The theme song of the day was that of the freed prisoner, the returning exile, 'Tie a Yellow Ribbon Round the Old Oak Tree'. This had been sung in the United States to greet the freed Iran hostages and it was thought appropriate to the occasion. Many in the emotional crowd were wearing yellow. People had turned out not just from respect for all that Ninoy had endured, but also in an expression of yearning that he might be the one man to rescue them from the post-martial law slough into which the country had so palpably fallen. His China Airlines plane landed and taxied up to the terminal from whose rooftop the crowd became ecstatic. A door opened, steps were pushed up and three security men (two from AVSECOM and one from METROCOM) hurried into the plane. Almost immediately Ninoy appeared in a pale suit at the top of the stairs with his three escorts behind him, took a step forward and was shot in the head, his body tumbling down the flight of stairs to land in an outflung heap at their foot. More shots followed, leaving Ninoy and a man in a uniform lying on the oil-stained concrete. All this in full view of the crowd.

Marcos was in bed in the Malacañang guest house, which had been converted to a sterile hospital suite, recovering from his kidney transplant of 7 August. 'He was in poor shape,' according to Greg Cendaña. 'He was out of it.' Imelda was lunching with friends in Gloria Maris, the restaurant behind her Folk Arts Centre. Almost as soon as the food was served an aide went and whispered something to her. She stood up abruptly and announced the party would have to return to the Palace. The meal was hastily abandoned. 'It was a real crisis,' as one of the guests said years later. 'Everyone was summoned to the Palace and they just went on arriving until 2 and 3 a.m. Ronnie Zamora was there in a three-piece suit looking as if he expected to be sworn in as President.'

Oddly enough, Marcos was the one person never to have been seriously blamed, on the simple grounds that it was far too blatant. It was emphatically not his style. Had he really wanted Aquino dead he could have organized a hit a hundred times over so that it took place in Boston or anywhere else other than on his own doorstep. Come to that, he need never have let him leave his prison cell in Fort Bonifacio alive. Yet if this was true of Marcos, it ought to have been true of everyone else on whom suspicion has since fallen. Why let the man return to be greeted by a great crowd of his supporters, and then kill him before their eyes? There seemed no sense in it.

Theories abounded as to who did it and why. Imelda came under the most immediate suspicion since it was popularly believed that she deeply hated Ninoy, above all for his passing Dovie Beams's tape to his leftist student friends up at the 'Diliman Republic' and urging them to broadcast it over the campus PA system. All speculation seemed inseparable from the succession issue. If it was not actually a *coup*, had it been preparing the ground for one? There were two official enquiries. The second, or fact-finding board (the Agrava Commission) remained deeply split on the evidence. Meanwhile, a consensus of opinion inclined to a result reminiscent of the Warren Commission's verdict on John Kennedy's assassination: a lone gunman (in this case a man named Galman) who was himself shot dead afterwards. And, as in the case of the Warren Commission, it satisfied almost nobody, least of all in a country in which conspiracy theories are as meat and drink. Ninoy had been shot in the back of the head, the bullet angled downwards, and not in the front from the foot of the steps as the Galman theory necessitated. But even after the Warren Commission's report not everybody had agreed on the number or angles of the shots in JFK's head, either. Galman had been killed well beforehand, people said, his body brought to the scene in an AVSECOM truck where it was bundled out at the moment of Ninoy's death and shot again by security men. Look at the pictures, they said: you can see Galman out there lying on his stomach, but he's got blood running the wrong way across his face, showing he must have been lying on his back when he died . . . The ailing Marcos said he was quite satisfied that this lone gunman had done the deed, almost certainly at the behest of the Communists or as part of a private vendetta. However, the Agrava Commission was unanimous about one thing. Regardless of who had actually committed the murder there had unquestionably been military connivance. This was not a comforting finding for the President since it exploded his claim that the assassin was probably Communist-backed.

Inevitably, the CIA was also widely proposed. The theory went that they had decided the regime had to be ditched, and this would do the trick neatly by terminally destabilizing it while also getting rid of Aquino, a man they intensely disliked as a loudmouth with dangerous alliances on the far left:

> The idea was that the CIA were acting in complicity with 'certain Filipino personalities' who realized Ninoy's political usefulness was over. He'd had a triple heart by-pass and the doctors were giving him a maximum of a few years. They were willing to sacrifice him for his symbolic effect. It's even conceivable Ninoy himself connived at his own assassination. His insistence on returning, to say nothing of his prediction that he would be shot in the head at the airport, is certainly suggestive. The main objective was to discredit the Marcos dynasty: not just Ferdinand (because of his own limited future due to ill-health) but also his likely successor, Imelda, or any conceivable Imelda/Enrile/Ver triumvirate. Somehow, Filipino military intelligence got wind of this plot – via Ver, almost certainly, since he and several CIA officials had a long history of mutual secrets and mutual aid. The Filipino military reasoned that there was no way they could finger the CIA directly, so they conspired to find a sacrificial goat to take the blame. Hence the Galman plot. There's no question of Ver's closeness to the CIA, even without knowing Oliver North's subsequent revelations about Ver signing the end-use certificates for all those arms being supplied to Nicaragua.
>
> The official 'Opposition' theory – in other words the one held by his widow, Cory Aquino – seems now to be that Ninoy was shot by Moreno, one of the fifteen men still languishing in Munti [Muntinlupa jail]. But the TV pictures of Cory hearing the news

in Boston make her reaction look strangely unemotional. It could be read as stoical, of course. But it could also suggest Ninoy had briefed her what to expect.

Quite a different theory comes from Dr Bernardo Villegas, a Harvard-trained economist at the University of Asia and the Pacific. He sees the warring factions in Malacañang as having separated out in the late seventies, with fatal results for Ninoy.

> This struggle became acute over the control of the coconut industry. In those days, the person who controlled the coconut industry practically controlled the Philippines. [Danding] Cojuangco had a brilliant scheme for monopolizing it, and Enrile was in with him, partly because his law firm handled Danding's affairs. Then in the early eighties Imelda and her brother Kokoy tried to muscle in on the coco industry.
>
> Marcos was torn between them. He couldn't make up his mind who to side with. Danding was perhaps even closer to him than Imelda, closer than his own wife. He certainly depended greatly on Danding for advice. Because he couldn't decide, he tried to balance the opposing forces . . . Ver actually sided with Imelda. Yet, of course, both camps were loyal to Ferdinand; their war was with each other. Ver simply decided that his future lay with the Romualdez family.
>
> That struggle became very intense, the more so the sicker Marcos became, and especially in 1983 when Ninoy came back. We'll probably never know if the assassination was the Imelda/Ver or the Cojuangco side's work. Cory always suspected the latter. She's a Cojuangco, of course, but famously estranged from her cousin Danding's side of the family.[26]

Against this are all those who say that, powerful and ambitious as she was, Imelda would hardly have dared be a party to such a plot while Ferdinand was still alive. She would never have taken on the appalling responsibility for an act whose consequences were bound to be both momentous and unreadable. Plenty of people are satisfied to see it as Ver's work, however, if not as co-plotter with the queen-in-waiting then as the loyal Ilocano knight ridding his monarch of a troublesome politician and threat to the throne:

Ninoy as St Thomas à Becket. A less quixotic, more self-interested Ver would long have acknowledged that his loyalty was to the existing regime, in other words to both Marcoses, without whose patronage he was nothing and would immediately be out of a job. Once having perceived that the President's health would soon render him incapable of governing, Fabian Ver and Imelda may have gambled disastrously on pre-emptive action. Bobby Ongpin, the Trade and Industry Minister who steadily found himself more and more at the centre of political events, is unequivocal and pithy. 'Galman did it. Ver set him up.'

Well before Ninoy's ill-fated return there was a widely believed story current in Manila that a psychic – quite possibly Bionic Boy himself – had predicted that if ever Ninoy Aquino were to touch Philippine soil again *alive* the whole Marcos dynasty would come to an end. Immediately after his assassination, therefore, there was much speculation as to whether he was still technically alive when his body hit the ground. In any case, from the instant of its impact with the concrete beneath his supporters' horrified gaze, Ninoy Aquino became a saint and martyr.

Whoever was responsible, whatever murky conspiracies the act had concealed, the outcome was immediately clear. In a great public outpouring of grief and rage, a genuine and proper Opposition began cohering around the figure of his widow, Cory. The political scene had at last become polarized into two camps: those who continued to support the President and those who swore they would not rest until Malacañang Palace and the Philippine body politic had been purged of every last Marcos and every last crony.

Aquino's murder was also recognized abroad as a turning-point. Suddenly the Marcos Administration, which the West had mostly been content to ignore as just another of those grim little client regimes of America's, leaped up through levels of indifference into public awareness. The steady pressure of organizations like the Movement for a Free Philippines had paid off and a large section of the US media embarked on an openly hostile anti-Marcos campaign. For the past few years some of the more thoughtful newspapers had been printing critical articles here and there (although it should be remembered that Boni Gillego's original exposé of Marcos's 'faked' war medals was released in California by the MFP's information service in 1982 in time for the state visit, but not properly taken up by a major US newspaper until the *Washington Post*'s article in December 1983). Now, however, the assassination at Manila airport in its full outrageousness (wasn't this supposed to be a democracy, for heaven's sake?) swung public opinion against the Supreme Dictator of Oz and his wife in a way which probably nothing else could have done.

Yet Reagan's White House went on doggedly supporting Marcos, even as the State Department leaked unattributed news, views and files to the media which enabled journalists – several of whom had never set foot in the Philippines – to paint the regime in the darkest possible shades. It was soon evident that the people who made policy decisions outside the Oval Office had agreed that Marcos had to be dumped. He had outlived his usefulness. Weakened by illness, he had allowed his otherwise convenient regime to be publicly exposed as murderous and inept in a way that could no longer be ignored. With this, at least, even erstwhile loyalists at home began reluctantly to agree. A year or two ago such a thing could never have happened; the President had been far too canny and far too much in control. But now . . . Even outside the Palace people were taking sides with one or other Malacañang faction. It was in 1983 that Kansulay villagers could be first heard airing their *tuba*-inspired wisdom in those nightly drinking sessions beneath the rustling palms: of how an ambitious and scheming woman was taking advantage of her sick husband, and would soon prove to be his ruin.

13

EDSA and after

For the first time since he had taken power in 1965, Marcos now had appreciable sections of the establishment ranged against him in an opposition that was growing ever more organized. Dispossessed oligarchs found themselves on the same side as students who had done their stint in the hills with the NPA; teachers began tacitly, then openly, supporting their more militant pupils. The judiciary might still have belonged to Marcos, but he had lost the Church. In many ways this was the biggest blow of all for Malacañang. Cardinal Sin, the radical bishops and all manner of leftish liberation theologians now took over the ground at the centre of the Church, squeezing the First Couple's old conservative elements out onto the ecclesiastical fringes. In this way the new centre carried with it many of the hitherto silent majority of the pious and respectable, who increasingly viewed political events as scenes in a morality play. The Manichaean characterization of Malacañang as home to the forces of evil was under way.

The first sign that these new alliances could wield real political power came in the 1984 Congressional elections. A friend of Cardinal Sin's, Jose Concepcion, reformed NAMFREL (National Citizens' Movement for Free Elections) which, it will be remembered, had originally been set up by the CIA for the 1952 Congressional elections. The new NAMFREL could call out 200,000 seminarians, nuns and lay religious nationwide as poll-watchers to counteract COMELEC (Commission on Elections), which the President controlled. NAMFREL was thus a demonstration of the Church's practical involvement in politics as guardian of the democratic process. Marcos won the election by two to one in the total number of seats, but only by the expedient of last-minute cheating in the provinces. Manila itself had been too closely watched by NAMFREL observers for wide-scale tampering with the capital's ballots. The left, meanwhile, had made a big error (the same mistake it was to make more catastrophically in the snap election of 1986) by calling for a boycott of the polls. Agapito ('Butz') Aquino, Ninoy's younger brother, announced that participating in Marcos's election would be 'conniving at a foregone sham'; but the voters' remarkably high turnout showed this strategy to be badly out of touch. It was as though the electorate had divined that the most telling way of opposing the President was by using his own tactics of constitutionalism and legality, but making sure they were properly policed. This, too, would give the US no excuse to intervene, whereas left-inspired rioting might provoke Washington to react if it appeared genuinely to threaten the Marcos administration. The point about Washington was that one never quite knew what it was thinking. The apparent split that seemed to have opened up between the Department of State and the White House on the question of Marcos's future was no guarantee that ranks might not abruptly close if the external threat were real enough.

Yet the left's anti-Marcos and anti-US stance did continue to attract a good number of middle-class liberals, intellectuals and even business people. Whenever the security forces went on the rampage against crowds of demonstrators, the left won new converts. Incidents like that on 20 September 1985, when twenty-seven protesters were gunned down in Escalante, northern Negros, only helped the left. Ferdinand, now constantly on and off oxygen and dialysis in the Palace's intensive care unit, knew this perfectly well, and raged impotently. It was yet another illustration of the limits of even a Filipino 'strongman's' ability to control his own forces outside Manila. It showed how crude a *datu*'s chain of command really was; how anything that required delicacy or subtlety at state level could simply be annulled in the provinces by traditional headbangers being loyal in the only way they understood. It was old-style politics caught with its cudgels raised by the cameras of a modern mass media. He could see this only too clearly, but there was little he could do now to alter the nature of the carefully organized structure that had guaranteed his incumbency for the past two decades.

The factors that were really to decide the President's fate were actually taking shape within his own armed forces. Ultimately, these were probably rooted in the long-standing rivalry between Fabian Ver and Fidel Ramos. Throughout most of the seventies and martial law, Marcos had kept Romeo Espino on as Chief-of-Staff in order to prevent the rift between Ver and Ramos from becoming glaring. Despite both men being his relatives, the two were poles apart in every way. Ver's entire career had been built on personal loyalty to Marcos rather than on professional military accomplishment. He was loyal in a way that gave rise to sundry jokes, the commonest being that if the President were to order Ver to jump out of one of the Palace windows the General would reply, 'Certainly, sir! Which floor?' He and the man he served had been together since the days when Ver had been young Senator Marcos's driver and adviser on military affairs. Since then, in his capacity as Ferdinand's chief security officer he had built up the Presidential Security Command into a private army of 6,000 men, all with the single task of protecting one man and his family.

Fidel Ramos's own career, by contrast, could scarcely have been more different. He was a career soldier, a West Point graduate who had served in both Korea and Vietnam. Marcos had appointed him chief of the paramilitary Philippine Constabulary before martial law, at a time when it was very much more powerful and widely feared than the Army. The Army's remit was merely that of national defence, hardly an onerous role given the US bases on Philippine soil and the mutual defence pact. The PC, on the other hand, was responsible for practically all the front-line skirmishing with Communist guerrillas and the MNLF rebels in Mindanao: vicious and demoralizing fighting in which heavy casualties but few prisoners were taken. Battle talismans were collected and cherished on both sides: scalps and ears and dried scrotums made into purses. On declaration of martial law the relative positions of the PC and the Army were swiftly reversed. The Army was expanded from 50,000 to over 200,000 men, making the PC suddenly look like a very poor cousin indeed. Practically overnight, Fidel Ramos found himself presiding over a lot of outdated equipment and battle-wearied men. Yet he too was intensely loyal to his cousin, the President, and went on heading the PC as conscientiously and professionally as he could in the circumstances. He had a reputation for being incorruptible while at the same time knowing almost all there was to know about where the regime's bodies were buried (as how could he not, in his position? By the time of the 'EDSA Revolution' he would have been PC chief for sixteen years).

By 1981 Marcos realized that if he were finally to lift martial law he would need to improve the Army. The military had in many ways become quite slack since measures of public control such as curfews had made much of its job comparatively simple and routine. Now its morale and efficiency would need boosting. He retired General Espino, appointing Fabian Ver Chief-of-Staff and Fidel Ramos Vice-Chief. Among the reasons why Marcos passed over the militarily better-qualified Ramos for the top Armed Forces of the Philippines (AFP) post was the President's boundless cynicism about Washington, from whom he always expected the worst. To him, Ramos the West-Pointer with his excellent Pentagon connections, was their eyes and ears in the Philippines. In addition, Ver was to keep control of the Presidential Security Command (it later passed to his son Irwin) as well as of the vast intelligence network he had created. Unable to resist his old tendency to concentrate power, Marcos established a 'regional unified command structure' which put the Constabulary, armed forces, special forces and intelligence network all under Ver's ultimate command as a kind of private, warlord army. Watching this with the direst misgivings, Fidel Ramos the good soldier kept his head down and aired his opinions only to retired senior officers whose military brotherhood he could trust absolutely.

The ending of martial law also meant that the President had problems with his former martial law administrator, Juan Ponce Enrile, who was now left without a job. Enrile was, of course, a civilian: an ex-Harvard corporate lawyer by training, very sharp, with an ambitious and wily politician's instincts. These were what had made him so valuable as a strategist back in the 'think-tank' days of 1964–5 when he joined the already-formed group of people like Blas Ople, Joe Aspiras, O. D. Corpuz and Rafael Salas to plan the campaign that first took Marcos to Malacañang. Years later, while Minister of Defence, it was his legal mind that earned him the chairmanship of the coconut corporations which Danding Cojuangco formed on his way to taking over the entire coconut industry as a crony monopoly. On Philippine Constabulary Day (8 August) 1983, the President announced during the celebrations at Camp Crame that the post of Minister of Defence was no longer in the AFP chain of command. Enrile was now out of the power structure (which was why, when Ninoy Aquino was assassinated a fortnight later, he was one of the few people in the hierarchy not to come under suspicion). Suddenly dispossessed, he made common cause with Ramos, who was in a similar position. The two men discussed resigning but were urgently talked into staying by retired Army officers alarmed by the idea that if they went there would be nobody left to act as a counterweight to Ver, whose own power was inseparable from that of Marcos himself. Once more, the thought of Ferdinand suddenly dying and Ver and Imelda forming an alliance was enough to make it imperative that a representative of the Army should remain in the senior command structure. Fidel Ramos was not identified with Ver, even though technically his Vice Chief-of-Staff, and as an untainted professional soldier he retained the trust of a group of junior officers in the Army who were about to play a critical role in Philippine history.

Those loyalists who stoutly maintain that the ailing President kept his wits – meaning his political acumen – about him to the last come up against insurmountable evidence to the contrary. A tactician whose antennae were properly honed and acute would have known that giving Ver complete charge of the country's security forces while not allowing for the man's own *datu* instinct was carrying trustingness to the point of idiocy. Ver rewarded dozens of senior officers by keeping them on instead of pensioning them off, with the result that the upper echelons of the military became increasingly filled with the 'GerCom' or 'Geriatric Command', as a young staffer unkindly put it. The normal system of promotions thus blocked, men found themselves frozen at junior rank and on junior ranks' pay. It caused a good deal of chafing among young officers, although if this had been the only source of their discontent it could probably have been contained. The fatal ingredient was the young men's anger at the way the AFP had been consistently 'Ilocanized' and turned into General

Ver's and the President's private army. Instead of being a fighting force with a long and honourable history of defending the country it had become subordinated to personal megalomania, and all with the connivance and support of a foreign power. The more the militarizing of the country and its politics had exposed the armed forces to the mockery and hatred of the Filipino people – who after martial law increasingly saw it as a tool which Marcos and his minions deployed against the very people it was designed to protect – the more the young officers' anger increased. Ninoy Aquino's assassination was the last straw since almost everybody, including even the Agrava Commission, believed the military was deeply implicated in the murder. It was a dishonour that could no longer be borne. It should be remembered that these young officers were products of the Philippine Military Academy, which was modelled along the lines of US academies like West Point and turned out fiercely patriotic soldiers with a very keen sense of honour, probity and loyalty to each other. As far as they could see, almost everything they had been trained to respect had been systematically subverted or outraged by those in charge of the armed forces. Civilians were brutalized, while scams and wholesale corruption were endemic at every level of the military (the Army's Logistics Command alone furnished examples of theft on an almost incredible scale).

It was out of this anger that the Reform the Armed Forces Movement (RAM) was born, centred to a large extent around the Military Academy's Class of '71. By the end of March 1983, eighty officers had issued a statement calling for loyalty to the Philippine Constitution rather than to one man, and the names of the Movement's leaders became known: Lt.-Colonels Gregorio ('Gringo') Honasan and Vic Batac; Colonels Red Kapunan, Eugene Ocampo and Hector Tarrazona; Captain Felix Turingan and Navy Captain Rex Robles. They were rumoured to have up to 1500 supporters of every rank in all three services. Marcos had, of course, followed RAM's growing influence through Fabian Ver's intelligence network. In April 1985 Ramos and Enrile persuaded him to meet RAM's leaders and hear their complaints. He did; but once again it was a sign of his increasing weakness that nothing came of the meeting. He could no longer recognize grievance; he only saw disloyalty. Rex Robles and Gringo Honasan were both assistants to

Enrile, which in turn brought Enrile under increasing suspicion. Ever since his *de facto* demotion, the Defence Minister had smouldered. Both he and Marcos seemed at a loss to know how to deal with each other. Too much dirty water had flowed under the bridge since the old days for easy accommodations. Enrile, Danding Cojuangco and even Jose Aspiras had been talked about as the President's likeliest successors, but the factional split in Malacañang between Ferdinand's Ilocanos and Imelda's Warays had now become critically deep. The Ilocano bloc had decided that they must at all costs consolidate power. They had also taken the decision that in one way or another Imelda had to go – to be sent somewhere where she could do no harm. Ferdinand must himself have recognized how essential it was to solve this pressing politico-domestic conundrum, but it was beyond him. He was too dependent on Imelda and too ill. Lesser problems could be dealt with, however, and he had already taken the decision to replace Enrile as Minister of Defence with either Cojuangco or Aspiras, and maybe also to reinstate the post to its original position of having power over the AFP. The ailing President's mind must often have been prey to thoughts of a Palace *coup* even as it was further worked on by Fabian Ver, who was no friend of Enrile's. In the General's view Enrile, although from the North-east (Cagayan), had never really been on the 'Ilocano team'. He was by nature too much of a loner for Ver's taste, even without the sinister and suggestive fact that his most trusted aide-de-camp and security officer was Gringo Honasan.

Ver and Marcos now drew up secret plans to have all the RAM plotters and their supporters arrested – including Enrile, who was so close to RAM that in the paranoid atmosphere of Malacañang it might have seemed that the passionate young officers and their supporters were beginning to constitute his own private army. By now, indeed, a little gang of RAM colonels was screening high-level AFP paperwork and were, in effect, running the Department of Defence. Also to be arrested were all sorts of civilian Oppositionists including Cory Aquino (around whom much of the anti-Marcos struggle had polarized), her advisers such as Cardinal Sin himself, and many other Church and lay leaders. Those nominated for arrest totalled more than 10,000. The idea was to imprison them on the Isla de Caballo in Manila Bay and keep them there. In retrospect, this plan arguably represents the nearest Ferdinand Marcos came to a kind of madness. Martial law was long past; how could a supposedly democratic President order the mass arrest and transportation of his entire Opposition, including large numbers of the Church and his own military? It is charitable to assume he was addled with illness and pharmaceuticals, his judgement further warped by Fabian Ver who, when under pressure, reverted naturally to the old-style Ilocano warlord his extraordinary powers had turned him into. Once again, these were the measures of another century being proposed for a political crisis in a late twentieth-century democracy, and as such they perhaps did have about them a small measure of pathos buried in the larger measure of pure lunacy.

Throughout 1985 a wide selection of US officials paid visits to Manila to evaluate for themselves the deteriorating situation. There was a broad consensus that the atmosphere in Malacañang was truly weird. The President was evidently sick and his regime as evidently beleaguered, besides being riven with factionalism and intrigue. The resemblance to the last days of a mediaeval court was becoming ever more marked, with a Shakespearian Act V in the offing. The aura of fantasy was scrupulously observed. The dinners and receptions went on as normal, Imelda's disco on the top floor of the Palace thudded and flashed in the evenings, the technocrats and the cronies bustled in and out with briefcases. Though virtually imprisoned in Malacañang by his need to be within constant reach of the dialysis machine that kept him from lapsing into coma, Marcos was still looking forward to an indefinite future of uninterrupted power. Although his scepticism about the United States embraced the fickleness of US Congress, he seemed convinced that the highest levels in Washington would never withdraw their support. His reasoning can only be guessed at, but he must have imagined that his consolidated control over the entire state apparatus would always dissuade the US from making any move that could endanger their strategic and business assets in the Philippines. There were still a few years to go before Mikhail Gorbachev's *glasnost* and *perestroika* foreshadowed the gradual collapse of Communism throughout the world, thereby radically altering the old balance of power and its strategic priorities. Yet Marcos's view of the Philippines as being irrevocably a part of those priorities had already become fossilized. After twenty years of power which had seen him and Washington cut some very raw deals, there might also have been an idea at the back of his mind that both parties had too much dirt on each other to risk public recriminations or upsetting a profitable arrangement. His mistake as a Filipino *datu* was to be incapable of seeing that he had gone too far. *Datu*s are not in the habit of having their actions and morals called to account, especially by people they know to have acted every bit as illegally and shabbily as they themselves. It is exactly this mutual stand-off that provides the system with its equilibrium. But this was to reckon without US public opinion, which made itself felt in the very Congress he believed he could safely ignore. To a *datu*, public opinion was simply something that could be manipulated and stage-managed, so in this respect American public opinion was surely no different from that in the Philippines. That reasoning was fine as far as it went; his problem was that he did not control American public opinion, and Washington was doing a very professional job of turning it against him.

By now the Manichaean view of the Philippine crisis was far advanced in the United States, and consequently in much of the world's media. Once dead, Ninoy Aquino was turned into a saint and martyr, and the sacred flame of liberty had passed to his widow. Her religious nature had been stressed to the point where she too had acquired a kind of sanctity. Her closeness to Cardinal Sin and the Church was evident; she even had her own version of Imelda's 'Blue Ladies' in the shape of her 'Pink Sisters' – nuns of the Holy Spirit of Perpetual Adoration order.

> The link between Cory and Cardinal Sin was the Jesuits. Cory herself had always been close to the Church, but her famous piety and devoutness was deliberately exaggerated as part of the political necessity for spectacle and typecasting. She is at best a Sunday Catholic, whereas her mother, Doña Aurora, was a genuine Mass-a-day type.

Cory's casting in the full-blown Passion play that was about to be staged was greatly helped by her appearance, for she looked exactly like a typical Filipina nun. This could never have been said of Imelda Marcos, for instance, who in world opinion these days was looking rather less like Maganda and quite plausibly like Jezebel. Much was also made of the idea of Cory as a 'humble housewife', which was pure blarney. The inadequacy of describing any wealthy Filipina with an army of servants in such terms ought by now to be obvious. To portray a highly politicized Opposition leader's wife from one of the richest landowning clans in the country as though she were Mrs Checkered Apron from Apple Pie, Iowa, was nothing short of grotesque. Not knowing any better, Western journalism tended to swallow this fiction whole.

One consequence of this reading of Cory Aquino as a Joan of Arc figure with a divine mission was a widespread impression abroad of an anti-Marcos Opposition unified behind her by solemn purpose. It was in nearly everyone's interest to promote this notion; but as usual in such circumstances, the more the political era was felt to be nearing its end, the more Marcos's opponents began jockeying for individual advantage. Beneath the surface, the 'unified' Opposition embraced a rabble of pretenders and conflicting ambitions collectively represented by the 'Convener Group', an umbrella organization advised by Cardinal Sin and made up of sundry interests including the Church, business, women, traditional politicians and so on. The pretenders to Malacañang, who strove to conceal their private designs with more or less adroitness, included Jose Diokno, Jovito Salonga, Ramon Mitra, Doy Laurel and Ninoy's own younger brother, Butz.

When airing their grievances at their April meeting with the President had produced no tangible results, the RAM officers decided there was nothing for it but to carry out a military *coup*. Gringo Honasan and the others made Enrile privy to their plan and it took him a week of careful thought before the Defence Minister agreed to join them. The *coup* was set for either Christmas 1985 or New Year's Day 1986. In August, meanwhile, the Opposition tried to impeach Marcos on the grounds of having illegally amassed secret wealth abroad, charges that were backed up with evidence collected by the New York Congressman Stephen Solarz and his investigators. The impeachment failed; but since the CIA had been reporting to the White House since the late sixties that both Marcoses had been sending huge sums of money abroad, much of it traceable as US aid, the charge ought to have come as no surprise to the American President. Carter had certainly known what the CIA told him was going on. However, there is no evidence Reagan knew. There were certain kinds of detail his staff realized it was no use troubling him with. If they did not accord with his fantasies he would not take them in. To him, President Marcos was still the version he had met in 1969 as Governor of California: a great war hero and friend of the United States who had made his fortune long before he became President. Moreover, Nancy Reagan and Imelda were close. All sorts of rumours circulated about the relationship between the Reagans and the Marcoses. At a Cory rally in Luneta huge banners asked: 'How much salted $ went to Reagan's campaign fund?' and 'Nancy, Nancy, how do you like Meldy's pearls?' It became street wisdom that Reagan went on supporting Marcos because the Philippine President had bought him with a $10 million contribution to his campaign fund 'taken in cash, in satchels, to Mexico City where it was "laundered", then deposited in a Houston bank in which [Vice-President] Bush had an interest, and from there turned over to the Reagan campaign fund.'[1] It was equally widely believed that Imelda had given Nancy Reagan $2 millons' worth of jewellery from Cartier's.

The RAM officers' plan for the military *coup* was now finalized, with both Enrile and Fidel Ramos in full support. The idea was that 400 commandos would attack Malacañang from the river as other units secured the main television and radio stations. If the takeover were successful a junta would be formed with Ramos heading the military and Enrile the civilian interests, pledged to conduct free elections after two years. The plan had the CIA's backing, and in Washington the State Department went into action with the old Communist bogy in an effort to convince conservative members of Congress that even as Marcos grew weaker the NPA were gaining strength in the Philippines, threatening US business interests and the bases. This was completely untrue, and in any case it was hard to see how bands of guerrillas from the hills could seriously threaten some of the biggest and best-supplied US bases outside the continental United States. That was a mere detail, though. It was just part of a strategy, a preliminary softening-up in preparation for the idea that it was at last time for that old friend and ally, Ferdinand Marcos, to step down. Meanwhile, the *coup* plans were coming along nicely with the raising of a substantial private army by Enrile in his home province of Cagayan to provide back-up, when in November Marcos announced that he was calling a snap election.

The idea for this seems to have come from a troika of Reagan himself, Senator Paul Laxalt and the CIA's Director, William Casey. They sold it to Marcos on the grounds that another of his famous victories at the polls would do much to silence the Opposition and defuse the crisis. It would be charitable to call this a naive mis-reading of the anti-Marcos movement; but since Casey was not a naive man one can only conclude it was astoundingly cynical. The troika's calculation must have been that Marcos could be relied on to use his normal techniques of guns, goons and gold, plus the good offices of the Commission on Elections and the military to make sure the election went his way. Exactly what Casey's relation was to his CIA agents who were backing RAM's plans for a purely military solution will no doubt become clearer when the relevant files are made public. Possibly he was calculating that a glaringly rigged election would spell the end for Marcos, which in the event was more or less what did happen; but it seems very doubtful that President Reagan would have shared this assessment. He really did believe his old friends Ferdinand and Imelda could weather the storm. Ferdinand's announcement that the snap election would be held on 7 February 1986 obliged Enrile, Ramos and RAM to post-pone their plans. To have interrupted an election backed by the US President himself would have made their *coup* appear completely illegitimate instead of an unavoidable expedient to remove a tyrant.

Ferdinand's kidney transplant of August 1983 had failed, and he had since had a second one. Swollen from drugs and dropsical, he was too ill to do much in the way of active campaigning. Even so, he demonstrated great courage. Some might call it stubbornness or even vanity, because he was living out a fantasy: that of the enduring righteousness of his mission. The ultimate Filipino *amo*, the father of his people, he believed he still had his duty to perform even if he was feeling a little poorly at the moment. His running-mate, Arturo Tolentino, a decent 'Manila boy' and yet another of Ferdinand's fraternity brothers, was left to do most of the campaigning.

The question of who would be the President's running-mate had actually revealed some crucial differences of opinion as well as conflicting strategy. O. D. Corpuz, who by then had resigned as

Minister of Education, was horrified by one possibility. 'The issue then was whether Imelda would run as Vice-President. Since at that time there was no Vice-President and we were managing quite well without one, I went to Marcos and said, "Mr President, the Papacy in the Vatican has no need of a Vice-Pope." What I *couldn't* tell him was that if he had Imelda as Vice-President the Leyte faction might well assassinate him to seize power. Eventually Marcos chose Tolentino. They were fraternity brothers. You must understand that the Philippines is like Japan in that respect. Politicians choose their fraternity brothers for office. If there is no one available they choose their classmates. If there is no classmate, then someone from their same graduation year.'[2]

But it hadn't been quite that simple. As soon as Marcos announced the snap election his Trade and Industry Minister, Bobby Ongpin, had met with five American heavyweights – mainly high-ranking businessmen but including Frank Zarb, who had been the US Secretary of Energy in the 1970s and was Chief Executive Officer of Lazard Brothers, and Admiral Weisner, the Commander-in-Chief, Pacific (CINCPAC). Between them they decided that Ferdinand's running-mate should be his Prime Minister, Cesar Virata.

> Cesar Virata was very honourable, sound, quite inarticulate, the very antithesis of a forceful individual. A strong character himself, but he never stood his ground, never argued with Marcos. That was probably why the President made him his Prime Minister. He was pliable, but nevertheless untainted and reliable and much respected by the US. So I went to the President and told him our choice, and he agreed. Then at the last minute he overturned the decision in a Cabinet meeting because Imelda had rejected Virata. I was so angry I did something I'd never done before. I objected publicly to a Presidential decision. There and then in the Cabinet meeting I protested, saying I thought he was making a big mistake.[3]

What all this seems to suggest is that, however much it may appear to us now that Marcos's imminent downfall was a foregone conclusion, this was not at all how it seemed to his more intelligent and impartial ministers at the time. That senior Americans met with his Trade Minister to decide his best running-mate does suggest they accepted the prospect of yet another term of office, as well as that they were strategically planning to thwart the possibility of a pre-emptive Waray takeover by Imelda's faction. At any rate they seem not to have been privy to the CIA's knowledge that a RAM *coup* was likely to render everything academic.

The snap election's polling day produced a very heavy turnout of voters and – for foreign news-gatherers and observers – a wondrous display of the entire gamut of electoral fraud techniques. It has always been made to seem that Cory Aquino's forces of good behaved impeccably since theirs was the mandate of heaven and, with virtue on their side, they had no need to cheat. This is cant. Both sides cheated, as they always did in Philippine elections, although as always the incumbent party did the lion's share since it controlled the military, the police and the electoral machinery. The real difference this time was that Cory's Laban ('fight'/'opposition') party made a considerable effort to expose what the KBL, the President's party, was up to; and since most of the foreign observers were with Corysta teams her moral victory was a foregone conclusion, regardless of the election's outcome. Traditional methods were much to the fore: 'extraordinary harassment and intimidation, the theft of voter lists and ballot boxes, and the flying of voters from district to district to cast multiple ballots,'[4] as well as violence, bribery and electoral registers with hundreds of names missing and those of dead people substituted. Other techniques were startlingly original. The lady who was shortly to wander around the grounds of Malacañang and come upon Imelda Marcos's private hoard of sandwich spread was a NAMFREL observer who had been posted out to Kalookan City in northern Manila. She found her poll-watching mission greatly hampered by being unable to reach the polling booths, along with everyone else, owing to their being ringed by people of ethereal aspect and unhealthy pallor. On enquiry, she learned the truth. They were lepers. *Noli me tangere*, literally. Some powerful local Marcos supporter, presumably the Mayor, had hit on this brilliantly simple, non-violent method of curbing the democratic process that relied on nothing more than most people's superstitious dread of the disease. It was rumoured that he had flown the lepers over from the colony in Palawan, but in fact he had simply trucked them over from Kalookan City's own Tala leprosarium. 'Bussed lepers! Only in the Philippines!' as the frustrated voters joked among themselves, more than half-admiringly.

The remainder of the story of those first two months of 1986 is best told briefly, not just because it is so well known but because after twelve years the day-to-day details that were so significant to those who lived through the epic events of the 'People Power Revolution' no longer seem so for those who were not there. Marcos declared himself the winner of the snap election while Cory Aquino made the announcement of her own victory at a huge rally where her claim was publicly endorsed by Cardinal Sin and the bishops. The US Senate passed a resolution condemning Marcos's conduct of the election. Senator Edward Kennedy stated flatly: 'Corazon Aquino won that election lock, stock, and barrel', although he had not been in Manila at the time. (The historian O. D. Corpuz still says 'I think Marcos won that last election, but so narrowly he felt it necessary to tamper with the results in order to make it seem like a landslide . . . [T]here was cheating on both sides . . . as usual.'[5])

If the main focus of dramatic attention is the 'EDSA Revolution' of the weekend of 23 February, that of political interest is surely the laborious process by which President Reagan was finally persuaded to renounce – but never to denounce – his old friend Ferdinand Marcos. Reagan's special envoy to Manila, Philip Habib, never intended to induce Marcos to step down. His mission was to tell him that he could stay on with US backing until his current (i.e. pre-snap election) term expired in 1987, on condition that he sacked Fabian Ver and replaced him with Fidel Ramos as well as making certain Cabinet changes. Marcos refused. Habib then went to Cory Aquino to talk her into doing a deal with Marcos. She, too, refused, holding out for nothing less than the ex-President (in her eyes) leaving office. Behind Habib's back, though, knowing better than he how such negotiations were doomed to fail, the RAM plotters with their CIA backing had decided to go ahead with their *coup*. Cory might have come out of the election the moral victor, but the electoral process had been a farce and the recriminations might drag on inconclusively for months. Neither Marcos nor Cory was likely to back down: Marcos argued he had constitutionalism on his side, Cory knew she had the angels. The time had come for surgical action.

The *coup* was accordingly fixed for 2 a.m. on Sunday 23rd. The Palace would be attacked and the Marcoses captured or killed. Enrile would then declare himself head of a 'National Reconciliation Council'. What the plotters did not know was that one of their men had been 'turned' by Ver and was keeping him fully briefed. Ver probably made an early mistake by not moving straight away and arresting Enrile, Ramos and the RAM officers. Instead, he had his Presidential Security Command turn Malacañang into a fortress. When their informants reported this back to RAM, the plotters realized there had been a leak and hastily aborted their plan. Knowing it could only be a matter of time before they were arrested, Enrile and Ramos hurried to their respective strongholds (Ramos to Camp Crame and Enrile to Camp Aguinaldo over the road on E. de los Santos Avenue [EDSA], the Ministry of Defence headquarters). They announced that they and the RAM troops were leading a revolt. At dawn next morning Enrile moved over to Camp Crame in order to concentrate their forces, 400-odd men nervously facing a potential quarter of a million troops commanded by Ver. A strange inertia now seemed to hamper the detachments Ver sent to picket Camp Crame and dislodge the rebels. Instead of attacking they played for time by calling for reinforcements. The previous evening Ninoy's brother 'Butz' Aquino had made a broadcast over the Church's radio station, Radio Veritas, calling for popular support. And the people came. From all over Manila they came until they formed a crowd of ten thousand which 'Butz' Aquino led down EDSA chanting 'Cory! Cory!', waving yellow flags and flashing the 'L' sign of Cory's Laban. Ferdinand tried to do a deal over the phone with Enrile, but his ex-Defence Minister and sometime Palace lawyer knew things had already gone too far for deals. In Crame, Ramos, Enrile and their RAM group kept in touch with Cory Aquino via Jimmy Ongpin, a leading Oppositionist despite being the brother of Marcos's Trade Minister. Now the commander of the Marines, Brigadier-General Tadiar, brought the tanks and armoured personnel carriers he had been mustering at Imelda's University of Life campus down to EDSA where they trundled towards Camp Crame, intending to ring it. This produced the most memorable demonstration of 'People Power' when the vehicles were brought to a halt by the crowds, by nuns kneeling in the road in front of the snorting monsters, holding up crucifixes as though to halt Count Dracula, by people climbing onto the tanks' turrets and giving flowers and cigarettes to the bemused young soldiers inside. More and more of the forces sent in by Ver either disobeyed, temporized or defected. This was *palabas* to outdo even the Filipinos' favourite art form: sheerest spectacle heightened by tears, prayers, roadside Masses and the inevitable apparition of the Virgin; an outpouring of hysterical emotion that became hysterical bravery, for over everything hung the imminent likelihood of carnage. There was nobody in the densely packed crowds who did not know what the armed forces were capable of once given their head, and many present had been in Marcos's jails and interrogation centres during martial law. In the bright sunshine the yellow banners and the nuns' white habits – the Vatican's own colours – seemed designed to place the regime's unarmed opponents beneath special protection.

There then occurred an extraordinary scene, televised live from Malacañang, in which Fabian Ver could be heard and seen begging Marcos not to waste any more time but to let him open fire, launch an all-out attack on Camp Crame and put down the revolt regardless of the crowds in the way. Yet the sick and exhausted Ferdinand stubbornly refused to give the order.* To many of those

---

* The actual dialogue on TV went as follows:

> *Ver:* We have to immobilize the helicopters they've got. We have two fighter planes flying now to strike at any time, sir.
>
> *Marcos:* My order is not to attack.
>
> *Ver:* They are massing civilians near our troops and we cannot keep on withdrawing. You asked me to withdraw yesterday.
>
> *Marcos* (*interrupting*): My order is to disperse [them] without shooting them.
>
> *Ver:* We cannot withdraw all the time . . .
>
> *Marcos:* No, no no! Hold on. You disperse the crowds *without* shooting them. You may use any other weapon.

This transcript was printed in the *Philippines Sunday Express* of 2 March 1986 (p. 6), and was quoted in Remigio Agpalo, *Ferdinand E. Marcos* (Manila, 1993).

who knew and worked with him, this is still regarded as Marcos's finest hour. It was the moment when, no matter what orders he might have given in the past in the name of expediency, he refused to give the instinctive *datu*'s command that would have translated into wholesale slaughter. At the very least it showed he had learned from those days spent impotently in his office in the Palace, unable to prevent his armed forces from opening fire on crowds of protesters in the provinces even as he knew it was playing into the Opposition's hands. 'At that moment, I loved the man,' Bobby Ongpin says to this day, and remains immovable on the subject however much he might criticize Marcos for other actions. 'If you can't see the significance of his refusal to fire, that it reveals everything about the man, then you've understood nothing. One could only make sense of some of the things he did if one was there at the time. He was totally autocratic but he was also humane to the point of weakness. The unique thing about the guy is that in the face of his need to cling onto power there was this basic inconsistency of his.'

Even if one accepts that Ferdinand had little taste for bloodshed at first hand, and could hardly have been seen on television openly delegating the task of slaughtering crowds of nuns to Fabian Ver and his Army, one can agree with Bobby Ongpin that there was a strange inconsistency to the man. This was partly because of the fantasy element in his character. One might say that just as he had for many years successfully played the role of war hero, so he had played that of President of the Philippines, maker of history: an act in which part of him sincerely believed. As a true *datu*, though, his whole career had in reality been given up to the sterile circularity of pursuing ever more power in order to consolidate the power he already had. It was his private cultural inheritance. And most of this power had been channelled not into necessary social reforms but into ingenious ways of filling his warchest. It had been a compulsive acquisitiveness reminiscent of a squirrel obliviously hoarding nuts even as men with chainsaws prepare to fell the forest. This confusion of private agenda with public image, further muddied by illness, drugs and imminent disaster, left him mentally unprepared for the sudden raw confrontation with hundreds of thousands of Filipino citizens massing on the street who alone, according to the loyal Ver's urging, stood between him and the retention of that power. It may well have been his fantasy self that saved the day. At some level he had convinced himself that, no matter what dictatorial or electoral methods he had been obliged to use in the past, the majority of his people still respected if not loved him. After all, had he not held power for twenty years? At the very least this meant he had a place in his country's history that would certainly be denied him if he ended his career in a bloodbath.

A more cynical version of this act of clemency at the height of the EDSA confrontation might run that Washington, in constant touch via their Ambassador in Manila, Stephen Bosworth, had made it very plain to Marcos that if his troops did open fire on unarmed crowds he could forget any idea of being given safe conduct out of the country by the United States. But there is every reason for thinking that Ferdinand neither expected nor wanted to leave the Philippines (not least because he was to spend the three remaining years of his life begging to be allowed to return). What he hoped for was safe escort from the Palace and back home to his fiefdom in Ilocos Norte. Yet whichever argument predominated in his con-fused mind, the incontrovertible fact remains that he did prevent Ver from opening fire, which given the circumstances was in its way a genuine act of heroism to make amends for the more dubi-ous acts of heroism of over forty years previously. Some time later General Ver also received a message from the National Security Council in Washington telling him in effect that if he, too, expected the US to get him out of Manila in one piece, he should at all costs prevent bloodshed.

In deep despair Ferdinand called up Senator Paul Laxalt in Washington to see if anything could be worked out. Laxalt went off to talk to President Reagan and Secretary of State George Shultz before he called back two hours later. A now-famous conversation then ensued. When Ferdinand croakily asked what he ought to do, Laxalt replied:

'Mr President, I'm not bound by diplomatic restraint. I'm talking only for myself. I think you should cut and cut cleanly. The time has come. [Here there was a long pause]. Mr President, are you still there?' 'Yes, I'm still here,' came Ferdinand's voice. 'I am so very, very disappointed.'[6]

'Disappointed' was the word that revealed his sense of having been betrayed by Washington, even as in the meantime over ninety percent of the military had defected to Fidel Ramos, who was receiving phone calls pledging support from commanding officers all over the country. A degree of pathos entered the proceedings. Ferdinand called up his friend Enrile and tried to sue for peace on Enrile's terms. He said he would cancel the result of the snap election, set up a provisional government with Enrile at its head and stay on in the background as honorary President until 1987 while letting Enrile run things as he liked. In this way constitutionality might be preserved. In fact, Enrile had been just about to leave for Cory Aquino's oath-taking ceremony; it was too late now for last-ditch compromises. Mrs Aquino, back in Manila again after spending the height of the crisis in Cebu guarded by nuns, was sworn in as President together with her Vice-President, Salvador 'Doy' Laurel (son of the wartime President Jose Laurel who had once acquitted the young Ferdinand Marcos of murder). Two hours later a sad ceremony was enacted in Malacañang as Ferdinand was also sworn in as President, surrounded by his family and supporters, many of them in tears. It was pure Shakespeare in its evocation of a king shorn of his power. At the climax of the oath-taking, as the old man raised his right hand, the television transmission relaying the proceedings to his former people was abruptly cut as his cousin's military captured the TV station. Even so, it was not quite the end. The First Couple – and to their sworn courtiers they always would remain the First Couple – made a brief appearance on the balcony where Imelda summoned up her courage and gave a last, tearful rendition of her theme-song 'Dahil sa Iyo', 'Because of You'. Thereafter, any remains of collective fantasy collapsed altogether in a mad scramble of packing for departure under escort. The *jacquerie* was already massing at the Palace gates and could not indefinitely be held off. It was not until later that night as the last helicopter staggered up from Malacañang grounds into the soft air over Manila that the Palace defenders themselves fell back and then, their uniforms hastily changed for jeans and T-shirts, tried to lose themselves in the cheering crowds who came bursting in through the gates and over the railings.

*

Each year since EDSA, commemorative rallies and Masses have been held on the ring road near Camp Crame in an effort to recreate the magic and significance of those few February days and nights in 1986. And each year, the ever-receding events have been invoked with increasing difficulty by the surviving participants. It is not that individual memories are less acute but that the collective image of what really happened, once so clear, has become increasingly uncertain. The tenth anniversary, with its fly-pasts and general panoply of a state occasion, was certainly a reminder that, like the event it commemorated, it was mainly an affair for Manileños. The people who had turned out for the original 'People Power Revolution' had been almost entirely locals, despite all efforts to imply that it was a nationwide uprising. People in the provinces had not risen as one and surrounded their local PC compound or picketed the nearest AFP camp. Instead, the sense of a regime's collapse had spread from the capital out to the country's periphery as the armed forces' commanders rallied by telephone and radio behind a new military leadership. Moreover, that tenth anniversary had a particularly uneasy hollowness behind it as though the gap between collective fantasy and actuality was no longer bridgeable by sentiment. What was finally obvious was something that few had chosen to notice in the fervour and emotion surrounding the Marcoses' ousting: that it never was a revolution. Worse, for all the spontaneity and extraordinary bravery of those EDSA crowds who were responsible for scripting the climax of a play, the entire production could clearly be seen as having been to a degree stage-managed from elsewhere for two and a half years before the curtain went up on the final act.

Back in 1983, the combination of near-economic collapse (helped along by notorious and uncurbed crony capitalism) and the outrageous public killing of Ninoy Aquino at the very moment of his homecoming from America had made it inevitable Washington would decide that the Presidency of a mortally ill Marcos, after almost eighteen years, was finished. A minor problem was President Reagan's unqualified support for the man. This could largely be ignored; indeed, it was probably quite useful, if embarrassing, that the White House should continue to pledge public support even as the downfall of America's Boy was being planned. Much weightier problems were the question of who his successor should be and how best to exploit the cracks that had opened up in General Ver's armed forces. From the moment Cory Aquino accepted her dead husband's mantle as Marcos's sworn political enemy, Washington began a careful nurturing of relations with both her and the Church, as also with the RAM leadership, whose officers regularly met with contacts from the US Embassy. For his part, Cardinal Sin was in constant touch with a variety of foreign diplomats. All this should have been obvious in retrospect. The United States had always been recognized as the power behind the throne in the Philippines; the withdrawal of that support changed little except the incumbent. The power remained.

This was the source of an enduring sense of grievance on the part of the Marcoses and many of their loyalist camp: not so much the withdrawal of support but the sheer hypocrisy of the way in which it was done. Once the Passion play had been cast with Cory as heaven's right hand and Ferdinand as the decrepit prince of darkness, the Americans inevitably appeared as the crusaders in white armour who had enabled good to triumph. It was as though their previous two decades' unflinching support for the prince of darkness were completely forgotten in EDSA's single long week-end. Yet almost no one at the time pointed this out. Everybody was too carried away by the simplistic drama as presented by Cardinal Sin himself. It had had nothing to do with politics, said the prelate, for the Church never meddled in politics. 'The issue was moral. It was a fight between the forces of Good and Evil.'[7] (Ferdinand's subsequent apotheosis, complete with the stigmata, was the *lumpen*-devotionalists' triumphant revenge.) 'Parachute journalists' – in a favourite contemptuous phrase of his – dropped in fresh from Haiti where a bare week earlier 'Baby Doc' Duvalier's regime had fallen to a military *coup*. As far as they could see Manila presented much the same scenario as Port-au-Prince. Another Third World tropical city, another sleazy old dictator.

Ferdinand and his supporters continued to nurture a deep sense of betrayal. Washington's switch in loyalties had seemed to them breathtakingly sudden and arbitrary. For the best part of two decades the US had appeared perfectly content with – or at least resigned to – his *datu*-style politics. Now, abruptly, the US Congress he had once so triumphantly addressed was rising to denounce the snap election as if it had only now woken up to what it was they had so long supported. The care Ferdinand had taken to rewrite the Constitution had paradoxically showed the store he set by constitutionalism, which was also something Washington valued highly in its client states. He and many of his supporters remained convinced that the KBL had won the snap election, and in any case a disputed electoral outcome in Manila could hardly be settled by a foreigner like Edward Kennedy getting to his feet in Washington and declaring Cory Aquino the victor. What of legality now? There should have been enquiries, investigations, even a re-run. But no; a declaration of a winner by American *fiat* and suddenly Cory Aquino is being sworn in as President even as President Marcos still occupies Malacañang. It seemed like a travesty of the law.

Later, and at a more private level, the Marcoses were shocked and hurt by their treatment from the moment the helicopters landed at Clark Field. So far had their American hosts identified with the terms of their own play that this was no longer a sick and ageing President hoping to return to his home province of Ilocos Norte, but a master criminal who could have no further say in where he was being taken, and whose party's private baggage was separated and ransacked before much of it vanished entirely.[8] This was when the Philippine currency came to light, proving beyond much doubt that the Marcoses had never expected to leave the country. Fabian Ver, on the other hand, had brought his entire family including servants, and had clearly packed for the duration, which suggested that his links to friends in Washington were now better than Ferdinand's own. It could never have occurred to Ferdinand and his family that Hawaii was to remain his permanent place of exile, but such it proved. He had another three and a half years to live, during which time he frequently petitioned Cory Aquino for permission to return home, but to no avail. He died in Hawaii at the end of September 1989, two weeks short of his seventy-second birthday.

It is only fair to point out that if Ferdinand felt America had betrayed him, the feeling was mutual. Even though successive White Houses went on supporting him, the State Department was frequently miffed at what they saw as his reneging on their deals. When Washington allowed him to declare martial law, it was conditional on certain guarantees, such as permitting Oppositionists to get out of the country first and not doing anything to interfere with

US business or military affairs. But in addition, Marcos had been expected to carry on with the Parity agreement. This was the post-war amendment to the Philippine Constitution that MacArthur had insisted on as a prerequisite for rehabilitation aid and inde-pendence. It gave US citizens parity with Filipinos to exploit Philippine natural resources and operate public utilities. These Parity rights were due to lapse in 1974, and Washington was rely-ing on Marcos to renew them. He never did. But that was not the only reason for US displeasure; there were macro-political consid-erations, too. Marcos had been expected to help bring other ASEAN countries into line behind US policy. The US wanted a firm foothold in Asia in order to do business with China. They agreed to the old South East Asia Treaty Organization (formed in Manila in 1954 to protect Southeast Asia from Communist aggression) being subsumed by ASEAN because they were counting on Marcos to induce the other members to adopt a pro-American alignment.

> Instead, to their fury, Marcos turned out to have his own agenda. He drove a wedge between Japan and the US and, worse, tried to get China as his client. The Japanese were wanting to expand into Southeast Asia – in those days Indonesia, Singapore and Thailand had still not opened up. Marcos welcomed the Japanese back to the Philippines during martial law by means of tourism, trade and industry. The Philippines was the first country in ASEAN to begin heavy trading with the Japanese. The US didn't like that a bit because the Japanese got to ASEAN before they did. Marcos played a major role in ensuring that ASEAN became much more independent of the US than the Americans had hoped. You have only to look at Mahathir's Malaysia today.
>
> Similarly, his China initiative upset them, despite Nixon's ping-pong diplomacy. It hinted at independence. So Marcos's big crimes in Washington's eyes were over ASEAN, China and the Parity Amendment. His ultimate sin was to try to become leader of the non-aligned countries at the Cancun Summit in 1981.[9]

It can be seen, therefore, that there were grievances on both sides – on all sides, soon, as it turned out, because even the sainted Cory appeared to renege on her tacit obligation to be a compliant friend of Washington's. The reason, they say, was less from nationalist zeal than from vindictiveness. When her husband had been exiled in Boston, Washington had ignored her. It only paid her attention after Ninoy's assassination, once she had become the focus for the Opposition and as such could serve Washington's purposes. She was not a forgiving person, and maybe this supposed snub gave impetus to a presidential decision she took during the US bases talks of 1990–1 not to meet US Defence Secretary Dick Cheney when he came to Manila in mid-February 1991. At the time, her Government was considerably miffed about what it saw as Washington's unfulfilled commitments as well as an attitude perceived as one of 'Cory-bashing'. So, 'in order to convey to the US the Philippine Government's displeasure', she decided to let her Defence Secretary, Fidel Ramos, see Cheney in her stead.[10] No Filipino head of state had ever done such a thing before. A good few people cheered.

It is doubtful if Marcos himself can ever have held out much hope that President Aquino would allow him to return to the Philippines, even just to die, although he might well have been amazed and slightly gratified had he known that she would not even so much as permit his corpse to be brought back. Evidently it still contained too much political voltage. (It was left to his own cousin, Fidel Ramos, to authorize its return.) As a Filipino, Ferdinand would ruefully have understood Mrs Aquino's motivation as being founded partly on political considerations, but mostly on vengeance. The Philippines' political system is not in practice based on abstract ideals of good governance so much as on emotional issues and *ad hominem* point-scoring. Those seen as allies are rewarded, enemies are punished. Ferdinand Marcos's ultimate responsibility for Ninoy Aquino's death, to say nothing of imprisonment, amply justified condemning him to die in exile. Unconstitutional though it might have been, it was a deal everyone understood.

To outsiders, though, and even to many Filipinos, the campaign this pious lady waged against the exiled Marcoses often seemed downright implacable. It was true her husband had been publicly murdered, but it was still quite unclear who had authorized the killing. Maybe her rancour would have been less conspicuous had not so much been made of her devout Christianity. Also, given

how long the Marcos era had lasted, how deeply through
Philippine society its roots ran, and the traumas caused by its
ending, it might have been thought that some sort of reconciliation
would be high on any wise incoming President's agenda once justice had been meted out to those with criminal charges against
them. Yet here was a strange thing. The Presidential Commission
on Good Government (PCGG) began investigating how much vanished wealth it could claw back from cronies and a complex array
of Swiss bank vaults and offshore hidey-holes. It could draw on all
sorts of help from Washington's voluminous files, for in the early
days of Cory's Presidency she could have asked for anything. And
yet remarkably little money was recovered and not a single person
of any stature was ever jailed, a situation that continues to be true
down to the present day. There was no lack of recriminations, but
there was also a complete absence of criminal proceedings or even
extraditions. Instead, there appeared to be a concentration of effort
on name-calling and petty measures. 'The Cory Government called
everyone who didn't support it a "Marcos Loyalist", even people
who hadn't supported Marcos. This produced a quite unnatural
polarity,' as O. D. Corpuz observed.[11] This polarity was, of course,
a hangover from EDSA with Washington's Manichaean casting.
Even perfectly proper and useful parts of the Marcoses' legacy
were allowed to collapse or were boycotted. Thus the Department
of Tourism stopped promoting all the successful resorts the previous Administration had developed up the northwestern coast of
Luzon. The various sites that Joe Aspiras had opened to the profit
of the Philippine Government were suddenly ignored. From
Bauang, La Union up to Vigan itself and encompassing all those
historic Spanish churches Imelda had taken such a fancy to – all
were as though written off the map. Indeed, almost anywhere
north of Cory's own home ground of Tarlac was practically abandoned as Marcos-tainted territory whenever it came to
governmental projects or assistance. In Metro Manila even the most
socially useful of Imelda's projects were starved of funds. As for the
arts and the Cultural Centre of the Philippines, they were ignored
altogether.

Those who still believed in the EDSA polarity must certainly
have had their faith severely tested in the months that followed
when EDSA's most photogenic hero, Enrile's right-hand man and

original RAM conspirator Gringo Honasan, led a failed *coup* against the Government he had helped install – one of several that dogged Cory's term of office. The *coup* was no kind of joke since it killed, among others, sixty-three homeless street people (including a large number of children), for whose deaths Honasan and his rebel friends were responsible. Honasan became an outlaw, the Philippines' most-hunted man who, like many a hunted man before him, actually spent a good deal of time living quietly at home in Quezon City. (Today he is a Senator.) This by itself should have alerted observers to the idea that Philippine political realities were stubbornly refusing to keep to Washington's script, even before Enrile's bitter retraction of EDSA in 1990 when he implied on a radio programme that his having helped install Cory Aquino had after all been a terrible mistake. ('I'm sorry . . . I apologize to our people for that event.') Long before then, awful divisions in President Aquino's own Cabinet had climaxed in a tragic act of utter disillusionment. This was the suicide of Bobby Ongpin's younger brother Jaime, who had courageously opposed Marcos for years, had been with the rebels throughout EDSA and become Cory's Finance Minister.

Nearly eleven months earlier, on 22 January 1987, there was a march-rally by farmers who had come to Manila to call on President Aquino to implement the agrarian reform she had resoundingly promised, maybe even to begin with her own family's gigantic Hacienda Luisita. Eleven thousand protesters converged on Mendiola Bridge, which marks the approach to Malacañang Palace. The underlying mood of the rally was serious but its tactics were non-threatening, being more an EDSA-style celebration with protest songs and street theatre. Towards evening, without warning, police and Marines opened fire on the unarmed peasants, killing thirteen and wounding scores. (Ten years later, the relatives of the dead are still trying to get justice.)

That the Mendiola Massacre, as it is nowadays known, was not merely an aberration or throwback to a previous era was borne out by other statistics. A report released by FIND (Families of Victims of Involuntary Disappearances) on 4 December 1992 revealed that 'more political activists disappeared during the six-year presidency of Corazon Aquino than during Ferdinand Marcos's 21-year rule,' putting the total number of *desaparecidos* at

1,586.[12] This came shortly after the Medical Action Group had held a symposium and a psychiatrist announced that most political prisoners had undergone torture during the post-Marcos era.[13] And within a matter of days, an ecumenical mission of Church and human rights organizations made an urgent pre-Christmas plea for 1,000 starved and ill families in Antique Province. These were the inhabitants of three villages which had been 'placed by the military under virtual siege for the last ten years' and further 'fortified' in 1991 by being ordered to amalgamate into one village with only one exit and entrance. (This was the same 'hamleting' technique of rural pacification pioneered in the Philippine–American war in the early years of the century and used extensively in the Vietnam war.) The villagers were even prevented from holding prayer groups:

> The military suspect such sessions to be fronts for rebel meetings. During Sunday, some paramilitary men would attend worship to spy on churchgoers, residents complain. Not only is the villagers' religious life affected . . . The traditions of evening courtships, serenades, fiestas and thanksgiving have been banned. The use of flashlights at night has also been forbidden. Farmers are prohibited from using axes. Residents are required to secure travel passes when they leave the village.[14]

If Cory Aquino's Washington-backed democracy now appears less than a holy revolution, it is hardly a surprise. In keeping with Philippine political tradition it was more like musical chairs, with the same élite families and datus merely switching around. Teodoro Locsin Jr.'s description of martial law as having been 'in a manner of speaking . . . an affair among friends' is equally true of the country's entire governmental system. Nothing else explains the way in which none of the notorious thieves and monsters of the Marcos era – all of whom are perfectly well known to most Filipinos – have ever been brought to justice. By late 1997 almost all those who fled before or with the Marcoses were back in the Philippines. Today newspaper published a partial list of the more prominent Marcos-era people in power, starting with Ferdinand's own cousin and police chief, President Fidel Ramos, and going on from there:

Eleven years after the EDSA People Power Revolt, the cronies of former President Marcos . . . now dominate both the ruling Lakas-NUCD and the opposition . . . Most of the 217 congressmen, from the Speaker down to the opposition, once belonged to Marcos's KBL. [It] has prompted a former anti-Marcos activist to say that the list of the members of the House is like the old guest book of Malacañang. 'The old guards [of the EDSA revolution] are gone. In their place are the praetorian guards of Marcos,' the source said. Most prominent of the KBL stalwarts is former First Lady and now Rep. Imelda Marcos of Leyte. Mrs Marcos and her husband's former pilot, Rep. Roque Ablan of Ilocos Norte now lead the KBL remnants. Lakas Rep. Luz Cleta Bakunawa of Masbate was Marcos's personal secretary. Speaker Jose de Venecia, President Ramos's chief political lieutenant and secretary-general of Lakas, was a Marcos-appointed diplomat to Saigon who became a congressman in the 1970s. Lakas Rep. Ricardo Silverio of Bulacan was the owner of the defunct Delta Motors and one of Marcos's business cronies. Three former Marcos Cabinet members are House Minority Leader Ronaldo Zamora, former presidential chief legal counsel; Lakas Reps. Carmencita Reyes of Marinduque, social welfare and development minister; Jose Aspiras of La Union, tourism minister; and Rodolfo del Rosario of Davao del Sur, natural resources minister . . .[15]

The complete list goes on endlessly. One of the proposals made to Cory Aquino when she became President was to put a special clause in the new Constitution banning all those who had served Marcos from public office for five years. This was modelled on the example of Argentina after the Colonels, though there the ban was for ten years. The idea was to give those who had set their aspirations on the high ideals of EDSA a chance of being elected in the first post-EDSA Congress. This motion was successfully opposed by Peping Cojuangco, Cory Aquino's younger brother. The ex-journalist and former Marcos-era Ambassador J. V. Cruz is his usual outspoken self on the subject:

Look around you for the Marcos era – it's still here. Look at Ramos himself. Look at the next crop of 'presidentiables' for 1998: Estrada, Maceda, De Venecia . . . The only one not tainted by having been a Marcos man is the current Chief Justice of the Supreme Court. The rest were not mere associates but *close* associates of Marcos. Look at the roll of the current House of Representatives. More than half are associated with, and tainted by, their Marcos connections. They won their seats by election, too, so obviously their constituents didn't give a damn. If a lot of Filipinos look back to Marcos with nostalgia – and they do – we owe it to Cory Aquino. It's only possible for most people to be nostalgic about Marcos because Aquino was so awful. . . . I give FVR [Fidel Ramos] high marks for retrieving us from the depths, though nothing *radical* has changed, of course. All he does is show the sort of minimal competence one has the right to expect in a President.[16]

If this sounds a harsh judgement on Cory Aquino there are many who would counter it by saying that her great contribution was to have weathered half a dozen *coup* attempts and to have restored the democratic process on which Ramos was able to build. But this was achieved at the cost of virtually no new infrastructural projects. The first of her legacies that Ramos inherited was a nationwide power crisis caused by a chronic lack of generating capacity, and the first years of his term were characterized by constant blackouts and power cuts that often brought the capital to a literal standstill, since the traffic lights also failed. If Ramos is remembered for nothing else, it should be for having restored Manila's electricity supply.

The political panic of 1997 was only the latest, but in some ways the best, illustration of how little had changed since the days of Marcos. President Ramos constantly had to deny that he had a secret plan to abrogate the Constitution in order to avoid having to leave office when his term expired in 1998. That he was not universally believed was proved by huge rallies led by those selfsame EDSA heroes, Cory Aquino and Cardinal Sin, to protest any idea of a second term of office for the professional soldier whose defection from Marcos's service they once lauded as a supreme act of patriotism. It was significant that Ramos's promise to step down was so distrusted. Rep. Joker Arroyo said 'Ramos doesn't care about the Constitution. The only way he can keep himself in power is to resort to extraconstitutional means.' In other words, the old spectre of martial law was once more floating about the corridors of power. It was hardly surprising, given that Filipinos knew their own history so well. The parallels between the perceived conduct of the present Government and that of the Marcos administration all those years ago suddenly surfaced alarmingly:

> Ramos, it has been said, has been acting like Marcos. Armed Forces Chief of Staff Arnulfo Acedera has been acting like Fabian Ver, the Armed Forces Chief during the dictatorship. National Security Adviser Jose Almonte is acting like Marcos's then-Defence Secretary Juan Ponce Enrile. And Gabriel Claudio, Ramos's adviser for political affairs, is acting like Leonardo Perez, who served Marcos in various capacities (like being COMELEC chairman) and whose loyalty to the dictator rivals Ver's . . . [17]

This degree of scepticism is most eloquent. If professional journalists have so little confidence in the democratic instincts of politicians they have known for so long, what can one say of Juan de la Cruz out there in the provinces? How does the great majority of Filipinos living outside Manila react to these ever-unchanging power games played out among the political élite charged with leading their country to peace and prosperity? To answer this question one final story may be cited. It is one I recounted some years ago in a book about the sea, but make no apology for updating here. Its appositeness grows with each year of official silence that goes by until it almost aspires to the status of parable. Moreover, it was an incident whose outward sign was witnessed from Kansulay.

1997 was the tenth anniversary of the world's worst-ever maritime disaster, the sinking in the Philippines of the M/V *Doña Paz*. Over three times as many people died in this as did in the *Titanic*, but owing to a complete absence of American millionaires and British socialites aboard the event is never likely to attract the attention of Broadway or Hollywood. That it involved a vessel ultimately owned by an American oil company has also been conveniently forgotten.

The *Doña Paz*, a 2,215-ton inter-island ferry, had been en route from Tacloban in Leyte province (coincidentally Imelda's home port) to Manila, grotesquely overladen with passengers for the Christmas holiday season. Not only was the ship's departure delayed fourteen hours to take on this illegal complement of passengers but she stopped a few hours later at Catbalogan in Samar to pick up still more. She was provisioned for a maximum of 3,000 and by the night of 20 December food and drinking water had long since run out. Life-rafts and life-jackets, which at best could never have sufficed for more than a fraction of those aboard, were variously holed, rusted, missing or locked inaccessibly away. Shortly before midnight in the Tablas Strait off Mindoro the *Doña Paz* collided with the M/T *Vector*, an unlighted and rusty tanker owned by Caltex (Philippines). This hulk was barely seaworthy and carrying a highly inflammable cargo which included over 8,000 barrels of fuel oil from a Batangas refinery. The two ships exploded in a fireball visible forty miles away over the horizon on Kansulay beach, a stupendous bonfire of children and diesel oil and Christmas presents. There were twenty-eight survivors.

The incident did cause headline news – albeit briefly – around the world. The Pope expressed his anguish, along with several heads of state. President Cory Aquino ordered an 'all-out probe' that was to leave 'no stone unturned'. Then everyone returned gratefully to Christmas. Not until November the following year – and then only after another accident involving one of its vessels – were the operations of Sulpicio Lines, who owned the *Doña Paz*, briefly suspended in an administrative slap-on-the-wrist. A survivor from the *Doña Paz* said that her captain, who did not himself survive, had been drunk and playing mah-jong at the time of the collision. A witness from the tanker testified that the *Vector*'s bridge had been completely empty. The charge filed against Caltex was for carrying 'a highly dangerous mix of cargo in a grossly inadequate and unseaworthy vessel'.[18]

The victims had been mainly from Leyte and Samar, and their relatives formed an organization (*Bulig Kita, Samar ug Leyte*, which means 'I'll help you, Samar and Leyte' in Cebuano) to press for an official enquiry and compensation. In a reference to the disaster in my book *Seven-Tenths* (1992) I said that the official estimate of the dead was 3,000, this being the maximum number of passengers the *Doña Paz* had been legally entitled to carry, but added 'it is certain to have been many more'. This was partly because children under the age of ten were never listed on passenger manifests at the time and it was a safe bet that travellers heading for Christmas family reunions in Manila would have taken every last infant. It is now generally accepted by journalists as well as by *Bulig Kita* that over 5,000 died, though the true figure can never be known. Whatever is left lies in 500 metres of water. In May 1989, eighteen months after the disaster, Sulpicio Lines claimed that '86 percent of the passengers aboard the *Doña Paz* have been paid for at ₱30,000 per victim' (about £600). That is, eighty-six percent of those whose names appeared on the ship's manifest – in other words 2,580 passengers, probably about half the real total. The company admitted no liability whatever for the passengers it had illegally carried and who could not now be reliably identified. The whole issue was further muddied for both the company and the victims' relatives by hundreds of impostors who, smelling money, came forward to file entirely fictitious claims of their own.

The one certainty is that no one has ever been arrested, prosecuted or tried, still less sentenced. President Aquino's 'all-out probe' soon withered into inertia in the usual way: sidetracked by allegations and counter-allegations, subjected to delaying tactics and blinded by legalistic smokescreens. Every stone of any weight was scrupulously left unturned. It remains a crime that to this day has gone completely unpunished. Not even the relevant coast guard official in Tacloban, who was technically responsible for assuring the shipping lines' compliance with lading regulations, was called to account or admonished. Credulity was further stretched when barely ten months later the *Doña Marilyn*, another Sulpicio Lines ferry, was lost in typhoon Unsang. Far from being an act of God, it was the direct consequence of an act of criminal stupidity in that the ship's captain, together with Manila port officials, the coast guard and Sulpicio directors had decided to risk their vessel leaving port at a time when the typhoon was forecast to hit its destination in the Visayas and was being monitored from as far away as Hong Kong. The *Doña Marilyn* made it as far as Samar, where it sank in pitiful circumstances. At the time the death toll was put at 340, but similar principles were involved as with the *Doña Paz*, and the unofficial toll soon went higher.

The case against Sulpicio Lines over the *Doña Paz* continues to this day as the families of victims who were not declared in the ship's manifest battle wearily for compensation. Even if their campaign is successful there will remain a deep sense of injustice over the way all those responsible for the crime have in effect been pardoned by the *de facto* amnesty of sheer lapse of time. Mrs Aquino has long since left office and nobody is tactless enough to remind this famous Christian lady of her promise of an 'all-out probe'. Sulpicio Lines has upgraded its fleet and the company's family administration has changed since 1987. As for the owners of the M/T *Vector*, they soon melted away behind a haze of PR. 'Doing its share to be a responsible corporate citizen,' as a headline described the company in a 1992 interview with its new president and CEO, William S. Tiffany.

> Caltex has always considered its role as a responsible corporate citizen of its host countries as an important part of its doing business all over the world. Tiffany has said that the company worldwide always 'tries to be a good citizen'. 'Wherever Caltex does business, it looks for ways to help the community around it,' he explained. 'We have a corporate philosophy of putting back into the community much more than the local taxman demands from us.'[19]

That the *Titanic* had only enough lifeboats for half its passengers was a good enough reason for successful lawsuits to be entered against her owners, whether or not the chance encounter with a stray iceberg had been an act of God. That the *Doña Paz* had virtually no safety equipment aboard – even though the explosion would have rendered it irrelevant – came as no surprise to anyone in the Philippines.

Wherein lies this story's near-parable status? What is remarkable is the seeming passivity, not just of the authorities, but of the Filipino public itself. After the original outcry, made all the more emotive for the juxtaposition with the festive season, the story quickly faded. Except when some new accident makes newspaper editors remember the ship, or a reporter covers a fresh campaign by *Bulig Kita* to draw attention to their still-unsettled case, the *Doña Paz* has simply vanished into gulfs of oblivion. In fact the public's resignation is entirely understandable. It was merely one more – albeit by far the worst – in a long line of sinkings and disasters which have gone unpunished and largely uncompensated. Nobody expected anything to happen, so nothing did. Ten years later it could be seen that the tragedy did have some salutary effect in that when President Ramos came to power the discrepancy between his vision of 'Philippines 2000' and the derelict hulks still plying his country's domestic sea lanes made a degree of change inevitable. There are many newer vessels today on inter-island routes. Even so, an impression is left that the impetus for this came as much from a desire for greater economic efficiency and to make the Philippines' image more attractive to foreign investors as out of interest for the safety of its citizens, for there are still plenty of 'floating coffins' (as the press calls them) on minor routes.

In this, then, lies a partial answer to that question of how the Juan de la Cruzes of Kansulay and elsewhere view the perennial shenanigans of Manila's governmental élite. One speaks of the 'seeming' passivity of the Filipino public advisedly. This has nothing to do with the Western racial stereotyping of Easterners as being more callous about death. It is not about callousness; it is about *despair*. The patient glance, the shrug, the half-smile, the joke: these are forms of a stoicism learned centuries ago. On and on it goes, keeping pace with the constant failure of the political merry-go-round to satisfy anything other than itself. One might even go so far as to argue that half the more bizarre cases that hit the headlines in the Philippines and catch the attention of foreign editors have their origins in sheer despair as much as in ordinary criminality.

This underlying despair, so brilliantly concealed by the culture's predominant cheerfulness ('Where Asia Wears a Smile!') seems to me what unites incidents like that of the *Doña Paz* – which in many another country could have led to the government's fall – with the Mendiola Massacre, even with the 'EDSA Revolution' itself. For what is as plain as the gap between Manila and the Philippines is that gulf between political process and the people. EDSA's bravery, characteristically masquerading beneath a fiesta-like atmosphere, was itself born of despair. This was partly twenty years' despondency that the country's mock-democratic system could only administer the nation it was supposed to serve by calling out the armed forces to dragoon it into submission, when all that the vast majority of its people had ever wanted were some basic living standards.

But another part of the despair would have stemmed from the hidden knowledge that substituting an oligarch for an autocrat was no kind of revolution. Only the hysteria of the moment could have prevented this glum awareness from surfacing. Shear away all the nonsense about good and evil and what really were the differences between Marcoses and Aquinos? Super-rich *datus* with their fraternity brotherhoods, intermarriages, internecine rows and reparations, scheming for power and yet more power; by turns advantageously flirting with the Church, Masonry, Communism, the United States; stealing the people's foreign aid and putting it into private bank accounts and property scattered throughout the world. What kind of leadership was this? The answer to which, of course, was the most despairing of all: the Filipino kind, the one we have; the one we might by now have long since rid ourselves had it not been for the global self-interests of a foreign power. There it is.

Away in Kansulay villagers survey the diminished river. Or else the subsistence fisherman gazes down at the dying reef. At night the city-like lights of the fishing fleets owned by powerful consortiums are sometimes bright enough to cast his shadow on the beach. He watches as, unpoliced, they illegally come inshore to sweep up his livelihood with their superior technology. Useless to complain. He is represented in Congress by a person who owns such a fleet. '*Ito*,' he says with that same smile. '*Ito*.' '*This*.' All there is to say.

14

First Couple redux

'The Marcoses were the best of us, and the worst. That's why we say we hate them so much.' Thus the journalist, Rod Dula, summing them up and adding 'This country looks for two things: either idols or demons.' This may sound suspiciously epigrammatic, even simplistic, but the role of the Church in the Marcoses' unseating, no less than that of Washington, made their demonizing inevitable. The myth of their being an outstanding evil whose complete purging from Philippine society somehow implied that the country would then return to a state of prelapsarian grace was the last great fantasy surrounding the Marcoses. It would have been an injustice if only because it singled them and their era out for damnation instead of blaming an entire political system that had too well suited its last colonials. Few people at the time said loudly enough that the antique philosophy of the robber barons had already prevailed for too long and it was high time such energy was channelled into the common good. If Ferdinand Marcos ran true to form by being a consummate old-style politician it was only what Washington and Filipinos – despair and all – had expected.

There is an irony here. The boy from Batac, despite his youthful dynamism, his early technocratic intentions, his infrastructural achievements and his progressive social legislation, remained profoundly out of date. He was old-fashioned in an old-fashioned system that required him to act as *amo* at *barangay* level as well as to the administrative classes, the judiciary and the military. And at that level, it is true, he was an expert. He had been brought up on exactly these techniques and had no real wish to shake himself free. If his war experiences had led him cynically to believe that anyone could be bought, he found nothing in Filipino public life to suggest he was mistaken. Even his critics readily concede how politically adroit he was in his understanding and manipulation of the grassroots politics of *utang na loob*, but will add 'and used it for his own purposes'. Well, of course. That is what politicians do. The critics go on to counter that a halfway enlightened Ferdinand might have harnessed his populist skill at least as much for the nation's good as for the Marcos family's fortunes. So he might; but that *was* old-style country politics. It was a consummate old-style politician thinly disguised as Prince Charming the Filipino electorate had voted into office in 1965. This being so, there was more than a touch of hypocrisy in the way he was summarily heaped with the nation's dirty laundry in 1986 and driven out into the wilderness as though what was left behind was miraculously shriven and already convalescent.

One can remain a cynic and say that Marcos had always intended to become President expressly to make a fortune, and that anything he might have done for his country along the way would be purely coincidental. Alternatively, one can say that despite being an old-style politician he had become President with some genuine ideals, but that something happened to him that made things go wrong. Greed, moral obliquity, arrogance, American pressures, his own wife, illness – all have been suggested as explanations for this genuine puzzle.

Ironically, given his constant description as a 'strongman' or 'dictator', Marcos turns out to have had a surprising streak of weakness in his character. No matter what those closest to him might say, much of his strength in office derived from practically unconditional US backing, and later from his own steady militarization of the political scene. Had he really been as determinedly idealistic as his judgement told him he should be, he would surely have done more to implement land reform, at least to the point where it might have defused the growing antagonism of the left. If he was unafraid during martial law to break the oligarchs who had annoyed him, he could surely have made large landowners agree to some concessions had he backed up his demands with real determination. He could certainly have counted on popular support for such a move. There again, given that he had manoeuvred himself into such a position that he needed to declare martial law, why did he not use those extraordinary powers to make far-reaching and effective changes over eight years? Instead of which, Malacañang presented the spectacle of an Administration facing two ways at once. At a Cabinet meeting some sensible and well-informed economic strategy might be agreed which an hour later could be completely nullified by a private deal with a crony. Undoubtedly there is something very Filipino about this.

When asked why Marcos had allowed himself to be distracted, and finally hamstrung, by corruption a man who had worked closely with him for many years thought for a moment and said: 'I sometimes think he became bored. One has to say it, unfortunately, but he was very greedy. Yet it wasn't ordinary greed. He never gave himself airs and graces like Imelda. I mean, he never for a moment came to believe he was an oligarch or one of the élite. Nor did he want to spend the money he made – at least, not on himself. Not on food and drink and houses and fast cars and rich men's toys and the usual things, although he must have spent a lot on women like Dovie Beams. I think he became bored after a year or two of martial law because he really didn't have that much daily *governing* to do, though he quite liked acting the Head of State and meeting foreign diplomats and so on. He played a lot of golf, actually. I quite favour the idea that his crony capitalism, as they call it, began with some genuine nationalistic motives. But when some of those cronies began to work out cunning schemes with him he was seduced by the intellectual challenge of it – you know, bending the law, intricate deals. He really wanted to know what he could get away with. It's a Filipino trait, this constant testing to see how far we can go. He loved all that. The money he made was almost irrelevant, a by-product. Not quite, though. Unfortunately for everyone, himself included, his greed won. Nobody will ever know what a remarkable President he could have made. That's the saddest part.'

And yet after all, the realistic comparison of Ferdinand Marcos was never with some ideal leader of a Western democracy, but with others of the same area – for example with that neighbouring *datu*,

President Suharto, whose own 'New Order' was his version of Ferdinand's 'New Society'. As the Indonesian economic crisis of early 1998 made plain, the *datu* habit of routing much of the nation's economy through the hands of his own First Family and friends was scarcely confined to the Marcoses' Philippines. That aside, there is no question that one can condemn Marcos once again for the great sums of money he undoubtedly did spirit out of the country during his twenty years of office. The fact that the exact amount has still not been agreed after twelve years' rummaging by Filipino and US investigators suggests it never will be, just as it suggests complicity on the part of several investigators on both sides of the Pacific who knew – or discovered – a lot more than they have told. Larceny on so grand a scale could only have happened with international connivance. The various cans of worms are left sealed and put up on the capacious shelves of modern history's oubliette along with those left over from RICO (Racketeer Influenced and Corrupt Organizations) trials in New York, the one labelled 'Ninoy Aquino' and dozens of others. These were not purely Filipino affairs. This, together with Ferdinand's famous Ilocano austerity, gives the whole issue of his theft as much a metaphorical as a moral status. It carries with it an odd note of helplessness. It was almost as if, having realized there was no way he could remedy the political system he had inherited without endangering either his job or his life, he might as well use it to make himself so grotesquely rich as almost to achieve a level of satire. This would at any rate have accorded with a historically life-saving national character trait: when something can't be beaten, make a mock of it. It was indeed a token of moral failure, but it also concealed a small gesture of despair.

Hence there undoubtedly is a certain pathos in the spectacle Ferdinand Marcos presented at the end: something of a prisoner within the bars of a cage he must almost have forgotten was there. Possibly he imagined that sending gold ingots outside the cage would give him a virtual kind of existence somewhere in freedom over the horizon. Even on the day of his political execution he was still hoping to do a deal with his jailers long after the death warrant had been signed in an office thousands of miles away. For all that lawyer's canniness of his he never really understood the position he was in. Nothing revealed this like the famous conversation he had with Senator Laxalt on the telephone. Not until the senator had told him to 'cut and cut cleanly' did he realize it was all over. The revelation is that this news had to come *from an American*. His own people had been telling him the same thing for weeks, months, years, but he was deaf to them. Only when an American senator told him he was no longer useful did this self-proclaimed nationalist Filipino patriot at last perceive how things stood. But then, he was not the only one to have been misled. The waiting crowds outside the Palace and on E. de los Santos Avenue were convinced they themselves had brought him to justice.

It could even be argued that ultimately it was not those largely middle-class crowds of nuns, priests, journalists, teachers, doctors, businesspeople and students at EDSA who proved to be Marcos's nemesis, nor even the policy-makers of Washington. No matter how indirectly, his undoing stemmed from Juan de la Cruz – from The People out in the provincial *barangays* whom he had so tirelessly and expensively wooed. It was none of their conscious doing, of course. Much of his loyal support came – still comes – from this grassroots level, from the folk that any traditional politician tried to put under an obligation of loyalty: the lowest but stoutest rung of his ladder to the Presidency. It was Ferdinand's desire to be every Filipino's personal *amo*, and it was surely this that premised his fall. The sheer ambitiousness of the scheme demanded unlimited amounts of cash for the Christmas tree; and in generating the requisite money he made an inherited system of corruption and graft work with unprecedented efficiency and on a scale never dreamed of by his predecessors.

It was his political intelligence that recognized this end and devised the means. It was his entrepreneurial skill, betrayed by a genuinely amoral pragmatism that he saw mirrored in Washington, which led him into the ever-deepening swamp he failed to perceive until it was too late. By then he was a sick man and probably lacked the energy to extricate himself, or even to want to. There were too many hands reaching out to grasp his own, pulling him not out but onward: too many allegiances, too many Ilocano blood ties, old debts, atavistic urgings. Too much uncritical American support, telling him that the White House was behind him all the way. There were also too many dire threats for him to dare stop and retrace his steps: NPA guerrillas re-grouping after the setbacks of early martial law, Palace factions who wanted his power, the legalistic tangle he himself had so skilfully woven to cover his tracks.

So onward he had to go, led as much by his own failings as by the lesser and greedier men who battened on him. It is notable that of all the cronies who tugged at his sleeves even as they helped ruin their country's economy, not one but made it to dry land at last, showered carefully in rose-water, and went off to stash his fortune in a safe place abroad. The Marcoses were left to sink alone in the mud, which in Ferdinand's case he did in exile with a curious dignity that increased the more the world rallied to pelt him.

What, then, of his wife? Had Imelda Marcos been a character in a novel she would have been one of the world's great literary creations. As it is, she is a remarkable work of her own imagination as well as of the Filipino psyche. Because the majority of her countrypeople has a weakness for glamour she gave them glamour, with the canny overkill which is yet another aspect of that Filipino disparagement of the worldly which makes them parody what they most affect to covet.

She was brought up a Catholic, inheriting the demure Spanish moral precepts appropriate to a lady. But the insidious cultural influences of the age were almost exclusively American. She and her school friends looked to Hollywood ('Favourite actress: Ingrid Bergman' – they must have just seen *Casablanca*). The values to which she and her friends aspired were inevitably those of the American way of life which in the triumphalist post-war era was proclaimed by every hoarding, billboard and advertisement. How could it have been otherwise, in an ex-colony which did not achieve full independence until Imelda was seventeen and was thereafter administered with a governmental, judicial and educational system cloned from that of the United States? Whether or not she knew it, she raised her own version of the American Dream (log cabin to Oval Office, garage floor to Malacañang) to a pitch of pure satire, winding up by having more money and power to throw around than all those tacky Mellons and Rockefellers put together. (For a time it became her practice to leave little bowls of pearls in the bedrooms of distinguished guests, much as an attentive hostess might leave pot-pourri; and what an infinite satisfaction it must have been to find that the little bowls were nearly always empty when the guest left!) What was it those moralizing school text-books of hers had quoted? 'If you can talk with crowds and keep your virtue,/Or walk with Kings – nor lose the common touch . . .' Not only did she talk with more crowds in a year than Kipling saw in a lifetime, she had kings eating out of her hand, while mere colonels simply rolled over and purred. And what of those awe-some social *ne plus ultras*, Hollywood and the White House? Hollywood stars trailed after her like lapdogs. (Brooke Shields, gaping at a black chiffon gown with a great diamanté collar Imelda was wearing on a gala night: 'Oo look! Those are real *diamonds* Mrs Marcos has sewn on her dress! That's really *neat!*' as her hostess's neck sparkled and flashed in the spotlight like one of those revolv-ing mirrored balls in a disco.) Indeed, Hollywood can clearly be seen as having exercised a formative influence on Imelda's cre-ation of her own myth. This is true in terms of style and imagery as well as in her choice of husband who, as a bright and ruthless country boy with glamorously shady connections, was a rougher diamond than she ever was. In this way he might be seen as having neatly filled that category of rough trade that certain ambitious female stars occasionally prefer.

What on earth could five successive American Presidents have thought, as this extraordinary creature who had so outrageously transcended her protégée status flitted and flirted and sang through their stolid courts? Beside Imelda their own First Ladies looked, well, a bit motherly and virtuous, to say the least. But even here the high ground went to this dazzling Filipina. She not only out-mothered them ('my *life*-story is Motherhood. Mothering is the centre of life') but her incredible list of public works and social projects made their own handful of drying-out clinics look like mere hobbies.

What was all this if not a superb kind of revenge? (For no one close to her ever doubted a steeliness within that occasionally escaped and caused mortal injury. The stories of her vindictiveness are legion, even in a culture that demands scores be settled.) Revenge for the garage floor on General Solano, revenge for the petty snobberies of the Manileño élite – these are indeed some-times mentioned as possible motivation for certain of her actions. But I have never yet seen America itself suggested as a major target

of her ire. Yet it is hard to think of a better explanation for her
having turned her office into a blatant travesty of the very values
and ideals the American colonizers of her country had brought
for the edification of the Filipino and which they themselves so frequently transgressed. How can one not see in the earnest
neo-Platonism of *Malakas at Maganda* a hilarious parody of all those
improving schoolbooks the Thomasites and missionaries brought
over to the Philippines at the turn of the century? Her book cap-
tures exactly the same Judaeo-Christian solemnities of thought
and expression, but turns them around completely so that instead
of describing the noble qualities of the white race they now extol
the *Maharlika*-like nobility of a proudly brown people striving for
freedom. It is the final nail in Hiawatha's coffin.

I do not for a moment think this was conscious on her part (especially given her dislike of the colour brown and its fecal
associations); but I see no reason why the deep residual nationalism
of her people (and they *were* her people) might not have inspired
much that she did. That this sometimes led to disaster, to gestures
that could look like someone cutting off their nose to spite their
face, is no argument against it. The frustration of centuries can
occasionally be glimpsed in Kansulay, too, as a sudden, black,
nihilistic streak amongst all the cheerful humour and religiosity.
Now and then this national trait leads to extravagant acts of violence which, though ostensibly directed against others, often seem
as much aimed at the self, at inherited ghosts. Running amok in a
great cathartic rampage can only end in one way, like Samson
pulling down the temple of Gaza onto his own head. Such an
image may appear wildly out of place when discussing Imelda
Marcos, an ex-beauty queen and a President's widow – 'a true
stateslady', as I heard one of her friends describe her. Yet some of
the things she did maybe constituted a super-rich, super-powerful
person's way of running amok, always with that bleak inner gleam
of self-destruction.

This is why I think she would have made a great literary creation. Since she is *sui generis* I am not sure whom she would have
resembled. Her court was indeed for years decadent and
debauched, though less in the self-indulgent manner of aesthetes
and voluptuaries than of mediaeval monarchs or Renaissance warlords. (By the early eighties, certain memorable dinner-parties in

Manila apartments resembled nothing so much as scenes from Petronius's *Satyricon*, complete with naked children as waiters.) Literary seekers of pleasure and sensation like Des Esseintes and Dorian Gray might have been fabulously vulgar in their refinement and silly Yellow Book amorality, but they were also disdainful and jaded. Imelda was anything but jaded. Her energy was voracious. Besides, the gold, the jewels, the gallons of scent and 'aerobic shopping' represented not an extreme of exquisiteness but an excess of commodities. Patrick Bateman, the hero of Brett Easton Ellis's brilliantly revolting satire of consumer society, *American Psycho*, was a beginner at brand-name shopping compared with Imelda. An entirely empty character, he was able to be defined only by what he bought. Imelda defined herself by being the buyer; *what* she bought scarcely seemed to matter so long as she had more of it than anybody else. It was enough to be the patron saint of conspicuous consumption. In any case, what all these literary characters lack is the least hint of tragic stature. Imelda Marcos unquestionably has it. It is as if she always knew that, far from defining her, this avalanche of objects was irretrievably burying her; and that if such were the case, then one might as well go for broke and add to the avalanche. (In this way she was perhaps not unlike her husband in his attitude to ludicrous wealth.) Hers was everybody's secret omnipotence made real, only thwarted at a far later stage than seemed possible for a mere mortal. It was all quite Greek in its way.

Imelda's ability to scandalize would have made any Wildean hero envious. It was a power she raised to the level of an art form in its flaunting of both the Catholic and American decorums of her upbringing. Once again, this was surely unconscious; and her unflagging espousal of that trademark litany of 'the Good, the True and the Beautiful' (as well as her assurance to me 'I have nothing to look back on with shame') is, I am convinced, perfectly sincere. Nevertheless, so successfully did she *épater* the international bourgeoisie that to this day at least half the world genuinely believes itself shocked by her. The terms are always the same: moral outrage and accusations of criminality or trust betrayed. This was summed up in an exchange I once had with the writer Frank Sionil José while driving down the Zambales coastal road. *FSJ*: 'She and Marcos were *evil*.' *JH-P*: 'Are you speaking as a religious person, Frankie?' *FSJ*: 'No. I'm speaking as a Filipino.'

Far be it from a foreigner, then, to attempt to overturn this stark verdict. Nevertheless I do think it interesting how, as a general rule, when public figures of Mrs Marcos's stature fall from grace they are almost never accorded a tithe of the understanding that is legally granted an arsonist or a mad axe-murderer. If such common criminals were not allowed to enter in their own defence details of miserable and abused childhoods it would quite properly be thought a denial of their rights. What woman accused of shoplifting might not expect a wave of sympathy to go around the court when her counsel described how she had as a child slept on wooden planks in the garage of her father's house and as a young bride had been driven to a nervous breakdown by her husband's nefarious way of life? Yet for some reason money and position are assumed to abrogate such a basic right, just as they are evidently believed to annul psychic damage. Sheer power and wealth are magically expected to exempt one from the malign legacy of one's own past, as if suddenly becoming rich could rewrite childhood and silence an ache and its echo.

This is by the way, however. To return to the question of the moral outrage Imelda can still provoke, much of it clearly contains an element of hypocrisy. The wave of condemnation that pursued her and her ailing husband to Hawaii in 1986 was predicated on something which was never stated. They had 'raped their country' and 'abused their position' and had 'acted like common thieves'; but it was as though no other Filipino politician had ever done so or would again. It was conveniently overlooked that plenty of Presidents before Marcos – some would say *all* of them – had abused their position, although perhaps 'exploited its possibilities' would be a more delicate phrase. And as for acting like common thieves, the two succeeding Administrations showed how commonplace thievery could be (to say nothing of prodigious corruption) even though both Presidents held themselves personally aloof from the time-honoured practice. In short, the subtext of the public outrage aimed at the Marcoses was that they had been aberrations, freakish exceptions; whereas in truth they were exceptional only for having taken normal political habits to new extremes. What was being packed off to Hawaii in disgrace was Caliban's mirror.

I used to ask friends in Kansulay what they would have done had they been in Ferdinand's or Imelda's position. They would assume a wistful expression. 'Well, taking care of the family is number one, of course,' they would say. 'That's only natural. After that, well . . .' The women often seemed more intrigued by the idea of Imelda's power than by a dream of diamonds. 'I'd soon sort some people out around here,' they would say darkly. 'But I'd be quite fair, of course.' Of course. Inevitably, the one thing they all left out of their fantasies of themselves-as-Imelda was her *style*, because it cannot be copied and is based on the private parodic certainty that nothing exceeds like excess. This was the other part of Imelda that used to enrage people, her apparent flouting of taste and convention. To have mocked the accepted pieties of Western-style government was one thing; but only she could have extended this demolition into the field of religion and deliciously confused the cult of the Santo Niño with that of herself.

This cult is of near-ubiquitous significance in the Philippines. It has its roots in Magellan's gift on her baptism to the Queen of Cebu in 1521 of a statue of the Holy Child. The figure of the Sto. Niño thenceforth spread with Christianity throughout the archipelago. The Sto. Niño, like the Manileños' Nazarene of Quiapo, is a spirit-manifestation of Jesus Christ. Naturally, the widespread belief during the 'EDSA revolution' that the crowds who defied the tanks were possessed and protected by the Sto. Niño was in no way affected by Mrs Marcos's being herself a prominent devotee of this powerful cult. Her devotion was such that she built an enormous – even flamboyant – shrine in Leyte which was widely accused of being quite as much about Imelda as it was about the Christ Child. (A prominent lady in the world of publishing tells of her mother visiting the shrine in the late seventies, where she found a diorama of Imelda's early life showing her as having been a *colegiala* at a convent school, implying private wealth. 'She was never any such thing!' said the mother indignantly. 'She had no private school education at all. It was a complete fiction, I'm afraid. Really, that all belonged to her image-building period. After that, she went into jet-setting.')

Yet to build a basilica to the greater glory of the Infant Jesus and then to fill it with bedrooms as well as displays of scenes from a private fictitious past was no ordinary lese-majesty. It is quite pointless to confront such things with conventional displays of outrage because Imelda never intended outrage. On such occasions she managed to transcend mere matters of taste and left people with little to do but goggle in helpless acknowledgement that she had always had this dumbfounding element in her.

In the case of her huge Sto. Niño shrine in Olot, there is perhaps a parallel with what she did in *Malakas at Maganda*. To insert herself and her own personal history into the Philippines' most popular religious cult is not dissimilar to having inserted herself retrospectively into Filipino history (even invoking Ancient Egypt) to the extent that she and her husband could appear as that history's destiny. Here is an egotism so exalted there is literally nothing it cannot subsume, even as it does so with sincere protestations of humility. *Toujours de l'audace!* Attempts to rewrite the past always do strike Westerners as particularly outrageous (one remembers those scornful jokes about Soviet Russia doctoring its photographs in order to eliminate faces since fallen out of favour). But from the moment the young Imelda Romualdez had successfully made Mayor Lacson change the results of a beauty contest even after it had been won and the winner announced, she must have known she had inherited to the point of genius an instinct already present in the national character: provided the accompanying pageantry is sufficiently over the top, anything can be made possible. This was the basic tenet behind her putting up 'ancestral homes' while set-dressing Ilocos Norte for daughter Irene's wedding, her confident invention of instant dynasties – another harmless piece of fantasy by no means unknown on the other side of the Pacific. People later made stern remarks about 'the arrogance of power'; but in its utter refusal to accept normal limits, Imelda's sense of her own power went way beyond mere arrogance and became something else, something like a sublime sense of mockery. (Looking for a parallel, one thinks of Stalin's famous *faux*-jovial warning to Lenin's widow who was fussing about his plans to change one of Moscow's boulevards. 'Dear Nadezhda Krupskaya,' he said. 'Do remember we can always find someone else to be Lenin's widow.') Lurking at the back of one's mind is the suspicion that Imelda's unconscious was holding up to ridicule the whole ethos of 'can-do' Americanism on which she had been brought up. 'Can-do' Imelda-ism went several unacceptable steps further.

Mrs Marcos has frequently been derided for having too easily fallen beneath the spell of intellectual 'mentors' with their own agendas (such as Dr Jolly Benitez) and becoming prey to any passing fashionable idea that takes her fancy. Strong men have testified to feeling faint at the prospect of one of her interminable lectures about Circles of Life or holes in the sky. Lifelong insomniacs have found the precious balm of sleep at last descending during one of Ma'am's explanations of intuitive intelligence or the Filipino ideology, though courtesy has obliged them to shake it off. From time to time when the mood was on her Mrs Marcos would hijack Cabinet meetings, haranguing a long table ringed with glazed ministers, each carrying on a bitter interior monologue. It was not unlike being invited to dinner in London in the seventies and finding oneself seated for the duration next to someone who had recently undergone an intellectual epiphany after reading Robert Pirsig or Edward de Bono. One knew one was in for some revelations about motorcycles or practical thinking more banal even than the inevitable quiche lorraine biding its time in the kitchen. At equivalent moments with Madame Marcos, hers was the implacable earnestness of the auto-didact. Ironically – for she would doubtless consider herself at such times as being at her most exalted and visionary – these bouts of dotty theorizing represent Imelda almost at her worst. This is because her major talents for spontaneity, warmth and humour temporarily desert her. She ploughs on with a discourse manifestly not her own, a spiel she has learned by rote. She becomes unstoppable, charmless, boring. Too many years of too many people suppressing their own intelligence through fear or good manners have led to her holding forth with impunity, when what she badly needed was for someone to have the courage to stand up and say 'Oh, for heaven's sake, this is just gibberish! Talk sense!' But nobody ever did; and the result is that people have increasingly come to think of her as roughly one-third mad. This is a pity, because she isn't. Like others of her class, her problem is partly that she has too seldom kept proper company, meaning unbeholden and disciplined intellects. There is an irony here in that unlike her husband, Imelda did to some extent surround herself with representatives of the liberal arts: not merely the Van Cliburns of the world stage but educated and bright Filipinos like Jolly Benitez as well as writers, artists, musicians and dancers.

Ferdinand, by contrast, really surrounded himself with Ilocano thugs and warlords, even though he had the native wit to ensure that behind the cronies and the yes-men some highly educated people were always working for him. Yet Imelda lacks the intellectual humility to benefit easily from people more intelligent than herself. She has a tendency to blot out whatever she finds disagreeable, too quick to forgo mental effort in favour of her famous grasshopper approach to novel ideas, pinging from one bright surface to another. This frivolity is a trait she shares with many other Filipinas of her generation and class; and it is hard not to see her at least partly as a victim of the macho Filipino social tendency that even today fears bright and articulate women, much preferring them to be demure homebodies or safely glamorous with their heads full of movie stars and tinsel and half-baked ideas.

Perhaps the idea Mrs Marcos espouses that comes closest to being fully-baked – or at least a genuine expression of a private conviction – is that about the importance of motherhood. This is not the apple-pie version, which is anyway a self-mocking American political shorthand. It probably does include a certain fashionable concept of the mother as the spiritual female principle that allegedly underwrites the universe; but I think it has a more specifically Asian aspect to it. A constant equation in her commissioned writings (above all in *Malakas at Maganda*) is made between the Philippine state and a family whose parents happen to be Imelda and Ferdinand Marcos. To a Westerner this merely looks like vulgar and literal paternalism raised to the level of a political cult. Yet the paradigm of the state as the family is Confucian, and no doubt also pre-dated him. The way in which old (i.e. pre-Japanese Imperial) Korea was administered was a good example of Confucian theory, and the system still lingers today in South Korea (even though barely visible) in relations between the state and the people. The Philippines' *amo* or *padrino* system could be seen as merely a regional variant.

Imelda's claims to maternalism may after all be worthy of passing consideration. Over the years one has watched the effect on families in Kansulay of mothers and fathers going off to Manila to earn the living they are unable to scratch at home, or vanishing abroad on three-year stints as remittance OCWs. It is hard to exaggerate the sad impact on the bereft family they leave behind, and no amount of dollars earned seems to make up for the splitting, for the crucial absence of a father or a mother and sometimes even both. Just occasionally, I have thought, it is possible to regard the entire country as a broken family, as though to explain a certain ingrained despair, a fleeting sense of moral delinquency, a chronic lack of leadership. According to this conceit the Philippines-as-household has indeed endured a succession of strange men – including a king, an emperor, several presidents and a homeboy borderline dictator – all of whom barged in, dallied for a while, swore undying love, protested total commitment to their children and drifted away again, their pockets jingling. In this casual, broken paradigm, Imelda's vision of herself as being not only a mother but her country's mother is maybe not so ludicrous after all. Many people might protest that she herself hardly merits such a self-proposed title; but the fact that she intuited such a role as representing a national psychic need does have a certain bizarre validity. At the very least it calls to mind some peculiar emotional damage, behind which lurks her nation's traumatic rejection of 'Mother Spain' in the Revolution of 1898 as well as the more general obsession with mothers characteristic of this intensely Catholic and matrilinear society. More immediate to Imelda might be the emotional consequences of her own divided childhood, of her father's second marriage, of the *indio* mother she half identified with and half repudiated.

Some may feel that I have gone on too long – even too admiringly – about Imelda Marcos, who is after all not a person I know beyond a six-hour acquaintance and to whom I owe nothing other than that and half an excellent roast fowl. Yet in her extravagant and complex character, in her wounded past and her naive sincerity, she expresses to an almost painful degree so much that I have seen in Kansulay over the last seventeen years. It seems absurd to imply that there could ever be the remotest link between those famous shopping sprees to Van Cleef & Arpels followed by dinner for the glitterati in one of her New York properties, and an evening in a clearing surrounded by bamboo huts where people drunkenly sing their hearts out to the accompaniment of a plywood guitar and edge-blown leaves. Yet there is something in common between Manhattan and Kansulay after all: a way of dealing with history, the pretence of a cure for longing, the concealing smile. I think there will come a time when Filipinos will learn to appreciate their own creative genius in inventing Imelda Marcos to express themselves. In her way, she was the logical culmination of centuries of inspired subversion, this being the national character's answer to repression. (We recall the Japanese officer in Chapter 4 glumly admitting 'fifty percent are comedians'.) If today the Philippines still occasionally seems to drift in and out of the shadow cast by a cloud of disapproving Western moralism, it is chiefly because with levity and wit Filipinos have all too accurately travestied their models.

15

Kansulay meets Babylon

After the typhoon, night elides into uneasy morning without any sense of awakening or renewal. Nobody in Kansulay has slept, in any case. Many abandoned their huts and sought shelter in cement-block buildings like the day-care centre or the captain's house, squashed together on the floor, wrapped in soaked cotton blankets and staring up at the corrugated iron roof as great bangs and thuds of decompression threatened to tear it off. In the hours after midnight everyone was inside, dressed for escape and hugging wet floors like soldiers under mortar fire. Outside was a lethal black maelstrom of whizzing fronds, coconuts hitting the grounds like shells and an occasional sheet of corrugated iron scything lethally through the air like a horizontal guillotine blade. Part of dawn's unreality is the absence not of wind but of the sound of wind: the constant roar of dark air, stiffened with salt, pouring past at over a hundred miles an hour accompanied by a tumultuous shaking. This shaking could be felt through the ground as well as heard. It was the sea 200 yards away, smashing into the land and invading the air so that spray lashed through palm fronds miles inland, leaving surfaces and skin sticky. This roaring howl lasted for hours, and its sudden absence has left the whole world gone under wool, as after excessively loud music or bombardment.

The sky is raw, abraded clear of clouds. Sometimes a small gust of wind picks up, a lost straggler detached from the main body of the storm now miles away over the South China Sea. In this scrubbed dawn dazed people wander among the huge litter of the village. The track leading from the coast road up to Turing's patch and the forest is a carpet of fronds and branches past which the swollen river pelts in a pinkish flood. Surprisingly, damage to the houses seems comparatively light. Their airy, sieve-like construction has allowed the gale to pass through them. A couple have lost their roofs entirely, while many have coconut-frond panels either missing or flipped up vertically like the air-brakes of an aircraft coming in to land. Village life, always slow, is halted as people retrieve their sodden belongings, try to get fires going with damp kindling and matches that won't strike. Wise home-owners extinguished all embers, lamps and candles before the height of the storm since typhoons do not always bring enough rain to put out the fires they so easily start. Now Kansulay presents a sight that José Rizal himself would have recognized, as also those long-buried villagers who left their broken cooking pots up at Turing's patch: people scurrying about carrying precious fire, a few live coals held in a coconut shell, a smouldering stick gripped in a pair of iron tongs and leaving a wavering smoke-trail on the air. Many of the families up by the forest have kept dry tinder in tins and, after a few minutes' rubbing, can actually make fire when matches are damp or disposable lighters empty.

There will be no traffic today along the coastal road. As far as the eye can see in either direction it is blocked with fallen trees and collapsed masses of vegetation. The scanty power and phone lines are down. In the space of a few hours the late twentieth century has been blown away and reveals what has always been: a village by the sea still beyond the reach of government. This province is too small and rugged ever to have had great agricultural estates, so there has never been widespread agrarian unrest and consequently no NPAs to attract the attention of the military. In this way it has largely escaped the sort of political involvement that might have brought it to a government's awareness. Stoically self-reliant, the people make fire, cook rice, spread clothes to dry in the strengthening sun. Battered hens wander about as if amazed by their own survival, having roosted up as always and clung to leeward branches throughout the long night as feathered fruit, their

plumage blown inside out like weak umbrellas. Yet here they are
again, foraging with pigs among the fallen debris.

Those villagers not immediately concerned with fire-lighting
and restoring normality are unresistingly drawn to the remaining
scene of drama, to where the night's tumult lives on with little sign
of slackening: the sea. The deep pounding sound increases as they
thread their way among the palms before emerging on the lip of the
beach where the sandy soil is matted with vines. It is a spectacle as
awesome as its sound. Beneath the blank, colourless sky waves
resembling *cappuccino* coffee thresh to the horizon, while in the
foreground immense combers burst on the inshore reef in explo-
sions whose tonnage can be felt through the soles of rubber
sandals. Shivering boys in T-shirts hug themselves and watch the
dramatic action transform a usually benign and tranquil scene.
They laugh and point to where somebody's pig rolls in the surf, its
trotters stuck stiffly out, disappearing like a log and reappearing
once again as the currents trundle it to and fro in the foam. It is an
illusion that the ocean is muddy to the horizon, of course. It is only
the inshore waters that are opaque with churned-up sand and silt
as well as with the soil washed off hills in the interior and borne
down by the river. In the absence of wind the sea will calm itself
quite quickly, but the silt in suspension will take a good fortnight to
precipitate out again and leave the water clear enough for night-
time spear fishing. In any case nobody will venture out for the next
three days, so it is back to dried salt fish. By the time it is worth
bringing the boats down to the beach again (they were carried well
inland before the typhoon arrived) the sand will have been cleared
of the worst of the jetsam, especially the rolling headless palm
trunks that will be left stranded at all angles with plastic cartons,
carrier bags and dead chicks trapped along their landward lengths.
By then it will be possible once more to see this shore as it usually
is: a working beach with people mending nets and painting boats,
with pigs rooting up and gulping the villagers' excrement, and
women and children wading out at low tide with empty pots and
tins for the little shells, seaweeds and other edible tidbits that can
be found on the reef flats.

Then once again this strand will become Kansulay's doorstep to
the planet, where the village can gather at night to sit around driftwood fires while children and dogs dash into the circle of light

and out again, their squeals and padding footsteps fading along the unseen water's margin. Overhead against the rash of stars the palm fronds hold their plumes motionless as drifts of fireflies eddy among them. Bats will come and go – although of course they may not be bats at all but *bantay-ginto*, the 'gold guardians' of buried treasure, estranged souls in search of a human host. This is the very spot from which, shortly before Christmas 1987, a group of fishermen drinking around just such a driftwood fire watched in astonishment as the sun rose at midnight in the western sky, not knowing that they were witnessing the deaths of 5,000 people, conscious only of unnatural events somewhere beyond their world's horizon.

Strangely, it is in the aftermath of typhoons, in the welter of felled banana boles and unroofed houses and ruined vegetable patches, that an underlying stability is made plainest. In the naked impermanence and fragility of life on these coasts a poet's words speak for something that transcends this village that happens to be Kansulay:

> Here we were born,
> here we live,
> here we will die –
> and here we will live once again.

Not quite mere continuity, this 'something' was likened at the end of Chapter 9 to a reagent that permits an etching to emerge. Now, as people clear away the storm's mess, they themselves are revealed as the reagent, and slowly a meta-Kansulay is glimpsed beneath the village's restored and tidied bones. This is a culture's solid underpinning. Only a foreigner's fond delusion pretends that these same villagers would not (given half the chance) become *datus* tomorrow and duly turn into the Marcos of their choice.

The only real casualty is the luckless grey-haired 'aunt' of Epdi and her siblings. Her flimsy house was largely flattened, reduced to its main uprights and the kitchen area's raised fire-tray. The floor of bamboo slats cants at an angle, plastered with brightly coloured rags and swatches of cotton. The Singer sewing machine has been unearthed but will need repairs before it can be used again. The 'aunt' moves through the ruins of her home dry-eyed, picking up this and that and putting it down again. A neighbour helping her clear up comes upon the little bamboo-handled whip trodden into the mud. Unnoticed, the helper quietly goes off to her own house and drops it into the fire. It is the only thing that is not restored to Epdi's foster aunt. In the meantime, though, where will the homeless children go? These professional brats (somewhat looked down on, to be frank, as though they had inherited their feckless parents' moral contamination) provide the classic test of that famous virtue, Filipino hospitality. Needless to say, they are all found temporary homes, as anyone always is. Yet like so much else in Kansulay it does not feel entirely like a straightforward act of charity. Instead, it suggests yet again something elusive, off at an angle and pointing to a world not quite ours; to a parallel universe, perhaps, or to a distant history that is somehow still coeval with the present. There is a fascinating passage dating from 1900, the second full year of the American Occupation, in the Philippine Commission's Annual Report. It addresses this very subject of hospitality with some amazement. What makes it doubly interesting is that the writer was describing the very province in which Kansulay lies, and might as well have been speaking of the village itself:

> They are hospitable by instinct, and it readily happens that he who has a house and food places both at the disposal of anyone who chances to come along, even though he is a complete stranger. This characteristic, good in itself, is carried to extremes as a result of innate timidity and weakness of character which cannot deny anything to anyone. Not only do they show their hospitality to relatives and acquaintances, but also to strangers, concealing their disgust or inconvenience that it occasions them. They even lodge evildoers in their houses and in spite of the trouble it occasions them, satisfy them with everything they have and cannot conceal from them, showing a pleasure which they do not really feel in their company.

One can disagree with the moral judgement ('weakness of character') without invalidating the account. It was not the American author's fault that, coming from a simple culture shaped by cheery precepts like 'One good turn deserves another', he picked up nothing of the aggression behind the supposed timidity and weakness, the will to throw a net of indebtedness over potential enemies, the taming with bonds. Epdi's brothers and sisters are taken in; the 'aunt' goes to lodge for a while with a 'cousin'; Kansulay congratulates itself yet again on its virtue.

By far the typhoon's oddest achievement is to have provoked an act of archaeology that goes unnoticed for much of the day. The day-care centre stands shaded by a great mango tree whose old hide, resembling a tribal African cheek, is scarred all over by ancient parallel cuts to provoke fruiting. A large branch of this tree was brought down by the storm and crashed into the front of the building in which people were sheltering, though without doing any real damage. When in the afternoon this immense swag of boskage is finally dragged away, a curiosity is revealed. It has knocked down the long tin sign from above the door that reads 'Kansulay Day Care Centre', disclosing a blank rectangle of cement beneath. Or rather, it *was* blank; but the impact of the branch against the wall has jarred the fillings out of forgotten lettering deeply incised across the façade which can now be read. 'Kansulay Day Care Centre,' it says. 'A Project of the First Lady, the Hon. Imelda Romualdez Marcos.'

Not Semiramis after all, but Ozymandias. Farewell to Babylon and Nineveh and Tyre. All long ago; and, to Kansulay, so very far away.

References

Introduction

1   *Horizons* (De La Salle College quarterly), March 1969.

1   Digging a well in Kansulay

1   O. D. Corpuz, *The Roots of the Filipino Nation*, vol. 1 (Manila, 1989), p. 29.
2   Ibid., pp. 17–18.
3   BBC World Service, 30 October 1990.

2   A history told by foreigners

1   William Henry Scott, *Prehispanic Source Materials* (Quezon City, 1984), p. 63.
2   See Alejandro R. Roces, *Fiesta* (Manila, 1980), p. 171.
3   O. D. Corpuz, *The Roots of the Filipino Nation*, vol. 1 (Manila, 1989), p. 22.
4   Joseph Earle Stevens, *Yesterdays in the Philippines* (Filipiniana Book Guild, vol. XIII, Manila, 1968).
5   Wallace Stevens, 'Lytton Strachey, Also, Enters into Heaven' in *The Palm at the End of the Mind* (New York, 1967).
6   José Rizal, *Noli Me Tangere* (Berlin, 1887; Madrid, 1992), ch. 54.
7   Benedict Anderson, 'The First Filipino', *London Review of Books*, 16 October 1997.

8   Gore Vidal, *New Statesman* (London, 13 January 1967).
9   Ibid.
10 Dean C. Worcester, *The Philippines Past and Present* (New York, 1921), pp. 830–1.
11 Thelma B. Kintanar and associates, *Cultural Dictionary for Filipinos* (University of the Philippines, 1996).
12 Quoted in Gore Vidal, 'The Day the American Empire Ran out of Gas', printed in *The Nation* and collected in *Armageddon?* (London, 1987).
13 Romeo V. Cruz, *America's Colonial Desk and the Philippines, 1898–1934* (Manila, 1974), p. 229.
14 *Los Angeles Times*, 26 November 1911.
15 Hartzell Spence, *For Every Tear a Victory* (New York, 1964).
16 Florentino Dauz, 'On the Philippines and Filipinos: Letter to an American Friend' in *Marcos and the Making of History* (Manila, 1980).
17 Hugh Brogan, *The Penguin History of the United States of America* (London, 1990), p. 454.
18 *The Far Eastern Review* (Shanghai), September 1923, p. 583.
19 All quotations from Katherine Mayo, *The Isles of Fear* (New York, 1925), ch. 10.
20 Sterling Seagrave, *The Marcos Dynasty* (New York, 1988), p. 70.
21 See Antonio C. Abaya, *Philippine Graphic*, 27 February 1995 (the fiftieth anniversary of the Japanese defeat in the Philippines).
22 Ibid.
23 Associated Press despatch, 7 February 1968.

3   Ferdinand Marcos makes a good start

1   Michael Taussig, *Shamanism, Colonialism and the Wild Man* (Chicago, 1991), p. 32.
2   Renato Constantino, 'Two First Ladies' in *The Marcos Watch* (Manila, 1972/1986).
3   David Wurfel, *Filipino Politics, Development and Decay* (Manila, 1988).
4   O. D. Corpuz, *The Roots of the Filipino Nation*, vol. 2 (Manila, 1989), p. 573.
5   Alfredo and Grace Roces, *Culture Shock! Philippines* (Times Books International, 1994).
6   Sterling Seagrave, *The Marcos Dynasty* (New York, 1988), p. 23.
7   Ibid., p. 44.
8   This photograph is reproduced in Arturo C. Aruiza, *Ferdinand E. Marcos: Malacañang to Makiki* (Manila, 1991).

4   The Second World War

1   Marcial P. Lichauco, *Dear Mother Putnam. A Diary of the Second World War in the Philippines* (privately published, Manila 1949/1996).
2   Ibid. 3 January 1942.
3   See Ian Sayer and Douglas Botting, *America's Secret Army. The Untold Story of the Counter Intelligence Corps* (London, 1989).
4   Lichauco, op. cit., 16 February 1942.
5   Benedict J. Kerkvliet, *The Huk Rebellion. A Study of Peasant Revolt in the Philippines* (Berkeley, CA, 1977).
6   See Louis Morton, *The Fall of the Philippines* (US Government Printing Office, Washington D.C., 1965), pp. 61–2.
7   See Hanson Baldwin, *Battles Lost and Won: Great Campaigns of World War II* (New York, 1966).
8   Carol M. Petillo, *Douglas MacArthur: The Philippine Years* (Indiana, 1981).
9   Dorris Clayton James, *The Years of MacArthur* (Boston, 1975), vol. 3.
10   Petillo, op. cit.
11   William Manchester, *American Caesar: Douglas MacArthur 1880–1964* (New York, 1978).
12   Carol M. Petillo, 'Douglas MacArthur and Manuel Quezon: A Note on an Imperial Bond', *Pacific Historical Review*, vol. 48 (1981).
13   Robert Ferrell ed., *The Eisenhower Diaries* (New York, 1981).
14   Lichauco, op. cit.
15   See Sterling Seagrave, *The Marcos Dynasty* (New York, 1988), p. 80.
16   Hartzell Spence, *For Every Tear a Victory* (New York, 1964), p. 158.
17   Ibid., p. 4.
18   *Time*, 21 October 1966.
19   *Washington Post*, 18 December 1983.
20   *New York Times*, 23 January 1986.
21   Seagrave, op. cit., Notes, p. 438.
22   *New York Times*, 23 January 1986.
23   Ibid.
24   *Philippine Daily Inquirer*, 24 May 1996.
25   Nick Joaquin, *The Aquinos of Tarlac* (Manila, 1972/1983), p. 13.
26   Lichauco, op. cit., 25 September 1943.
27   Ibid.
28   Kerkvliet, op. cit., pp. 73 *et seq.*
29   Seagrave, op. cit., p. 27.
30   See Pio Andrade, Jr., *The Fooling of America. The Untold Story of Carlos P. Romulo* (Manila, 1990), pp. 189–90.
31   Lichauco, op. cit., 12 April 1943.
32   Seagrave, op. cit., pp. 126–7.

5   The haunting of Kansulay

1   José Rizal, *Noli Me Tangere*, XXXII (Berlin 1887; Madrid, 1992). [Author's translation]
2   Exodus 3: 14.
3   Pedro Murillo Velarde, *Jesuit Missions in the Seventeenth Century* (Manila, 1749).

6   Imelda Romualdez, too, makes a good start

1   Beatriz Romualdez Francia, *Imelda* (Manila, 1992).
2   Ibid., p. 69.
3   Carmen Navarro Pedrosa, *The Rise and Fall of Imelda Marcos* (Manila, 1987), p. 50.
4   Ibid., p. 52.
5   Imelda Romualdez Marcos, *Circles of Life* (privately published, Manila ?1995).
6   Pedrosa, op. cit., p. 58.
7   See Manila press reports for 3 March 1953.
8   See Lewis E. Gleeck, *The Rise & Fall of Harry Stonehill in the Philippines* (Manila, 1989).
9   In conversation, 2 February 1997.
10 In conversation, 2 February 1997.
11 Kerima Polotan, *Imelda Romualdez Marcos* (New York, 1969).
12 Francia, op. cit., p. 156.
13 Ibid.
14 Polotan, op. cit., p. 84.
15 Francia, op. cit., p. 158.
16 Polotan, op. cit., p. 85.
17 Francia, op. cit., p. 159.
18 Pedrosa, *The Untold Story of Imelda Marcos* (Manila, 1970), p. 192.
19 In conversation, 2 February 1997.

7   Communists, nationalists, and America's Boy

1   Garry Wills, *Reagan's America* (New York, 1988), ch. 27.
2   *Playboy*, April 1971.
3   Quoted in Sidney Zion, *The Autobiography of Roy Cohn* (New Jersey, 1988), p. 48.
4   Nick Joaquin, *The Aquinos of Tarlac* (Manila, 1972/1983), p. 199.
5   Ibid., p. 209.
6   T. R. Fehrenbach, *This Kind of War* (New York, 1963).

7   Ibid.
8   Joaquin, op. cit., p. 229.
9   Michael Maclear, *Vietnam: The Ten Thousand Day War* (London, 1981).
10   Ibid., p. 23.
11   Alfredo B. Saulo, *Communism in the Philippines* (Manila, 1969/1990).
12   Quoted in Benedict J. Kerkvliet, *The Huk Rebellion. A Study of Peasant Revolt in the Philippines* (Berkeley, CA, 1977), p. 59.
13   AFPAC Regulations, GHQ, AFPAC, 'Counter Intelligence Corps: General Provisions,' 1 August 1945.
14   Neil Sheehan, *A Bright Shining Lie* (New York, 1988).
15   See Joaquin, op. cit., p. 240.
16   See Sterling Seagrave, *The Marcos Dynasty* (New York, 1988), p. 131. Among Seagrave's sources was Valeriano's widow.
17   William J. Lederer and Eugene Burdick, *The Ugly American* (New York, 1958).
18   Seagrave, op. cit., p. 152.
19   Frances FitzGerald, *Fire in the Lake* (London, 1972).
20   Joaquin, op. cit., p. 268.
21   Quoted in Albert E. Kahn, *The Unholy Hymnal* (New York, 1971).
22   Gore Vidal, *Palimpsest* (London, 1995), p. 362.
23   Arthur M. Schlesinger, Jr., *A Thousand Days* (Boston, 1967), p. 312.
24   Jonathan Mirsky and Stephen E. Stonefield, 'The Nam Tha Crisis: Kennedy and the New Frontier on the Brink', in ed. Alfred W. McCoy and Nina S. Adams, *Laos: War and Revolution* (New York, 1970), p. 161.
25   Kahn, op. cit., Foreword.

8   The Marcoses of Malacañang

1   6 October 1968. These manuscript letters form part of the Addis Papers archive (PPMS 25) in the library of the School of Oriental and African Studies, London.
2   1 September 1963.
3   Ibid.
4   Ibid., 22 September 1963.
5   In conversation, 2 February 1997.
6   Victor G. Heiser, 'Sanitation in the Philippines', *Journal of Race Development*, October 1912.
7   Kerima Polotan, *Imelda Romualdez Marcos* (New York, 1969), p. 149.
8   Sterling Seagrave, *The Marcos Dynasty* (New York, 1988), pp. 175–6.
9   See Fred Poole and Max Vanzi, *Revolution in the Philippines* (New York, 1984), p. 264.

10   Speech before the Inland Press Association, 23 February 1966.
11   Nathan F. Twining, *Neither Liberty Nor Safety* (New York, 1966).
12   James Kirkup, *Filipinescas* (London, 1968).
13   Addis Papers archive (PPMS 25), 21 May 1967.
14   Quoted in Kirkup, op. cit., p. 44.
15   Quoted in Quijano de Manila [Nick Joaquin], 'Art in the Palace' (1968), *Doveglion and Other Cameos* (Manila, 1977).
16   Ibid. [Author's partial translation]
17   From *Action Programmes*, a booklet edited by Ileana Maramag and published in Manila in about 1969.
18   In conversation, 10 January 1997.
19   Adrian Cristobal, in conversation, 16 January 1997.
20   PD (Presidential Decree) 27, the Tenants' Emancipation Act.
21   Under-Secretary Jose Medina of the Department of Agrarian Reform, Manila. In conversation, 29 February 1996.
22   Presidential Decree 442.
23   Presidential Decree 704.
24   Blas Ople, in conversation, 24 January 1997.
25   Beatriz Romualdez Francia, *Imelda: A Story of the Philippines* (Manila, 1992), p. 196.
26   Ibid., p. 196.
27   Speech before joint session of Congress, 15 September 1966.
28   Speech before the National Press Club, Washington DC, 15 September 1966.
29   Ibid.
30   Speech before the Joint Luncheon of the Philippine–American Chamber of Commerce, the Far East American Council and the Asia Society, 20 September 1966 (author's italics).
31   In conversation, 2 February 1997.
32   Seagrave, op. cit., p. 257.
33   Ibid., p. 207.
34   In conversation, 24 January 1997.
35   Francia, op. cit., p. 211.
36   Quoted in *Newsweek*, 3 January 1966.
37   See Gary Wills, *Reagan's America* (New York, 1988), chapter 18.
38   In conversation, 2 February 1997.
39   Addis Papers (PPMS 25), 17 September 1967.
40   1 January 1970.
41   In conversation, January 1997.
42   In conversation, 5 February 1997.
43   President's Report of the Cultural Centre of the Philippines (CCP), 1984.

44   Imelda Marcos's speech at the inauguration of the CCP, September 1969.
45   Addis Papers (PPMS 25), 26 June 1967.
46   Ibid., 2 July 1967.
47   Ibid., 23 February 1969.
48   Ibid., 7 September 1969.
49   Ibid., 9 November 1969.
50   Ibid., 15 November 1969.

9   Villagers and élites

1   Addis Papers (PPMS 25), 8 June 1969.
2   Ibid., 20 April 1969.
3   Speech delivered at the Third European Conference on Philippine Studies at Aix-en-Provence, 27–29 April 1997.
4   In conversation, 22 January 1997.
5   See William Henry Scott, *Barangay* (Manila, 1994).
6   Stephen Jay Gould, *The Panda's Thumb* (New York/London, 1980).
7   Editorial, *Philippine Daily Inquirer*, 15 December 1992.

10   Love-nests, leftists and riots

1   John Addis to A. J. de la Mare at the Foreign Office, 27 April 1967.
2   In conversation, 2 February 1997.
3   Quoted in Beatriz Romualdez Francia, *Imelda: A Story of the Philippines* (Manila, 1992), p. 333.
4   Ibid., p. 355.
5   In conversation, 17 January 1997.
6   Hermie Rotea, *Marcos' Lovey Dovie* (Los Angeles, 1984), p. 3.
7   Ibid., p. 188.
8   Ibid., p. 75.
9   In conversation, 17 January 1997.
10   Remarks at the state dinner in honour of President and Mrs Richard M. Nixon, Malacañang Palace, 26 July 1969.
11   Ibid.
12   Ibid.
13   Speech, 31 December 1969 at Luneta, quoted in Rotea, op. cit., p. 144.
14   In conversation, 7 January 1997.
15   Sterling Seagrave, *The Marcos Dynasty* (New York, 1988), p. 225.
16   Diary entry, 11 November 1970.
17   Rotea, op. cit., p. 232.
18   *Republic Weekly*, 26 February 1971.

19 Carmen Navarro Pedrosa, *The Rise and Fall of Imelda Marcos* (Manila, 1987), p. 124.
20 Col. Arturo C. Aruiza, *Ferdinand E. Marcos: Malacañang to Makiki* (Manila, 1991), p. 104.
21 *Manila Times*, 30 July 1967.
22 Quoted in *Horizons*, issue of November 1968–March 1969.
23 Ricardo Malay, in conversation, 28 January 1997.
24 Seagrave, op. cit., p. 242.
25 See *Philippine Daily Inquirer*, 9 November 1993.
26 Imelda Marcos, in conversation, 2 February 1997.
27 Ricardo Malay, in conversation, 28 January 1997.
28 Satur Ocampo, in conversation, 4 February 1997.
29 Seagrave, op. cit., pp. 240–1.
30 In conversation, 24 January 1997.
31 In conversation, 28 January 1997.
32 See *Guiding Principles of the New Society* (Manila, 1976), p. 13.
33 Quoted in Ricardo Manapat, *Some Are Smarter Than Others* (New York, 1991), p. 552.
34 Primitivo Mijares, *The Conjugal Dictatorship . . .* (San Francisco, 1976), p. 90.
35 Blas Ople, in conversation, 24 January 1997.

11   Martial law

1 In conversation, 20 February 1997.
2 Quoted in Nick Joaquin, *The Aquinos of Tarlac* (Manila, 1972/88).
3 Ibid.
4 An informed gossip and ex-Indios denizen, in conversation, 16 February 1997.
5 In conversation, 24 February 1997.
6 A senior civil servant (and ex-Marcos opponent) at the Department of Justice, in conversation, 1996.
7 Ibid.
8 Quoted in Nimia P. Arroyo, *Auditing the Accounting Profession* (Manila, 1971), p. 62.
9 In conversation, 24 February 1997.
10 In conversation, 1996.
11 In conversation, January 1997.
12 Alfred W. McCoy, in ed. Alfred McCoy, *An Anarchy of Families* (Manila, 1994), p. 429.
13 Teodoro L. Locsin, Jr., in conversation, 6 February 1997; and Bernardo M. Villegas, in conversation, 7 February 1997.

14 McCoy, op. cit., p. 430.
15 In conversation, 21 February 1997.
16 In conversation, 10 February 1997.
17 *Wall Street Journal*, 4 November 1983.
18 Ricardo Manapat, *Some Are Smarter Than Others* (New York, 1991), p. 559.
19 *Times Journal*, 21 December 1980.
20 Ricardo Malay, in conversation, 28 January 1997.
21 In conversation, 26 February 1997.
22 In conversation, 30 January 1997.
23 In conversation, 4 February 1997.
24 *Today*, 21 February 1997.
25 See Jack Anderson and Les Whitten, 'Washington Merry-Go-Round', 2 July 1975.
26 *Philippines Free Press*, 10 January 1970.
27 Quoted in Mario V. Bolasco, *Points of Departure* (Manila, 1994), 'The Church and the Social Question', p. 119.
28 Arturo C. Aruiza, *Ferdinand E. Marcos: Malacañang to Makiki* (Manila, 1991), p. 377.

12   The politics of fantasy

1 Frank L. Baum, *Glinda of Oz* (1920).
2 In conversation, 16 January 1997.
3 Arturo C. Aruiza, *Ferdinand E. Marcos: Malacañang to Makiki* (Manila, 1991), p. 107.
4 Addis Papers archive (PPMS 25/138).
5 Ibid., PPMS 25/142.
6 In conversation, 2 February 1997.
7 See David Blundy and Andrew Lycett, *Qaddafi and the Libyan Revolution* (Boston, 1987), p. 23; and Geoff Simons, *Libya: The Struggle for Survival* (London, 1993), pp. 281–3.
8 See James Hamilton-Paterson, 'Theatre of Blood', *The Independent Magazine* (London, 14 May 1994).
9 Quoted in Eric Gamalinda, *The Empire of Memory* (Manila, 1992), p. 177.
10 *The Philippine Star*, 16 February 1997, L-1.
11 See Arnold Molina Azurin, *Reinventing the Filipino* (Manila, 1993).
12 In conversation, 2 February 1997.
13 Ricardo Manapat, *Some Are Smarter Than Others* (New York, 1991), p. 260.
14 Imelda Romualdez Marcos, *Si Malakas at Si Maganda* (Manila, 1980), p. 269. [Author's translation]

15 *Philippines Free Press*, 16 August 1997.
16 In conversation, 2 February 1997.
17 Jacqueline Rose, *States of Fantasy* (Oxford, 1996).
18 Sterling Seagrave, *The Marcos Dynasty* (New York, 1988), p. 4.
19 Quoted in *We Forum* (Manila, 8–10 October 1982).
20 *Seattle Times*, 17 September 1982.
21 *Pacific Stars and Stripes*, 16 October 1982. Quoted in Charles McDougald, *The Marcos File* (San Francisco, 1987), p. 247.
22 In conversation, 20 February 1997.
23 In conversation, 21 February 1997.
24 In conversation, 20 February 1997.
25 Rodolfo Dula, in conversation, 10 February 1997.
26 In conversation, February 1997.

13   EDSA and after

1 *Philippines Free Press*, 11 November 1995.
2 In conversation, 10 January 1997.
3 In conversation, 11 January 1997 and 26 February 1997.
4 Sterling Seagrave, *The Marcos Dynasty* (New York, 1988), p. 403.
5 Roberto V. Ongpin, in conversation, 10 January 1997.
6 *Time* , 10 March 1986.
7 *San Francisco Examiner*, 7 May 1986, p. A-3.
8 See Arturo Aruiza, *Ferdinand E. Marcos: Malacañang to Makiki* (Manila, 1991), pp. 169–70.
9 Rod Dula, in conversation, 10 February 1997.
10 See Alfredo R. A. Bengzon with Raul Rodrigo, *A Matter of Honour: The Story of the 1990–91 Bases Talks* (Manila, 1997).
11 In conversation, 10 January 1997.
12 *Philippine Daily Inquirer*, 5 December 1992.
13 Ibid., 22 November 1992.
14 Ibid., 7 December 1992.
15 *Today*, 25 February 1997.
16 In conversation, 22 January 1997.
17 *Philippines Free Press*, 27 September 1997.
18 See *Manila Bulletin*, 20 December 1987 *et seq.*, but also almost any other Manila newspaper *passim* throughout the following month.
19 *Philippine Daily Inquirer*, 7 December 1992.

Bibliography

Addis, John Mansfield, Addis Papers archive (PPMS 25), SOAS, London

Agpalo, Remigio, *Ferdinand E. Marcos: War Hero, National Leader, and Great Man of Peace* (Manila, 1993)

Anderson, Benedict, 'The First Filipino', *London Review of Books*, 16 October 1997

Andrade, Pio, Jr., *The Fooling of America: The Untold Story of Carlos P. Romulo* (Manila, 1990)

Arroyo, Nimia P., *Auditing the Accounting Profession* (Manila, 1971)

Aruiza, Arturo C., *Ferdinand E. Marcos: Malacañang to Makiki* (Manila, 1991)

Azurin, Arnold Molina, *Reinventing the Filipino* (Manila, 1993)

Baldwin, Hanson, *Battles Lost and Won: Great Campaigns of World War II* (New York, 1966)

Baum, L. Frank, *The Wonderful Wizard of Oz* (1900)

—— *Glinda of Oz* (1920)

Bengzon, Alfredo R. A. with Rodrigo, Raul, *A Matter of Honor: The Story of the 1990–91 RP-US Bases Talks* (Manila, 1997)

Blundy, David and Andrew Lycett, *Qaddafi and the Libyan Revolution* (Boston, 1987)

Bolasco, Mario V., *Points of Departure* (Manila, 1994)

Bulatao, Jaime C., *Phenomena and their Interpretation* (Manila, 1992)

Chirino, Pedro, *Relación de las Islas Filipinas*, 2nd ed. (Manila, 1890)

Constantino, Renato, *The Marcos Watch* (Manila, 1972 [suppressed]; republished 1986)

Cooper, James Fenimore, *The Last of the Mohicans* (1826)

Corpuz, Onofre D., *The Roots of the Filipino Nation* (Manila, 1989)

Cruz, Romeo V., *America's Colonial Desk and the Philippines, 1898–1934* (Manila, 1974)

Dauz, Florentino, *Marcos and the Making of History* (Manila, 1980)

Fehrenbach, T. R., *This Kind of War: A Study in Unpreparedness* (New York, 1963)

Ferrell, Robert (ed.), *The Eisenhower Diaries* (New York, 1981)

FitzGerald, Frances, *Fire in the Lake* (Boston, 1972)

Forster, E. M., *Two Cheers for Democracy* (London, 1951) 'What I believe'

Francia, Beatriz Romualdez, *Imelda: A Story of the Philippines* (3rd ed., Manila, 1992)

Gamalinda, Eric, *The Empire of Memory* (Manila, 1992)

Gleeck, Lewis E., Jr., *The Rise and Fall of Harry Stonehill in the Philippines* (Manila, 1989)

—— *President Aquino: Sainthood Postponed* (Manila, 1992)

Gould, Stephen Jay, *The Panda's Thumb* (New York, 1980)

Greene, Graham, *The Quiet American* (London, 1955)

Heiser, Victor G., 'Sanitation in the Philippines', *Journal of Race Development*, October 1912

Hamilton-Paterson, James, *Playing with Water* (London, 1987)

—— 'Theatre of Blood', *The Independent* Magazine (London, 14 May 1994)

Horizons (De La Salle College quarterly), March 1969

James, Dorris Clayton, *The Years of MacArthur* (Boston, 1975), vol. 3

Joaquin, Nick, 'Art in the Palace' (1968), in *Doveglion and Other Cameos* (Manila, 1977)

—— *The Aquinos of Tarlac* (Manila, 1972/1988)

—— *Jaime Ongpin the Enigma* (Manila, 1990)

Kahn, Albert E., *The Unholy Hymnal* (New York, 1971)

Kerkvliet, Benedict J., *The Huk Rebellion* (Berkeley, CA, 1977)

Kintanar, Thelma B. and associates, *Cultural Dictionary for Filipinos* (Manila, 1996)

Kirkup, James, *Filipinescas* (London, 1968)

Lederer, William J. and Burdick, Eugene, *The Ugly American* (New York, 1958)

Lichauco, Marcial P., *Dear Mother Putnam* (privately published, Manila, 1949/1996)

Longfellow, Henry Wadsworth, *The Song of Hiawatha* (1855)

Maclear, Michael, *Vietnam: The Ten Thousand Day War* (London, 1981)

Manapat, Ricardo, *Some Are Smarter Than Others* (New York, 1991)

Manchester, William, *American Caesar: Douglas MacArthur 1880–1964* (New York, 1978)

Maramag, Ileana (ed.), *Action Programmes* (Manila, 1969)

—— *Portrait of a First Lady with Vision* (Manila, 1970)

Marcos, Ferdinand E. (as titular author):

—— *New Filipinism: The Turning Point* (State of the Nation Address to Congress, 27 January 1969)

—— *Today's Revolution: Democracy* (Manila, 1971)

—— *Notes on the New Society of the Philippines* (Manila, 1973)

—— *The Democratic Revolution in the Philippines* (New Jersey, 1974)

—— *Guiding Principles of the New Society* (Manila, 1976)

—— *Five Years of the New Society* (Manila, 1978)

—— *Tadhana: The History of the Filipino People*, vol. I Part I (Manila, 1980)

—— *An Ideology for Filipinos* (Manila, 1980)

—— *Marcos Notes for the Cancun Summit 1981* (Manila, 1981)

—— *The New Philippine Republic: A Third World Approach to Democracy* (Manila, ?1982)

—— *The Philippines Today: Stability Amid Change* (The President's Center for Special Studies, Office of the President, 1984)

(*see also under* PACRIS *and* National Media Production Center)

Marcos, Imelda Romualdez, (as titular author):

—— *The Compassionate Society* (selected speeches) (Manila, 1977)

—— *The Ideas of Imelda Romualdez Marcos* (ed. Ileana Maramag), Vols I, II . . . *et seq., ad infinitum* (Manila, 1978–)

—— *Si Malakas at Si Maganda* (privately published, Manila, 1980)

—— *Circles of Life* (privately published, Manila, ?1995)

Mayo, Katherine, *The Isles of Fear* (New York, 1925)

McCoy, Alfred W. (as author and editor), *An Anarchy of Families* (Manila, 1994)

McCoy, Alfred W. and Adams, Nina S. (eds.), *Laos: War and Revolution* (New York, 1970)

McDougald, Charles C., *The Marcos File* (San Francisco, 1987)

—— *Asian Loot* (San Francisco, 1993)

Mijares, Primitivo, *The Conjugal Dictatorship* (San Francisco 1976/Manila 1986)

Mirsky, Jonathan and Stonefield, Stephen E., 'The Nam Tha Crisis' in *Laos: War and Revolution* (New York, 1970) (*see also* McCoy, Alfred W.)

Morga, Antonio, *Sucesos de las Islas Filipinas* (2nd ed., Paris, 1890)

Morton, Louis, *The Fall of the Philippines* (Washington D.C., 1965)

Nakpil, Carmen Guerrero, *Woman Enough* (essays) (Manila, 1963)

National Media Production Center of the Philippines, *A Meeting of Friends* (The Marcoses' state visit to Washington, 16–30 September 1982) (Manila, 1983)

Nituda, Victor G., *The Young Marcos* (Manila, 1980)

PACRIS (Philippine Army Civil Relations and Information Service),

Guiding Principles of the New Society (ed. Maj. Adrian E. Cristobal) (Fort Bonifacio, 1976)

—— *Marcos and Humanism* (Fort Bonifacio, 1977)

Pedrosa, Carmen Navarro, *The Untold Story of Imelda Marcos* (Manila, 1969)

—— *The Rise and Fall of Imelda Marcos* (Manila, 1987)

Petillo, Carol M., *Douglas MacArthur: The Philippine Years* (Bloomington, IN, 1981)

—— 'Douglas MacArthur and Manuel Quezon: A Note on an Imperial Bond', *Pacific Historical Review*, vol. 48 (1981)

Pineda, Macario, 'Talambuhay ng Aming Nayon' (quoted in Jaime C. Bulatao, op. cit.)

Polotan, Kerima, *Imelda Romualdez Marcos* (Ohio, 1969)

Poole, Fred and Vanzi, Max, *Revolution in the Philippines* (New York, 1984)

Quijano de Manila, *see* Nick Joaquin

Rizal, Jose, *Noli Me Tangere* (Berlin, 1887; Madrid, 1992)

—— *Filipinas dentro de cien años* (Barcelona, 1889)

—— *Sucesos de las Islas Filipinas* by Antonio de Morga, annotated by Rizal (Paris, 1890)

—— *El Filibusterismo* (Ghent, 1891)

—— 'Ultimo Adiós' (Hong Kong, 1897)

Roces, Alejandro R., *Fiesta* (Manila, 1980)

Roces, Alfredo and Grace, *Culture Shock! Philippines* (London, 1994)

Rohmer, Sax, *Emperor Fu Manchu* (London, 1959)

Rose, Jacqueline, *States of Fantasy* (Oxford, 1996)

Rotea, Hermie, *Marcos' Lovey Dovie* (Los Angeles, 1984)

Russell, Dick, *The Man Who Knew Too Much* (New York, 1993)

Santos, Vito C., *Pilipino–English Dictionary* (Manila, 1978)

Saulo, Alfredo B., *Communism in the Philippines* (Manila, 1969/1990)

Sayer, Ian and Botting, Douglas, *America's Secret Army* (London, 1989)

Scott, William Henry, *Cracks in the Parchment Curtain* (Quezon City, 1982)

—— *Prehispanic Source Materials* (Quezon City, 1984)

—— *Barangay* (Manila, 1994)

Schlesinger, Arthur M., Jr., *A Thousand Days* (Boston, 1967)

Seagrave, Sterling, *The Soong Dynasty* (New York, 1985)

—— *The Marcos Dynasty* (New York, 1988)

Sheehan, Neil, *A Bright Shining Lie* (New York, 1988)

Simons, Geoff, *Libya: The Struggle for Survival* (London, 1993)

Spence, Hartzell, *For Every Tear a Victory* (New York, 1964); also published in expanded version as *Marcos of the Philippines* (Cleveland, OH, 1969)

Stevens, Joseph Earle, *Yesterdays in the Philippines* (New York, 1898; Manila, 1968: Filipiniana Book Guild, vol. XIII)

Stevens, Wallace, *The Palm at the End of the Mind*, Selected Poems (New York, 1967)

Taussig, Michael, *Shamanism, Colonialism and the Wild Man* (Chicago, 1991)

Twining, Nathan F., *Neither Liberty Nor Safety* (New York, 1966)

Velarde, Pedro Murillo, *Jesuit Missions in the Seventeenth Century* (Manila, 1749)

Vidal, Gore, *New Statesman* (London, 13 January 1967)

—— *Armageddon* (essays, 1983–7) (London, 1987)

—— *Palimpsest* (London, 1995)

Wills, Garry, *Reagan's America* (New York, 1988)

Worcester, Dean C., *The Philippine Islands and their People* (New York, 1899)

—— *The Philippines Past and Present* (New York, 1921)

Wurfel, David, *Filipino Politics, Development and Decay* (Manila, 1988)

Yabes, Criselda, *The Boys From The Barracks* (Manila, 1991)

Zion, Sidney, *The Autobiography of Roy Cohn* (New Jersey, 1988)

Index

Hamilton-Paterson,
James.

America's boy.

10/99

$30.00